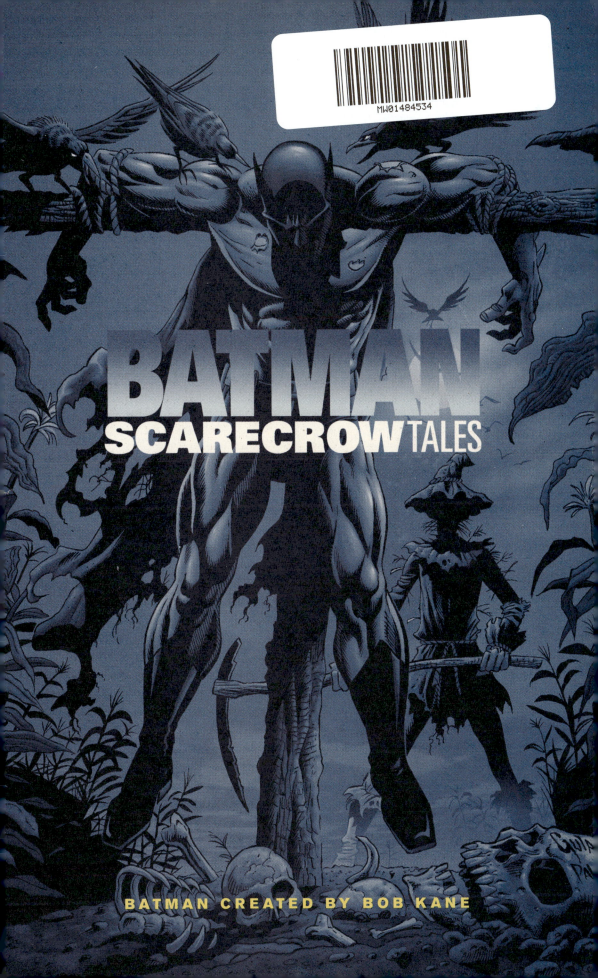

BATMAN
SCARECROW TALES

BATMAN CREATED BY BOB KANE

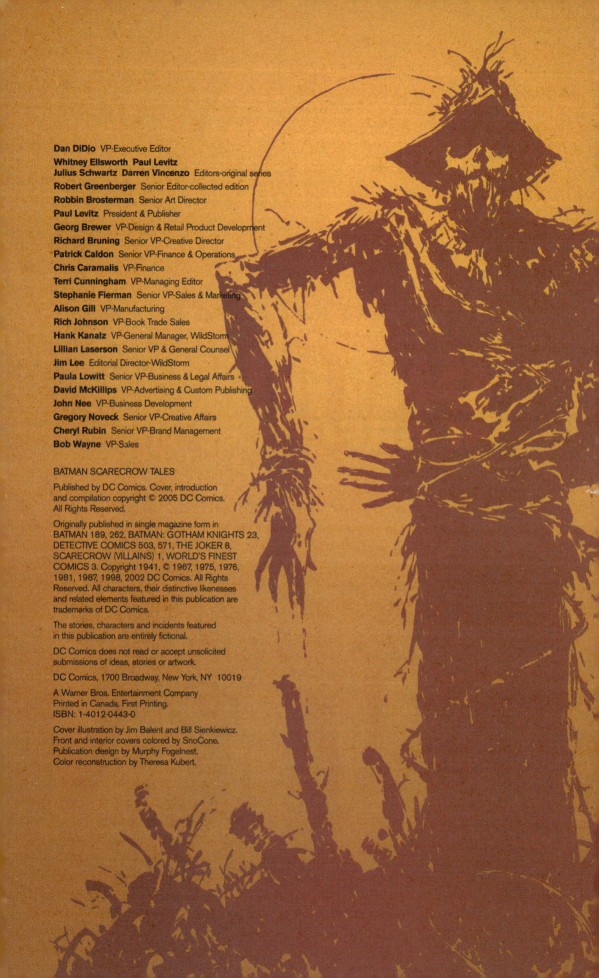

BATMAN SCARECROW TALES

Published by DC Comics. Cover, introduction
and compilation copyright © 2005 DC Comics.
All Rights Reserved.

Originally published in single magazine form in
BATMAN 189, 262, BATMAN: GOTHAM KNIGHTS 23,
DETECTIVE COMICS 503, 571, THE JOKER 8,
SCARECROW (VILLAINS) 1, WORLD'S FINEST
COMICS 3. Copyright 1941, © 1967, 1975, 1976,
1981, 1987, 1998, 2002 DC Comics. All Rights
Reserved. All characters, their distinctive likenesses
and related elements featured in this publication are
trademarks of DC Comics.

The stories, characters and incidents featured
in this publication are entirely fictional.

DC Comics does not read or accept unsolicited
submissions of ideas, stories or artwork.

DC Comics, 1700 Broadway, New York, NY 10019

A Warner Bros. Entertainment Company
Printed in Canada. First Printing.
ISBN: 1-4012-0443-0

Cover illustration by Jim Balent and Bill Sienkiewicz.
Front and interior covers colored by SnoCone.
Publication design by Murphy Fogelnest.
Color reconstruction by Theresa Kubert.

TABLE OF CONTENTS

WHO'S WHO #20, 1986   **4**
Art by Art Adams

RIDDLE OF THE HUMAN SCARECROW   **5**
Originally presented in WORLD'S FINEST COMICS #3, Fall 1941
Story: Bill Finger **Art:** Bob Kane, Jerry Robinson & George Roussos

Pinup   **18**
Originally presented in WHO'S WHO, 1990
Art by George Pratt

FRIGHT OF THE SCARECROW   **19**
Originally presented in BATMAN #189, February 1967
Story: Gardner Fox **Artist:** Bob Kane & Joe Giella **Letters:** Gaspar Saladino

Pinup   **42**
Art by Mark Stutzman

THE SCARECROW'S TRAIL OF FEAR!   **43**
Originally presented in BATMAN #262, April 1975
Story: Denny O'Neil **Pencils:** Ernie Chua **Inks:** Dick Giordano

THE SCARECROW'S FEARSOME FACE-OFF!   **61**
Originally presented in THE JOKER #8, July-August 1976
Story: Elliot S! Maggin **Pencils:** Irv Novick **Inks:** Tex Blaisdell

THE 6 DAYS OF THE SCARECROW   **78**
Originally presented in DETECTIVE COMICS #503, JUNE 1981
Story: Gerry Conway **Pencils:** Don Newton **Inks:** Dan Adkins **Letters:** Ben Oda

Pinup   **103**
Originally presented in BATMAN CHRONICLES GALLERY, 1997
Art by Jim Balent & Bill Sienkiewicz

FEAR FOR SALE   **104**
Originally presented in DETECTIVE COMICS #571, February 1987
Story: Mike W. Barr **Pencils:** Alan Davis **Inks:** Paul Neary
Letters: John Workman **Color:** Adrienne Roy

Pinup   **126**
Originally presented in BATMAN: SAGA OF THE DARK KNIGHT trading card #51
Artist: Mike Mignola

MISTRESS OF FEAR   **127**
Originally presented in SCARECROW (VILLAINS) #1, February 1998
Story: Peter Milligan **Artist:** Duncan Fegredo **Colorist:** Bjarne Hansen
Letterer: Albert DeGuzman

Pinup   **149**
Originally presented in BATMAN MASTERPIECES
Art by Dermot Power

FEAR OF SUCCESS   **150**
Originally presented in BATMAN: GOTHAM KNIGHTS #23, January 2002
Story: Devin Grayson **Pencils:** Roger Robinson **Inks:** John Floyd
Letters: Bill Oakley **Color:** WildStorm FX

COVER GALLERY   **172**

THE SCARECROW

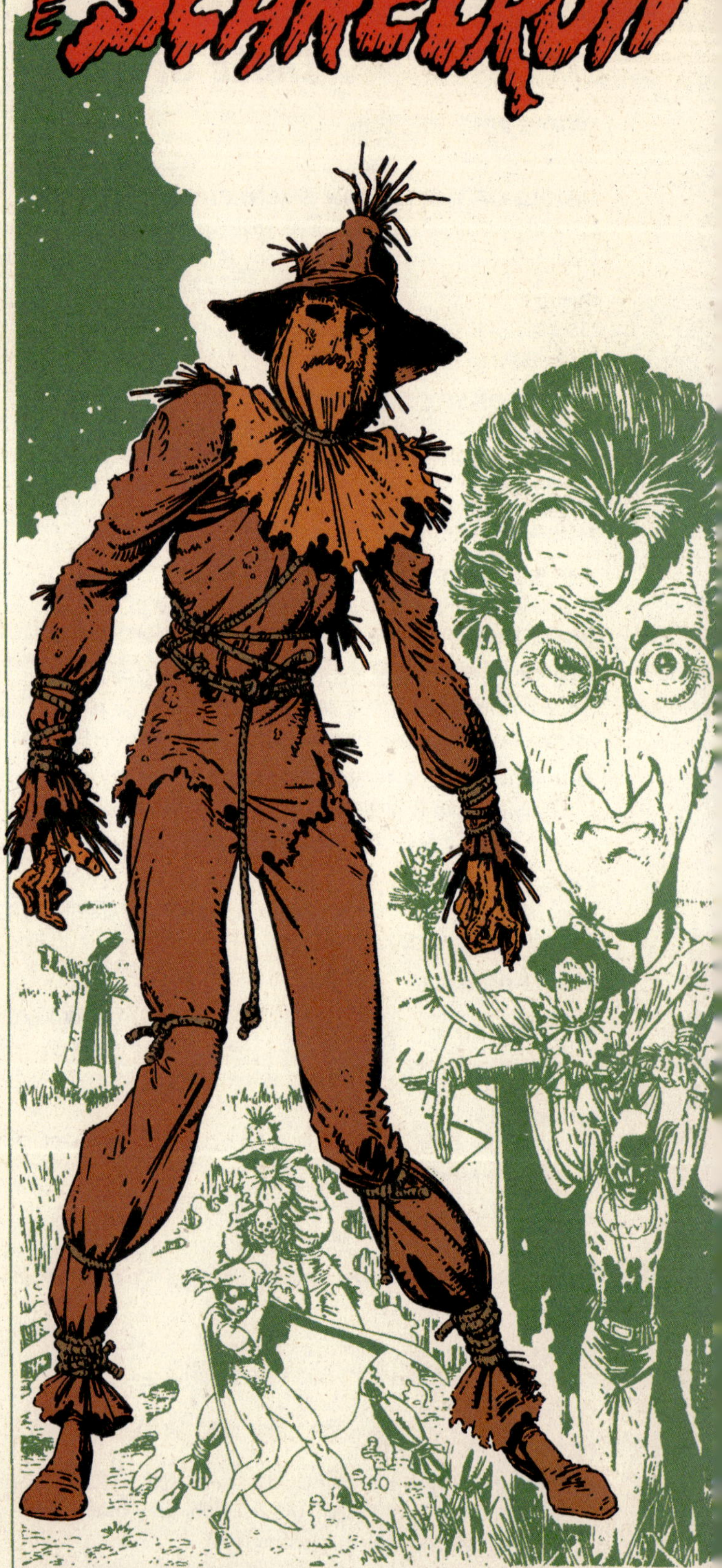

PERSONAL DATA

Alter Ego: Jonathan Crane
Occupation: Former Professor of Psychology, now Professional Criminal
Marital Status: Single
Known Relatives: None
Group Affiliation: Injustice Gang of the World
Base of Operations: Gotham City
First Appearance: WORLD'S FINEST COMICS #3
Height: 6' *Weight:* 140 lbs.
Eyes: Blue *Hair:* Black

HISTORY

When he was a small boy, Jonathan Crane liked to frighten birds. His fascination with the subject of fear persisted into adulthood. Crane became a professor of psychology at Gotham University and was known as an authority on the psychology of fear.

Crane was a tall, spindly figure who dressed shabbily, choosing to spend his money on books rather than clothing. His faculty colleagues disliked and derided Crane, mockingly referring to him as "Scarecrow" Crane due to his appearance.

Crane's strange obsession with creating fear led him one day, while lecturing students on the subject of fear, suddenly to fire a bullet at a flower pot, shattering it. The students were unnerved to see their professor wielding a loaded gun in class.

One afternoon Crane overheard some of his colleagues mocking his shabby, scarecrow-like appearance. Bitterly, Crane decided that if he had much more money, he would gain his colleagues' respect, and be able to dress better and buy still more books. The next day he lectured about the ways criminals extorted "protection" money from victims through fear. Later, Crane decided to turn criminal himself, utilizing his knowledge of creating fear. He took the guise of the Scarecrow, believing it to be the perfect symbol of fear and poverty combined.

As the Scarecrow, Crane hired himself out to people who wanted others intimidated through illegal means. Crane was fired from the university for his fanatical teachings and classroom behavior. The Batman deduced that Crane was the Scarecrow, and he and Robin captured him (see *Batman II, Nightwing*).

The Scarecrow, who has become a notorious master thief and has clashed repeatedly with The Batman, leaves straws behind at the scenes of his crimes. Besides using conventional means of terrorizing his victims and opponents, the Scarecrow has also devised various scientific means of affecting the human brain to create the sensation of fear. It has become apparent over the years, however, that Crane himself is subject to fears, including fear of capture by The Batman.

POWERS & WEAPONS

The Scarecrow is a brilliantly cunning criminal mastermind and psychologist who is an expert at creating terror. He can induce fear in a person by affecting his or her mind with a special fear-inducing gas, high frequency waves transmitted by electronic devices, or a fear-inducing pheromone chemical.

The Scarecrow has little skill at hand-to hand combat.

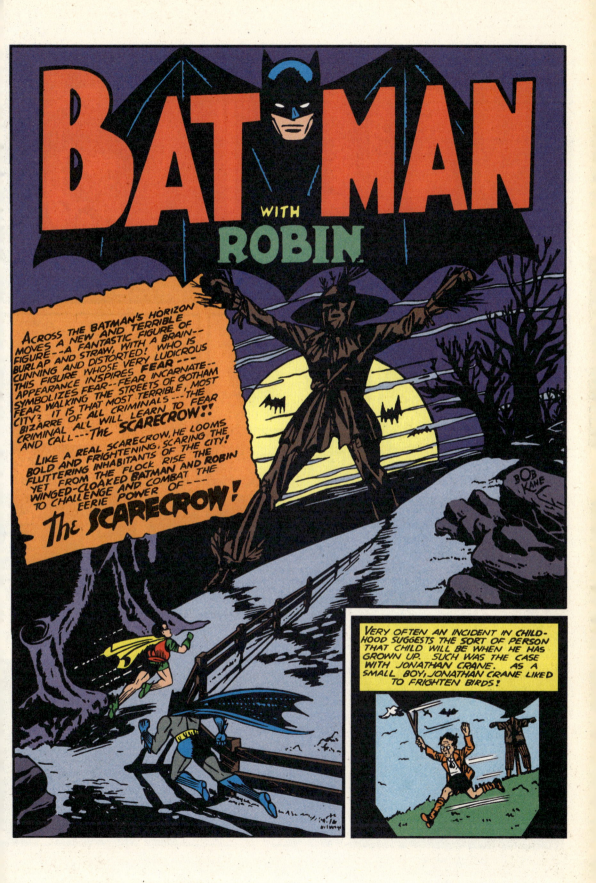

BAT MAN
WITH ROBIN

Across the Batman's horizon moves a new and terrible figure--a fantastic figure of burlap and straw, with a brain-cunning and distorted! Who is this figure whose very ludicrous appearance inspires FEAR--symbolizes FEAR--fear incarnate--fear walking the streets of Gotham City? It is that most terrible, most bizarre of all criminals---the criminal all will learn to fear and call---THE SCARECROW!!

Like a real scarecrow, he looms bold and frightening, scaring the fluttering inhabitants of the city! Yet from the flock rise the winged-cloaked Batman and Robin to challenge and combat the eerie power of---

The SCARECROW!

Very often an incident in childhood suggests the sort of person that child will be when he has grown up. Such was the case with Jonathan Crane. As a small boy, Jonathan Crane liked to frighten birds!

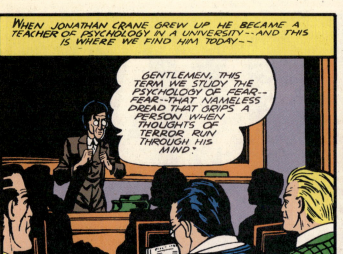

When Jonathan Crane grew up he became a teacher of psychology in a university--and this is where we find him today--

Gentlemen, this term we study the psychology of fear--fear--that nameless dread that grips a person when thoughts of terror run through his mind!

Notice this gun! Should I point it at you, you would be afraid-- but you would be more afraid--

--if I did this!

Now you see what the gun can do. It can destroy! Before, you only guessed what it could do. Now that you have seen --you are even more afraid! Simple psychology, gentlemen--

After the class is over-- Crane nears some other professors--

You're coming to the party I'm giving tonight-- don't forget!

All except one, eh? He looks so shabby in those old clothes-- positively weird--

He earns the same salary we do-- why doesn't he buy some decent clothes?

Poor Crane! He looks like a scarecrow in those clothes-- he certainly is a queer fellow--

He spends every cent he earns to buy new books--

And later--in his home-- Crane ponders--

The fools! Do they think I would give up my precious books just to buy clothes? Bah! They think I'm strange and I look like a scarecrow-- a scarecrow?

They judge human values by money-- if I had money they'd respect me --and I could buy more books! Yes---if I only had money--lots of money--

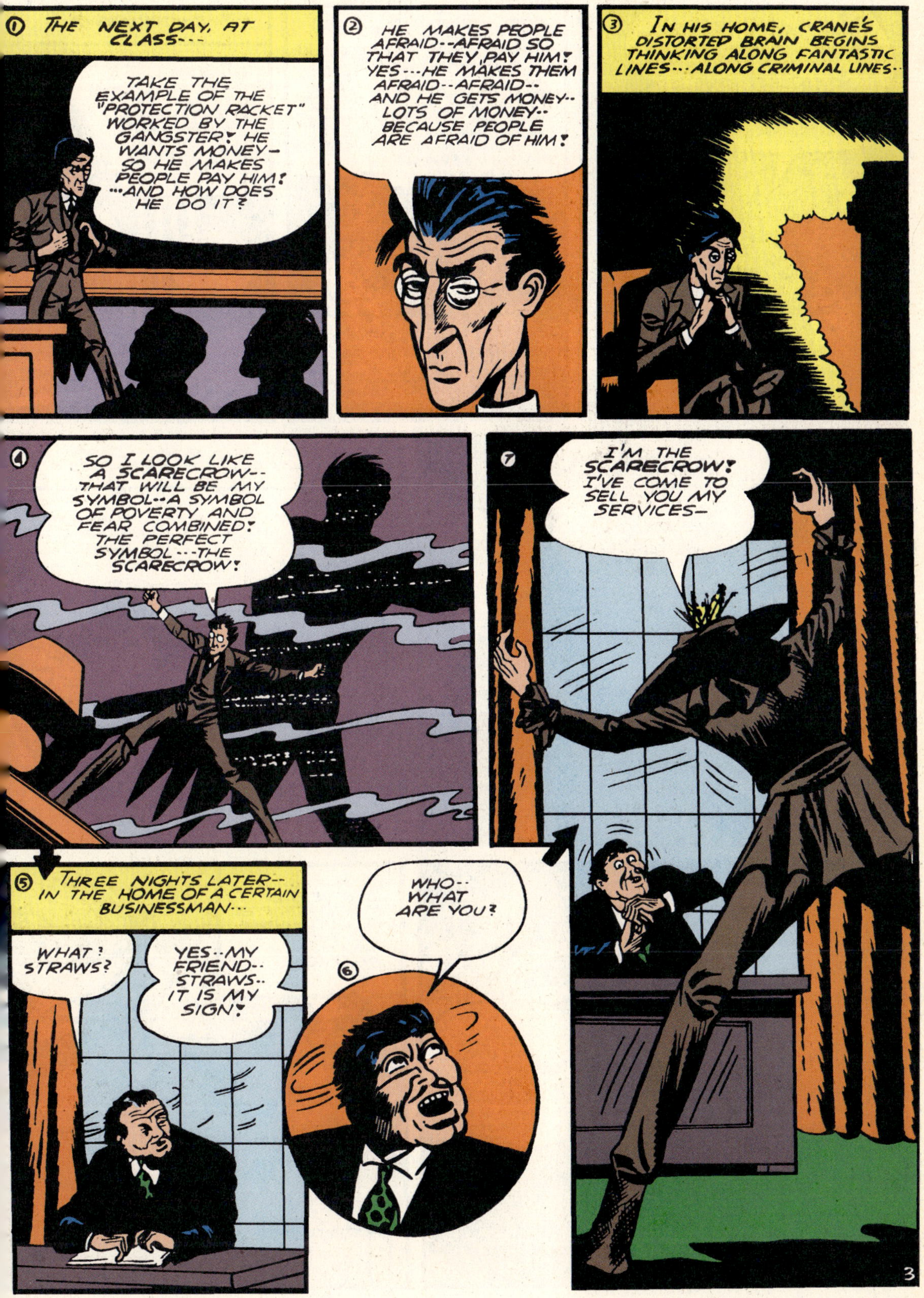
THE NEXT DAY, AT CLASS---
TAKE THE EXAMPLE OF THE "PROTECTION RACKET" WORKED BY THE GANGSTER! HE WANTS MONEY-- SO HE MAKES PEOPLE PAY HIM! ...AND HOW DOES HE DO IT?
HE MAKES PEOPLE AFRAID--AFRAID SO THAT THEY PAY HIM! YES---HE MAKES THEM AFRAID--AFRAID-- AND HE GETS MONEY-- LOTS OF MONEY-- BECAUSE PEOPLE ARE AFRAID OF HIM!
IN HIS HOME, CRANE'S DISTORTED BRAIN BEGINS THINKING ALONG FANTASTIC LINES--- ALONG CRIMINAL LINES--
SO I LOOK LIKE A SCARECROW-- THAT WILL BE MY SYMBOL--A SYMBOL OF POVERTY AND FEAR COMBINED! THE PERFECT SYMBOL---THE SCARECROW!
THREE NIGHTS LATER-- IN THE HOME OF A CERTAIN BUSINESSMAN---
WHAT? STRAWS?
YES..MY FRIEND-- STRAWS.. IT IS MY SIGN!
WHO-- WHAT ARE YOU?
I'M THE SCARECROW! I'VE COME TO SELL YOU MY SERVICES—
3

YOU ARE FRANK KENDRICK? YOUR BUSINESS PARTNER IS SUING YOU BECAUSE YOU STOLE SOME MONEY FROM THE BUSINESS YOU TWO OWN!

FOR A CERTAIN SUM OF MONEY, I WILL SCARE YOUR PARTNER SO THAT HE WILL BE AFRAID TO PROSECUTE YOU--HE WILL DROP THE SUIT! DO YOU WANT TO BUY MY SERVICES?

I...I SUPPOSE SO. WHY NOT? IF YOU CAN STOP MY PARTNER!

THAT VERY NIGHT---

I AM THE SCARECROW! YOU ARE FRANK KENDRICK'S BUSINESS PARTNER! I'VE COME TO TELL YOU, YOU MUST WITHDRAW YOUR SUIT AGAINST HIM!

WHO?

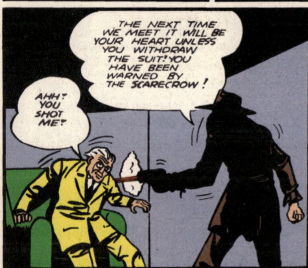

THE NEXT TIME WE MEET IT WILL BE YOUR HEART UNLESS YOU WITHDRAW THE SUIT! YOU HAVE BEEN WARNED BY THE SCARECROW!

AHH! YOU SHOT ME!

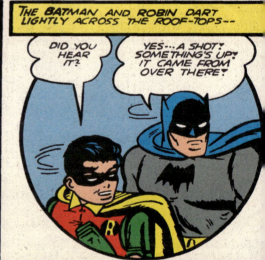

THE BATMAN AND ROBIN DART LIGHTLY ACROSS THE ROOF-TOPS--

DID YOU HEAR IT?

YES...A SHOT! SOMETHING'S UP! IT CAME FROM OVER THERE!

WHAT IS IT?

LOOKS LIKE A WALKING SCARECROW-- COME ON, ROBIN!

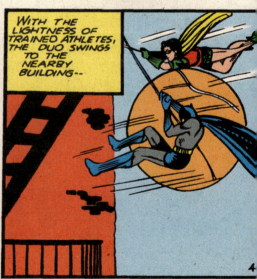

WITH THE LIGHTNESS OF TRAINED ATHLETES, THE DUO SWINGS TO THE NEARBY BUILDING--

4

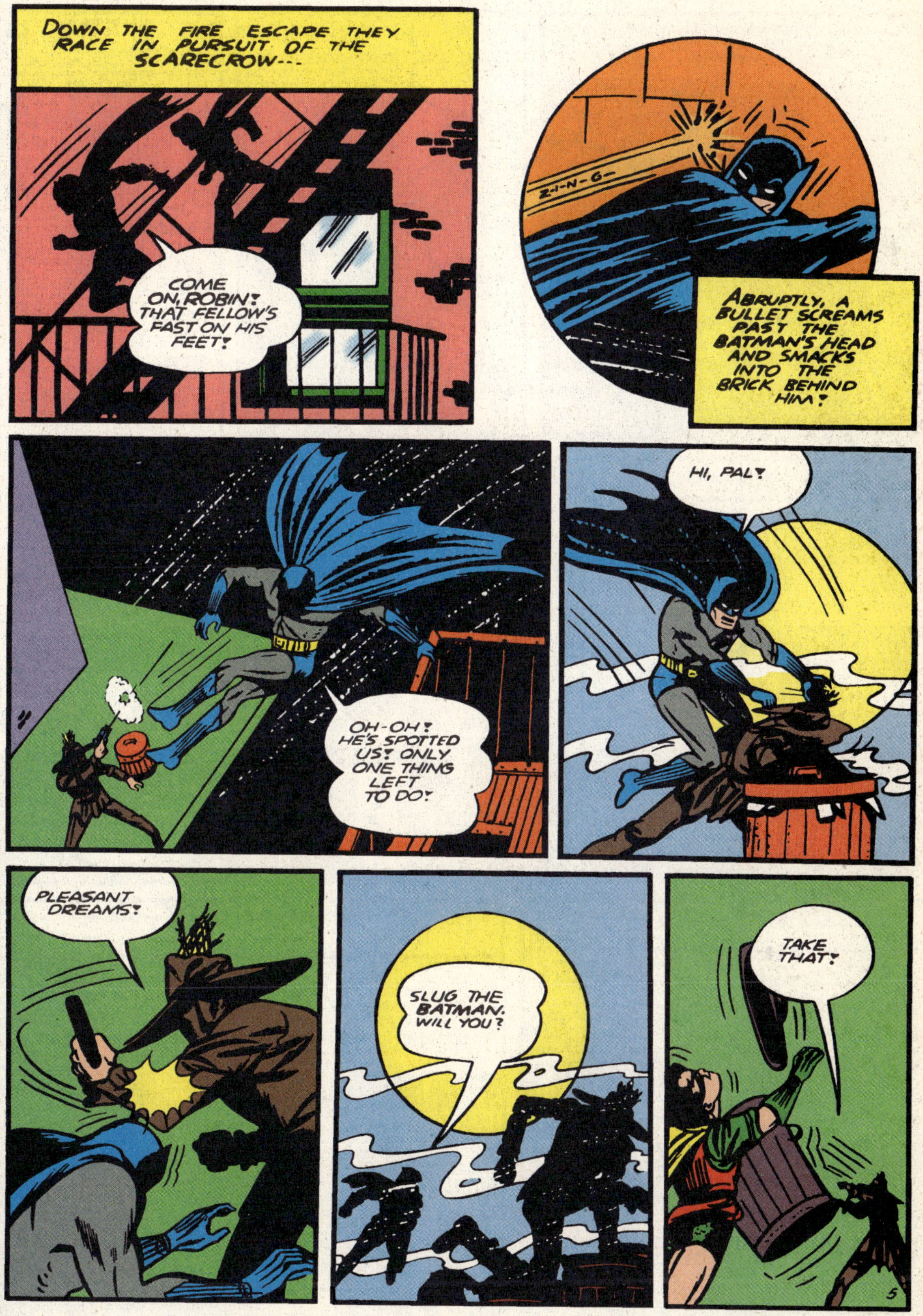
DOWN THE FIRE ESCAPE THEY RACE IN PURSUIT OF THE SCARECROW---
COME ON, ROBIN! THAT FELLOW'S FAST ON HIS FEET!
Z-I-N-G-
ABRUPTLY, A BULLET SCREAMS PAST THE BATMAN'S HEAD AND SMACKS INTO THE BRICK BEHIND HIM!
OH-OH! HE'S SPOTTED US! ONLY ONE THING LEFT TO DO!
HI, PAL!
PLEASANT DREAMS!
SLUG THE BATMAN. WILL YOU?
TAKE THAT!
5

AND WITH QUEER GRASSHOPPER LEAPS THE SCARECROW DISAPPEARS INTO THE BLACK NIGHT!

ARE YOU ALL RIGHT?

JUST A BIT WOOZY! THAT WAS QUITE A CLOUT! OH-OH SIRENS! SOMEBODY HEARD THAT SHOT AND PHONED THE POLICE!

THE IS

2 Cents   New York

BUSINESSMAN SHOT BY SCARECROW

WALKING SCARECROW WARNS HEROLD

PAUL HEROLD ACCUSES

AND FRANK KENDRICK SAYS--

DO YOU DENY HIRING THIS SCARECROW TO FRIGHTEN HEROLD INTO DROPPING HIS LAW SUIT?

OF COURSE I DO! CAN I HELP IT IF THIS SCARECROW PERSON TAKES AN INTEREST IN MY AFFAIRS?

YOU KNOW WE CAN'T ARREST YOU WITHOUT PROOF! C'MON, BOYS! I DON'T LIKE THE AROMA IN THIS PLACE--SMELLS LIKE A SKUNK IS LOOSE HERE-

AND THAT VERY NIGHT, AS PAUL HEROLD READS, GUNFIRE CRASHES THROUGH HIS ROOM—

THE SCARECROW WARNS ONLY ONCE!

AND WHEN THE POLICE ARRIVE---

HEROLD-- MURDERED- AND LOOK AT THIS I FOUND!

STRAW! THE SCARECROW LEFT HIS CALLING CARD-

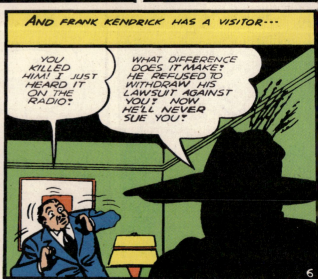

AND FRANK KENDRICK HAS A VISITOR---

YOU KILLED HIM! I JUST HEARD IT ON THE RADIO!

WHAT DIFFERENCE DOES IT MAKE! HE REFUSED TO WITHDRAW HIS LAWSUIT AGAINST YOU! NOW HE'LL NEVER SUE YOU!

6

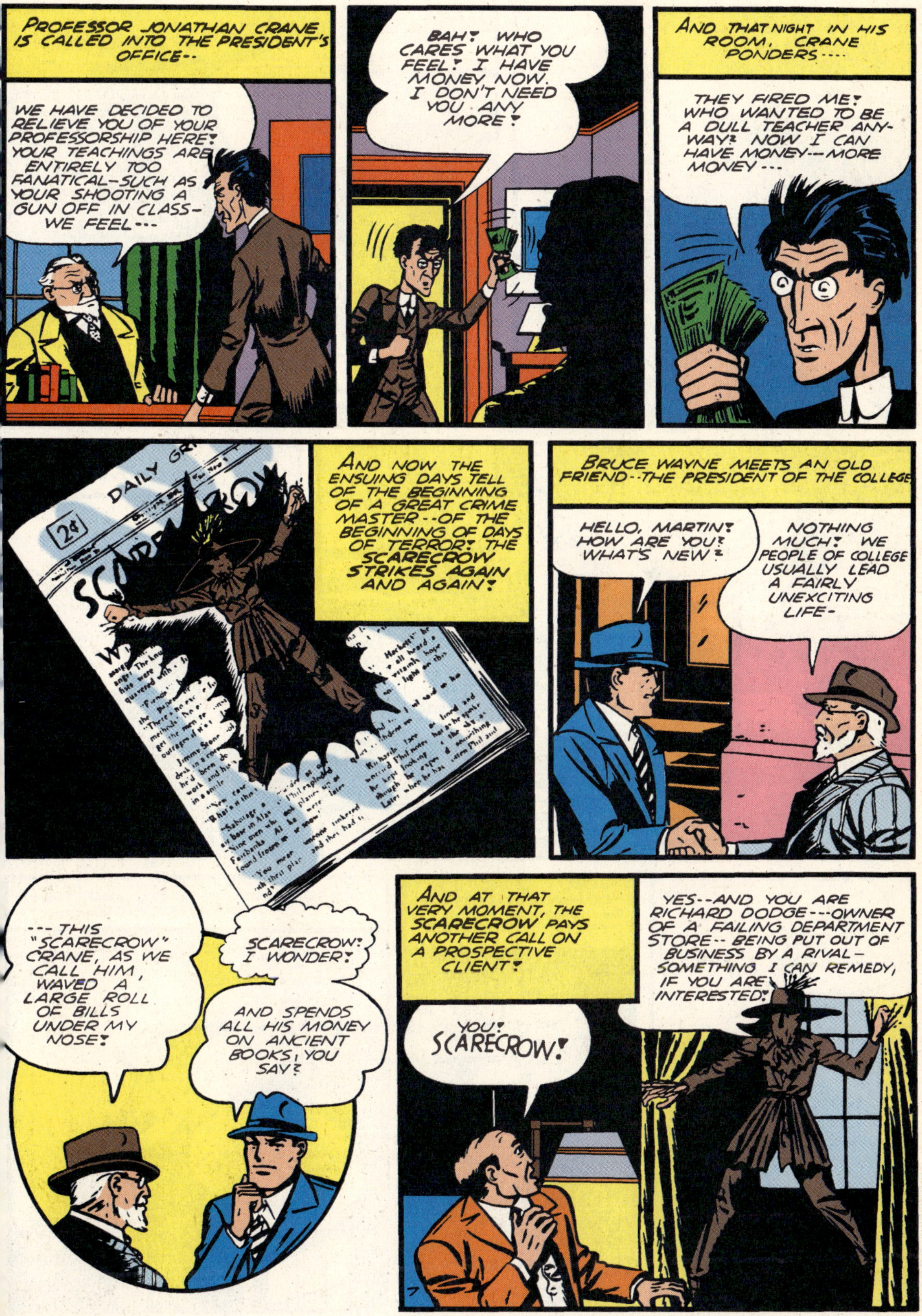
PROFESSOR JONATHAN CRANE IS CALLED INTO THE PRESIDENT'S OFFICE--
WE HAVE DECIDED TO RELIEVE YOU OF YOUR PROFESSORSHIP HERE! YOUR TEACHINGS ARE ENTIRELY TOO FANATICAL--SUCH AS YOUR SHOOTING A GUN OFF IN CLASS--WE FEEL---
BAH! WHO CARES WHAT YOU FEEL! I HAVE MONEY NOW. I DON'T NEED YOU ANY MORE!
AND THAT NIGHT IN HIS ROOM, CRANE PONDERS----
THEY FIRED ME! WHO WANTED TO BE A DULL TEACHER ANYWAY? NOW I CAN HAVE MONEY--MORE MONEY---
DAILY
2¢
AND NOW THE ENSUING DAYS TELL OF THE BEGINNING OF A GREAT CRIME MASTER--OF THE BEGINNING OF DAYS OF TERROR! THE SCARECROW STRIKES AGAIN AND AGAIN!
BRUCE WAYNE MEETS AN OLD FRIEND--THE PRESIDENT OF THE COLLEGE
HELLO, MARTIN! HOW ARE YOU! WHAT'S NEW?
NOTHING MUCH! WE PEOPLE OF COLLEGE USUALLY LEAD A FAIRLY UNEXCITING LIFE--
---THIS "SCARECROW" CRANE, AS WE CALL HIM, WAVED A LARGE ROLL OF BILLS UNDER MY NOSE!
SCARECROW! I WONDER!
AND SPENDS ALL HIS MONEY ON ANCIENT BOOKS, YOU SAY?
AND AT THAT VERY MOMENT, THE SCARECROW PAYS ANOTHER CALL ON A PROSPECTIVE CLIENT!
YOU! SCARECROW!
YES--AND YOU ARE RICHARD DODGE---OWNER OF A FAILING DEPARTMENT STORE--BEING PUT OUT OF BUSINESS BY A RIVAL--SOMETHING I CAN REMEDY, IF YOU ARE INTERESTED!
7

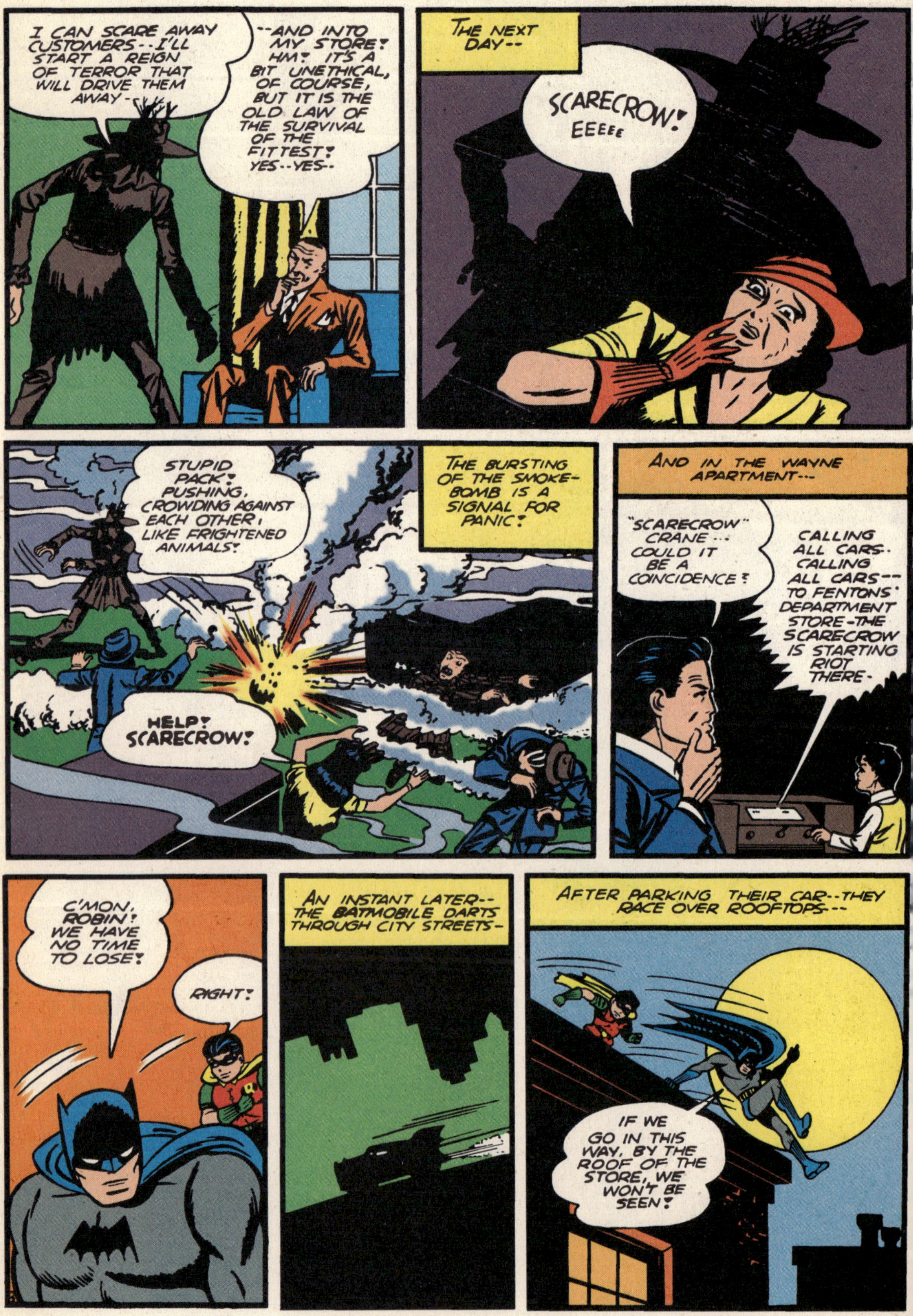
I CAN SCARE AWAY CUSTOMERS--I'LL START A REIGN OF TERROR THAT WILL DRIVE THEM AWAY--
--AND INTO MY STORE! HM! IT'S A BIT UNETHICAL, OF COURSE, BUT IT IS THE OLD LAW OF THE SURVIVAL OF THE FITTEST! YES--YES--
THE NEXT DAY--
SCARECROW! EEEEE
STUPID PACK! PUSHING, CROWDING AGAINST EACH OTHER, LIKE FRIGHTENED ANIMALS!
THE BURSTING OF THE SMOKE-BOMB IS A SIGNAL FOR PANIC!
HELP! SCARECROW!
AND IN THE WAYNE APARTMENT---
"SCARECROW" CRANE--- COULD IT BE A COINCIDENCE?
CALLING ALL CARS-CALLING ALL CARS--TO FENTONS' DEPARTMENT STORE-THE SCARECROW IS STARTING RIOT THERE-
C'MON, ROBIN! WE HAVE NO TIME TO LOSE!
RIGHT!
AN INSTANT LATER--THE BATMOBILE DARTS THROUGH CITY STREETS-
AFTER PARKING THEIR CAR--THEY RACE OVER ROOFTOPS--
IF WE GO IN THIS WAY, BY THE ROOF OF THE STORE, WE WON'T BE SEEN!

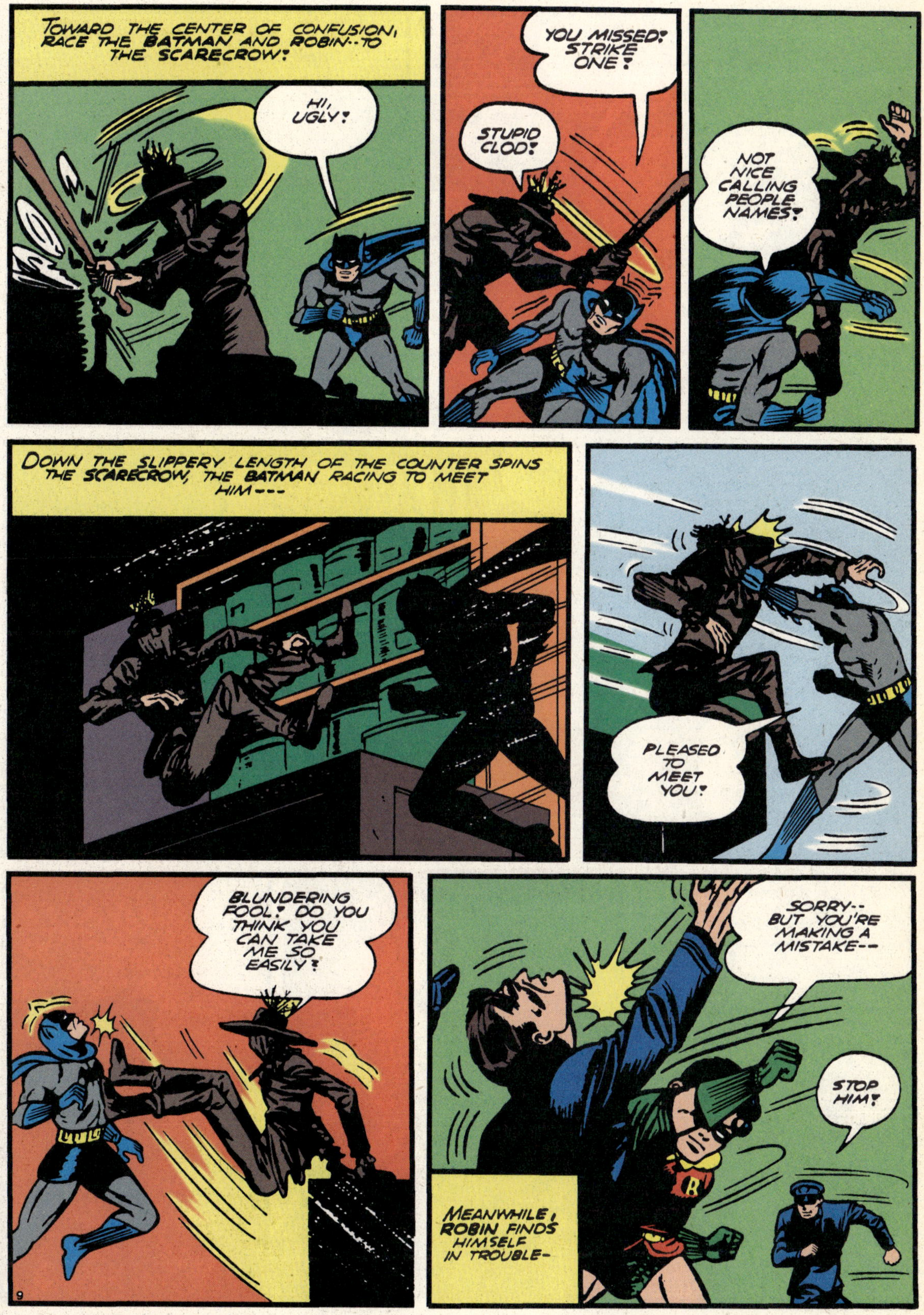
TOWARD THE CENTER OF CONFUSION, RACE THE BATMAN AND ROBIN--TO THE SCARECROW!
HI, UGLY!
YOU MISSED! STRIKE ONE!
STUPID CLOD!
NOT NICE CALLING PEOPLE NAMES!
DOWN THE SLIPPERY LENGTH OF THE COUNTER SPINS THE SCARECROW, THE BATMAN RACING TO MEET HIM---
PLEASED TO MEET YOU!
BLUNDERING FOOL! DO YOU THINK YOU CAN TAKE ME SO EASILY?
9
SORRY--BUT YOU'RE MAKING A MISTAKE--
STOP HIM!
MEANWHILE, ROBIN FINDS HIMSELF IN TROUBLE-

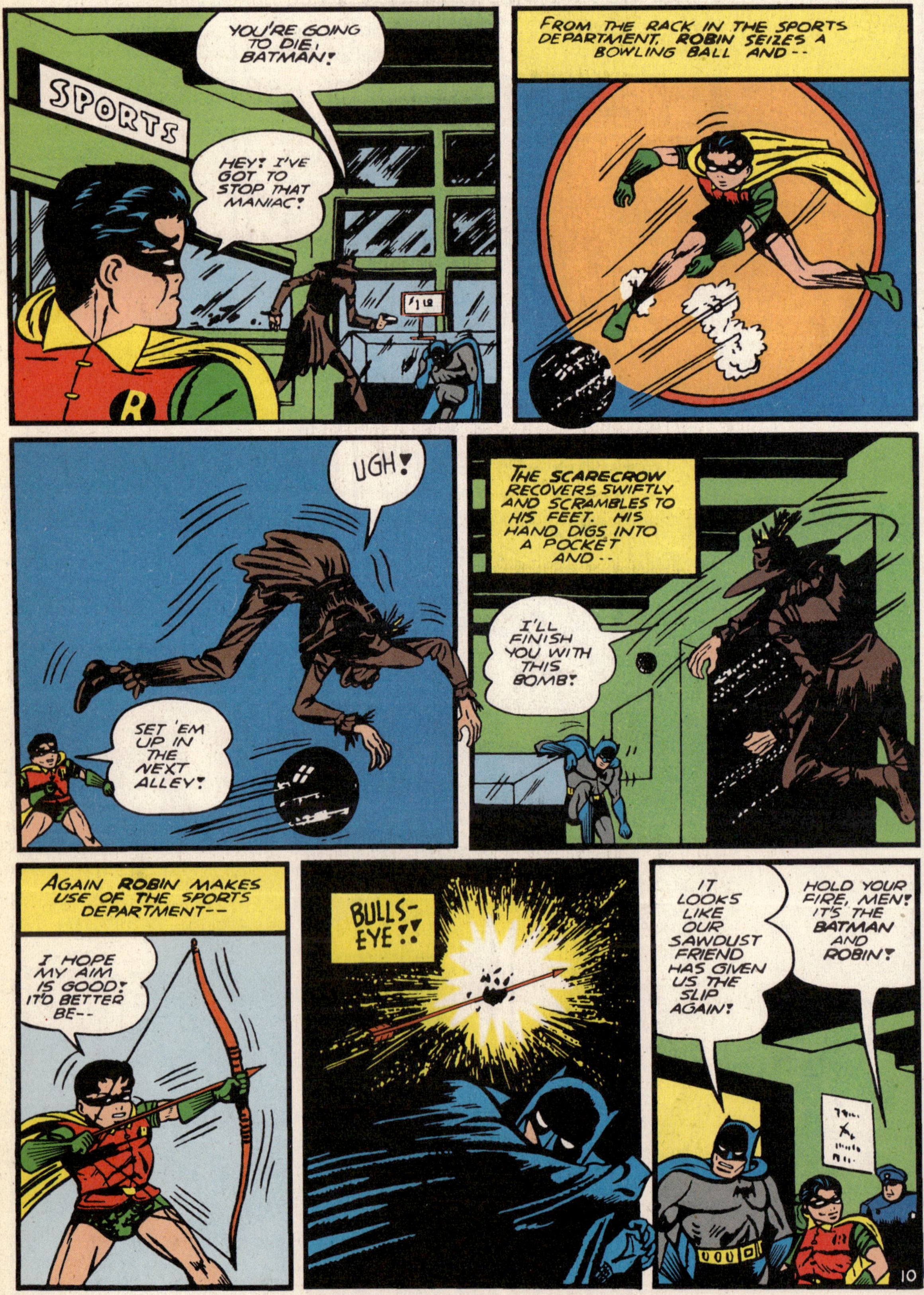
SPORTS
YOU'RE GOING TO DIE, BATMAN!
HEY! I'VE GOT TO STOP THAT MANIAC!
FROM THE RACK IN THE SPORTS DEPARTMENT, ROBIN SEIZES A BOWLING BALL AND--
UGH!
SET 'EM UP IN THE NEXT ALLEY!
THE SCARECROW RECOVERS SWIFTLY AND SCRAMBLES TO HIS FEET. HIS HAND DIGS INTO A POCKET AND--
I'LL FINISH YOU WITH THIS BOMB!
AGAIN ROBIN MAKES USE OF THE SPORTS DEPARTMENT--
I HOPE MY AIM IS GOOD! IT'D BETTER BE--
BULLS-EYE!!
IT LOOKS LIKE OUR SAWDUST FRIEND HAS GIVEN US THE SLIP AGAIN!
HOLD YOUR FIRE, MEN! IT'S THE BATMAN AND ROBIN!
10

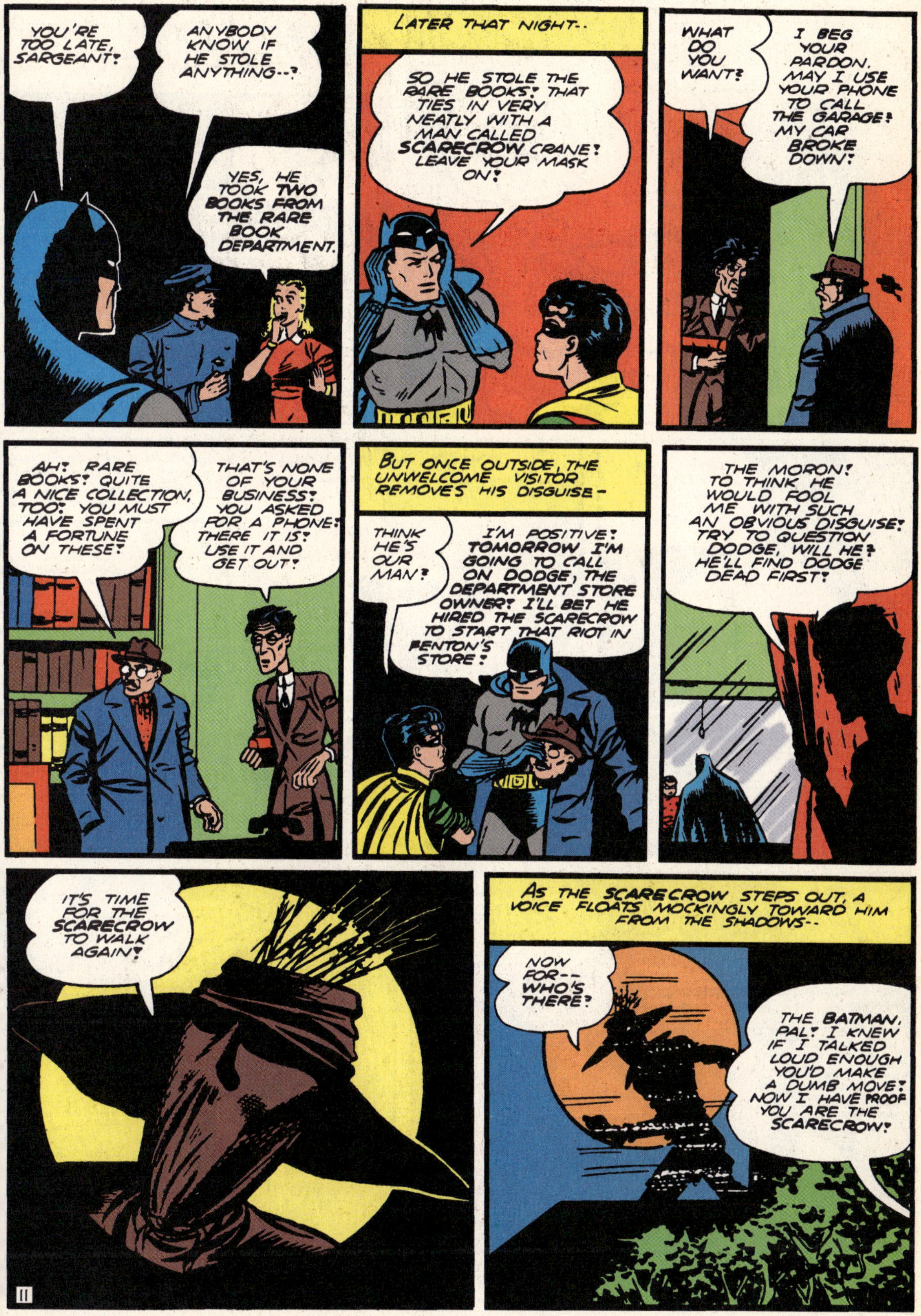
YOU'RE TOO LATE, SARGEANT?
ANYBODY KNOW IF HE STOLE ANYTHING--?
YES, HE TOOK TWO BOOKS FROM THE RARE BOOK DEPARTMENT.
LATER THAT NIGHT--
SO HE STOLE THE RARE BOOKS? THAT TIES IN VERY NEATLY WITH A MAN CALLED SCARECROW CRANE! LEAVE YOUR MASK ON!
WHAT DO YOU WANT?
I BEG YOUR PARDON. MAY I USE YOUR PHONE TO CALL THE GARAGE? MY CAR BROKE DOWN!
AH! RARE BOOKS! QUITE A NICE COLLECTION, TOO! YOU MUST HAVE SPENT A FORTUNE ON THESE!
THAT'S NONE OF YOUR BUSINESS! YOU ASKED FOR A PHONE! THERE IT IS! USE IT AND GET OUT!
BUT ONCE OUTSIDE, THE UNWELCOME VISITOR REMOVES HIS DISGUISE-
THINK HE'S OUR MAN?
I'M POSITIVE! TOMORROW I'M GOING TO CALL ON DODGE, THE DEPARTMENT STORE OWNER! I'LL BET HE HIRED THE SCARECROW TO START THAT RIOT IN FENTON'S STORE!
THE MORON! TO THINK HE WOULD FOOL ME WITH SUCH AN OBVIOUS DISGUISE! TRY TO QUESTION DODGE, WILL HE? HE'LL FIND DODGE DEAD FIRST!
IT'S TIME FOR THE SCARECROW TO WALK AGAIN!
11
AS THE SCARECROW STEPS OUT, A VOICE FLOATS MOCKINGLY TOWARD HIM FROM THE SHADOWS--
NOW FOR-- WHO'S THERE?
THE BATMAN, PAL! I KNEW IF I TALKED LOUD ENOUGH YOU'D MAKE A DUMB MOVE! NOW I HAVE PROOF YOU ARE THE SCARECROW!

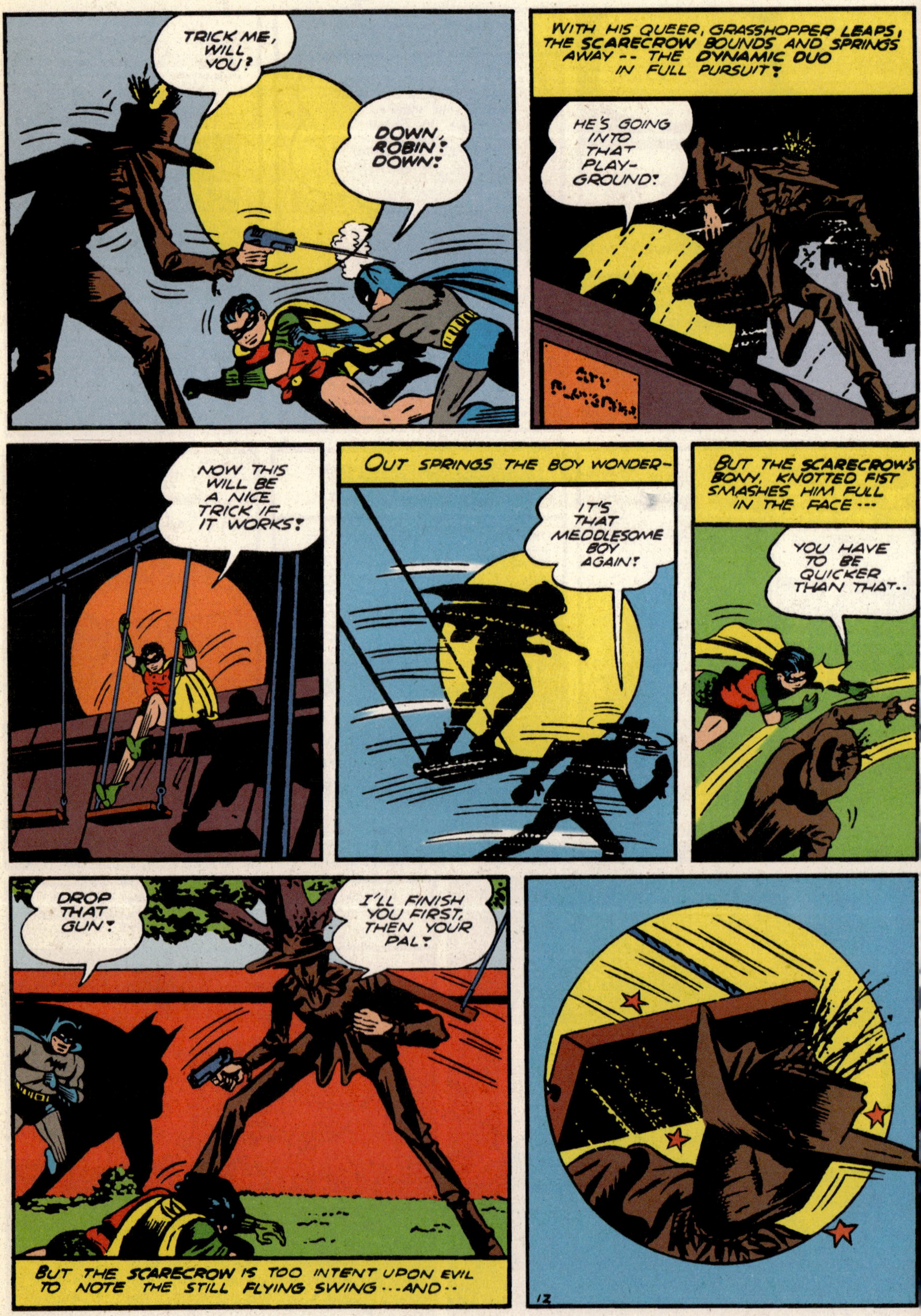
TRICK ME, WILL YOU?
DOWN, ROBIN! DOWN!
WITH HIS QUEER, GRASSHOPPER LEAPS, THE SCARECROW BOUNDS AND SPRINGS AWAY -- THE DYNAMIC DUO IN FULL PURSUIT!
HE'S GOING INTO THAT PLAY-GROUND!
NOW THIS WILL BE A NICE TRICK IF IT WORKS!
OUT SPRINGS THE BOY WONDER-
IT'S THAT MEDDLESOME BOY AGAIN!
BUT THE SCARECROW'S BONY, KNOTTED FIST SMASHES HIM FULL IN THE FACE---
YOU HAVE TO BE QUICKER THAN THAT--
DROP THAT GUN!
I'LL FINISH YOU FIRST, THEN YOUR PAL!
BUT THE SCARECROW IS TOO INTENT UPON EVIL TO NOTE THE STILL FLYING SWING---AND--
12

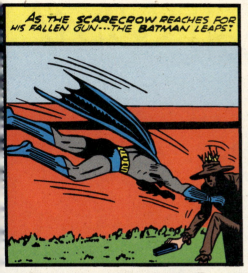

As the SCARECROW reaches for his fallen gun...the BATMAN leaps!

A shot blasts past the BATMAN'S face as they lock in a terrible struggle!

YOU'LL FIND I'M AS GOOD AT FIGHTING AS YOU ARE, BATMAN!

Once again, the SCARECROW stoops for his fallen gun when--ROBIN enters the fray!

HOLD THAT POSITION!

BOB KANE

NICE TIMING, KID!

WOW! IS HE REALLY OUT AT LAST!

I DON'T KNOW! HE CERTAINLY GAVE ME THE FIGHT OF MY CAREER, BUT FROM NOW ON THE ONLY FIGHTING HE'LL DO IS IN A PRISON CELL!

AND SO THE INFAMOUS, SHORT-LIVED CAREER OF THE SCARECROW COMES TO AN END AT LAST!

THE STUPID FOOLS ACTUALLY THINK THEY'RE GOING TO KEEP ME HERE--

THE End-

WILL THE SCARECROW RETURN? ONLY TIME... ONLY INSCRUTABLE TIME CAN TELL!

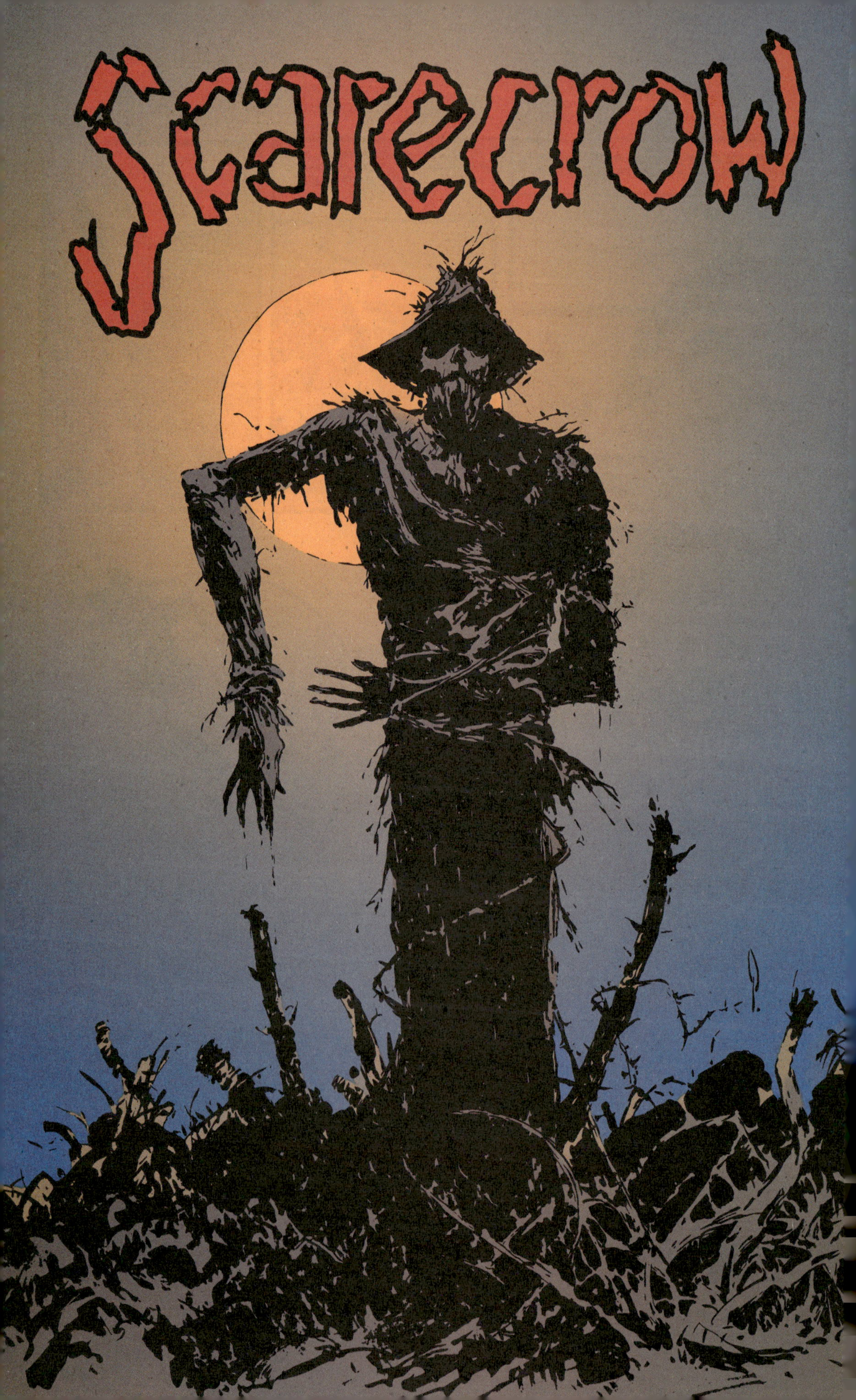
Scarecrow

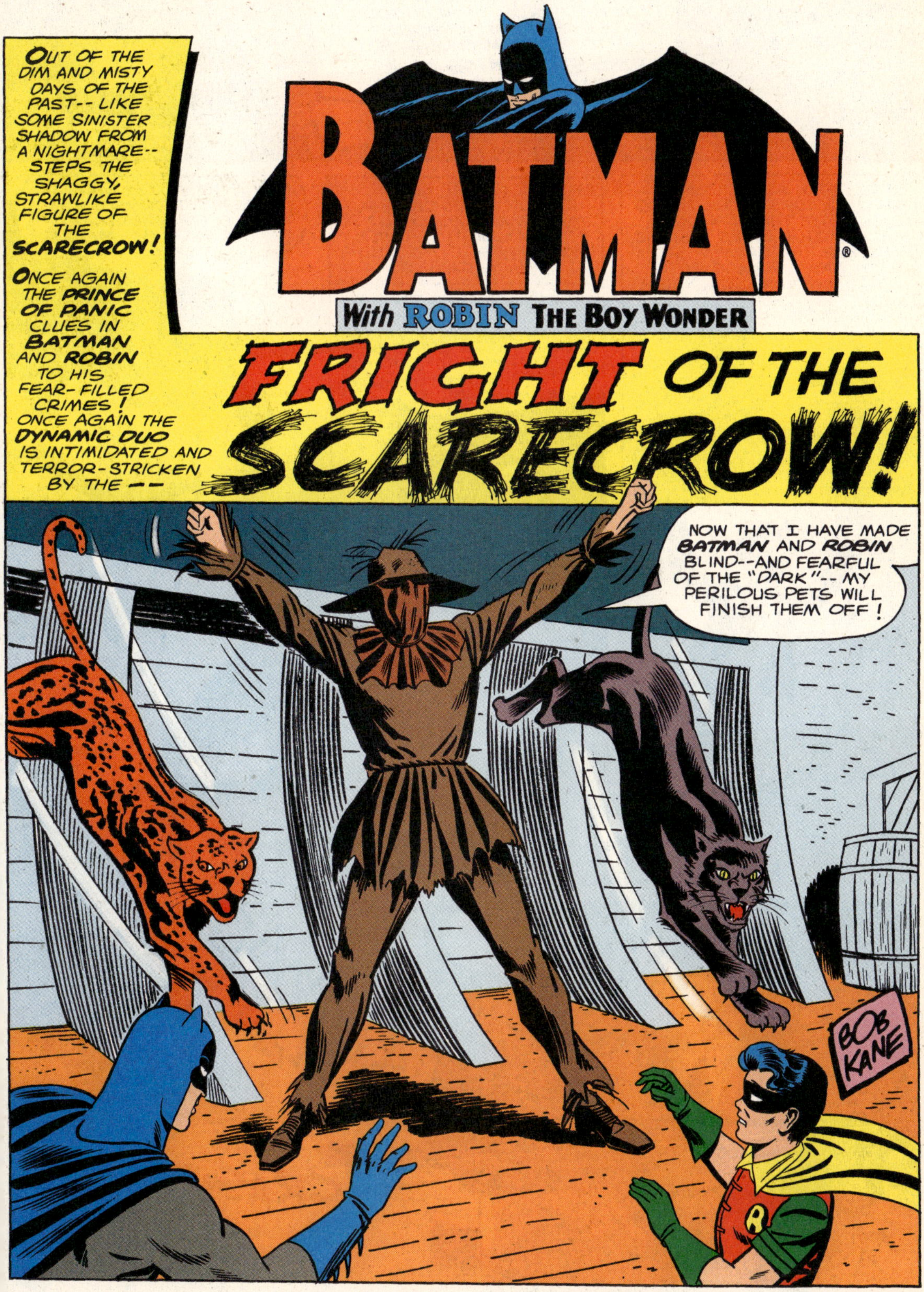
OUT OF THE DIM AND MISTY DAYS OF THE PAST-- LIKE SOME SINISTER SHADOW FROM A NIGHTMARE-- STEPS THE SHAGGY, STRAWLIKE FIGURE OF THE SCARECROW!
ONCE AGAIN THE PRINCE OF PANIC CLUES IN BATMAN AND ROBIN TO HIS FEAR-FILLED CRIMES! ONCE AGAIN THE DYNAMIC DUO IS INTIMIDATED AND TERROR-STRICKEN BY THE --
BATMAN®
With ROBIN THE BOY WONDER
FRIGHT OF THE SCARECROW!
NOW THAT I HAVE MADE BATMAN AND ROBIN BLIND--AND FEARFUL OF THE "DARK"-- MY PERILOUS PETS WILL FINISH THEM OFF!
BOB KANE

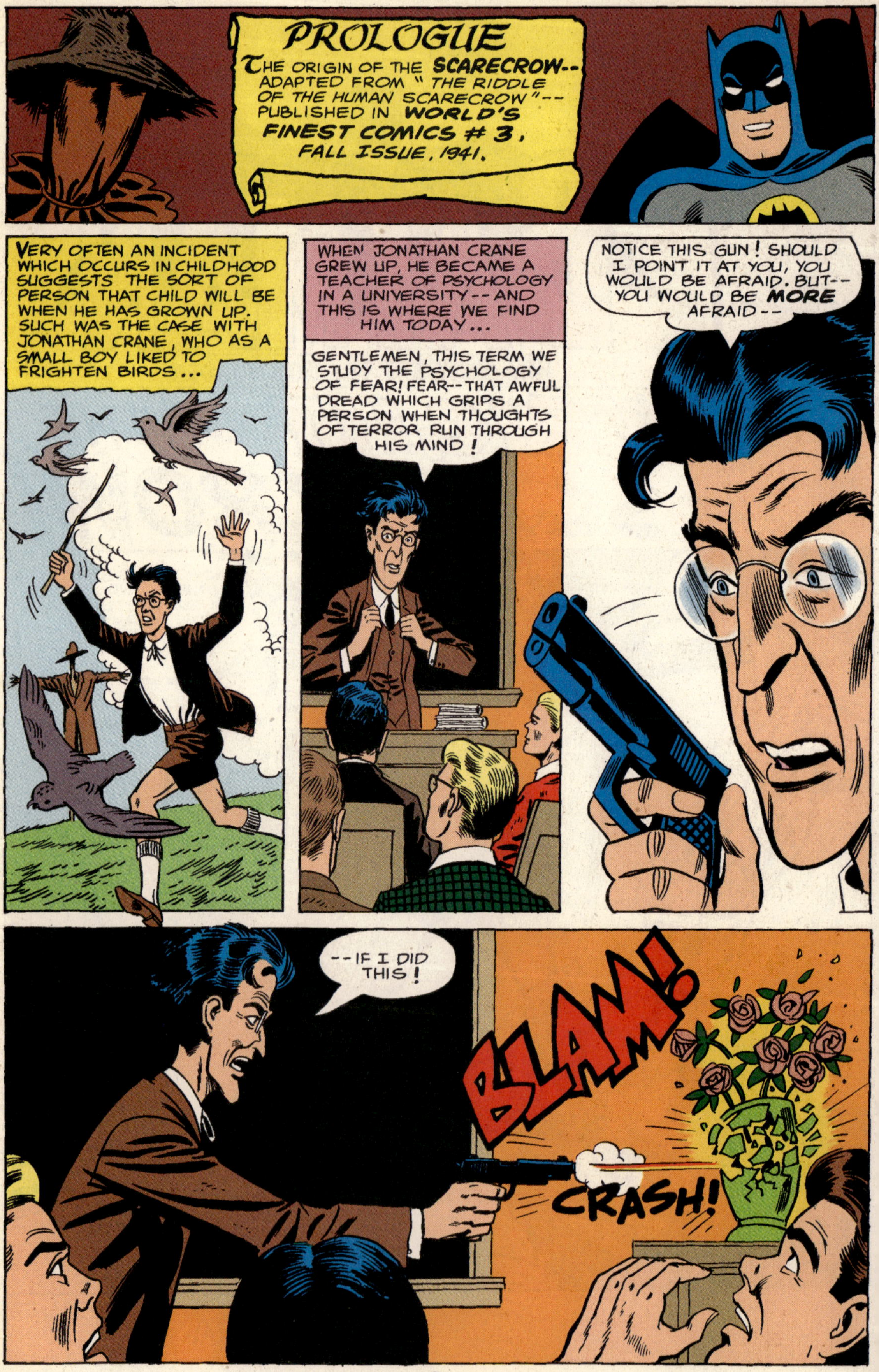
PROLOGUE
THE ORIGIN OF THE SCARECROW-- ADAPTED FROM "THE RIDDLE OF THE HUMAN SCARECROW"-- PUBLISHED IN WORLD'S FINEST COMICS #3, FALL ISSUE, 1941.
VERY OFTEN AN INCIDENT WHICH OCCURS IN CHILDHOOD SUGGESTS THE SORT OF PERSON THAT CHILD WILL BE WHEN HE HAS GROWN UP. SUCH WAS THE CASE WITH JONATHAN CRANE, WHO AS A SMALL BOY LIKED TO FRIGHTEN BIRDS...
WHEN JONATHAN CRANE GREW UP, HE BECAME A TEACHER OF PSYCHOLOGY IN A UNIVERSITY -- AND THIS IS WHERE WE FIND HIM TODAY...
GENTLEMEN, THIS TERM WE STUDY THE PSYCHOLOGY OF FEAR! FEAR-- THAT AWFUL DREAD WHICH GRIPS A PERSON WHEN THOUGHTS OF TERROR RUN THROUGH HIS MIND!
NOTICE THIS GUN! SHOULD I POINT IT AT YOU, YOU WOULD BE AFRAID. BUT-- YOU WOULD BE MORE AFRAID --
-- IF I DID THIS!
BLAM!
CRASH!

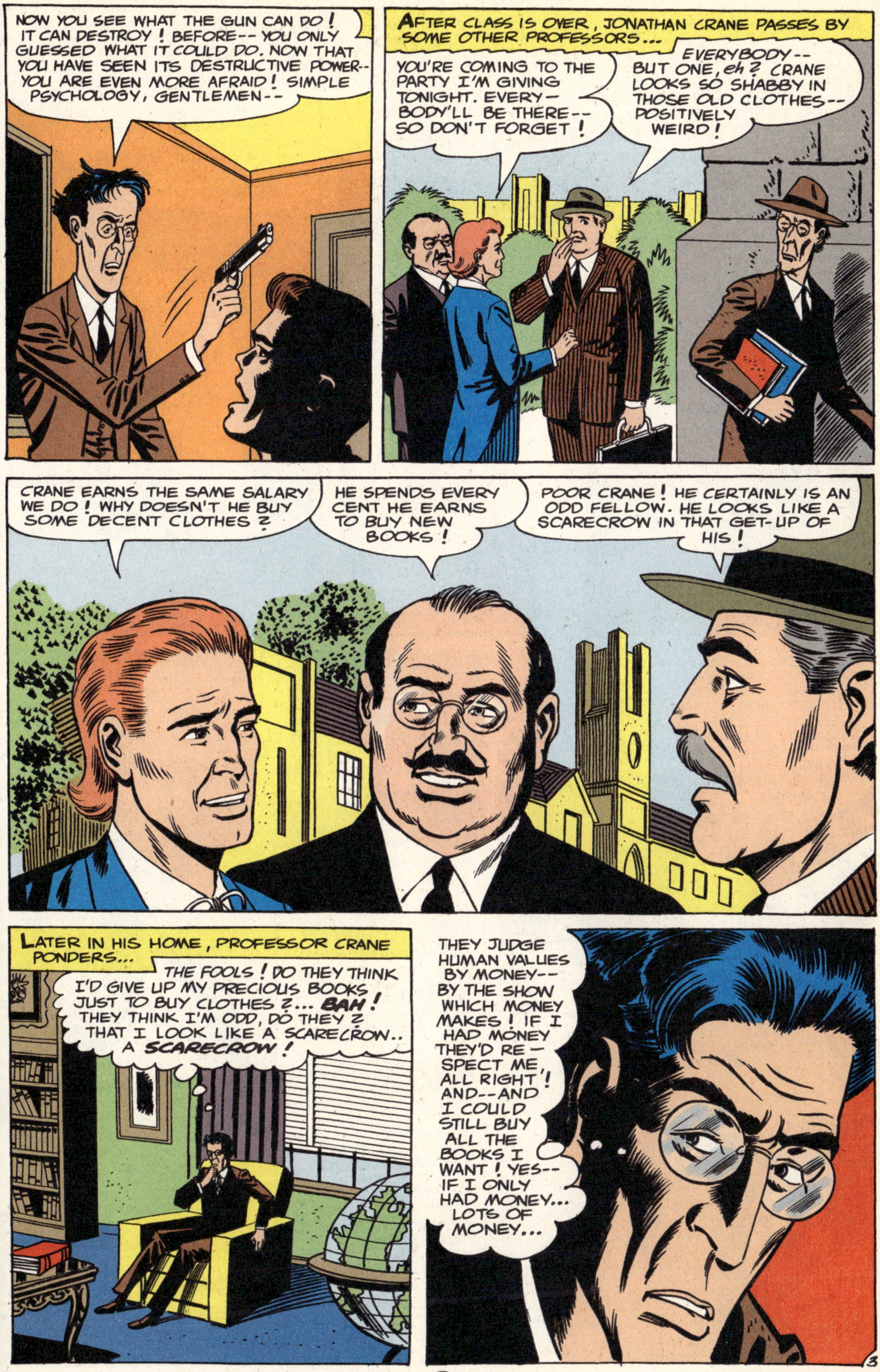
NOW YOU SEE WHAT THE GUN CAN DO! IT CAN DESTROY! BEFORE-- YOU ONLY GUESSED WHAT IT COULD DO. NOW THAT YOU HAVE SEEN ITS DESTRUCTIVE POWER-- YOU ARE EVEN MORE AFRAID! SIMPLE PSYCHOLOGY, GENTLEMEN--
AFTER CLASS IS OVER, JONATHAN CRANE PASSES BY SOME OTHER PROFESSORS...
YOU'RE COMING TO THE PARTY I'M GIVING TONIGHT. EVERY-BODY'LL BE THERE-- SO DON'T FORGET!
EVERYBODY-- BUT ONE, eh? CRANE LOOKS SO SHABBY IN THOSE OLD CLOTHES-- POSITIVELY WEIRD!
CRANE EARNS THE SAME SALARY WE DO! WHY DOESN'T HE BUY SOME DECENT CLOTHES?
HE SPENDS EVERY CENT HE EARNS TO BUY NEW BOOKS!
POOR CRANE! HE CERTAINLY IS AN ODD FELLOW. HE LOOKS LIKE A SCARECROW IN THAT GET-UP OF HIS!
LATER IN HIS HOME, PROFESSOR CRANE PONDERS...
THE FOOLS! DO THEY THINK I'D GIVE UP MY PRECIOUS BOOKS JUST TO BUY CLOTHES?... BAH! THEY THINK I'M ODD, DO THEY? THAT I LOOK LIKE A SCARECROW.. A SCARECROW!
THEY JUDGE HUMAN VALUES BY MONEY-- BY THE SHOW WHICH MONEY MAKES! IF I HAD MONEY THEY'D RE-SPECT ME, ALL RIGHT! AND--AND I COULD STILL BUY ALL THE BOOKS I WANT! YES-- IF I ONLY HAD MONEY... LOTS OF MONEY...
3

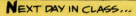

NEXT DAY IN CLASS...

TAKE THE EXAMPLE OF THE "PROTECTION RACKET," AS WORKED BY THE GANGSTER. HE WANTS MONEY--SO HE MAKES PEOPLE PAY HIM. AND HOW DOES HE DO THIS?

HE MAKES PEOPLE AFRAID--SO TERRIBLY AFRAID THEY PAY HIM WHAT HE ASKS! YES-- HE PUTS REAL *FEAR* INTO THEIR HEARTS-- AND HE GETS *MONEY!* LOTS OF *MONEY*--ALL BECAUSE PEOPLE ARE *AFRAID* OF HIM!

IN HIS HOME THAT NIGHT, THE DISTORTED BRAIN OF PROFESSOR CRANE BEGINS THINKING ALONG FANTASTIC LINES-- ALONG *CRIMINAL* LINES ...

ODD, AM I? AND-- A *SCARECROW!* FEAR MAKES *MONEY* FOR THE GANGSTER SO WHY NOT FOR--*ME?* HMMMM...

IF I LOOK LIKE A *SCARECROW*-- THEN THAT WILL BE MY SYMBOL! A SYMBOL OF POVERTY AND FEAR COMBINED! THE PERFECT SYMBOL TO REPRESENT JONATHAN CRANE-- THE *SCARE-CROW!*

AND SO IS BORN AN EVIL FIGURE OF THE NIGHT! ACROSS *BATMAN'S* HORIZON STALKS THIS NEW AND FRIGHTENING FORM-- A SCARY SHAPE OF STRAW AND SHAGGY BURLAP, WITH A BRAIN BOTH CUNNING AND DISTORTED!

WHO IS THIS FIGURE WHOSE VERY LUDICROUS APPEARANCE INSPIRES *FEAR*--SYMBOLIZES FEAR--FEAR INCARN-ATE--FEAR WALKING THE STREETS OF *GOTHAM CITY?*

IT IS THAT MOST TERRIBLE--MOST BIZARRE OF ALL CRIMINALS--THE CRIMINAL ALL WILL LEARN TO FEAR-- AND CALL ...

THE SCARECROW!

4

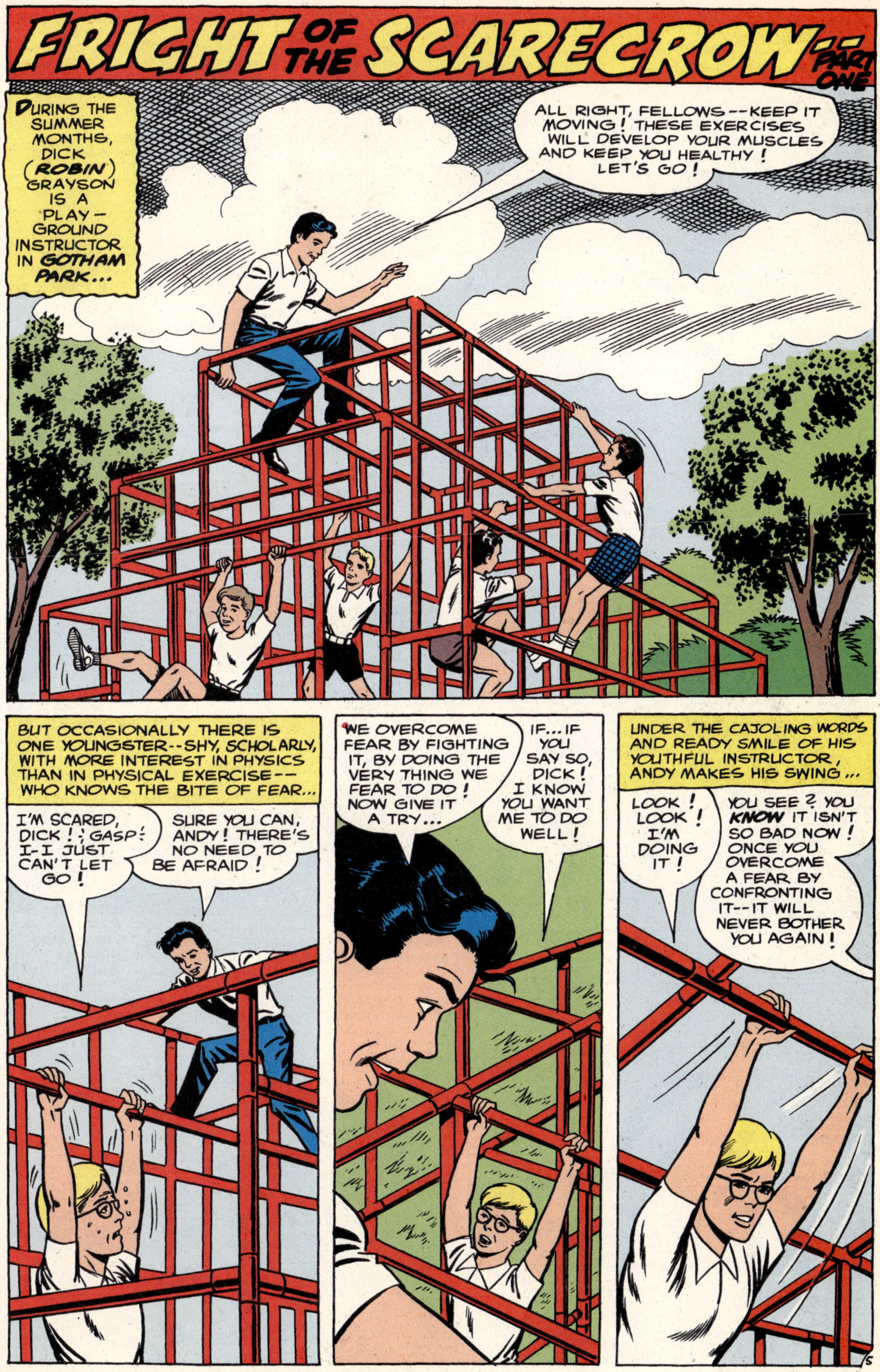

FRIGHT OF THE SCARECROW-- PART ONE
DURING THE SUMMER MONTHS, DICK (ROBIN) GRAYSON IS A PLAY-GROUND INSTRUCTOR IN GOTHAM PARK...
ALL RIGHT, FELLOWS--KEEP IT MOVING! THESE EXERCISES WILL DEVELOP YOUR MUSCLES AND KEEP YOU HEALTHY! LET'S GO!
BUT OCCASIONALLY THERE IS ONE YOUNGSTER--SHY, SCHOLARLY, WITH MORE INTEREST IN PHYSICS THAN IN PHYSICAL EXERCISE--WHO KNOWS THE BITE OF FEAR...
I'M SCARED, DICK! GASP! I-I JUST CAN'T LET GO!
SURE YOU CAN, ANDY! THERE'S NO NEED TO BE AFRAID!
WE OVERCOME FEAR BY FIGHTING IT, BY DOING THE VERY THING WE FEAR TO DO! NOW GIVE IT A TRY...
IF...IF YOU SAY SO, DICK! I KNOW YOU WANT ME TO DO WELL!
UNDER THE CAJOLING WORDS AND READY SMILE OF HIS YOUTHFUL INSTRUCTOR, ANDY MAKES HIS SWING...
LOOK! LOOK! I'M DOING IT!
YOU SEE? YOU KNOW IT ISN'T SO BAD NOW! ONCE YOU OVERCOME A FEAR BY CONFRONTING IT--IT WILL NEVER BOTHER YOU AGAIN!
5

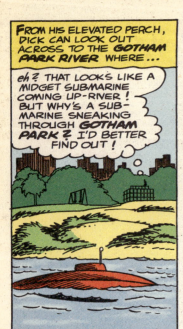

FROM HIS ELEVATED PERCH, DICK CAN LOOK OUT ACROSS TO THE *GOTHAM PARK RIVER* WHERE...

eh? THAT LOOKS LIKE A MIDGET SUBMARINE COMING UP-RIVER! BUT WHY'S A SUBMARINE SNEAKING THROUGH GOTHAM PARK? I'D BETTER FIND OUT!

OKAY, FELLOWS--TIME OUT FOR EATS! GRAB YOUR LUNCH BOXES AND MAKE FOR THE PICNIC AREA!

MOMENTS AFTERWARD, KEEN EYES FOLLOWING THE UNDERSEA CRAFT, DICK MOVES ALONG THE RIVERBANK...

MY LUNCH--AND MY ROBIN OUTFIT--ARE IN MY BASKET SO I'M PREPARED IF SOMETHING DEVELOPS! HMMM-- THE SUB IS TURNING IN TOWARD THIS BANK--

MOMENTS LATER...

HOLY SHOCKEROO! IT'S--THE-- SCARECROW!! ON THE LOOSE AGAIN! WH--WHAT KIND OF CROOKED BUSINESS CAN HE PULL OFF HERE IN THE PARK?

SHORTLY, A CHEERY VOICE HAILS THE YOUTHFUL SLEUTH...

HI, THERE, DICK! ALFRED AND I CAME OVER TO SURPRISE YOUR YOUNG CHARGES WITH SOME ICE CREAM TREATS!

MASTER DICK LOOKS AS IF HE'S SEEN A GHOST!

BRUCE! ALFRED! AM I EVER GLAD YOU'RE HERE! WAIT'LL I TELL YOU WHO JUST SHOWED UP!

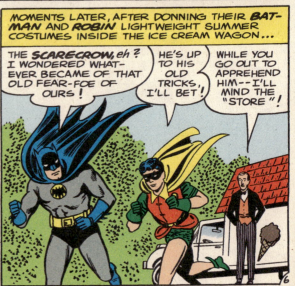

MOMENTS LATER, AFTER DONNING THEIR *BATMAN* AND *ROBIN* LIGHTWEIGHT SUMMER COSTUMES INSIDE THE ICE CREAM WAGON...

THE SCARECROW, eh? I WONDERED WHATEVER BECAME OF THAT OLD FEAR-FOE OF OURS!

HE'S UP TO HIS OLD TRICKS, I'LL BET!

WHILE YOU GO OUT TO APPREHEND HIM--I'LL MIND THE "STORE"!

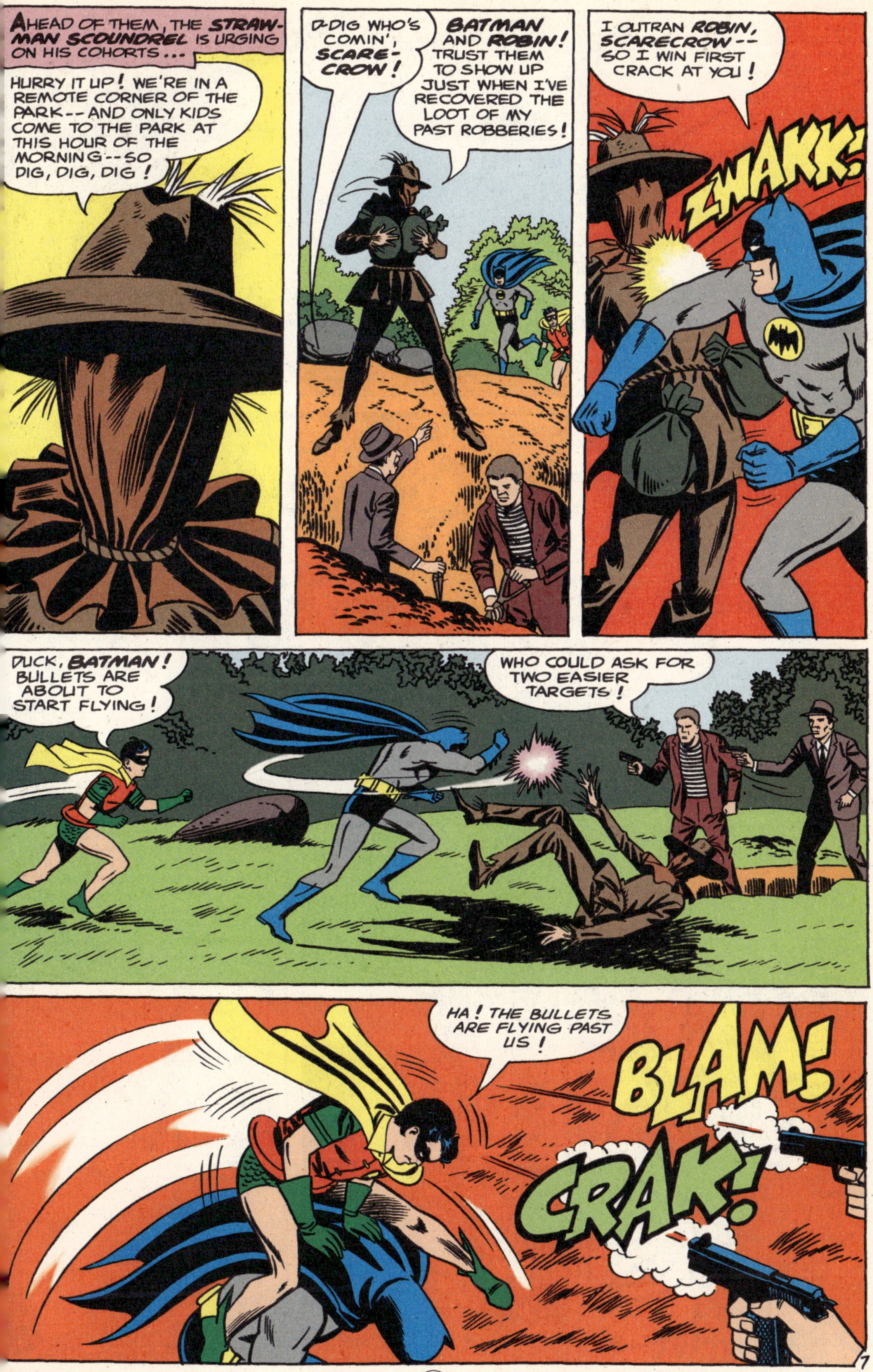
AHEAD OF THEM, THE STRAW-MAN SCOUNDREL IS URGING ON HIS COHORTS...
HURRY IT UP! WE'RE IN A REMOTE CORNER OF THE PARK--AND ONLY KIDS COME TO THE PARK AT THIS HOUR OF THE MORNING--SO DIG, DIG, DIG!
D-DIG WHO'S COMIN', SCARE-CROW!
BATMAN AND ROBIN! TRUST THEM TO SHOW UP JUST WHEN I'VE RECOVERED THE LOOT OF MY PAST ROBBERIES!
I OUTRAN ROBIN, SCARECROW--SO I WIN FIRST CRACK AT YOU!
ZWAKK!
DUCK, BATMAN! BULLETS ARE ABOUT TO START FLYING!
WHO COULD ASK FOR TWO EASIER TARGETS!
HA! THE BULLETS ARE FLYING PAST US!
BLAM!
CRAK!
7

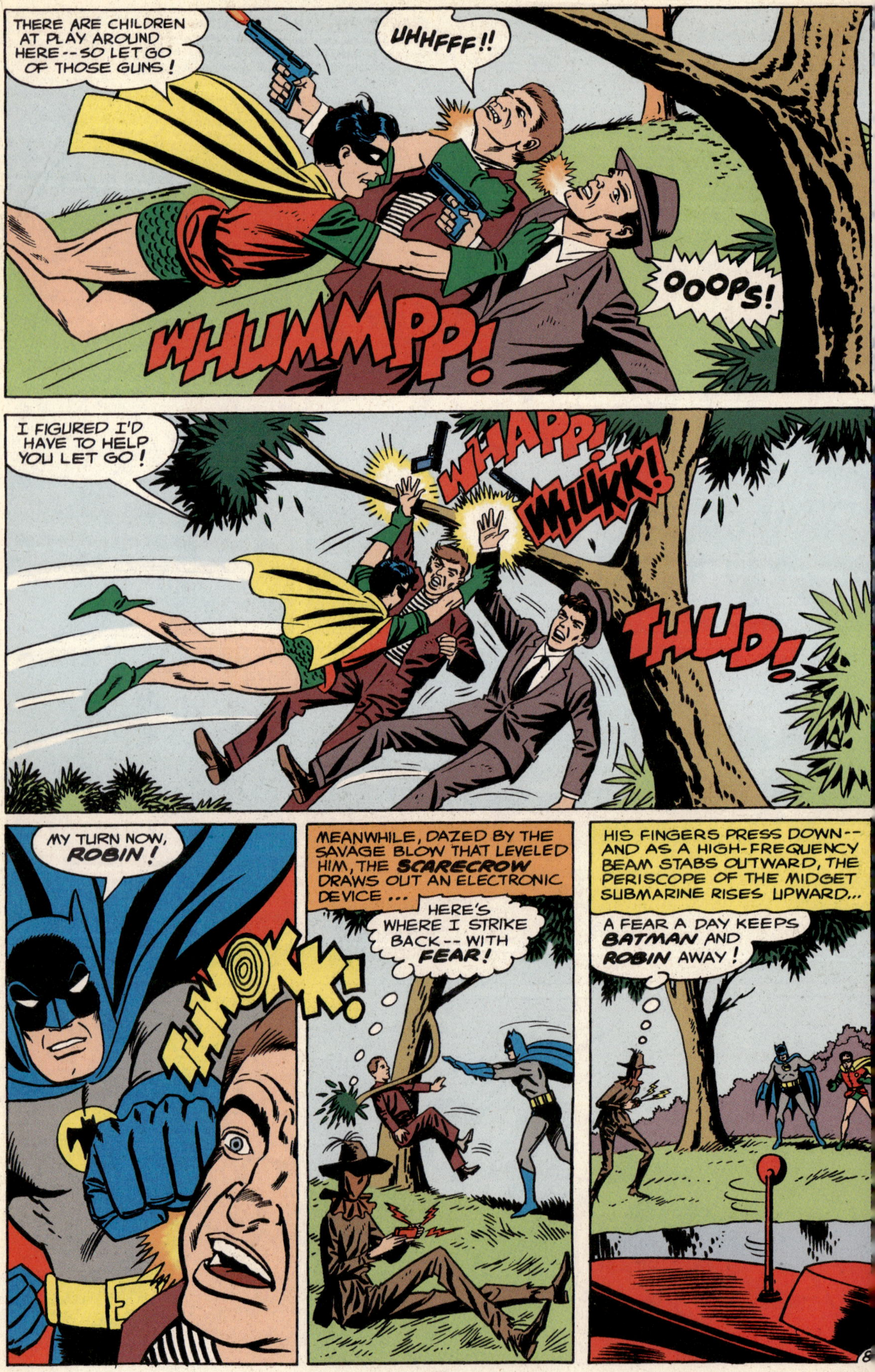
THERE ARE CHILDREN AT PLAY AROUND HERE--SO LET GO OF THOSE GUNS!
UHHFFF!!
OOOPS!
WHUMMPP!
I FIGURED I'D HAVE TO HELP YOU LET GO!
WHAPP!
WHUKK!
THUD!
MY TURN NOW, ROBIN!
THWOKK!
MEANWHILE, DAZED BY THE SAVAGE BLOW THAT LEVELED HIM, THE SCARECROW DRAWS OUT AN ELECTRONIC DEVICE...
HERE'S WHERE I STRIKE BACK--WITH FEAR!
HIS FINGERS PRESS DOWN--AND AS A HIGH-FREQUENCY BEAM STABS OUTWARD, THE PERISCOPE OF THE MIDGET SUBMARINE RISES UPWARD...
A FEAR A DAY KEEPS BATMAN AND ROBIN AWAY!
8

FROM THE PERISCOPE ARCHES A CHEMICAL SPRAY--A SPECIAL CONCOCTION OF THE TYRANT OF TERROR...

YULP! I'M FALLING...

LOSING MY BALANCE--GOING TO TOPPLE OVER--FALL INTO A BOTTOMLESS PIT...

YES, YOU TWO ARE FALLING.. INTO MY TRAP OF FEAR!

GOT TO HOLD TIGHT! C-CAN'T LET GO--OR I'LL DROP DOWN THROUGH THE GROUND!

DON'T HOG THE WHOLE TREE, ROBIN-- GIVE ME GRABBING ROOM TOO!

FEAR OF FALLING--AN INNATE FEAR OF MANKIND! IT'S ENGULFING THEM BOTH AS I LEAVE BEHIND MY CALLING CARDS--THESE STRAWS!

LOOK WELL AT THOSE STRAWS, DYNAMIC DUO! KNOW THEM FOR A SYMBOL OF THE MIGHTY POWER I WIELD AS THE--SCARECROW! FAREWELL, MY FEARFUL FELON-CHASERS-- FOR NOW!

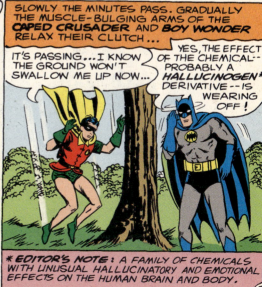

SLOWLY THE MINUTES PASS. GRADUALLY THE MUSCLE-BULGING ARMS OF THE CAPED CRUSADER AND BOY WONDER RELAX THEIR CLUTCH...

IT'S PASSING... I KNOW THE GROUND WON'T SWALLOW ME UP NOW...

YES, THE EFFECT OF THE CHEMICAL-- PROBABLY A HALLUCINOGEN* DERIVATIVE--IS WEARING OFF!

*EDITOR'S NOTE: A FAMILY OF CHEMICALS WITH UNUSUAL HALLUCINATORY AND EMOTIONAL EFFECTS ON THE HUMAN BRAIN AND BODY.

9

RACING TOWARD THE RIVER BANK, THEY FIND THE MIDGET SUBMARINE GONE-- BUT NOT FORGOTTEN...

AS HE DID ON HIS LAST ENCOUNTER WITH US, THE *SCARECROW* HAS LEFT US CRYPTIC CLUES! *PARK*-- OBVIOUSLY HIS FIRST VENTURE HERE TO REGAIN THE LOOT OF HIS MANY PAST ROBBERIES...

ARK! AND-- *MARK!* IF ONLY *THEIR* MEANING WERE AS OBVIOUS!

PARK ARK MARK

A LITTLE LATER, AS THEY ARE DISPENSING ICE CREAM TREATS, THE DEJECTED BRUCE WAYNE AND DICK GRAYSON LOSE A LITTLE OF THEIR GLOOM IN THE WARM GRINS OF THE BOYS...

THOSE CHEERY FACES SURE MAKE A FELLOW FEEL GOOD-- BUT I'D FEEL BETTER IF THE *SCARECROW* WERE BEHIND BARS!

I'M GLAD I GOT THIS IDEA OF HANDING OUT FREE ICE CREAM-- EVEN IF IT DID MEAN A SETBACK AT THE HANDS OF THE *SCARECROW!*

STORY CONTINUES ON THE NEXT PAGE ... 10

FRIGHT OF THE SCARECROW PART 2

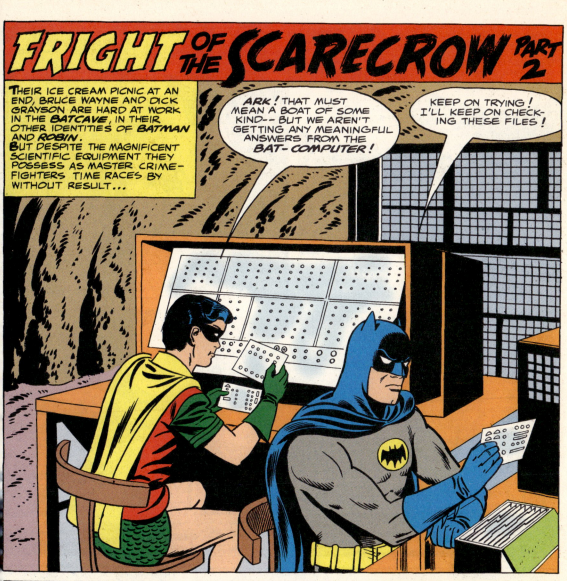

THEIR ICE CREAM PICNIC AT AN END, BRUCE WAYNE AND DICK GRAYSON ARE HARD AT WORK IN THE *BATCAVE*, IN THEIR OTHER IDENTITIES OF *BATMAN* AND *ROBIN*. BUT DESPITE THE MAGNIFICENT SCIENTIFIC EQUIPMENT THEY POSSESS AS MASTER CRIME-FIGHTERS TIME RACES BY WITHOUT RESULT...

ARK! THAT MUST MEAN A BOAT OF SOME KIND-- BUT WE AREN'T GETTING ANY MEANINGFUL ANSWERS FROM THE *BAT-COMPUTER!*

KEEP ON TRYING! I'LL KEEP ON CHECKING THESE FILES!

HERE'S A *"PROBABLE"!* THE *FLOATING PALACE*, A GAMBLING SHIP ANCHORED OUT BEYOND THE THREE-MILE LIMIT!

Hmm... BY STRETCHING THE IMAGINATION, IT MIGHT FIT--

WE'LL BE ON OUR WAY-- ALFRED! ARE THOSE *NEW* INFORMATION CARDS FOR THE *BAT-COMPUTER?*

INDEED THEY ARE, SIR! AUNT HARRIET'S BEEN KEEPING ME SO BUSY MOVING FURNITURE I AM AFRAID I'VE NEGLECTED MY MORE IMPORTANT DUTIES!

EAGERLY THE DEFT FINGERS OF THE *BOY WONDER* GRASP THE CARDS--FEED THEM THROUGH THE INTRICATE RELAY SYSTEMS OF THE INFORMATION MACHINE AND..

YIPPEE! WE'VE CAUGHT THE BRASS RING! LOOK--

THE *ARK*-- A REPLICA OF THE ORIGINAL *NOAH'S ARK* MADE FOR THE SILENT MOVIE OF THAT NAME...

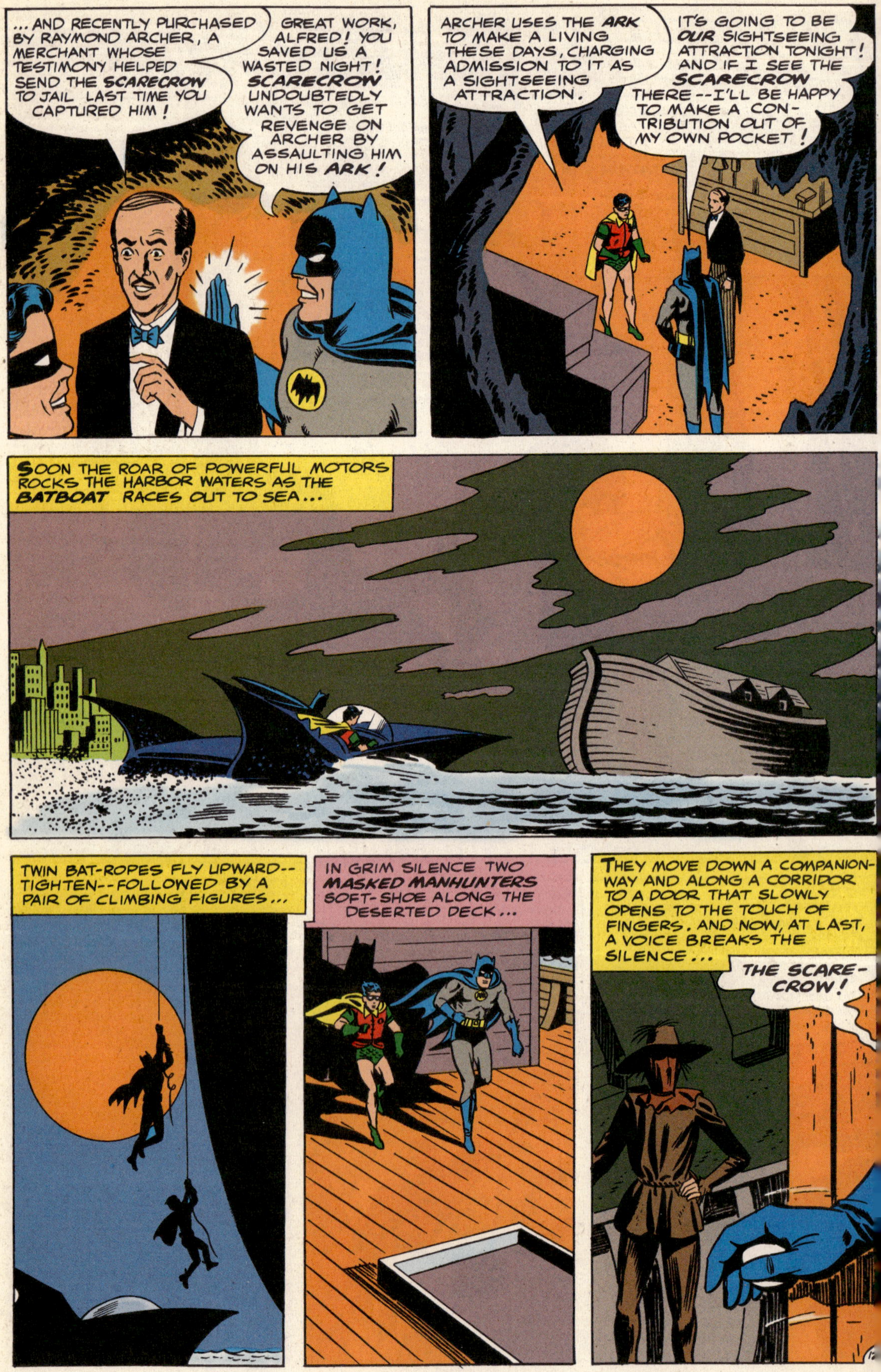

...AND RECENTLY PURCHASED BY RAYMOND ARCHER, A MERCHANT WHOSE TESTIMONY HELPED SEND THE SCARECROW TO JAIL LAST TIME YOU CAPTURED HIM!
GREAT WORK, ALFRED! YOU SAVED US A WASTED NIGHT! SCARECROW UNDOUBTEDLY WANTS TO GET REVENGE ON ARCHER BY ASSAULTING HIM ON HIS ARK!
ARCHER USES THE ARK TO MAKE A LIVING THESE DAYS, CHARGING ADMISSION TO IT AS A SIGHTSEEING ATTRACTION.
IT'S GOING TO BE OUR SIGHTSEEING ATTRACTION TONIGHT! AND IF I SEE THE SCARECROW THERE--I'LL BE HAPPY TO MAKE A CONTRIBUTION OUT OF MY OWN POCKET!
SOON THE ROAR OF POWERFUL MOTORS ROCKS THE HARBOR WATERS AS THE BATBOAT RACES OUT TO SEA...
TWIN BAT-ROPES FLY UPWARD--TIGHTEN--FOLLOWED BY A PAIR OF CLIMBING FIGURES...
IN GRIM SILENCE TWO MASKED MANHUNTERS SOFT-SHOE ALONG THE DESERTED DECK...
THEY MOVE DOWN A COMPANIONWAY AND ALONG A CORRIDOR TO A DOOR THAT SLOWLY OPENS TO THE TOUCH OF FINGERS. AND NOW, AT LAST, A VOICE BREAKS THE SILENCE...
THE SCARECROW!

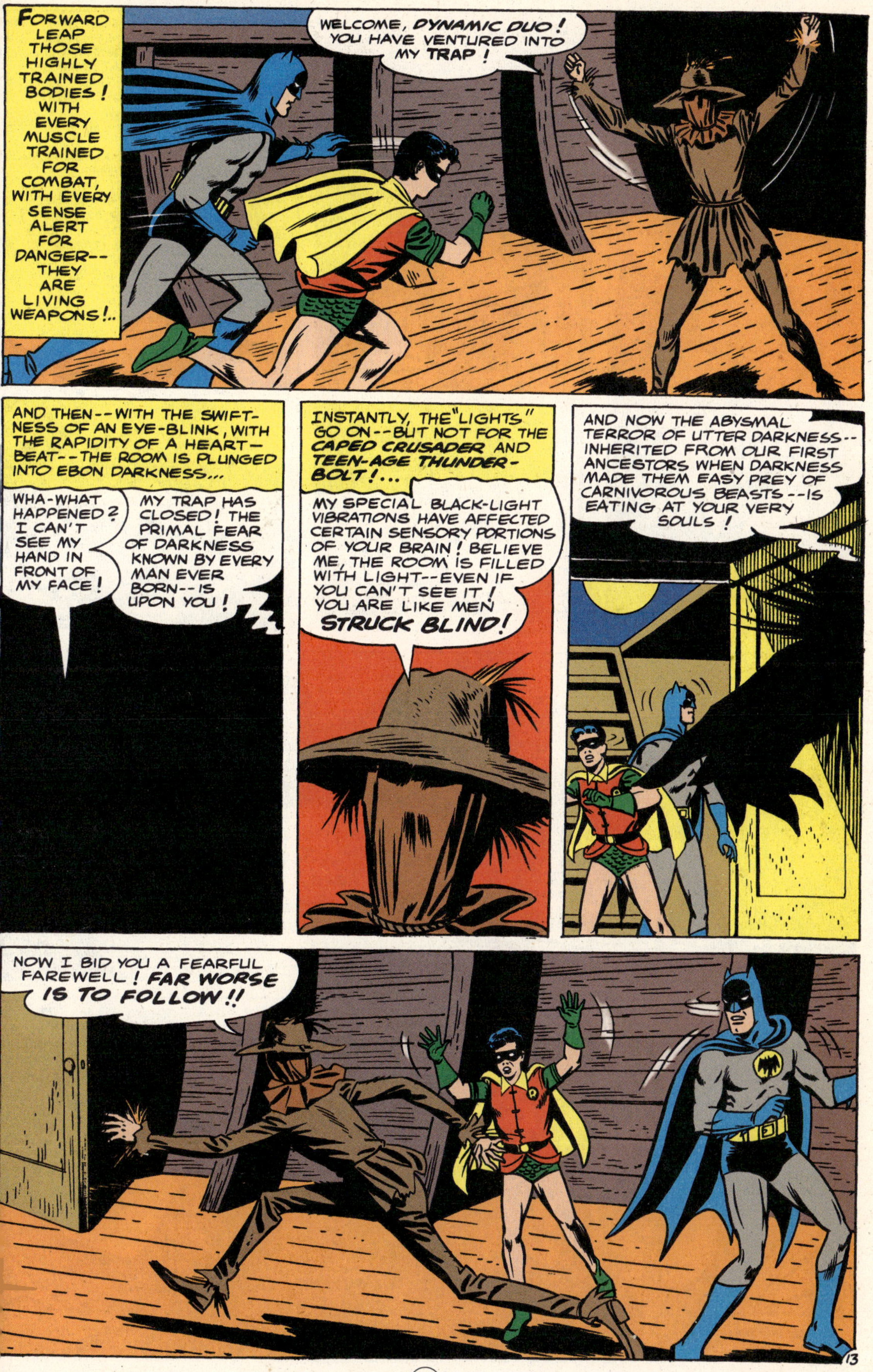
FORWARD LEAP THOSE HIGHLY TRAINED BODIES! WITH EVERY MUSCLE TRAINED FOR COMBAT, WITH EVERY SENSE ALERT FOR DANGER--THEY ARE LIVING WEAPONS!..
WELCOME, DYNAMIC DUO! YOU HAVE VENTURED INTO MY TRAP!
AND THEN--WITH THE SWIFTNESS OF AN EYE-BLINK, WITH THE RAPIDITY OF A HEART-BEAT--THE ROOM IS PLUNGED INTO EBON DARKNESS...
WHA-WHAT HAPPENED? I CAN'T SEE MY HAND IN FRONT OF MY FACE!
MY TRAP HAS CLOSED! THE PRIMAL FEAR OF DARKNESS KNOWN BY EVERY MAN EVER BORN--IS UPON YOU!
INSTANTLY, THE "LIGHTS" GO ON--BUT NOT FOR THE CAPED CRUSADER AND TEEN-AGE THUNDER-BOLT!...
MY SPECIAL BLACK-LIGHT VIBRATIONS HAVE AFFECTED CERTAIN SENSORY PORTIONS OF YOUR BRAIN! BELIEVE ME, THE ROOM IS FILLED WITH LIGHT--EVEN IF YOU CAN'T SEE IT! YOU ARE LIKE MEN STRUCK BLIND!
AND NOW THE ABYSMAL TERROR OF UTTER DARKNESS--INHERITED FROM OUR FIRST ANCESTORS WHEN DARKNESS MADE THEM EASY PREY OF CARNIVOROUS BEASTS--IS EATING AT YOUR VERY SOULS!
NOW I BID YOU A FEARFUL FAREWELL! FAR WORSE IS TO FOLLOW!!
13

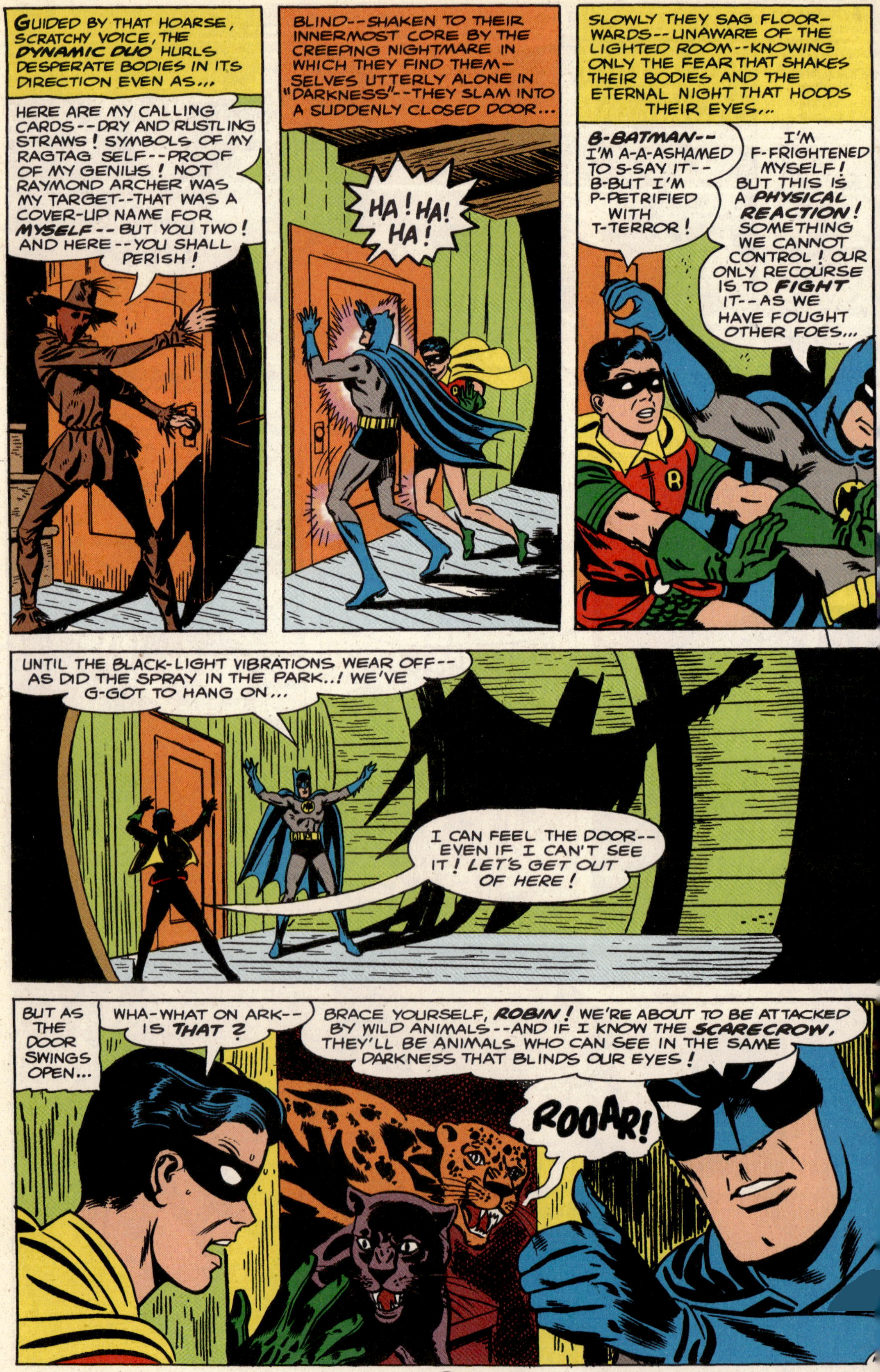
GUIDED BY THAT HOARSE, SCRATCHY VOICE, THE DYNAMIC DUO HURLS DESPERATE BODIES IN ITS DIRECTION EVEN AS...
HERE ARE MY CALLING CARDS--DRY AND RUSTLING STRAWS! SYMBOLS OF MY RAGTAG SELF--PROOF OF MY GENIUS! NOT RAYMOND ARCHER WAS MY TARGET--THAT WAS A COVER-UP NAME FOR MYSELF--BUT YOU TWO! AND HERE--YOU SHALL PERISH!
BLIND--SHAKEN TO THEIR INNERMOST CORE BY THE CREEPING NIGHTMARE IN WHICH THEY FIND THEM-SELVES UTTERLY ALONE IN "DARKNESS"--THEY SLAM INTO A SUDDENLY CLOSED DOOR...
HA! HA! HA!
SLOWLY THEY SAG FLOOR-WARDS--UNAWARE OF THE LIGHTED ROOM--KNOWING ONLY THE FEAR THAT SHAKES THEIR BODIES AND THE ETERNAL NIGHT THAT HOODS THEIR EYES...
B-BATMAN--I'M A-A-ASHAMED TO S-SAY IT--B-BUT I'M P-PETRIFIED WITH T-TERROR!
I'M F-FRIGHTENED MYSELF! BUT THIS IS A PHYSICAL REACTION! SOMETHING WE CANNOT CONTROL! OUR ONLY RECOURSE IS TO FIGHT IT--AS WE HAVE FOUGHT OTHER FOES...
UNTIL THE BLACK-LIGHT VIBRATIONS WEAR OFF--AS DID THE SPRAY IN THE PARK..! WE'VE G-GOT TO HANG ON...
I CAN FEEL THE DOOR--EVEN IF I CAN'T SEE IT! LET'S GET OUT OF HERE!
BUT AS THE DOOR SWINGS OPEN...
WHA-WHAT ON ARK--IS THAT?
BRACE YOURSELF, ROBIN! WE'RE ABOUT TO BE ATTACKED BY WILD ANIMALS--AND IF I KNOW THE SCARECROW, THEY'LL BE ANIMALS WHO CAN SEE IN THE SAME DARKNESS THAT BLINDS OUR EYES!
ROOAR!

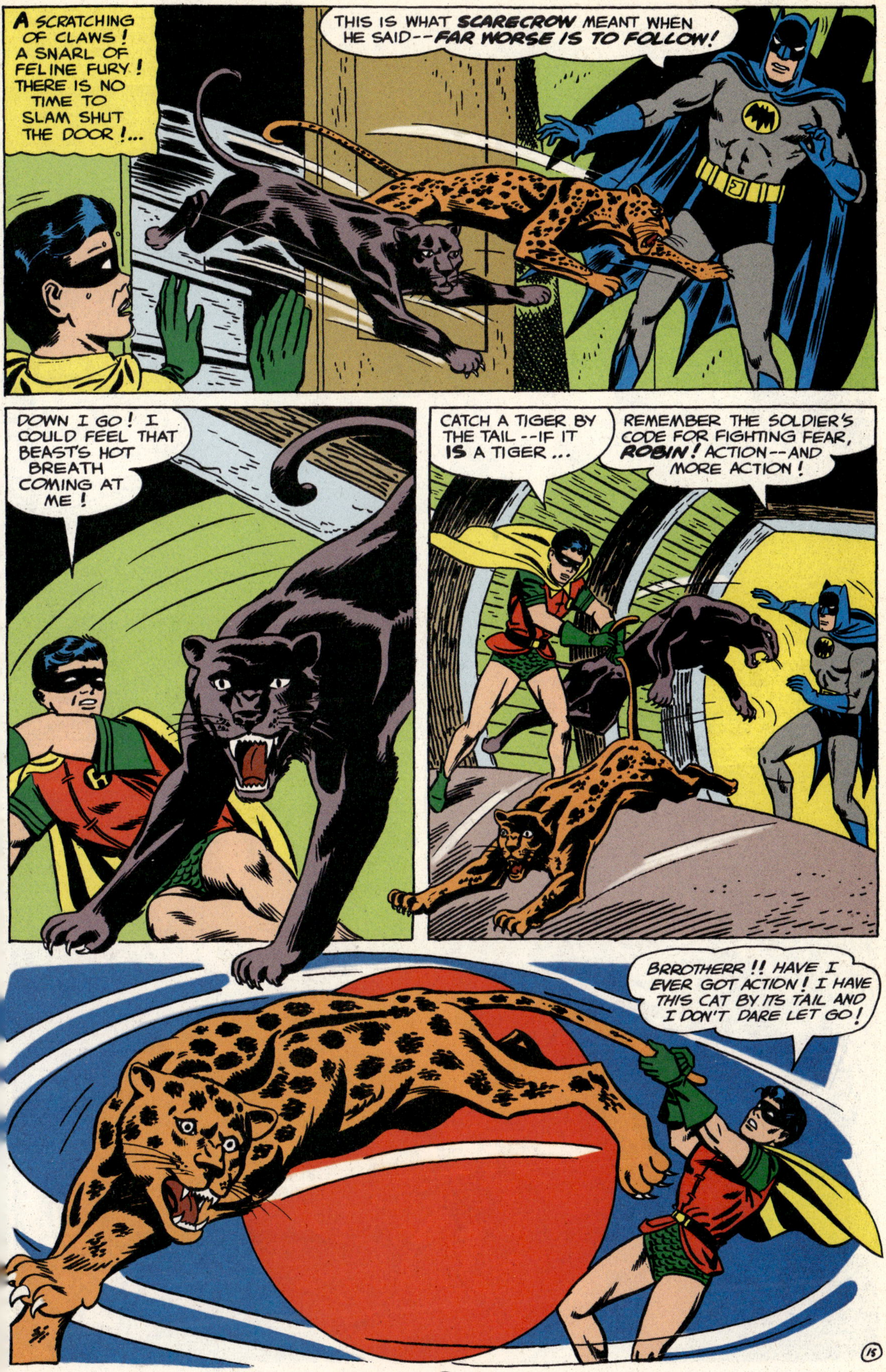
A SCRATCHING OF CLAWS! A SNARL OF FELINE FURY! THERE IS NO TIME TO SLAM SHUT THE DOOR!...
THIS IS WHAT SCARECROW MEANT WHEN HE SAID-- FAR WORSE IS TO FOLLOW!
DOWN I GO! I COULD FEEL THAT BEAST'S HOT BREATH COMING AT ME!
CATCH A TIGER BY THE TAIL --IF IT IS A TIGER...
REMEMBER THE SOLDIER'S CODE FOR FIGHTING FEAR, ROBIN! ACTION--AND MORE ACTION!
BRROTHERR!! HAVE I EVER GOT ACTION! I HAVE THIS CAT BY ITS TAIL AND I DON'T DARE LET GO!
15

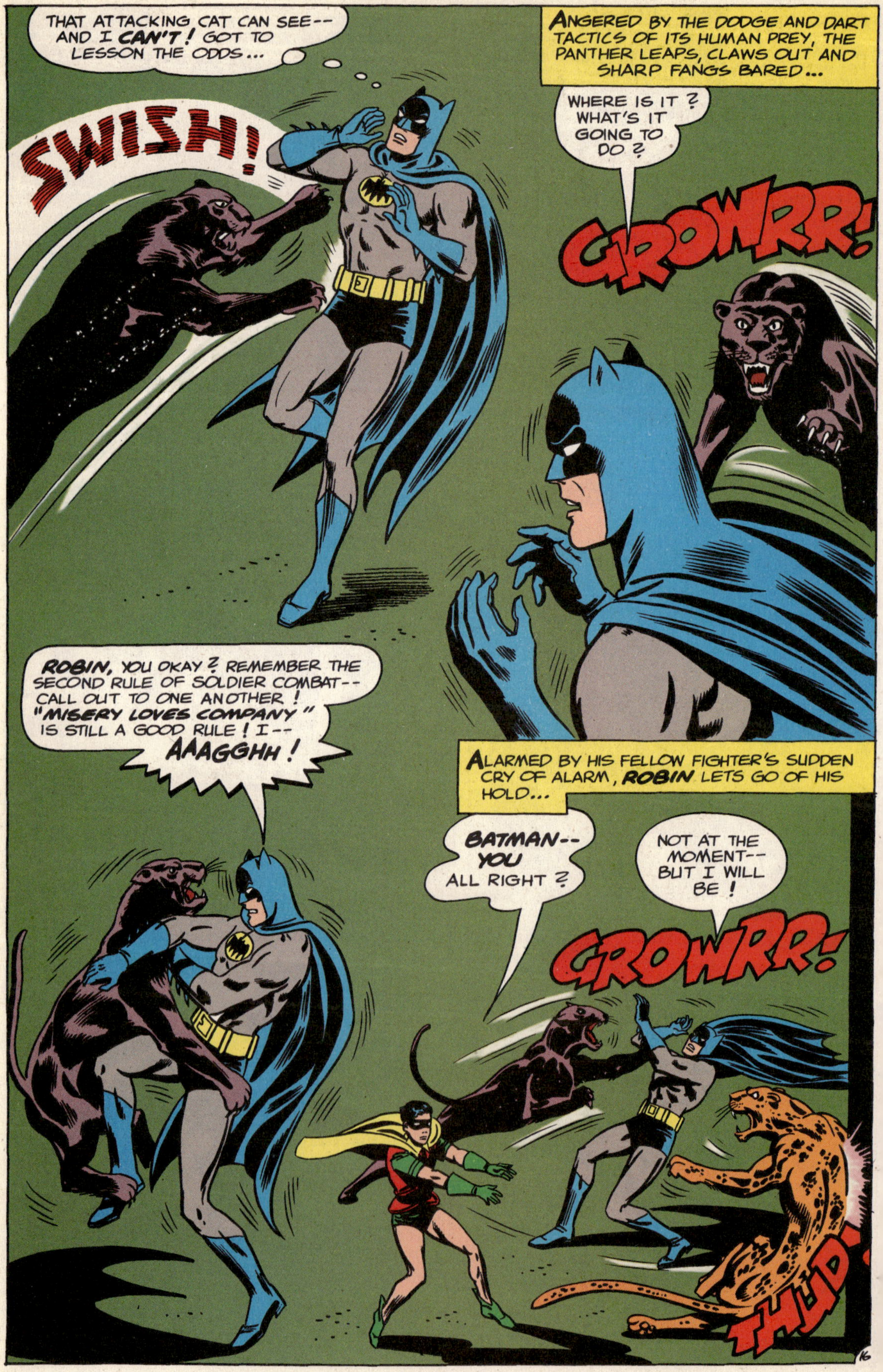
THAT ATTACKING CAT CAN SEE-- AND I CAN'T! GOT TO LESSON THE ODDS...
SWISH!
ANGERED BY THE DODGE AND DART TACTICS OF ITS HUMAN PREY, THE PANTHER LEAPS, CLAWS OUT AND SHARP FANGS BARED...
WHERE IS IT? WHAT'S IT GOING TO DO?
GROWRR!
ROBIN, YOU OKAY? REMEMBER THE SECOND RULE OF SOLDIER COMBAT-- CALL OUT TO ONE ANOTHER! "MISERY LOVES COMPANY" IS STILL A GOOD RULE! I-- AAAGGHH!
ALARMED BY HIS FELLOW FIGHTER'S SUDDEN CRY OF ALARM, ROBIN LETS GO OF HIS HOLD...
BATMAN-- YOU ALL RIGHT?
NOT AT THE MOMENT-- BUT I WILL BE!
GROWRR!
THUD!
16

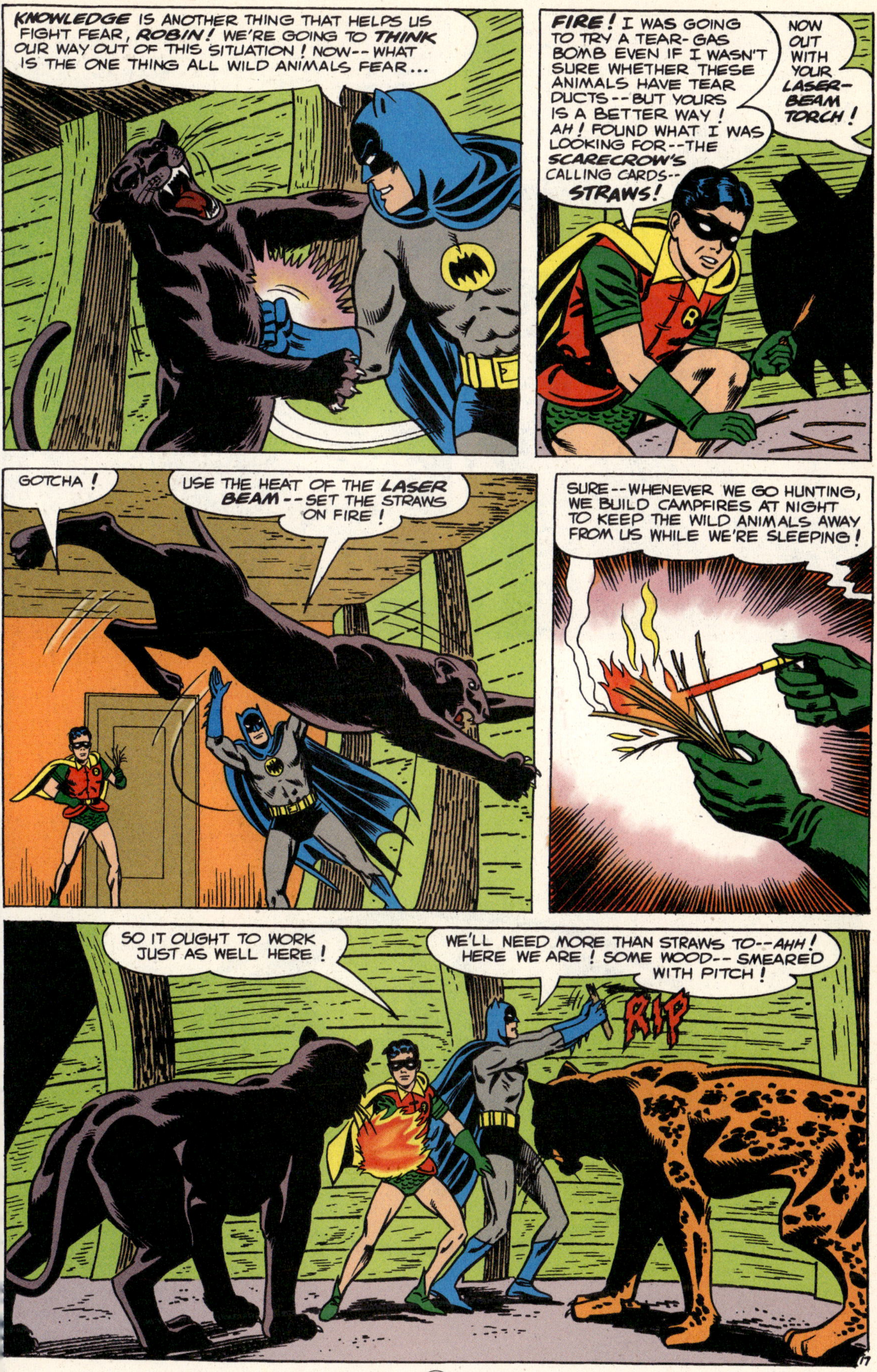
KNOWLEDGE IS ANOTHER THING THAT HELPS US FIGHT FEAR, ROBIN! WE'RE GOING TO THINK OUR WAY OUT OF THIS SITUATION! NOW--WHAT IS THE ONE THING ALL WILD ANIMALS FEAR...
FIRE! I WAS GOING TO TRY A TEAR-GAS BOMB EVEN IF I WASN'T SURE WHETHER THESE ANIMALS HAVE TEAR DUCTS--BUT YOURS IS A BETTER WAY! AH! FOUND WHAT I WAS LOOKING FOR--THE SCARECROW'S CALLING CARDS--STRAWS!
NOW OUT WITH YOUR LASER-BEAM TORCH!
GOTCHA!
USE THE HEAT OF THE LASER BEAM--SET THE STRAWS ON FIRE!
SURE--WHENEVER WE GO HUNTING, WE BUILD CAMPFIRES AT NIGHT TO KEEP THE WILD ANIMALS AWAY FROM US WHILE WE'RE SLEEPING!
SO IT OUGHT TO WORK JUST AS WELL HERE!
WE'LL NEED MORE THAN STRAWS TO--AHH! HERE WE ARE! SOME WOOD--SMEARED WITH PITCH!
RIP
17

ANGRY SNARLS RISE FROM THE THROATS OF THE FURRY, FRUSTRATED FELINES AS...
IT'S WORKING! THEY'RE KEEPING AT A SAFE DISTANCE!
NOW WE'VE GOT TO PUT OURSELVES AT AN EVEN SAFER DISTANCE--OUTSIDE THIS ROOM!
"RUNNING THE GAUNTLET" BETWEEN CLAWS AND FANGS, THE PAIR GROPES FOR THE DOORWAY...
GRAB THAT DOORKNOB, ROBIN!
I WILL--SOON AS I FIND IT!

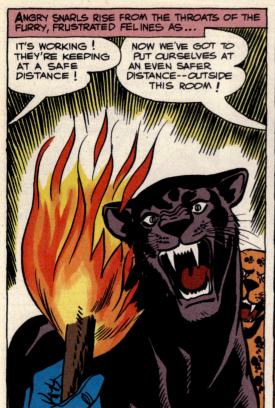

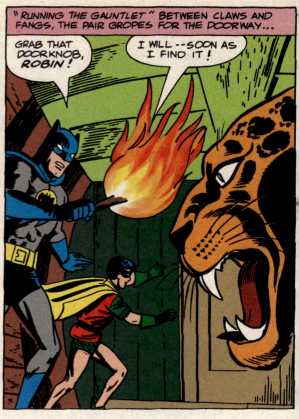

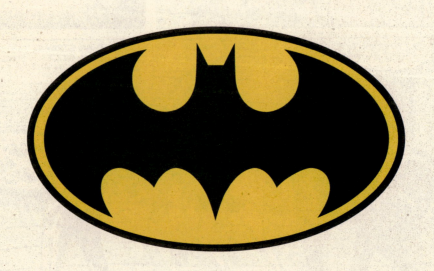

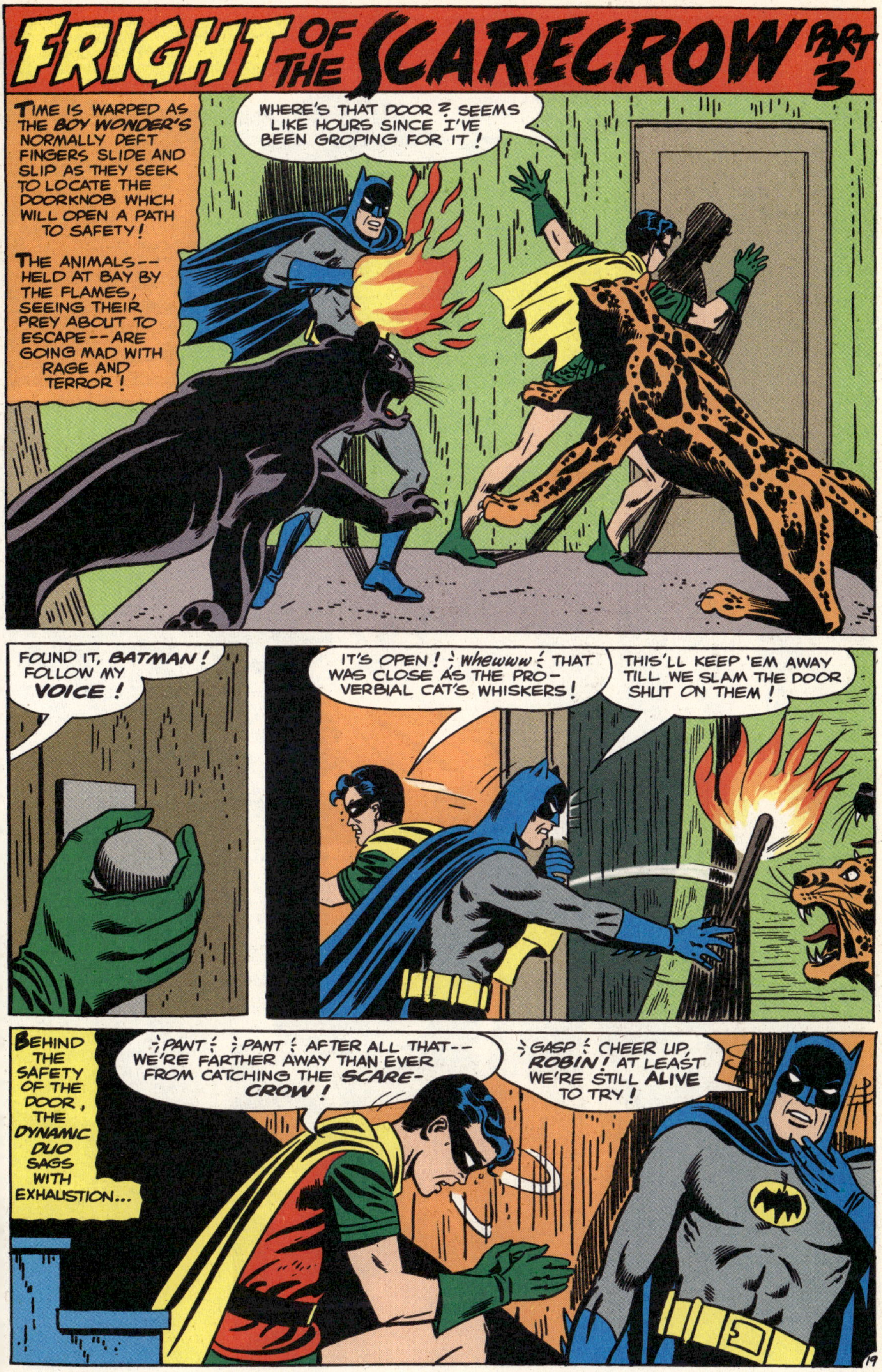
FRIGHT OF THE SCARECROW PART 3
TIME IS WARPED AS THE BOY WONDER'S NORMALLY DEFT FINGERS SLIDE AND SLIP AS THEY SEEK TO LOCATE THE DOORKNOB WHICH WILL OPEN A PATH TO SAFETY!
THE ANIMALS--HELD AT BAY BY THE FLAMES, SEEING THEIR PREY ABOUT TO ESCAPE--ARE GOING MAD WITH RAGE AND TERROR!
WHERE'S THAT DOOR? SEEMS LIKE HOURS SINCE I'VE BEEN GROPING FOR IT!
FOUND IT, BATMAN! FOLLOW MY VOICE!
IT'S OPEN! WHEWWW! THAT WAS CLOSE AS THE PRO-VERBIAL CAT'S WHISKERS!
THIS'LL KEEP 'EM AWAY TILL WE SLAM THE DOOR SHUT ON THEM!
BEHIND THE SAFETY OF THE DOOR, THE DYNAMIC DUO SAGS WITH EXHAUSTION...
PANT! PANT! AFTER ALL THAT--WE'RE FARTHER AWAY THAN EVER FROM CATCHING THE SCARE-CROW!
GASP! CHEER UP, ROBIN! AT LEAST WE'RE STILL ALIVE TO TRY!
19

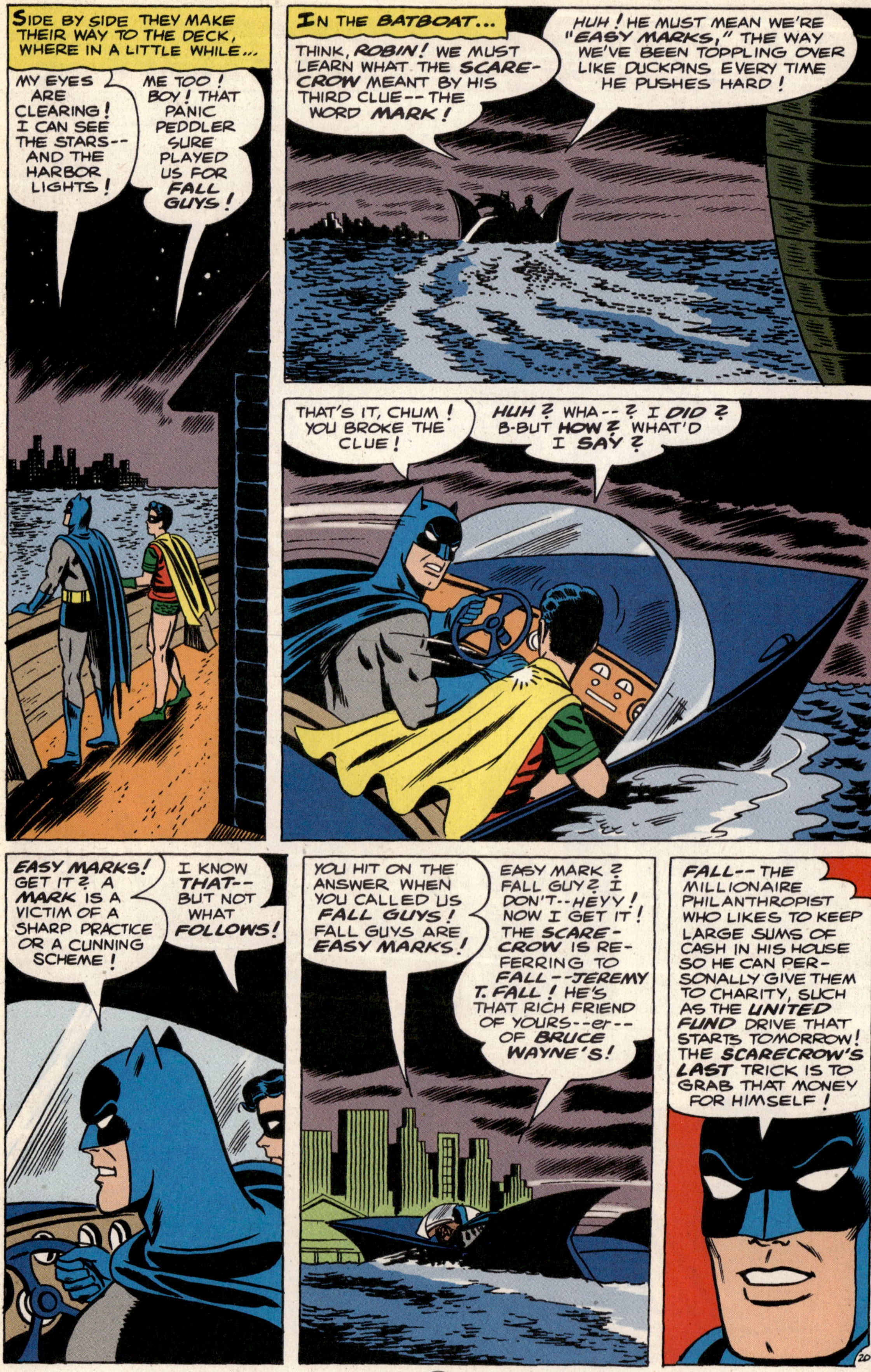
SIDE BY SIDE THEY MAKE THEIR WAY TO THE DECK, WHERE IN A LITTLE WHILE...
MY EYES ARE CLEARING! I CAN SEE THE STARS-- AND THE HARBOR LIGHTS!
ME TOO! BOY! THAT PANIC PEDDLER SURE PLAYED US FOR FALL GUYS!
IN THE BATBOAT...
THINK, ROBIN! WE MUST LEARN WHAT THE SCARE-CROW MEANT BY HIS THIRD CLUE-- THE WORD MARK!
HUH! HE MUST MEAN WE'RE "EASY MARKS," THE WAY WE'VE BEEN TOPPLING OVER LIKE DUCKPINS EVERY TIME HE PUSHES HARD!
THAT'S IT, CHUM! YOU BROKE THE CLUE!
HUH? WHA--? I DID? B-BUT HOW? WHAT'D I SAY?
EASY MARKS! GET IT? A MARK IS A VICTIM OF A SHARP PRACTICE OR A CUNNING SCHEME!
I KNOW THAT-- BUT NOT WHAT FOLLOWS!
YOU HIT ON THE ANSWER WHEN YOU CALLED US FALL GUYS! FALL GUYS ARE EASY MARKS!
EASY MARK? FALL GUY? I DON'T--HEYY! NOW I GET IT! THE SCARE-CROW IS RE-FERRING TO FALL--JEREMY T. FALL! HE'S THAT RICH FRIEND OF YOURS--er-- OF BRUCE WAYNE'S!
FALL-- THE MILLIONAIRE PHILANTHROPIST WHO LIKES TO KEEP LARGE SUMS OF CASH IN HIS HOUSE SO HE CAN PER-SONALLY GIVE THEM TO CHARITY, SUCH AS THE UNITED FUND DRIVE THAT STARTS TOMORROW! THE SCARECROW'S LAST TRICK IS TO GRAB THAT MONEY FOR HIMSELF!
20

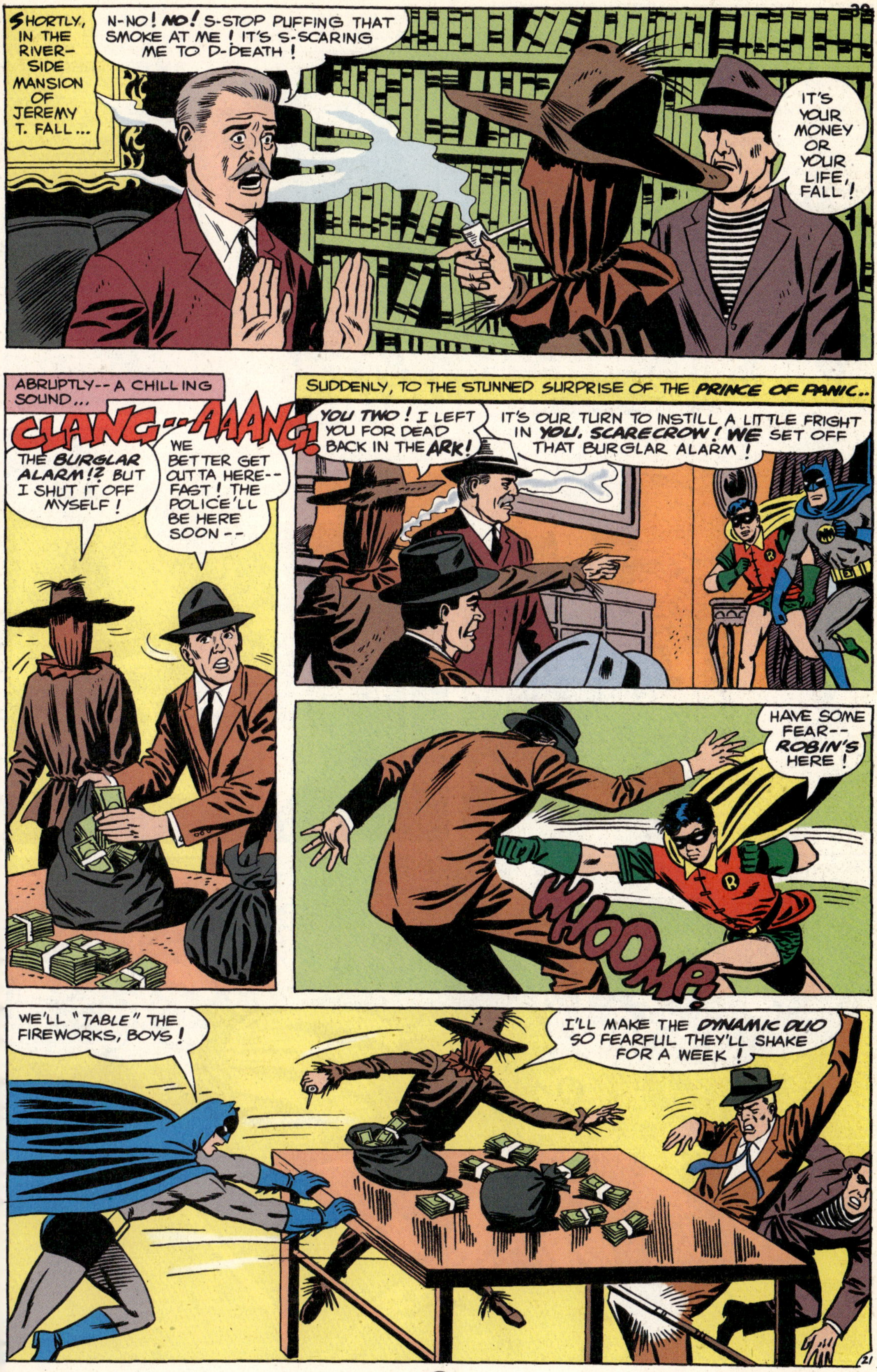

39
SHORTLY, IN THE RIVER-SIDE MANSION OF JEREMY T. FALL...
N-NO! NO! S-STOP PUFFING THAT SMOKE AT ME! IT'S S-SCARING ME TO D-DEATH!
IT'S YOUR MONEY OR YOUR LIFE, FALL!
ABRUPTLY-- A CHILLING SOUND...
CLANG--AAANG!
THE BURGLAR ALARM!? BUT I SHUT IT OFF MYSELF!
WE BETTER GET OUTTA HERE-- FAST! THE POLICE'LL BE HERE SOON--
SUDDENLY, TO THE STUNNED SURPRISE OF THE PRINCE OF PANIC..
YOU TWO! I LEFT YOU FOR DEAD BACK IN THE ARK!
IT'S OUR TURN TO INSTILL A LITTLE FRIGHT IN YOU, SCARECROW! WE SET OFF THAT BURGLAR ALARM!
HAVE SOME FEAR-- ROBIN'S HERE!
WHOOMP!
WE'LL "TABLE" THE FIREWORKS, BOYS!
I'LL MAKE THE DYNAMIC DUO SO FEARFUL THEY'LL SHAKE FOR A WEEK!
21

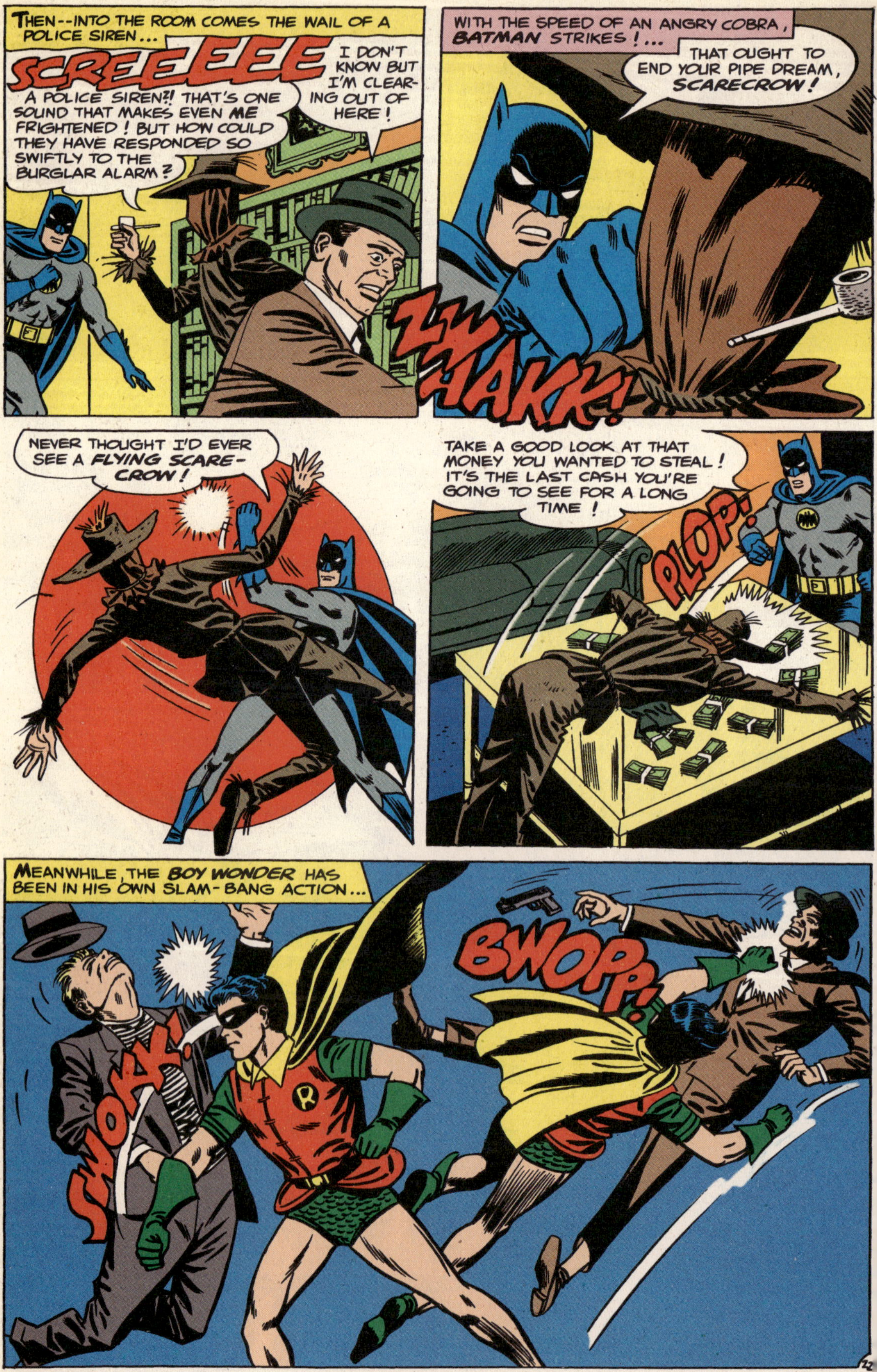
THEN--INTO THE ROOM COMES THE WAIL OF A POLICE SIREN...
SCREEEEEE
A POLICE SIREN?! THAT'S ONE SOUND THAT MAKES EVEN ME FRIGHTENED! BUT HOW COULD THEY HAVE RESPONDED SO SWIFTLY TO THE BURGLAR ALARM?
I DON'T KNOW BUT I'M CLEARING OUT OF HERE!
WITH THE SPEED OF AN ANGRY COBRA, BATMAN STRIKES!...
THAT OUGHT TO END YOUR PIPE DREAM, SCARECROW!
ZWHAKK!
NEVER THOUGHT I'D EVER SEE A FLYING SCARE-CROW!
TAKE A GOOD LOOK AT THAT MONEY YOU WANTED TO STEAL! IT'S THE LAST CASH YOU'RE GOING TO SEE FOR A LONG TIME!
PLOP!
MEANWHILE, THE BOY WONDER HAS BEEN IN HIS OWN SLAM-BANG ACTION...
BWOPP!
SWOKK!

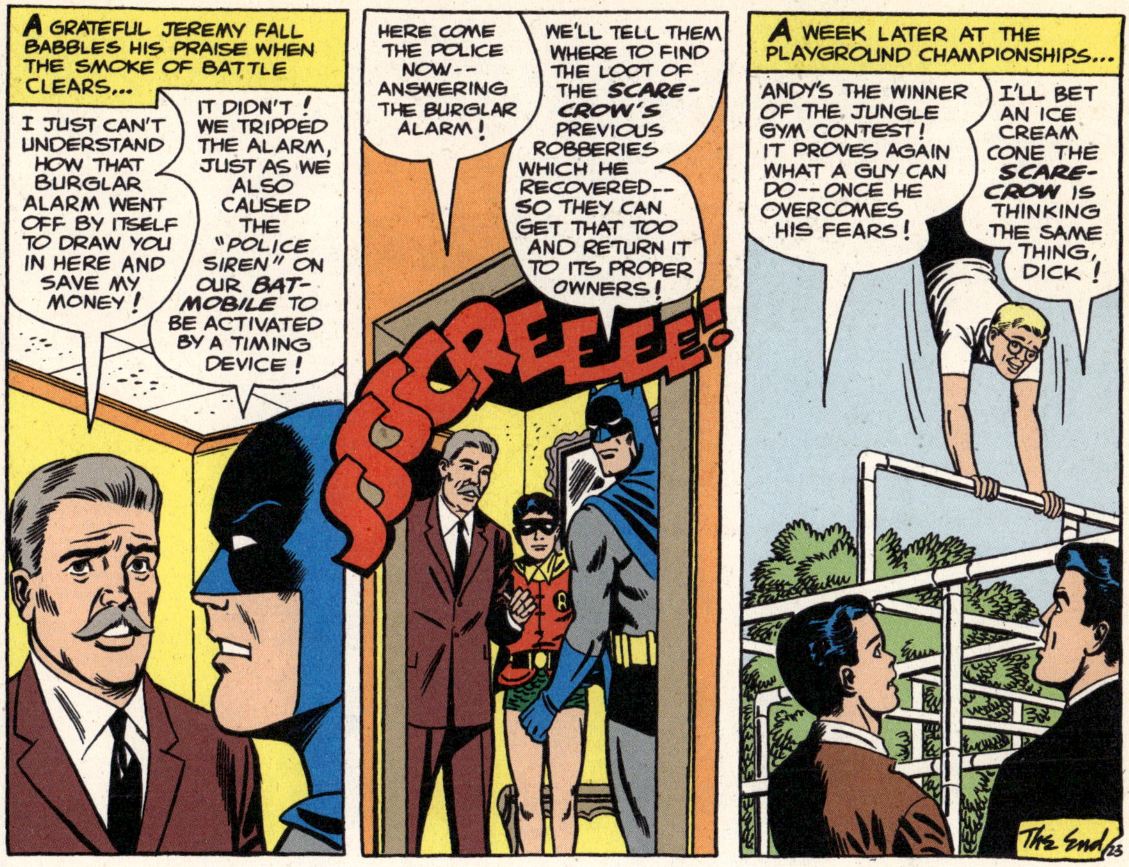

A GRATEFUL JEREMY FALL BABBLES HIS PRAISE WHEN THE SMOKE OF BATTLE CLEARS...

I JUST CAN'T UNDERSTAND HOW THAT BURGLAR ALARM WENT OFF BY ITSELF TO DRAW YOU IN HERE AND SAVE MY MONEY!

IT DIDN'T! WE TRIPPED THE ALARM, JUST AS WE ALSO CAUSED THE "POLICE SIREN" ON OUR *BAT-MOBILE* TO BE ACTIVATED BY A TIMING DEVICE!

HERE COME THE POLICE NOW-- ANSWERING THE BURGLAR ALARM!

WE'LL TELL THEM WHERE TO FIND THE LOOT OF THE *SCARE-CROW'S* PREVIOUS ROBBERIES WHICH HE RECOVERED-- SO THEY CAN GET THAT TOO AND RETURN IT TO ITS PROPER OWNERS!

SCREEEEE!

A WEEK LATER AT THE PLAYGROUND CHAMPIONSHIPS...

ANDY'S THE WINNER OF THE JUNGLE GYM CONTEST! IT PROVES AGAIN WHAT A GUY CAN DO-- ONCE HE OVERCOMES HIS FEARS!

I'LL BET AN ICE CREAM CONE THE *SCARE-CROW* IS THINKING THE SAME THING, DICK!

The End 23

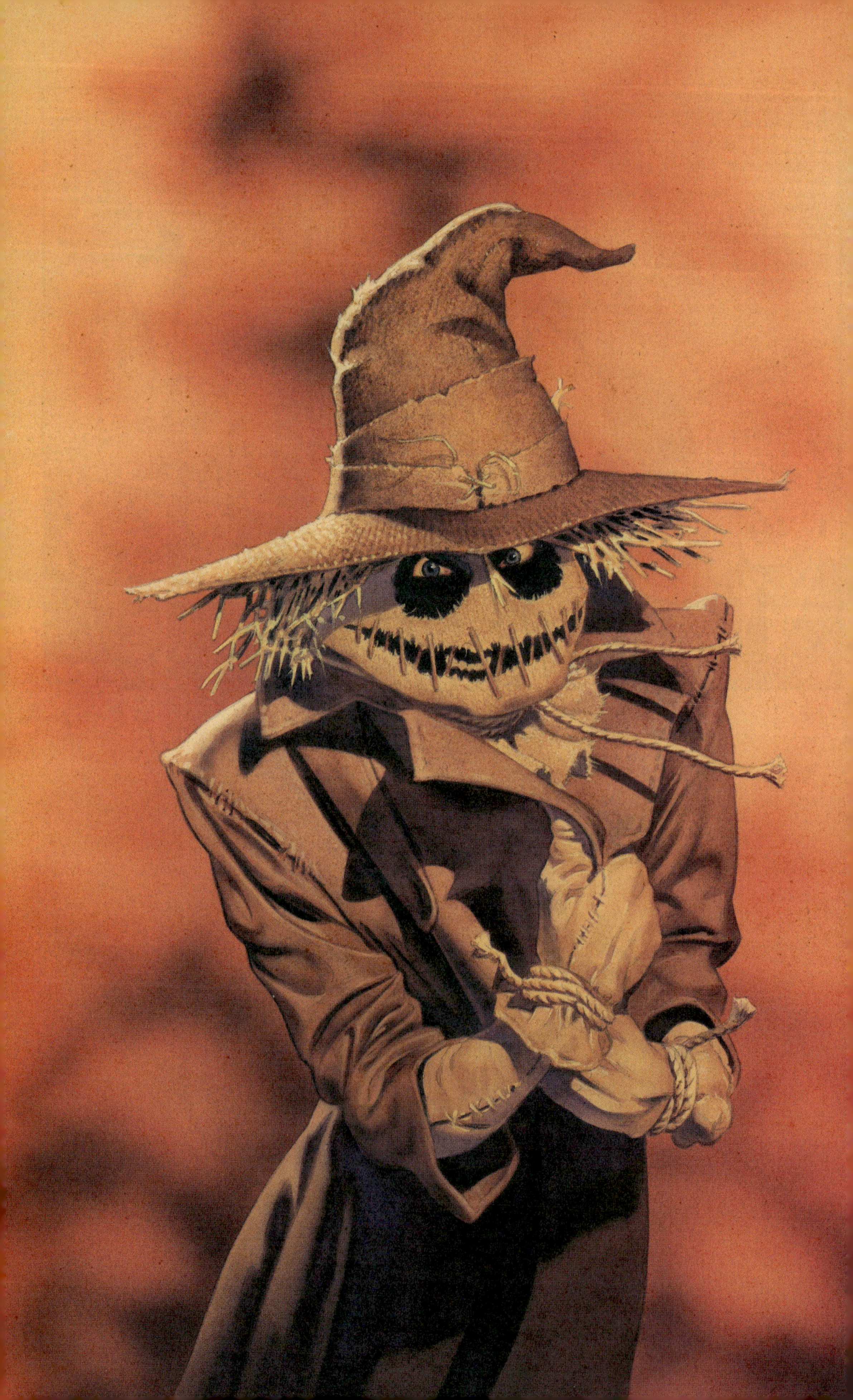

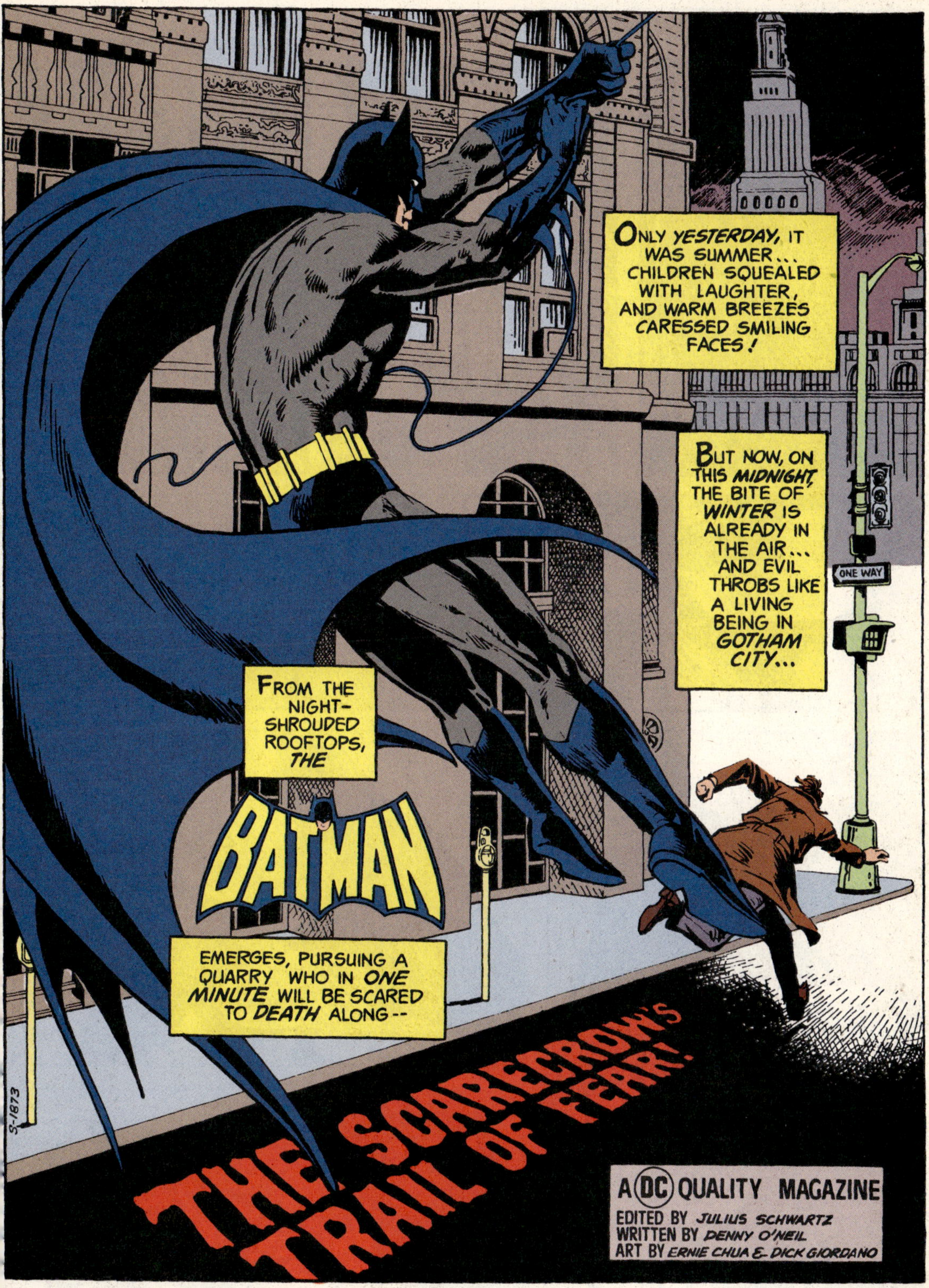

ONLY YESTERDAY, IT WAS SUMMER... CHILDREN SQUEALED WITH LAUGHTER, AND WARM BREEZES CARESSED SMILING FACES!
BUT NOW, ON THIS MIDNIGHT, THE BITE OF WINTER IS ALREADY IN THE AIR... AND EVIL THROBS LIKE A LIVING BEING IN GOTHAM CITY...
FROM THE NIGHT-SHROUDED ROOFTOPS, THE
BATMAN
EMERGES, PURSUING A QUARRY WHO IN ONE MINUTE WILL BE SCARED TO DEATH ALONG--
THE SCARECROW'S TRAIL OF FEAR!
ONE WAY
A DC QUALITY MAGAZINE
EDITED BY JULIUS SCHWARTZ
WRITTEN BY DENNY O'NEIL
ART BY ERNIE CHUA & DICK GIORDANO
S-1873

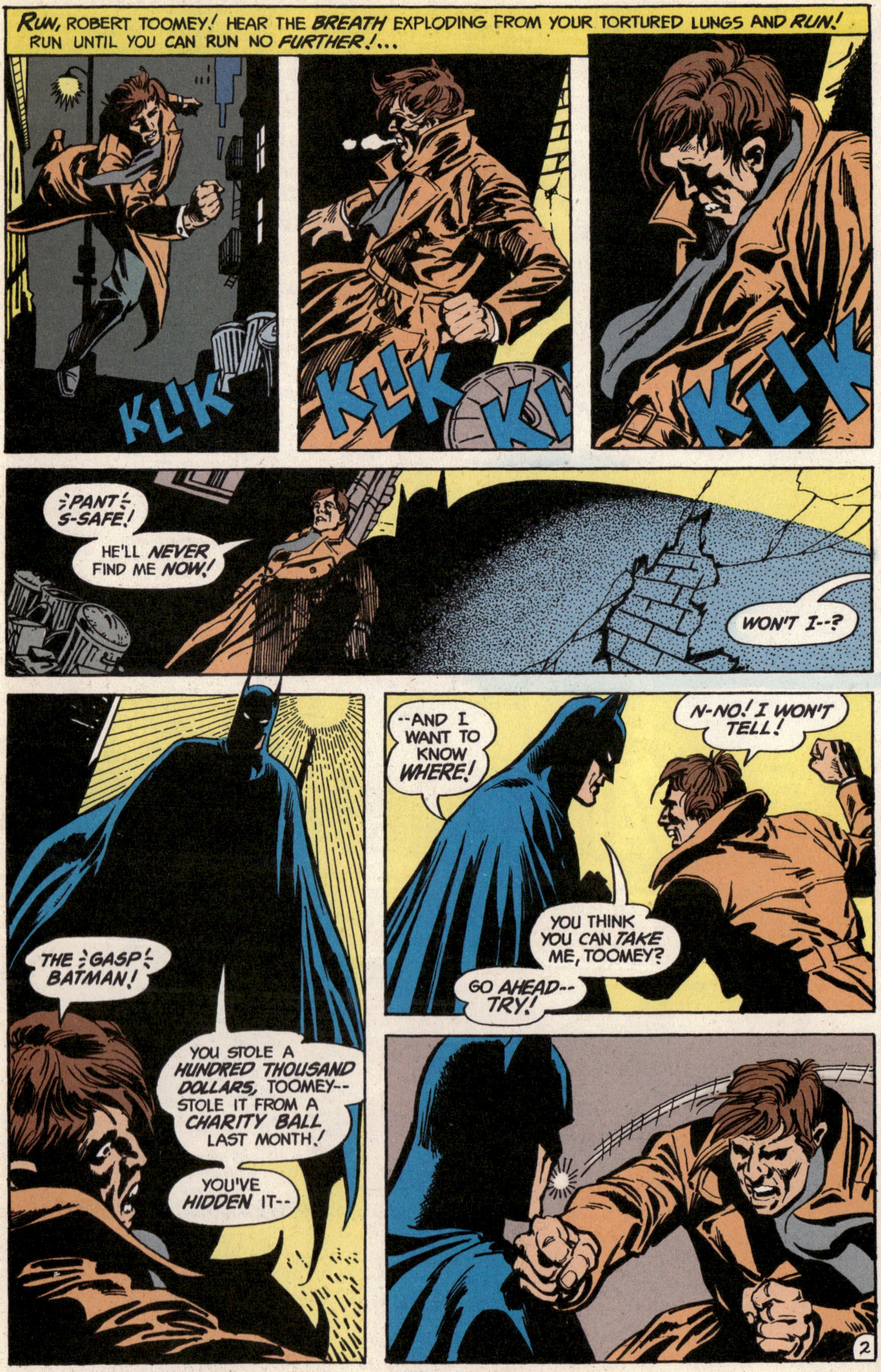
RUN, ROBERT TOOMEY! HEAR THE BREATH EXPLODING FROM YOUR TORTURED LUNGS AND RUN! RUN UNTIL YOU CAN RUN NO FURTHER!...
KLIK
KLIK
KLI
KLIK
PANT S-SAFE!
HE'LL NEVER FIND ME NOW!
WON'T I--?
THE GASP BATMAN!
YOU STOLE A HUNDRED THOUSAND DOLLARS, TOOMEY-- STOLE IT FROM A CHARITY BALL LAST MONTH!
YOU'VE HIDDEN IT--
--AND I WANT TO KNOW WHERE!
N-NO! I WON'T TELL!
YOU THINK YOU CAN TAKE ME, TOOMEY?
GO AHEAD-- TRY!
2

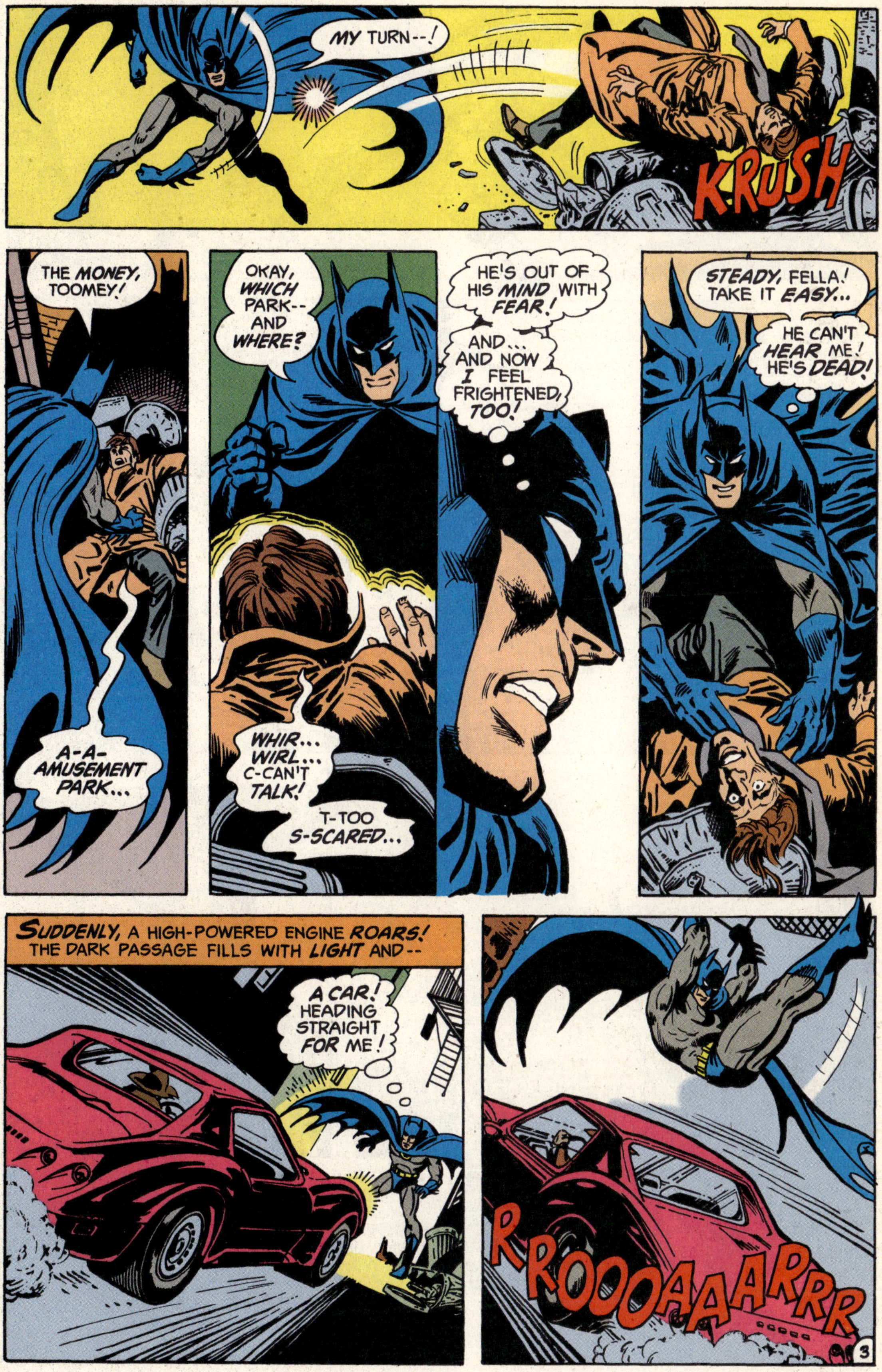
MY TURN--!
KRUSH
THE MONEY, TOOMEY!
A-A-AMUSEMENT PARK...
OKAY, WHICH PARK--AND WHERE?
WHIR... WIRL... C-CAN'T TALK!
T-TOO S-SCARED...
HE'S OUT OF HIS MIND WITH FEAR!
AND... AND NOW I FEEL FRIGHTENED, TOO!
STEADY, FELLA! TAKE IT EASY...
HE CAN'T HEAR ME! HE'S DEAD!
SUDDENLY, A HIGH-POWERED ENGINE ROARS! THE DARK PASSAGE FILLS WITH LIGHT AND--
A CAR! HEADING STRAIGHT FOR ME!
RROOOAAARRR
3

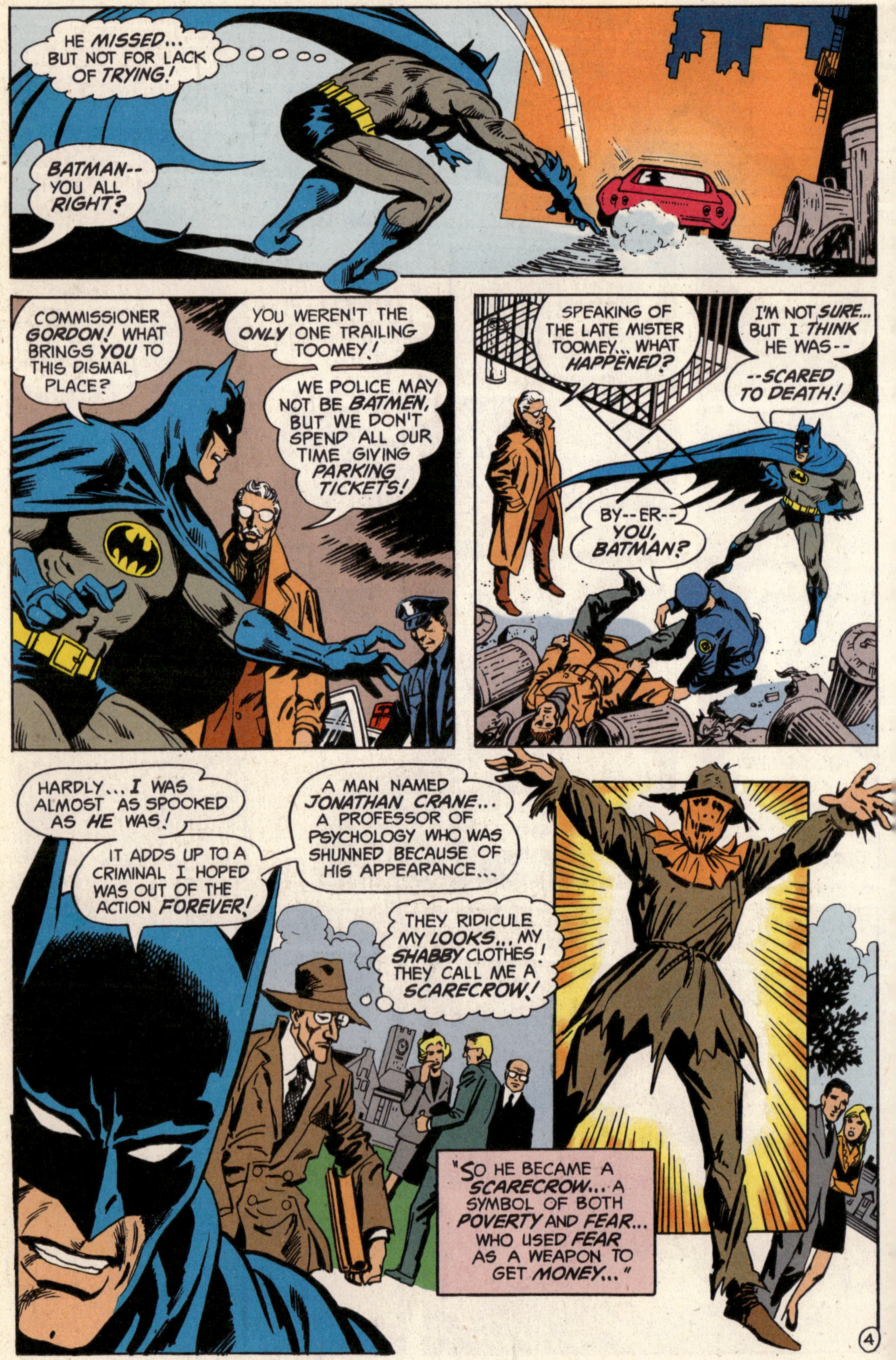
HE MISSED... BUT NOT FOR LACK OF TRYING!
BATMAN-- YOU ALL RIGHT?
COMMISSIONER GORDON! WHAT BRINGS YOU TO THIS DISMAL PLACE?
YOU WEREN'T THE ONLY ONE TRAILING TOOMEY!
WE POLICE MAY NOT BE BATMEN, BUT WE DON'T SPEND ALL OUR TIME GIVING PARKING TICKETS!
SPEAKING OF THE LATE MISTER TOOMEY... WHAT HAPPENED?
I'M NOT SURE... BUT I THINK HE WAS--
--SCARED TO DEATH!
BY--ER-- YOU, BATMAN?
HARDLY... I WAS ALMOST AS SPOOKED AS HE WAS!
IT ADDS UP TO A CRIMINAL I HOPED WAS OUT OF THE ACTION FOREVER!
A MAN NAMED JONATHAN CRANE... A PROFESSOR OF PSYCHOLOGY WHO WAS SHUNNED BECAUSE OF HIS APPEARANCE...
THEY RIDICULE MY LOOKS... MY SHABBY CLOTHES! THEY CALL ME A SCARECROW!
"SO HE BECAME A SCARECROW... A SYMBOL OF BOTH POVERTY AND FEAR... WHO USED FEAR AS A WEAPON TO GET MONEY..."
4

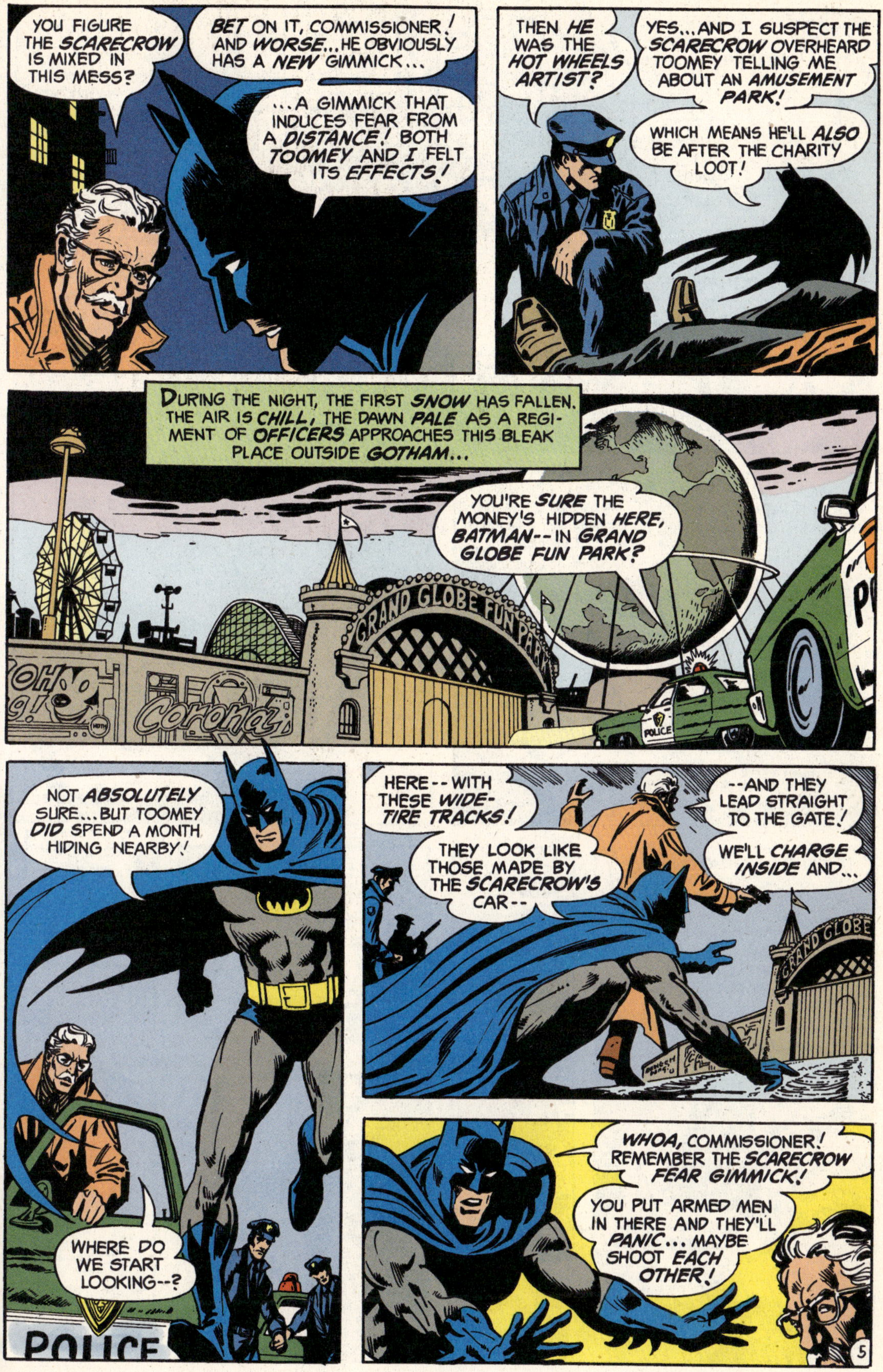
YOU FIGURE THE SCARECROW IS MIXED IN THIS MESS?
BET ON IT, COMMISSIONER! AND WORSE...HE OBVIOUSLY HAS A NEW GIMMICK...
...A GIMMICK THAT INDUCES FEAR FROM A DISTANCE! BOTH TOOMEY AND I FELT ITS EFFECTS!
THEN HE WAS THE HOT WHEELS ARTIST?
YES...AND I SUSPECT THE SCARECROW OVERHEARD TOOMEY TELLING ME ABOUT AN AMUSEMENT PARK!
WHICH MEANS HE'LL ALSO BE AFTER THE CHARITY LOOT!
DURING THE NIGHT, THE FIRST SNOW HAS FALLEN. THE AIR IS CHILL, THE DAWN PALE AS A REGIMENT OF OFFICERS APPROACHES THIS BLEAK PLACE OUTSIDE GOTHAM...
YOU'RE SURE THE MONEY'S HIDDEN HERE, BATMAN--IN GRAND GLOBE FUN PARK?
GRAND GLOBE FUN PARK
Corona
POLICE
NOT ABSOLUTELY SURE...BUT TOOMEY DID SPEND A MONTH HIDING NEARBY!
WHERE DO WE START LOOKING--?
POLICE
HERE--WITH THESE WIDE-TIRE TRACKS!
THEY LOOK LIKE THOSE MADE BY THE SCARECROW'S CAR--
--AND THEY LEAD STRAIGHT TO THE GATE!
WE'LL CHARGE INSIDE AND...
GRAND GLOBE
WHOA, COMMISSIONER! REMEMBER THE SCARECROW FEAR GIMMICK!
YOU PUT ARMED MEN IN THERE AND THEY'LL PANIC... MAYBE SHOOT EACH OTHER!
5

I'VE FOUGHT THE *SCARECROW* BEFORE-- AND *WON!*

I'LL STAND A BETTER CHANCE *ALONE!*

ALL RIGHT-- I'LL GIVE YOU *ONE HOUR...* NOT A *SECOND* LONGER!

THEN WE'RE COMING IN... *SHOOTING!*

AT THAT MOMENT, INSIDE...

THE BATMAN SHOULD ARRIVE SHORTLY!

I TRUST YOU WILL BE EQUAL TO THE *OCCASION!*

YOU *BETCHA!!* I BEEN WAITIN' FOR A CRACK AT HIM EVER SINCE HE PUT ME IN THE *JOINT!*

I WISH YOU *GOOD HUNTING!* HOWEVER, SHOULD YOU *FAIL...THIS* WON'T!

YOU GONNA BEAT *BATS* WITH A *WALKIE-TALKIE?* COME *ON!*

NOT A WALKIE-TALKIE-- A *MIND-BOGGLING INVENTION!*

OBSERVE! I HAVE MERELY TO SWITCH IT *ON* AND--

--YOU ARE *FROZEN WITH DREAD!*

S-S-STOP!

E-E-ENOUGH!

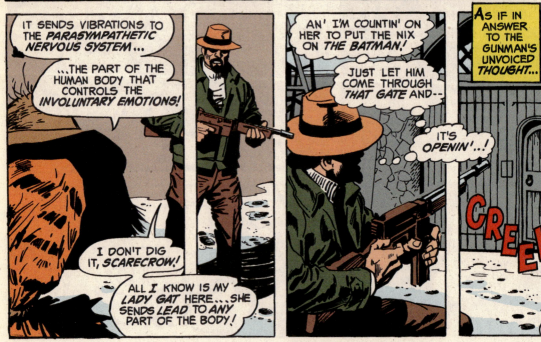

IT SENDS VIBRATIONS TO THE *PARASYMPATHETIC NERVOUS SYSTEM...*

...THE PART OF THE HUMAN BODY THAT CONTROLS THE *INVOLUNTARY EMOTIONS!*

I DON'T DIG IT, *SCARECROW!*

ALL *I* KNOW IS MY *LADY GAT* HERE...SHE SENDS *LEAD* TO ANY PART OF THE BODY!

AN' I'M COUNTIN' ON HER TO PUT THE NIX ON *THE BATMAN!*

JUST LET HIM COME THROUGH *THAT GATE* AND--

IT'S *OPENIN'*...!

AS IF IN ANSWER TO THE GUNMAN'S UNVOICED *THOUGHT...*

CREEK

6

Snik

BRAK BRAK

BRAK BRAK
BRAK

WOMP

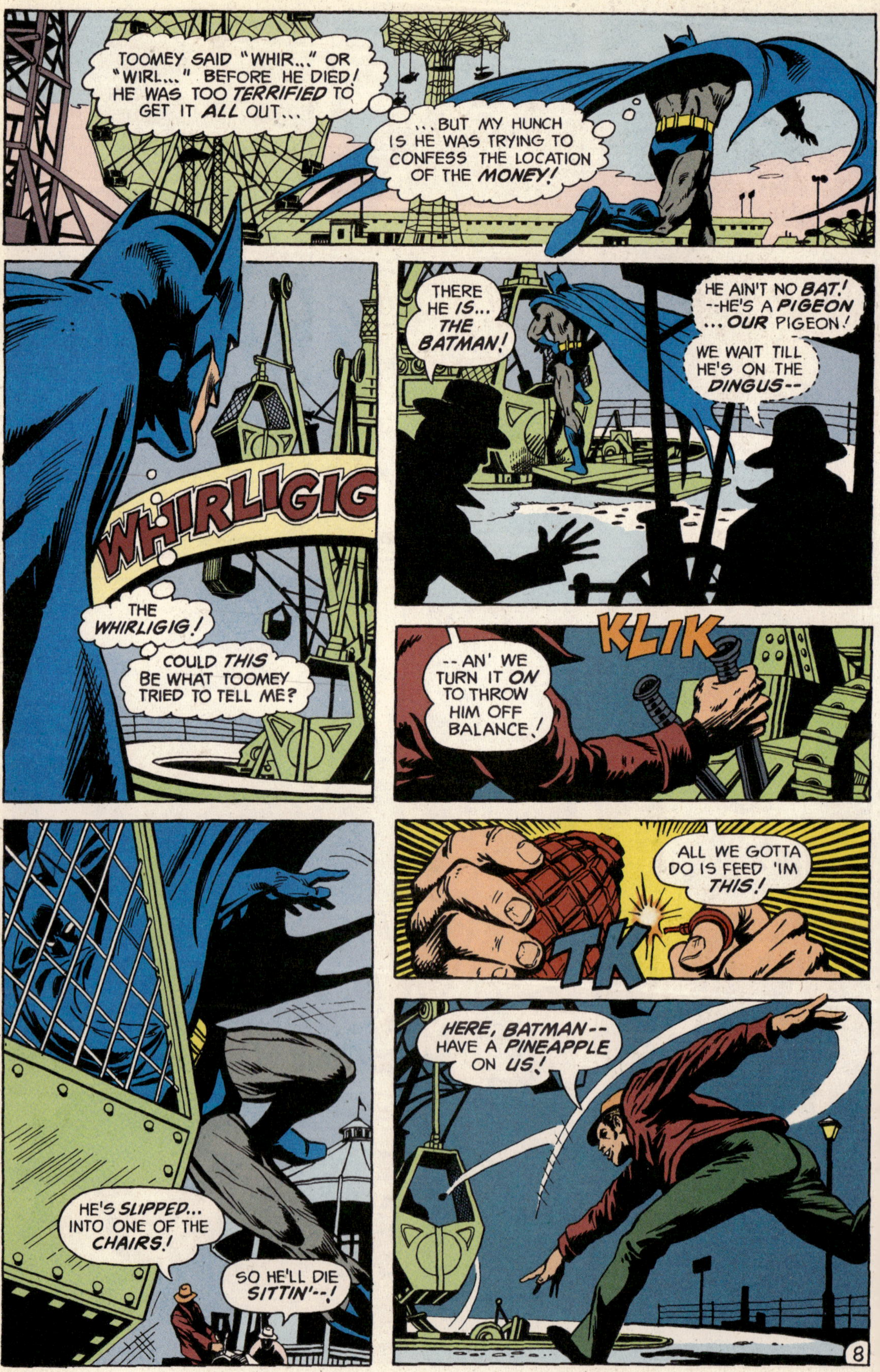

TOOMEY SAID "WHIR..." OR "WIRL..." BEFORE HE DIED! HE WAS TOO TERRIFIED TO GET IT ALL OUT...
...BUT MY HUNCH IS HE WAS TRYING TO CONFESS THE LOCATION OF THE MONEY!
WHIRLIGIG
THE WHIRLIGIG!
COULD THIS BE WHAT TOOMEY TRIED TO TELL ME?
THERE HE IS... THE BATMAN!
HE AIN'T NO BAT! --HE'S A PIGEON ...OUR PIGEON!
WE WAIT TILL HE'S ON THE DINGUS--
KLIK
--AN' WE TURN IT ON TO THROW HIM OFF BALANCE!
ALL WE GOTTA DO IS FEED 'IM THIS!
TK
HE'S SLIPPED... INTO ONE OF THE CHAIRS!
SO HE'LL DIE SITTIN'--!
HERE, BATMAN-- HAVE A PINEAPPLE ON US!
8

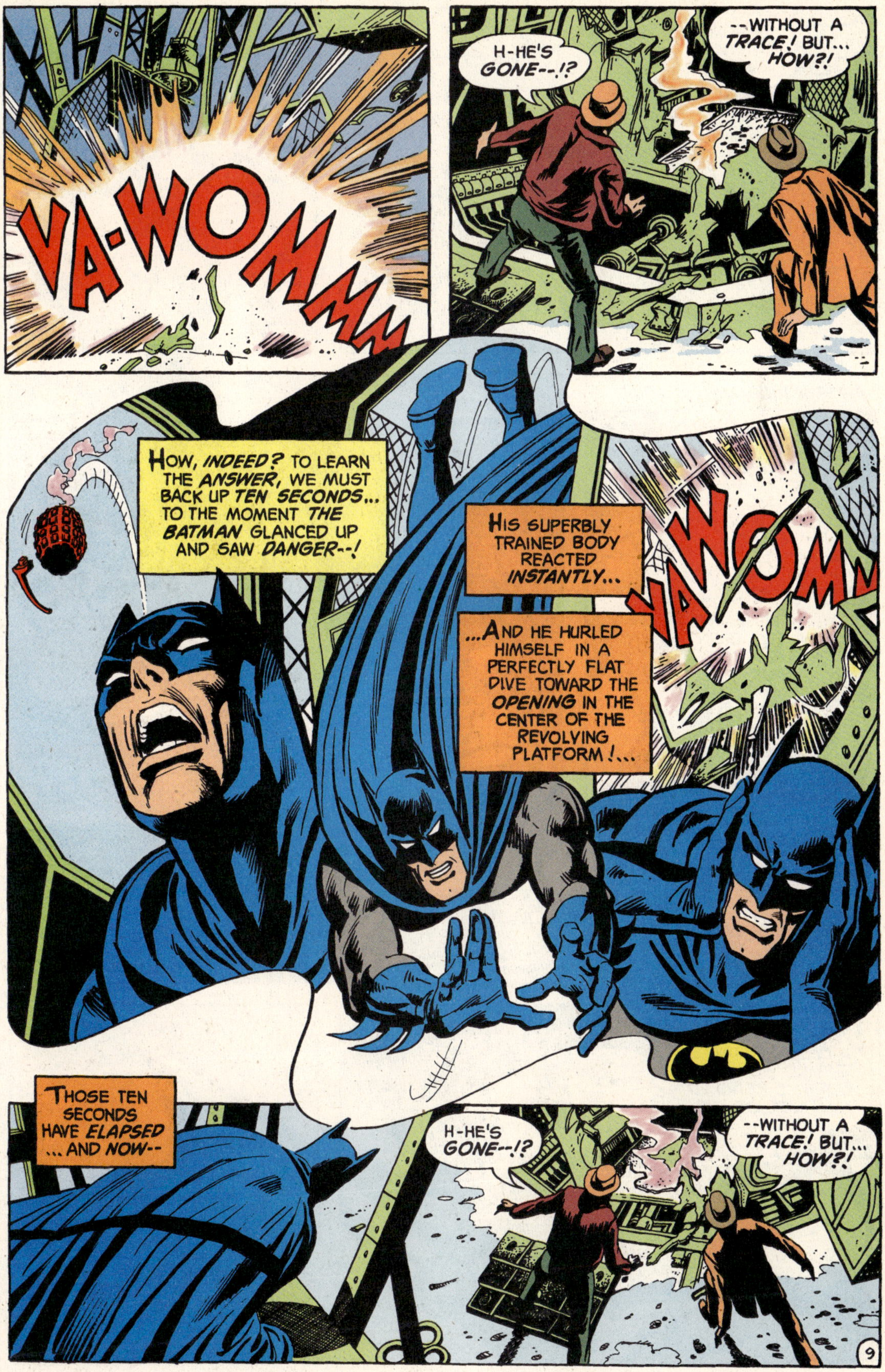
VA-WOMMM
H-HE'S GONE--!?
--WITHOUT A TRACE! BUT... HOW?!
HOW, INDEED? TO LEARN THE ANSWER, WE MUST BACK UP TEN SECONDS... TO THE MOMENT THE BATMAN GLANCED UP AND SAW DANGER--!
HIS SUPERBLY TRAINED BODY REACTED INSTANTLY...
...AND HE HURLED HIMSELF IN A PERFECTLY FLAT DIVE TOWARD THE OPENING IN THE CENTER OF THE REVOLVING PLATFORM!...
VA-WOMM
THOSE TEN SECONDS HAVE ELAPSED ...AND NOW--
H-HE'S GONE--!?
--WITHOUT A TRACE! BUT... HOW?!
9

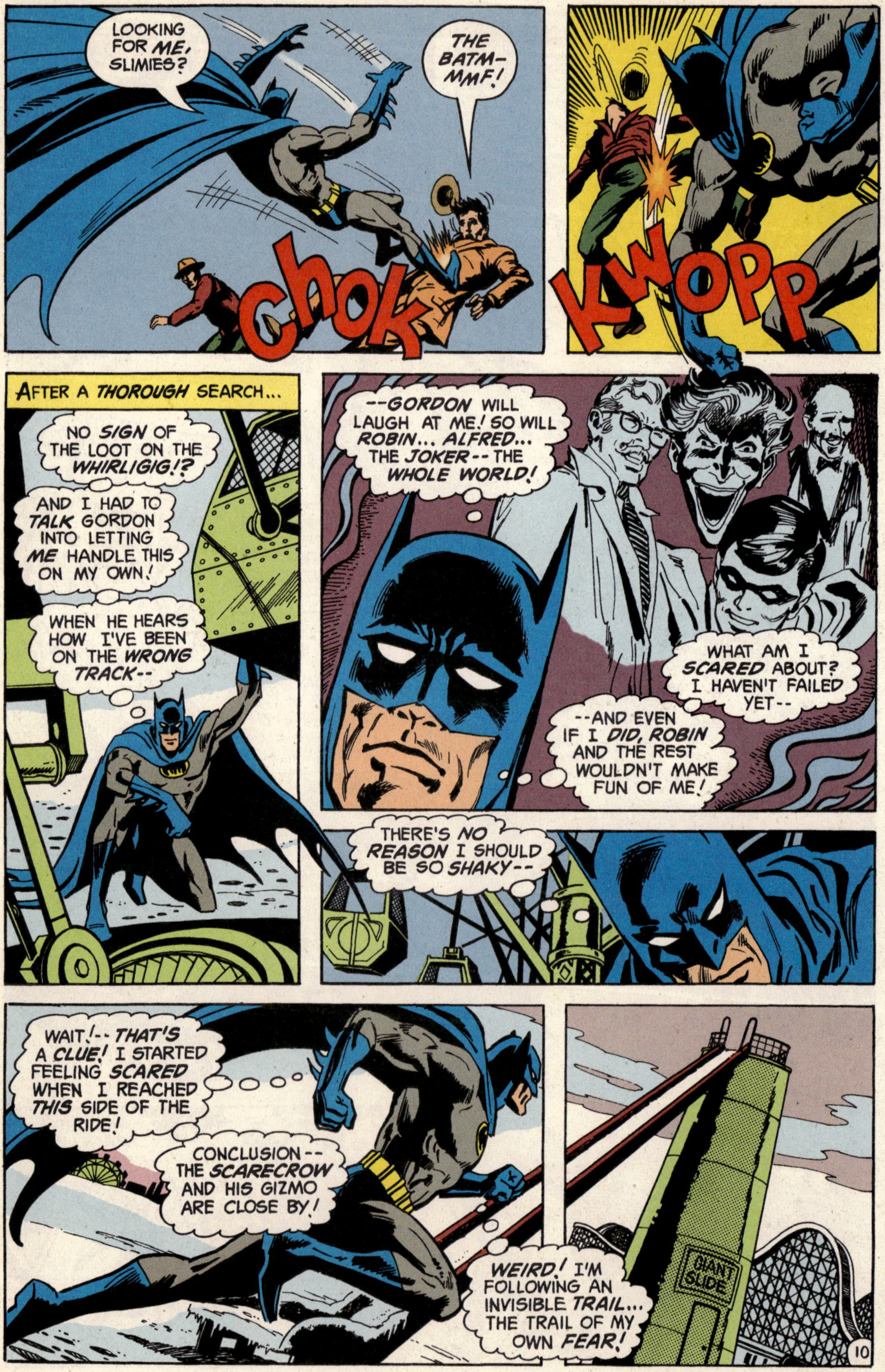
LOOKING FOR ME, SLIMIES?
THE BATM-MMF!
CHOK
KWOPP
AFTER A THOROUGH SEARCH...
NO SIGN OF THE LOOT ON THE WHIRLIGIG!?
AND I HAD TO TALK GORDON INTO LETTING ME HANDLE THIS ON MY OWN!
WHEN HE HEARS HOW I'VE BEEN ON THE WRONG TRACK--
--GORDON WILL LAUGH AT ME! SO WILL ROBIN... ALFRED... THE JOKER--THE WHOLE WORLD!
WHAT AM I SCARED ABOUT? I HAVEN'T FAILED YET--
--AND EVEN IF I DID, ROBIN AND THE REST WOULDN'T MAKE FUN OF ME!
THERE'S NO REASON I SHOULD BE SO SHAKY--
WAIT!--THAT'S A CLUE! I STARTED FEELING SCARED WHEN I REACHED THIS SIDE OF THE RIDE!
CONCLUSION--THE SCARECROW AND HIS GIZMO ARE CLOSE BY!
GIANT SLIDE
WEIRD! I'M FOLLOWING AN INVISIBLE TRAIL... THE TRAIL OF MY OWN FEAR!
10

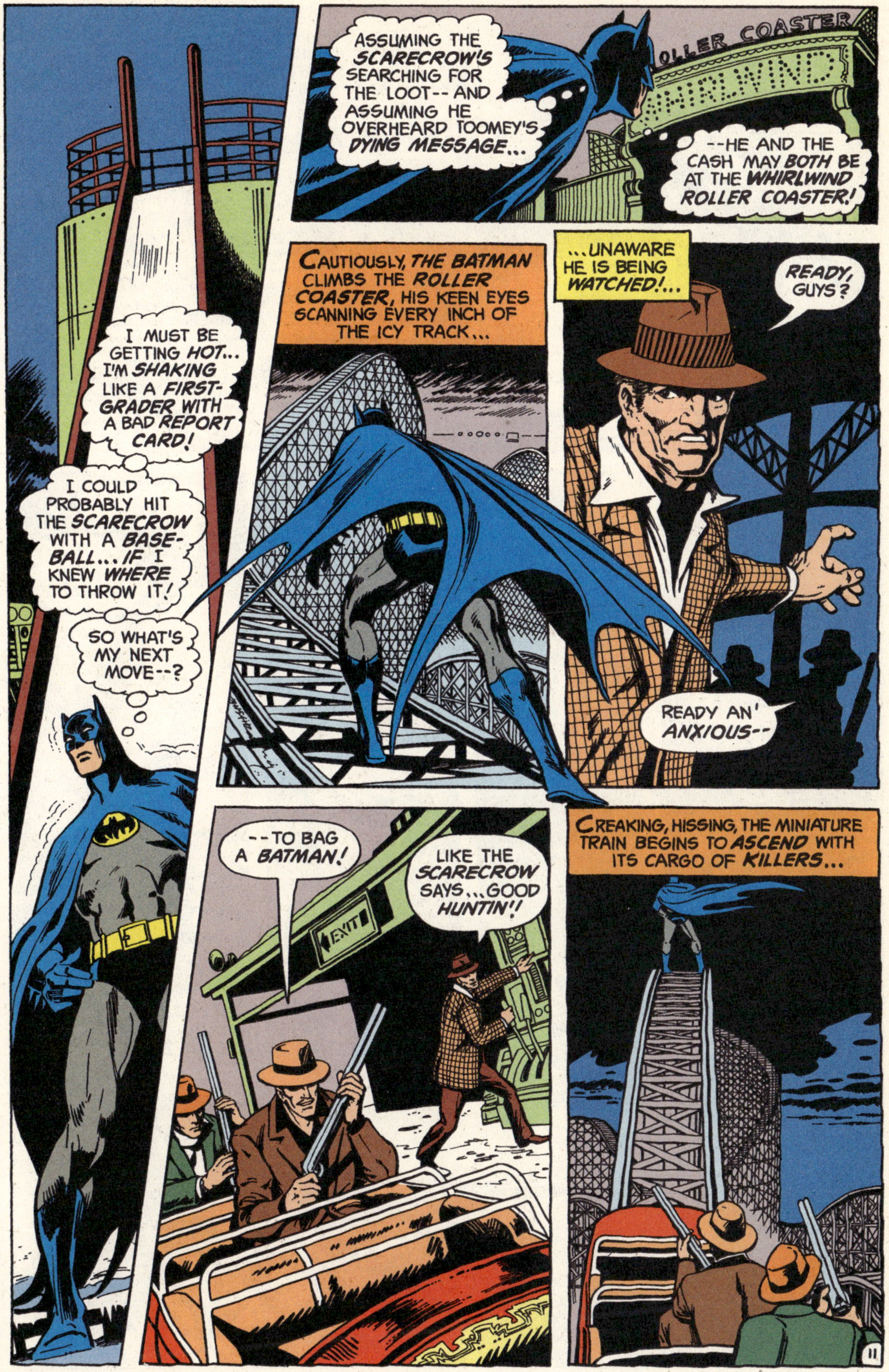
I MUST BE GETTING HOT... I'M SHAKING LIKE A FIRST-GRADER WITH A BAD REPORT CARD!
I COULD PROBABLY HIT THE SCARECROW WITH A BASE-BALL... IF I KNEW WHERE TO THROW IT!
SO WHAT'S MY NEXT MOVE--?
ASSUMING THE SCARECROW'S SEARCHING FOR THE LOOT-- AND ASSUMING HE OVERHEARD TOOMEY'S DYING MESSAGE...
ROLLER COASTER
WHIRLWIND
--HE AND THE CASH MAY BOTH BE AT THE WHIRLWIND ROLLER COASTER!
CAUTIOUSLY, THE BATMAN CLIMBS THE ROLLER COASTER, HIS KEEN EYES SCANNING EVERY INCH OF THE ICY TRACK...
...UNAWARE HE IS BEING WATCHED!...
READY, GUYS?
READY AN' ANXIOUS--
--TO BAG A BATMAN!
EXIT
LIKE THE SCARECROW SAYS... GOOD HUNTIN'!
CREAKING, HISSING, THE MINIATURE TRAIN BEGINS TO ASCEND WITH ITS CARGO OF KILLERS...
11

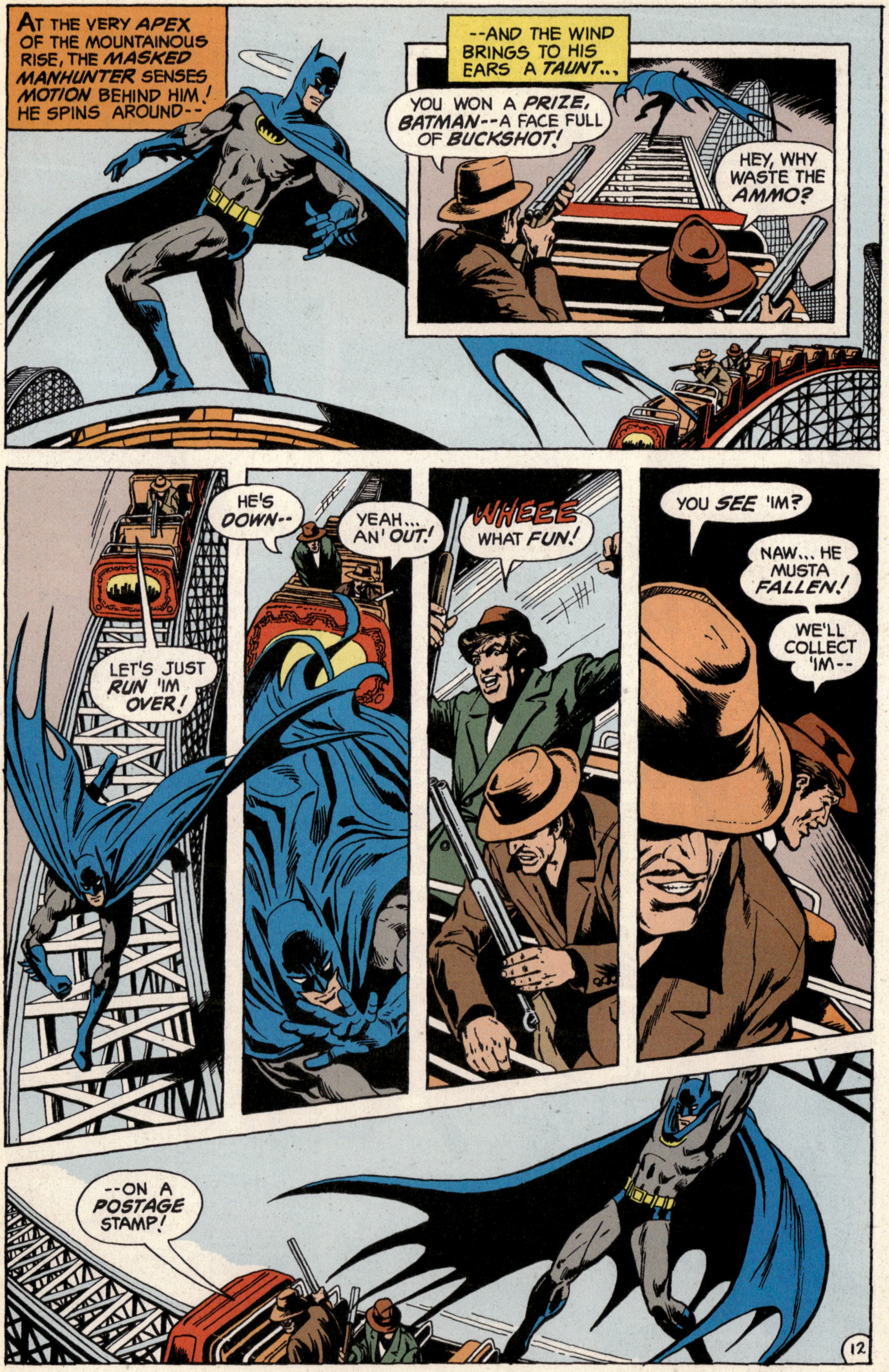
AT THE VERY APEX OF THE MOUNTAINOUS RISE, THE MASKED MANHUNTER SENSES MOTION BEHIND HIM! HE SPINS AROUND--
--AND THE WIND BRINGS TO HIS EARS A TAUNT...
YOU WON A PRIZE, BATMAN--A FACE FULL OF BUCKSHOT!
HEY, WHY WASTE THE AMMO?
LET'S JUST RUN 'IM OVER!
HE'S DOWN--
YEAH... AN' OUT!
WHEEE
WHAT FUN!
YOU SEE 'IM?
NAW... HE MUSTA FALLEN!
WE'LL COLLECT 'IM--
--ON A POSTAGE STAMP!
12

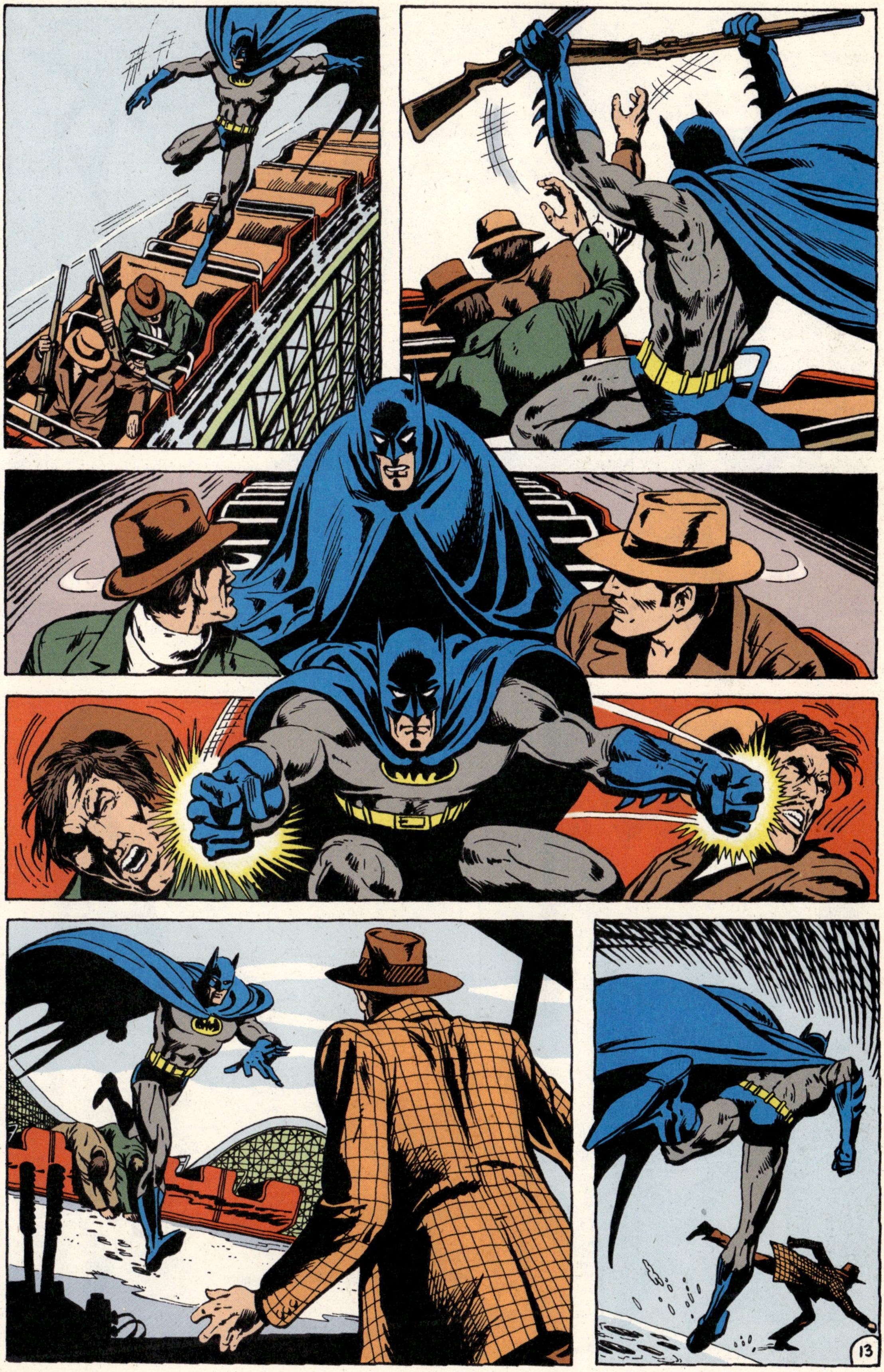
13

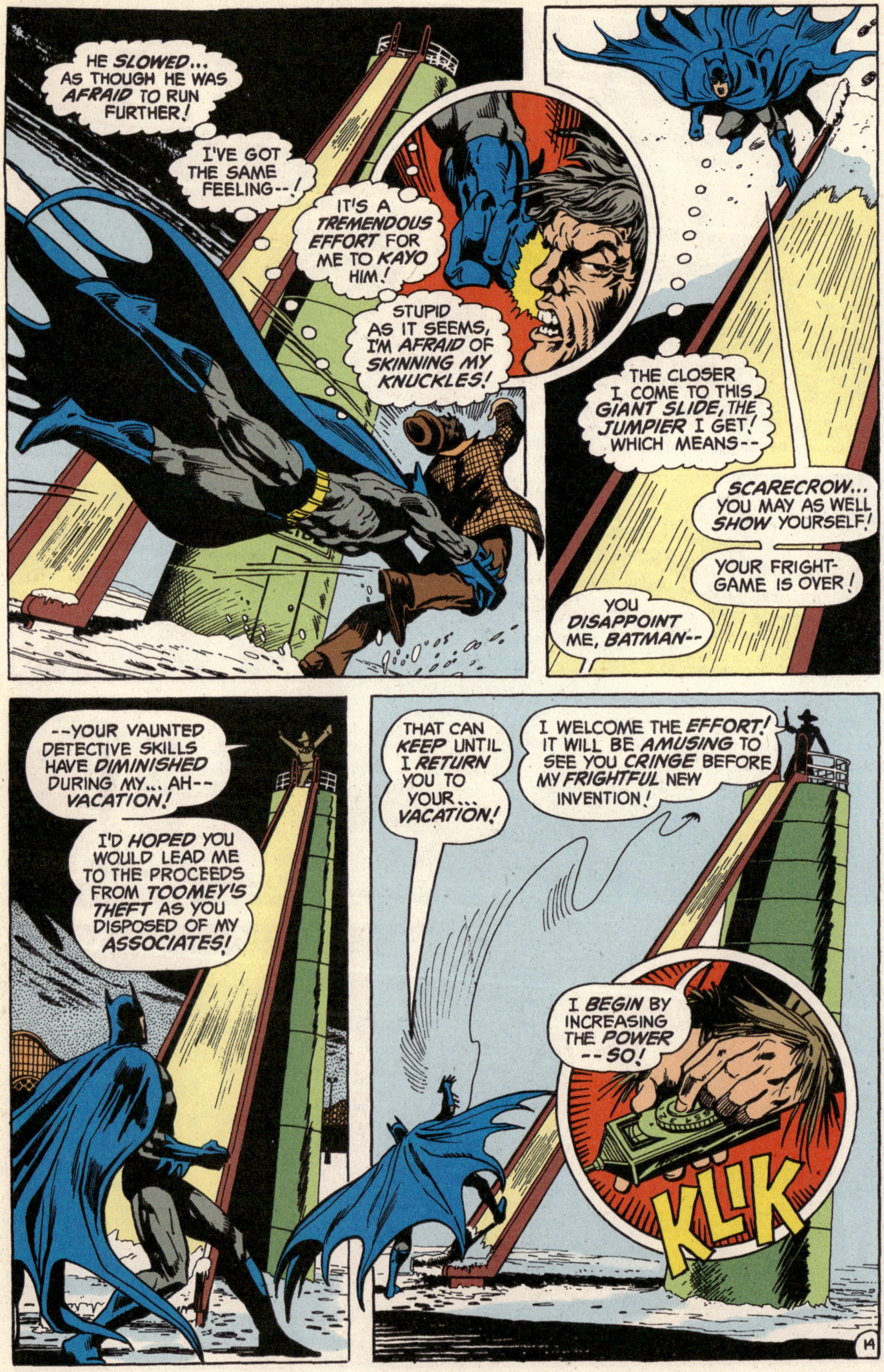
HE SLOWED... AS THOUGH HE WAS AFRAID TO RUN FURTHER!
I'VE GOT THE SAME FEELING--!
IT'S A TREMENDOUS EFFORT FOR ME TO KAYO HIM!
STUPID AS IT SEEMS, I'M AFRAID OF SKINNING MY KNUCKLES!
THE CLOSER I COME TO THIS GIANT SLIDE, THE JUMPIER I GET! WHICH MEANS--
SCARECROW... YOU MAY AS WELL SHOW YOURSELF!
YOUR FRIGHT-GAME IS OVER!
YOU DISAPPOINT ME, BATMAN--
--YOUR VAUNTED DETECTIVE SKILLS HAVE DIMINISHED DURING MY... AH-- VACATION!
I'D HOPED YOU WOULD LEAD ME TO THE PROCEEDS FROM TOOMEY'S THEFT AS YOU DISPOSED OF MY ASSOCIATES!
THAT CAN KEEP UNTIL I RETURN YOU TO YOUR... VACATION!
I WELCOME THE EFFORT! IT WILL BE AMUSING TO SEE YOU CRINGE BEFORE MY FRIGHTFUL NEW INVENTION!
I BEGIN BY INCREASING THE POWER --SO!
KLIK
14

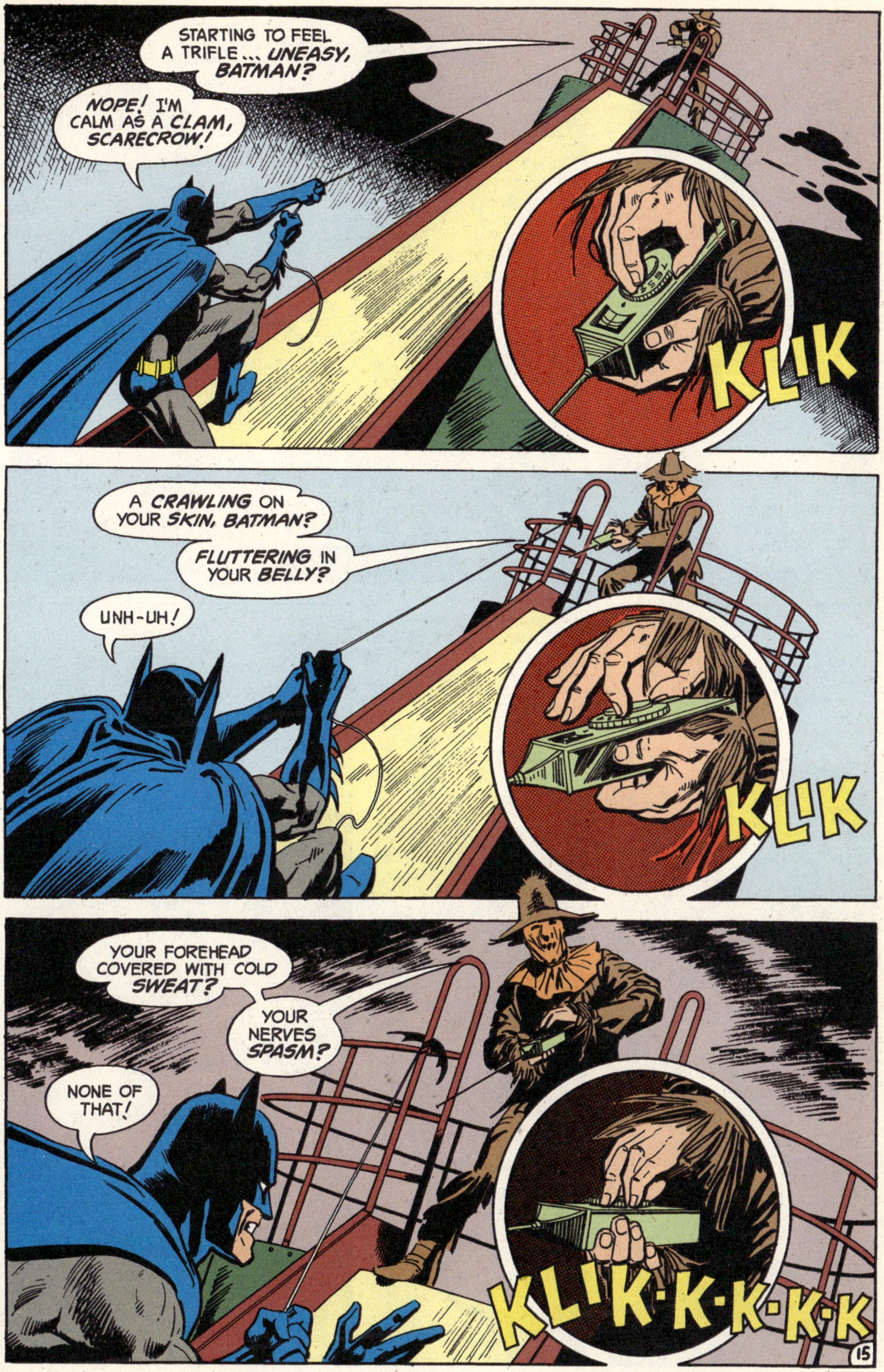
STARTING TO FEEL A TRIFLE... UNEASY, BATMAN?
NOPE! I'M CALM AS A CLAM, SCARECROW!
KLIK
A CRAWLING ON YOUR SKIN, BATMAN?
FLUTTERING IN YOUR BELLY?
UNH-UH!
KLIK
YOUR FOREHEAD COVERED WITH COLD SWEAT?
YOUR NERVES SPASM?
NONE OF THAT!
KLIK-K-K-K-K
15

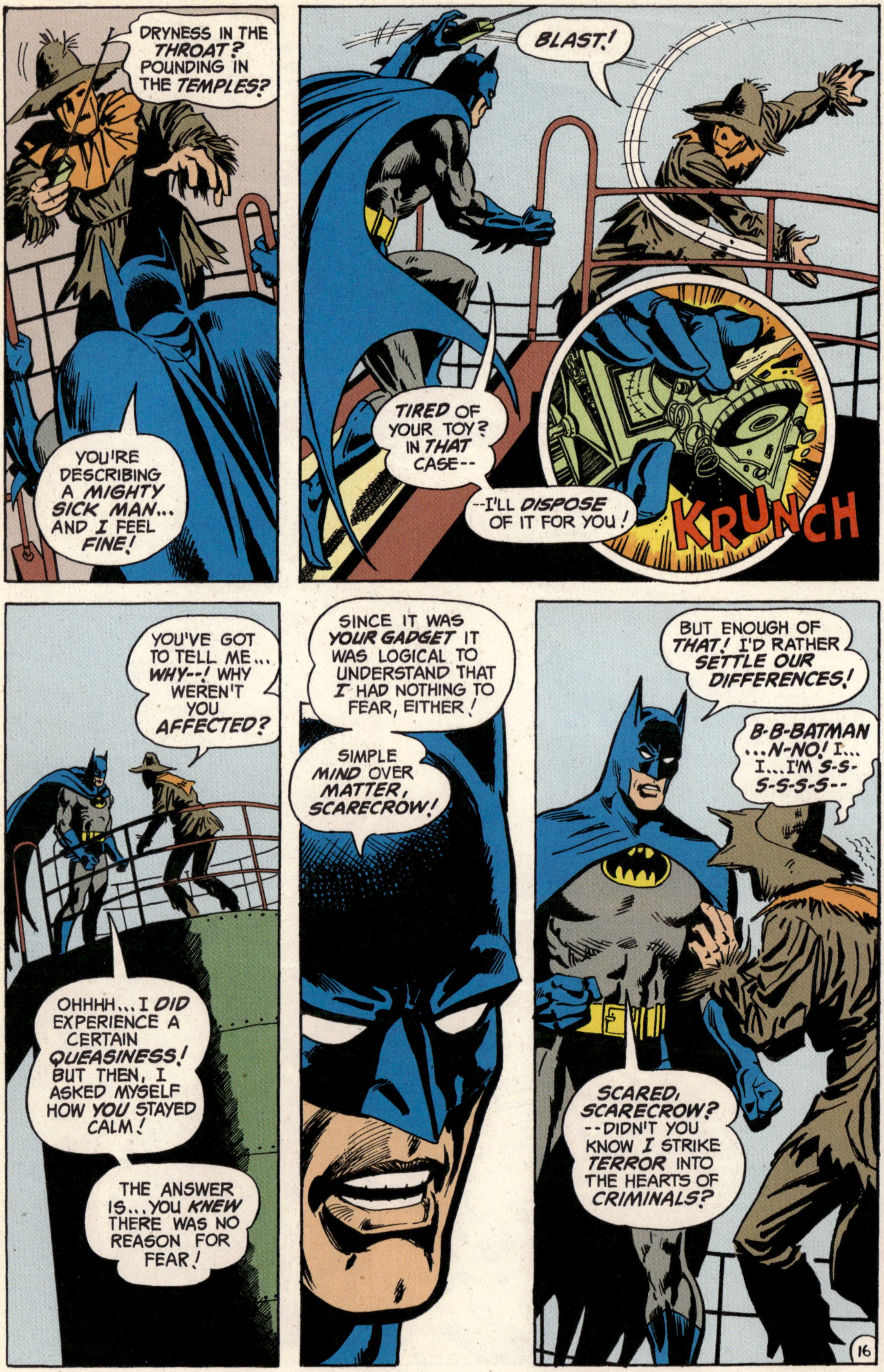
DRYNESS IN THE THROAT? POUNDING IN THE TEMPLES?
YOU'RE DESCRIBING A MIGHTY SICK MAN... AND I FEEL FINE!
BLAST!
TIRED OF YOUR TOY? IN THAT CASE--
--I'LL DISPOSE OF IT FOR YOU!
KRUNCH
YOU'VE GOT TO TELL ME... WHY--! WHY WEREN'T YOU AFFECTED?
OHHHH... I DID EXPERIENCE A CERTAIN QUEASINESS! BUT THEN, I ASKED MYSELF HOW YOU STAYED CALM!
THE ANSWER IS... YOU KNEW THERE WAS NO REASON FOR FEAR!
SINCE IT WAS YOUR GADGET IT WAS LOGICAL TO UNDERSTAND THAT I HAD NOTHING TO FEAR, EITHER!
SIMPLE MIND OVER MATTER, SCARECROW!
BUT ENOUGH OF THAT! I'D RATHER SETTLE OUR DIFFERENCES!
B-B-BATMAN ...N-NO! I... I...I'M S-S-S-S-S-S--
SCARED, SCARECROW? --DIDN'T YOU KNOW I STRIKE TERROR INTO THE HEARTS OF CRIMINALS?
16

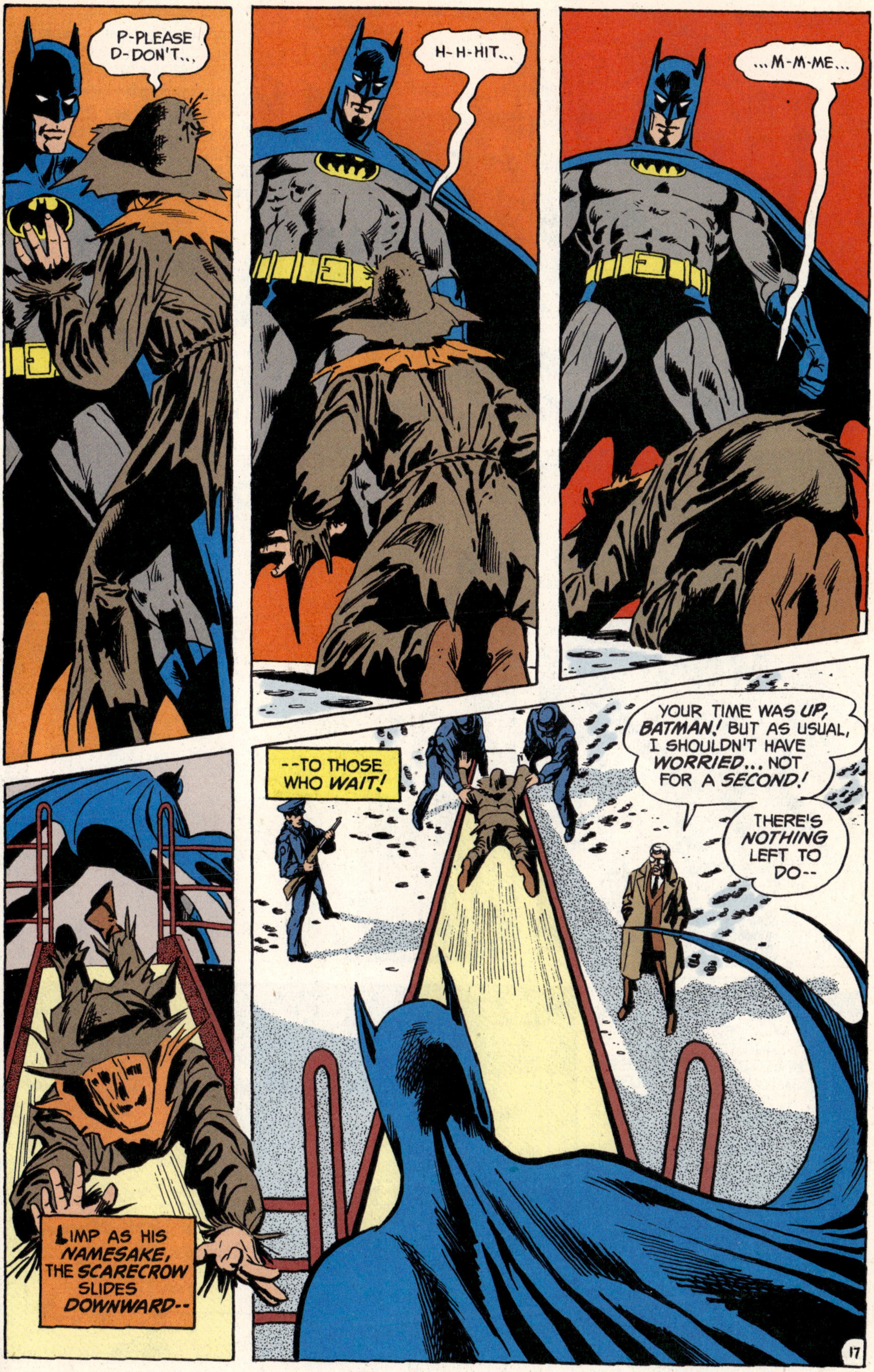
P-PLEASE D-DON'T...
H-H-HIT...
...M-M-ME...
LIMP AS HIS NAMESAKE, THE SCARECROW SLIDES DOWNWARD--
--TO THOSE WHO WAIT!
YOUR TIME WAS UP, BATMAN! BUT AS USUAL, I SHOULDN'T HAVE WORRIED... NOT FOR A SECOND!
THERE'S NOTHING LEFT TO DO--
17

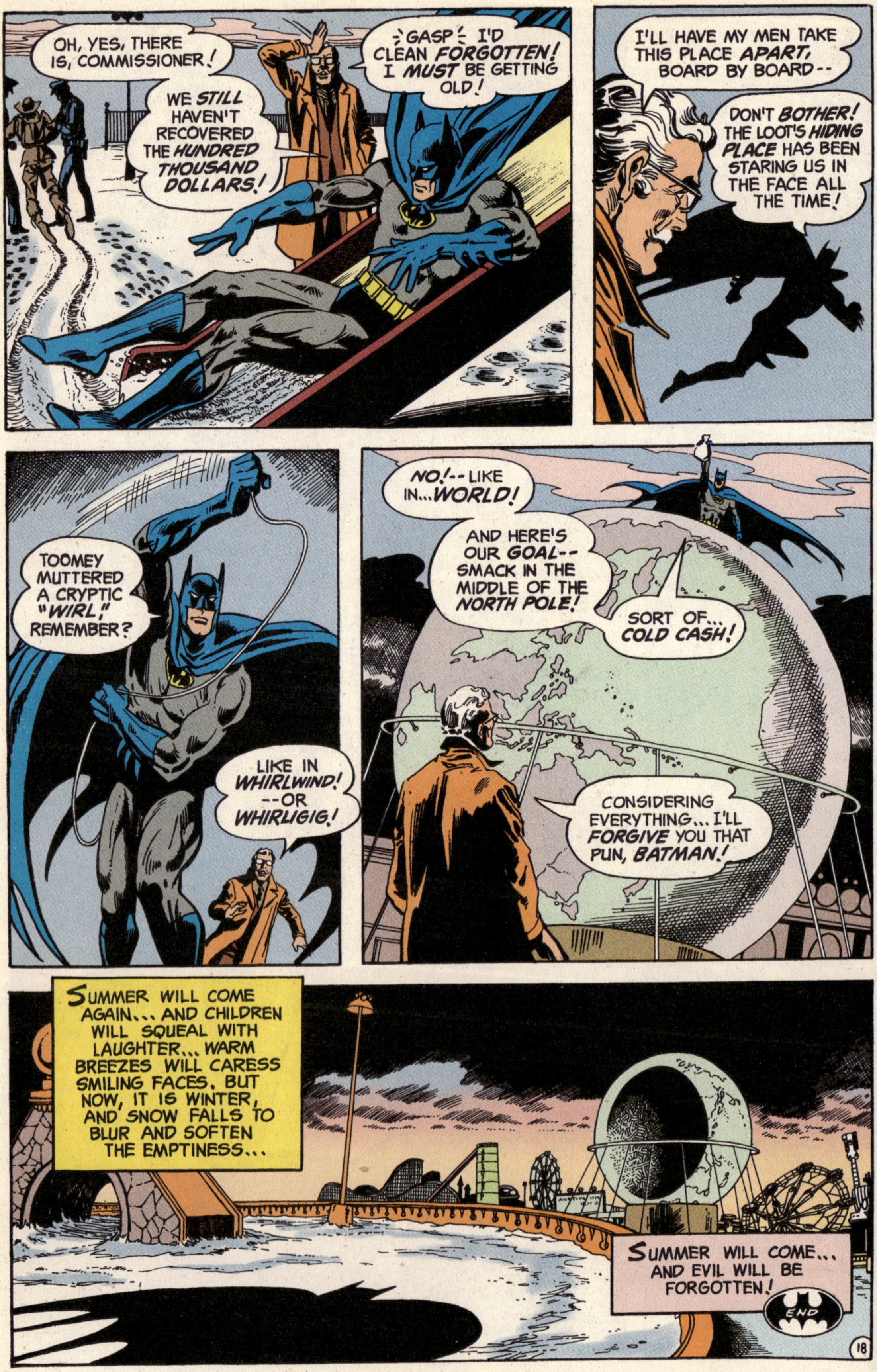
OH, YES, THERE IS, COMMISSIONER!
WE STILL HAVEN'T RECOVERED THE HUNDRED THOUSAND DOLLARS!
GASP I'D CLEAN FORGOTTEN! I MUST BE GETTING OLD!
I'LL HAVE MY MEN TAKE THIS PLACE APART, BOARD BY BOARD--
DON'T BOTHER! THE LOOT'S HIDING PLACE HAS BEEN STARING US IN THE FACE ALL THE TIME!
TOOMEY MUTTERED A CRYPTIC "WIRL," REMEMBER?
LIKE IN WHIRLWIND! --OR WHIRLIGIG!
NO!--LIKE IN...WORLD!
AND HERE'S OUR GOAL--SMACK IN THE MIDDLE OF THE NORTH POLE!
SORT OF... COLD CASH!
CONSIDERING EVERYTHING... I'LL FORGIVE YOU THAT PUN, BATMAN!
SUMMER WILL COME AGAIN... AND CHILDREN WILL SQUEAL WITH LAUGHTER... WARM BREEZES WILL CARESS SMILING FACES. BUT NOW, IT IS WINTER, AND SNOW FALLS TO BLUR AND SOFTEN THE EMPTINESS...
SUMMER WILL COME... AND EVIL WILL BE FORGOTTEN!
END
18

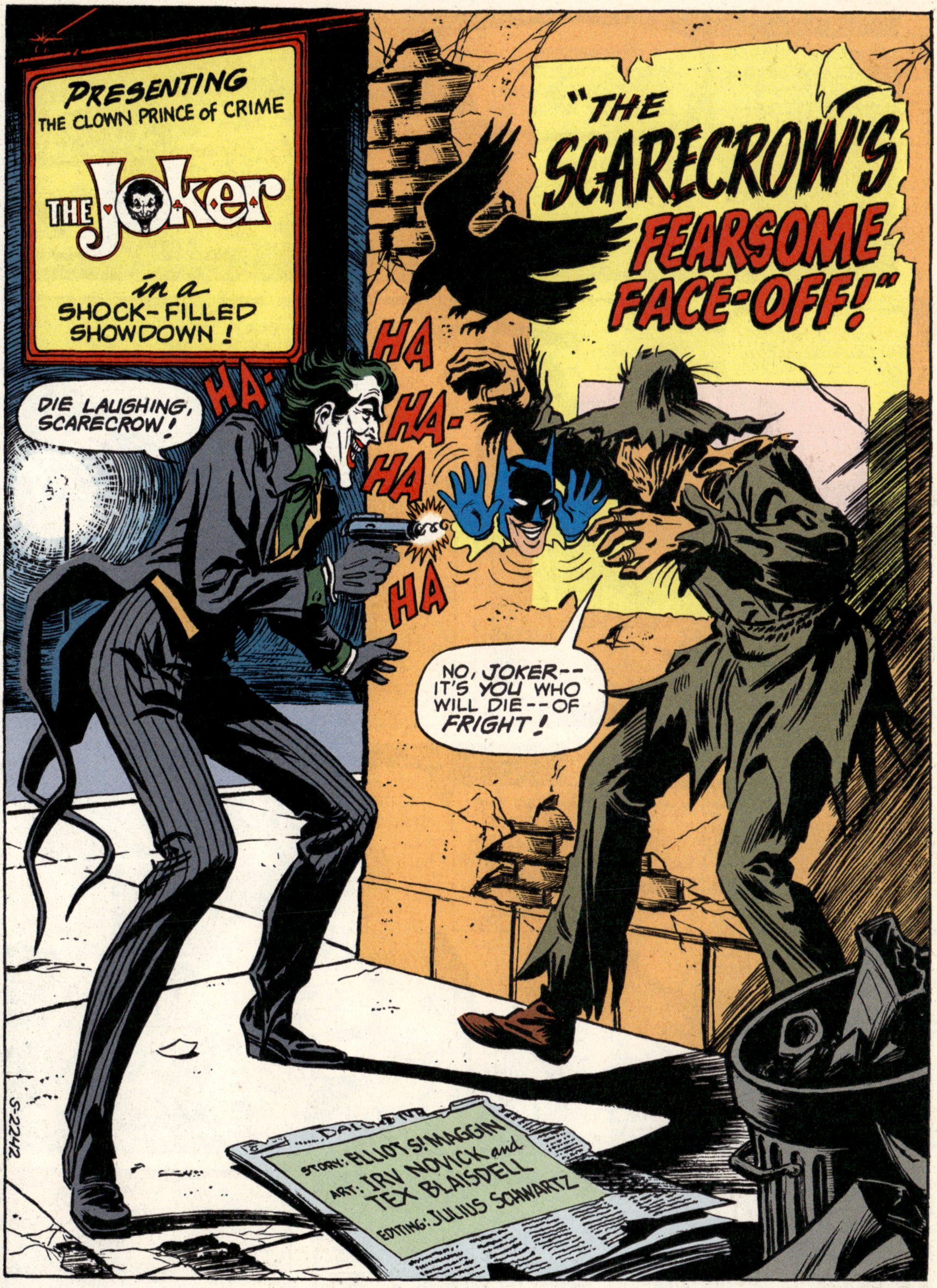

PRESENTING THE CLOWN PRINCE of CRIME
THE Joker
in a SHOCK-FILLED SHOWDOWN!
"THE SCARECROW'S FEARSOME FACE-OFF!"
DIE LAUGHING, SCARECROW!
HA- HA HA- HA HA HA
NO, JOKER-- IT'S YOU WHO WILL DIE--OF FRIGHT!
STORY: ELLIOT S! MAGGIN
ART: IRV NOVICK and TEX BLAISDELL
EDITING: JULIUS SCHWARTZ
S-2242

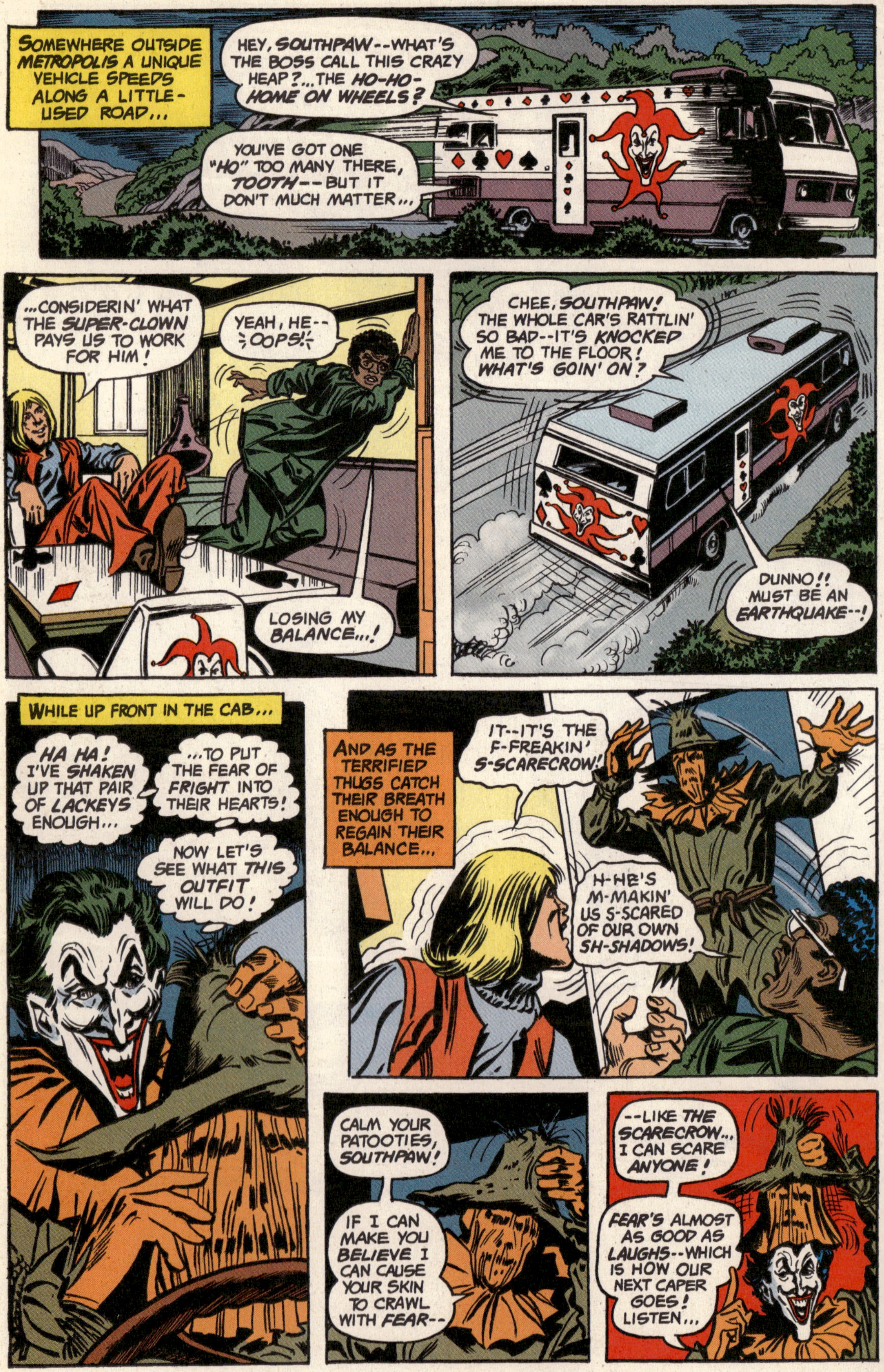
SOMEWHERE OUTSIDE METROPOLIS A UNIQUE VEHICLE SPEEDS ALONG A LITTLE-USED ROAD...
HEY, SOUTHPAW--WHAT'S THE BOSS CALL THIS CRAZY HEAP?...THE HO-HO-HOME ON WHEELS?
YOU'VE GOT ONE "HO" TOO MANY THERE, TOOTH--BUT IT DON'T MUCH MATTER...
...CONSIDERIN' WHAT THE SUPER-CLOWN PAYS US TO WORK FOR HIM!
YEAH, HE-- OOPS!
LOSING MY BALANCE...!
CHEE, SOUTHPAW! THE WHOLE CAR'S RATTLIN' SO BAD--IT'S KNOCKED ME TO THE FLOOR! WHAT'S GOIN' ON?
DUNNO!! MUST BE AN EARTHQUAKE--!
WHILE UP FRONT IN THE CAB...
HA HA! I'VE SHAKEN UP THAT PAIR OF LACKEYS ENOUGH...
...TO PUT THE FEAR OF FRIGHT INTO THEIR HEARTS!
NOW LET'S SEE WHAT THIS OUTFIT WILL DO!
AND AS THE TERRIFIED THUGS CATCH THEIR BREATH ENOUGH TO REGAIN THEIR BALANCE...
IT--IT'S THE F-FREAKIN' S-SCARECROW!
H-HE'S M-MAKIN' US S-SCARED OF OUR OWN SH-SHADOWS!
CALM YOUR PATOOTIES, SOUTHPAW!
IF I CAN MAKE YOU BELIEVE I CAN CAUSE YOUR SKIN TO CRAWL WITH FEAR--
--LIKE THE SCARECROW... I CAN SCARE ANYONE!
FEAR'S ALMOST AS GOOD AS LAUGHS--WHICH IS HOW OUR NEXT CAPER GOES! LISTEN...

THAT VERY NIGHT, AT *STAR LABORATORIES*...

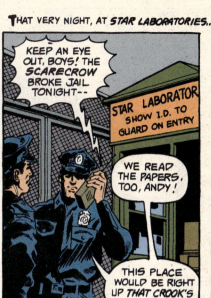

KEEP AN EYE OUT, BOYS! THE *SCARECROW* BROKE JAIL TONIGHT--

STAR LABORATOR
SHOW I.D. TO
GUARD ON ENTRY

WE READ THE PAPERS, TOO, ANDY!

THIS PLACE WOULD BE RIGHT UP *THAT CROOK'S* ALLEY!

YEAH, WE'D BE THE LOGICAL SPOT FOR THE *SCARECROW* TO BOWL OVER!

TIM--?

HEE-HEE..., HO! HO! HO!

TIM... WHAT'S SO--

THWIP!

--SO...HEH-HEH...*FUNNY?*

HAH! HAH! HO! HO!

DON'T KNOW, JONNY...HO! HO! BUT I'M HA...

...LAUGHING MY *HAH-HAH* GUTS OUT--!

AND WITHIN MINUTES...

JONNY?...TIM? WHAT'S GOING ON OUT THERE--?

SOUNDS LIKE THERE'S SOMETHING *SPOOKY* COMING OFF...!

NOW--FOR MY "SKELETON" KEY...

...WHICH CAN OPEN ANY DOOR... HA HA HA!

INSIDE THE HIGH SECURITY BUILDING...

WHERE ARE YOU MEN RUNNING IN THE MIDDLE OF THE NIGHT?

DR. FARR

TROUBLE AT THE MAIN ENTRANCE, DR. FARR! COULD BE *BIG TROUBLE!*

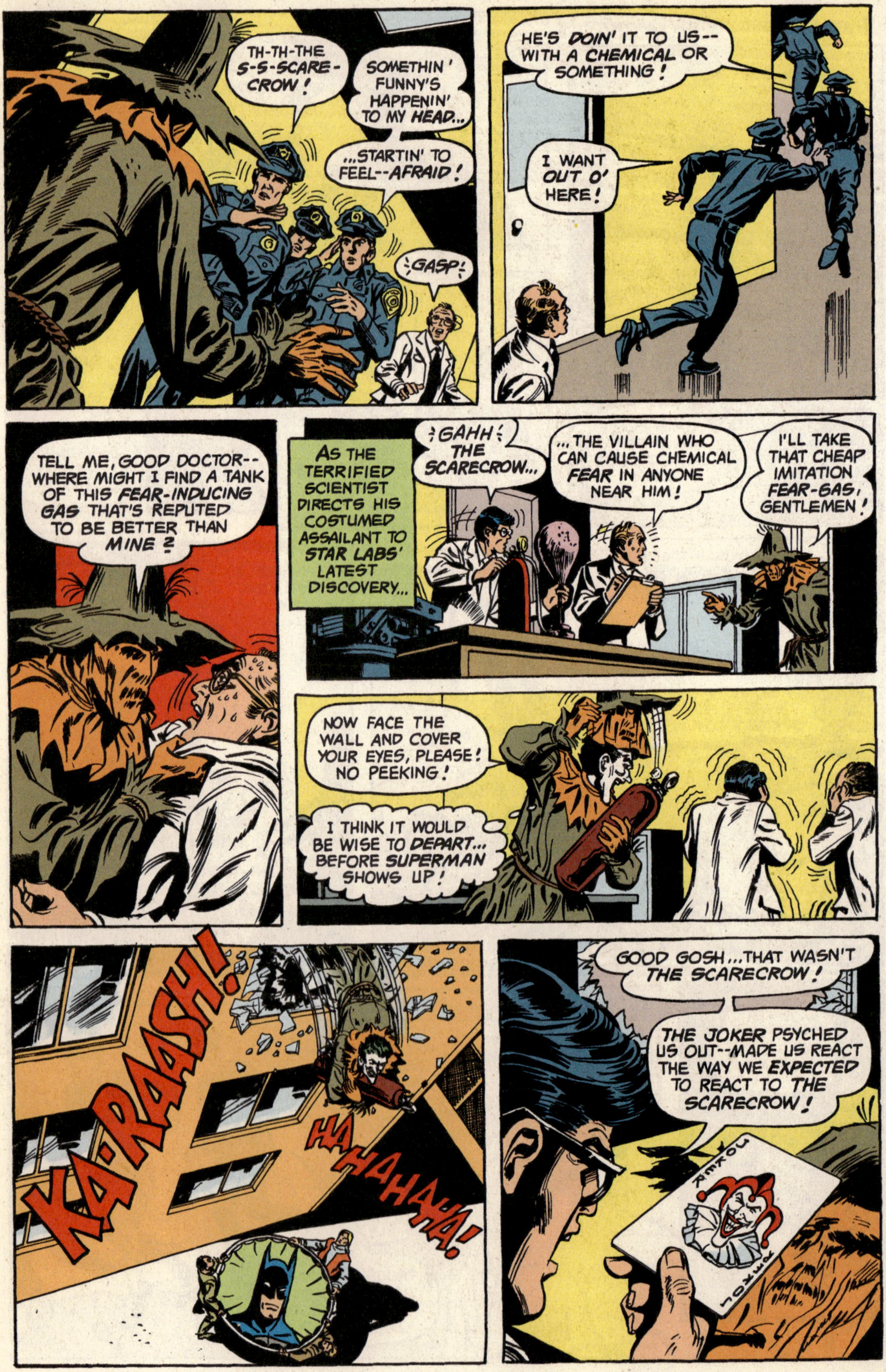
TH-TH-THE S-S-SCARE-CROW!
SOMETHIN' FUNNY'S HAPPENIN' TO MY HEAD...
...STARTIN' TO FEEL--AFRAID!
GASP!
HE'S DOIN' IT TO US--WITH A CHEMICAL OR SOMETHING!
I WANT OUT O' HERE!
TELL ME, GOOD DOCTOR--WHERE MIGHT I FIND A TANK OF THIS FEAR-INDUCING GAS THAT'S REPUTED TO BE BETTER THAN MINE?
AS THE TERRIFIED SCIENTIST DIRECTS HIS COSTUMED ASSAILANT TO STAR LABS' LATEST DISCOVERY...
GAHH! THE SCARECROW...
...THE VILLAIN WHO CAN CAUSE CHEMICAL FEAR IN ANYONE NEAR HIM!
I'LL TAKE THAT CHEAP IMITATION FEAR-GAS, GENTLEMEN!
NOW FACE THE WALL AND COVER YOUR EYES, PLEASE! NO PEEKING!
I THINK IT WOULD BE WISE TO DEPART... BEFORE SUPERMAN SHOWS UP!
KA-RAASH!
HA HA HA HA HA!
GOOD GOSH... THAT WASN'T THE SCARECROW!
THE JOKER PSYCHED US OUT--MADE US REACT THE WAY WE EXPECTED TO REACT TO THE SCARECROW!
JOKER

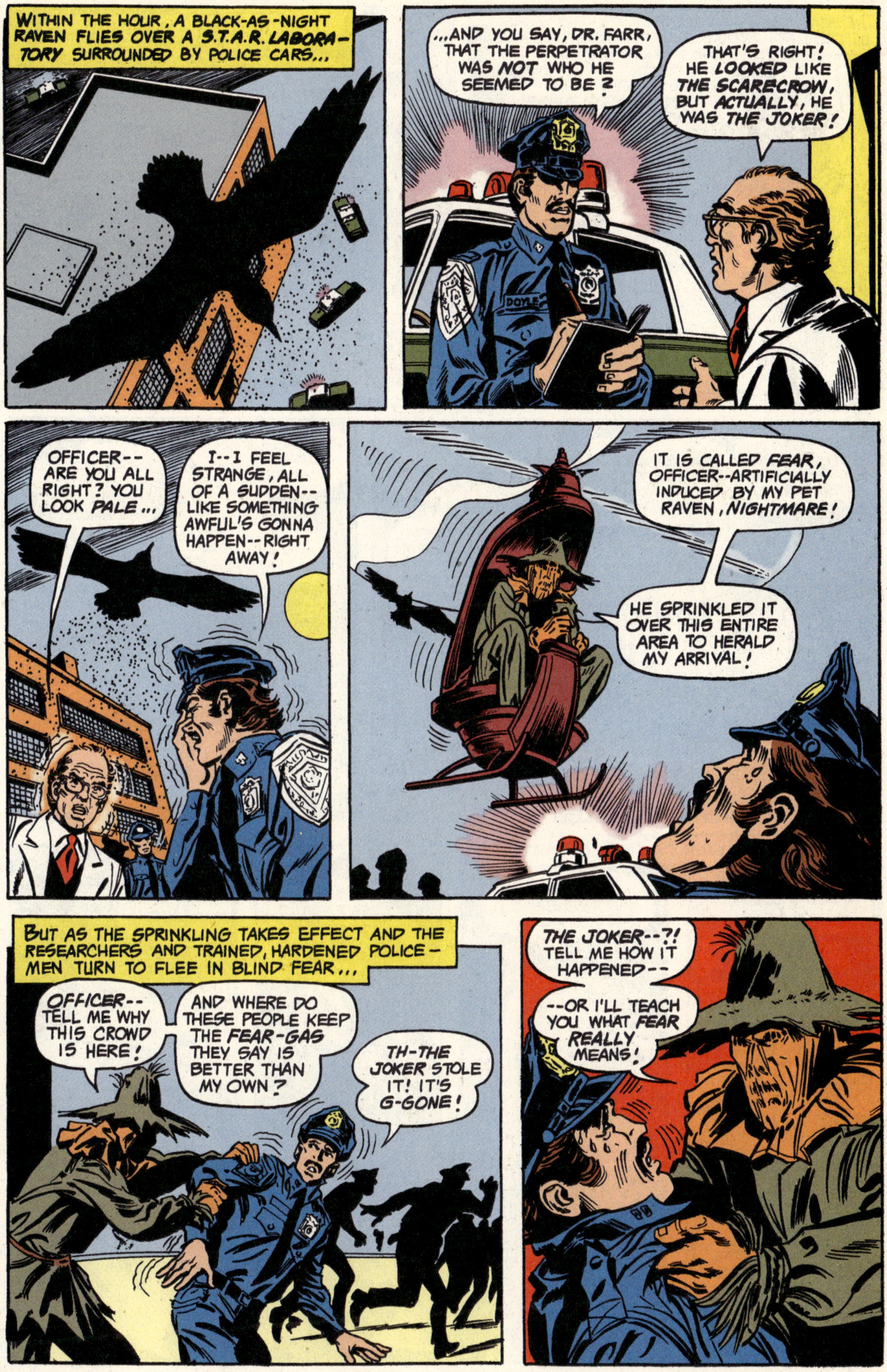
WITHIN THE HOUR, A BLACK-AS-NIGHT RAVEN FLIES OVER A S.T.A.R. LABORATORY SURROUNDED BY POLICE CARS...
...AND YOU SAY, DR. FARR, THAT THE PERPETRATOR WAS NOT WHO HE SEEMED TO BE?
THAT'S RIGHT! HE LOOKED LIKE THE SCARECROW, BUT ACTUALLY, HE WAS THE JOKER!
DOYLE
OFFICER-- ARE YOU ALL RIGHT? YOU LOOK PALE...
I--I FEEL STRANGE, ALL OF A SUDDEN-- LIKE SOMETHING AWFUL'S GONNA HAPPEN--RIGHT AWAY!
IT IS CALLED FEAR, OFFICER--ARTIFICIALLY INDUCED BY MY PET RAVEN, NIGHTMARE!
HE SPRINKLED IT OVER THIS ENTIRE AREA TO HERALD MY ARRIVAL!
BUT AS THE SPRINKLING TAKES EFFECT AND THE RESEARCHERS AND TRAINED, HARDENED POLICEMEN TURN TO FLEE IN BLIND FEAR...
OFFICER-- TELL ME WHY THIS CROWD IS HERE!
AND WHERE DO THESE PEOPLE KEEP THE FEAR-GAS THEY SAY IS BETTER THAN MY OWN?
TH-THE JOKER STOLE IT! IT'S G-GONE!
THE JOKER--?! TELL ME HOW IT HAPPENED--
--OR I'LL TEACH YOU WHAT FEAR REALLY MEANS!

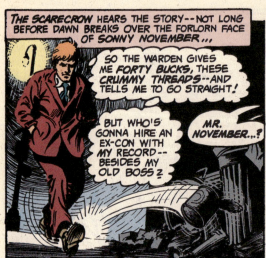

THE SCARECROW HEARS THE STORY--NOT LONG BEFORE DAWN BREAKS OVER THE FORLORN FACE OF SONNY NOVEMBER...

SO THE WARDEN GIVES ME FORTY BUCKS, THESE CRUMMY THREADS--AND TELLS ME TO GO STRAIGHT!

BUT WHO'S GONNA HIRE AN EX-CON WITH MY RECORD--BESIDES MY OLD BOSS?

MR. NOVEMBER...?

I WILL PAY A SUBSTANTIAL SUM OF MONEY FOR THE LOCATION OF YOUR FORMER EMPLOYER'S HEADQUARTERS!

SCARECROW!

GEE, I CAN SURE USE THE BREAD--

--BUT I CAN'T TELL YA WHERE THE JOKER'S HA-HACIENDA IS!

VERY WELL, THEN CONSIDER MY CASH OFFER WITHDRAWN!

NOW--MR. NOVEMBER YOU WILL TELL ME WHERE THIS... HA-HACIENDA IS!

HEY! WHAT'RE YA SPRAYIN' ON ME--?

¡GASP! THAT'S THE STUFF YOU USE ... TO MAKE PEOPLE AFRAID!

I DON'T WANNA BE AFRAID!... I'M S-SCARED OF BEIN' AFRAID!

P-PLEASE...DON'T SCARE ME NO MORE!

MAYBE IT WON'T COUNT IF I WHISPER WHERE THE HA-HACIENDA IS!

AH, YES, I KNOW THE GENERAL AREA!

THANK YOU, MR. NOVEMBER!

AND AS THE MASTER OF FEAR DEPARTS...

IT DON'T COUNT... HA HA HA...

...'CAUSED I WHISPERED IT... HA HA HA ...

...IT WASN'T MY F-FAULT... HA HA HA...

HO HO HEE HEE ¡CHOKE!

THE DAY THREATENS TO BE A SCORCHER AS THE CLOWN PRINCE OF CRIME SITS IN HIS *HA-HACIENDA*...

...AND THE THEFT OF A RARE CHEMICAL FROM S.T.A.R. LABORATORIES WAS CARRIED OUT BY THE JOKER--NOT THE SCARECROW, AS FIRST REPORTED!

HEY, BOSS, WHAT'RE YOU--

SHUT UP, MEATHEAD... OR I'LL MISS HEARING MY *NAME* OVER THE RADIO!

...THE MAN WHO SUCCUMBED TO THE LAUGHING DEATH HAS BEEN IDENTIFIED AS SONNY NOVEMBER!

DIDJA HEAR THAT--? SONNY'S DEAD!

QUIET, YOU NERD, AND LET'S HEAR THE DETAILS!

A FORMER MEMBER OF THE JOKER'S GANG, SONNY IS THOUGHT TO HAVE BEEN MURDERED BY HIS FORMER BOSS!

LET THAT BE A LESSON TO YOU, MY LEFT-HAND MAN--

--DON'T SQUEAL!

THE HYPNOTIC COMMAND I GAVE SONNY AUTOMATICALLY KILLED HIM WHEN HE REVEALED MY HIDEAWAY!

I'LL BET I KNOW WHO I'VE NOW MADE ANGRY ENOUGH TO WANT TO *FIND* ME, TOO!

SOUTHPAW, TAKE THIS MOTH TO THAT CROOKED ENTOMOLOGIST WE KNOW AND TELL HIM I WANT 2,000 LIVE ONES JUST LIKE IT!

BUT FIRST WE MUST TELL OUR ANGRY FRIEND WHERE WE WENT!

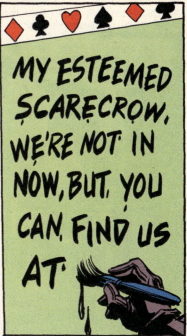

MY ESTEEMED SCARECROW, WE'RE NOT IN NOW, BUT YOU CAN FIND US AT

However, *THE SCARECROW*--ALIAS *JONATHAN CRANE,* PSYCHOLOGIST--HAS BUSINESS FIRST AT A NEARBY UNIVERSITY CAMPUS...

LUCKILY NO ONE'S SPOTTED ME SO FAR-- BUT I'M WELL-KNOWN ENOUGH HERE TO SOME FORMER COLLEAGUES...

...TO MAKE IT PRUDENT NOT TO BE RECOGNIZED!

THIS WILL KEEP PEOPLE AWAY AS SURE AS IF MY *BREATH* WERE SUFFERING THE EFFECTS OF A CRATE OF *GARLIC!*

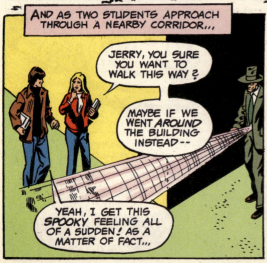

AND AS TWO STUDENTS APPROACH THROUGH A NEARBY CORRIDOR...

JERRY, YOU SURE YOU WANT TO WALK THIS WAY?

MAYBE IF WE WENT *AROUND* THE BUILDING INSTEAD--

YEAH, I GET THIS *SPOOKY* FEELING ALL OF A SUDDEN! AS A MATTER OF FACT...

...I THINK I'M *SCARED* OUT OF MY *SKIN!*

WAIT FOR *ME,* JERRY! DON'T LEAVE ME ALONE!

AND PRESENTLY, IN A LABORATORY CLASSROOM...

THIS ACIDIC MIXTURE IS IDEAL FOR *VAPORIZING* A CERTAIN ALUMINUM ALLOY...

WHILE OUTSIDE THE LAB...

...THE VERY ALLOY USED TO CONTAIN A CERTAIN GAS IN A CERTAIN *CANISTER!*

I-I FEEL STRANGE!

LABORAT0 1

I DON'T THINK I'LL GO INTO MY CLASSROOM TODAY--

LABORATORY 1

--OR EVER AGAIN!

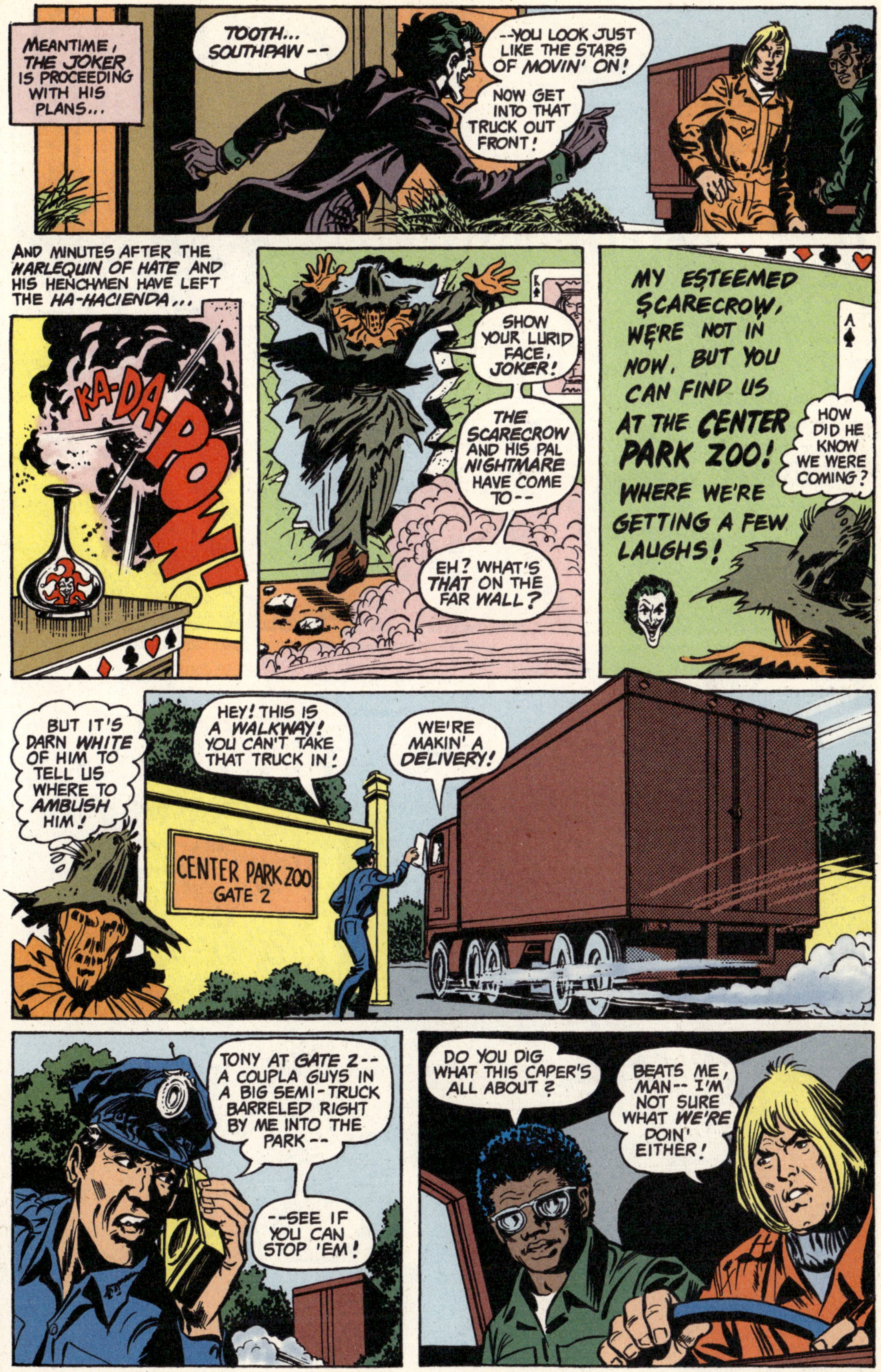

MEANTIME, THE JOKER IS PROCEEDING WITH HIS PLANS...
TOOTH... SOUTHPAW --
--YOU LOOK JUST LIKE THE STARS OF MOVIN' ON!
NOW GET INTO THAT TRUCK OUT FRONT!
AND MINUTES AFTER THE HARLEQUIN OF HATE AND HIS HENCHMEN HAVE LEFT THE HA-HACIENDA...
KA-DA-POW!
SHOW YOUR LURID FACE, JOKER!
THE SCARECROW AND HIS PAL NIGHTMARE HAVE COME TO --
EH? WHAT'S THAT ON THE FAR WALL?
MY ESTEEMED SCARECROW, WE'RE NOT IN NOW. BUT YOU CAN FIND US AT THE CENTER PARK ZOO! WHERE WE'RE GETTING A FEW LAUGHS!
HOW DID HE KNOW WE WERE COMING?
BUT IT'S DARN WHITE OF HIM TO TELL US WHERE TO AMBUSH HIM!
HEY! THIS IS A WALKWAY! YOU CAN'T TAKE THAT TRUCK IN!
WE'RE MAKIN' A DELIVERY!
CENTER PARK ZOO GATE 2
TONY AT GATE 2-- A COUPLA GUYS IN A BIG SEMI-TRUCK BARRELED RIGHT BY ME INTO THE PARK --
--SEE IF YOU CAN STOP 'EM!
DO YOU DIG WHAT THIS CAPER'S ALL ABOUT?
BEATS ME, MAN-- I'M NOT SURE WHAT WE'RE DOIN' EITHER!

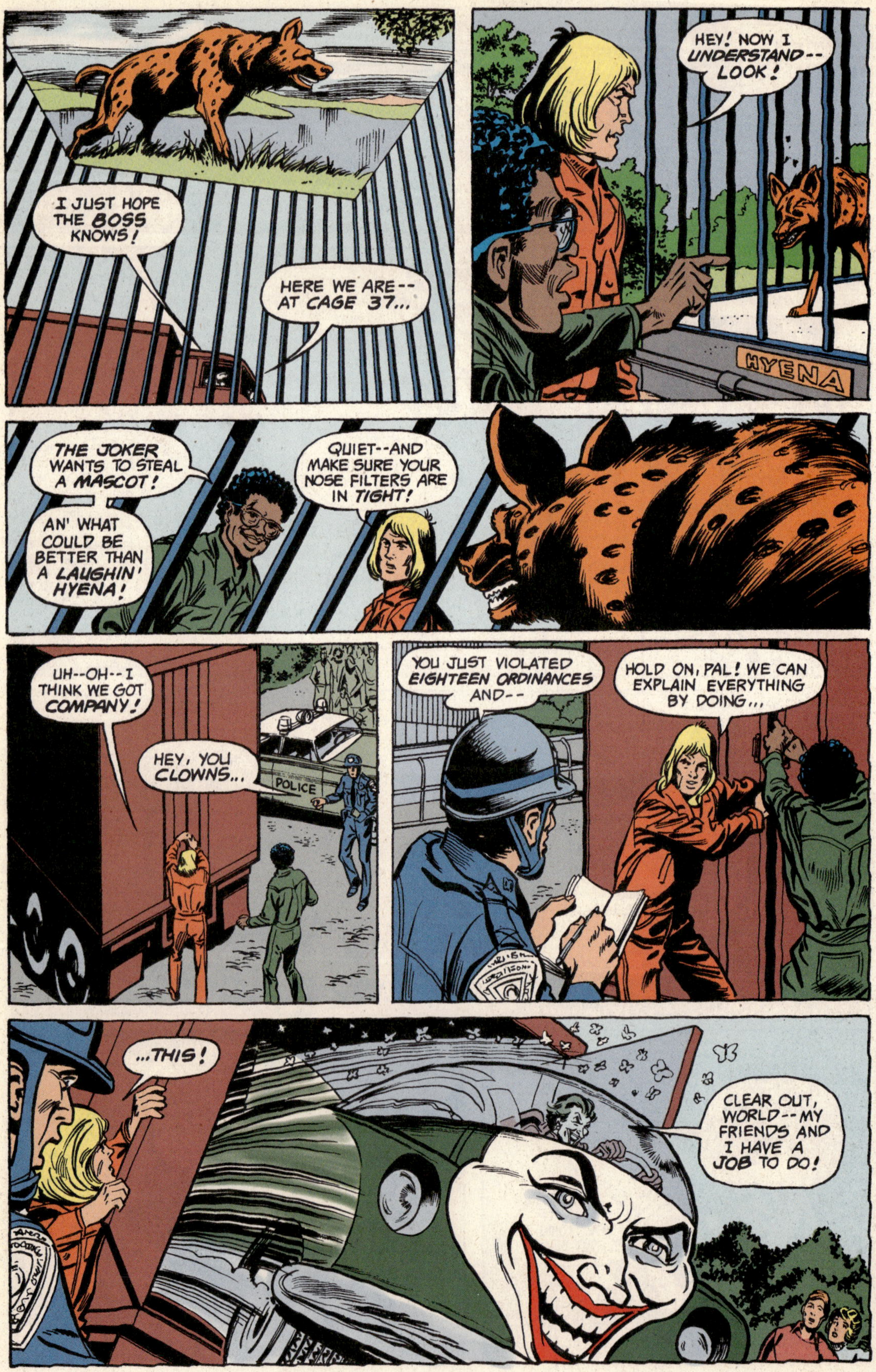

I JUST HOPE THE BOSS KNOWS!
HERE WE ARE--AT CAGE 37...
HEY! NOW I UNDERSTAND--LOOK!
HYENA
THE JOKER WANTS TO STEAL A MASCOT!
AN' WHAT COULD BE BETTER THAN A LAUGHIN' HYENA!
QUIET--AND MAKE SURE YOUR NOSE FILTERS ARE IN TIGHT!
UH--OH--I THINK WE GOT COMPANY!
HEY, YOU CLOWNS...
POLICE
YOU JUST VIOLATED EIGHTEEN ORDINANCES AND--
HOLD ON, PAL! WE CAN EXPLAIN EVERYTHING BY DOING...
...THIS!
CLEAR OUT, WORLD--MY FRIENDS AND I HAVE A JOB TO DO!

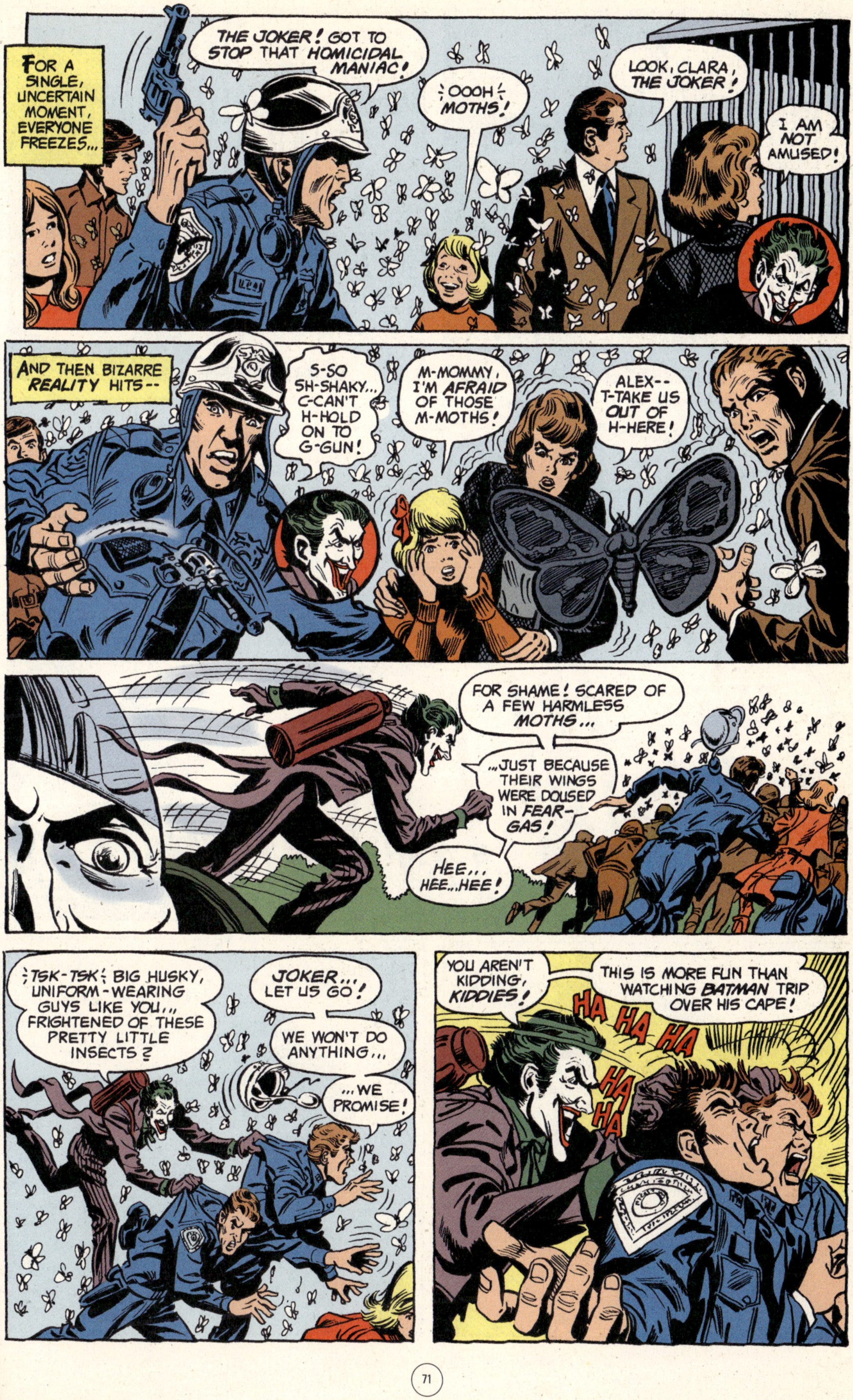
FOR A SINGLE, UNCERTAIN MOMENT, EVERYONE FREEZES...
THE JOKER! GOT TO STOP THAT HOMICIDAL MANIAC!
OOOH MOTHS!
LOOK, CLARA, THE JOKER!
I AM NOT AMUSED!
AND THEN BIZARRE REALITY HITS--
S-SO SH-SHAKY... C-CAN'T H-HOLD ON TO G-GUN!
M-MOMMY, I'M AFRAID OF THOSE M-MOTHS!
ALEX-- T-TAKE US OUT OF H-HERE!
FOR SHAME! SCARED OF A FEW HARMLESS MOTHS...
...JUST BECAUSE THEIR WINGS WERE DOUSED IN FEAR-GAS!
HEE... HEE...HEE!
TSK-TSK! BIG HUSKY, UNIFORM-WEARING GUYS LIKE YOU... FRIGHTENED OF THESE PRETTY LITTLE INSECTS?
JOKER... LET US GO!
WE WON'T DO ANYTHING...
...WE PROMISE!
YOU AREN'T KIDDING, KIDDIES!
THIS IS MORE FUN THAN WATCHING BATMAN TRIP OVER HIS CAPE!
HA HA HA
HA HA HA

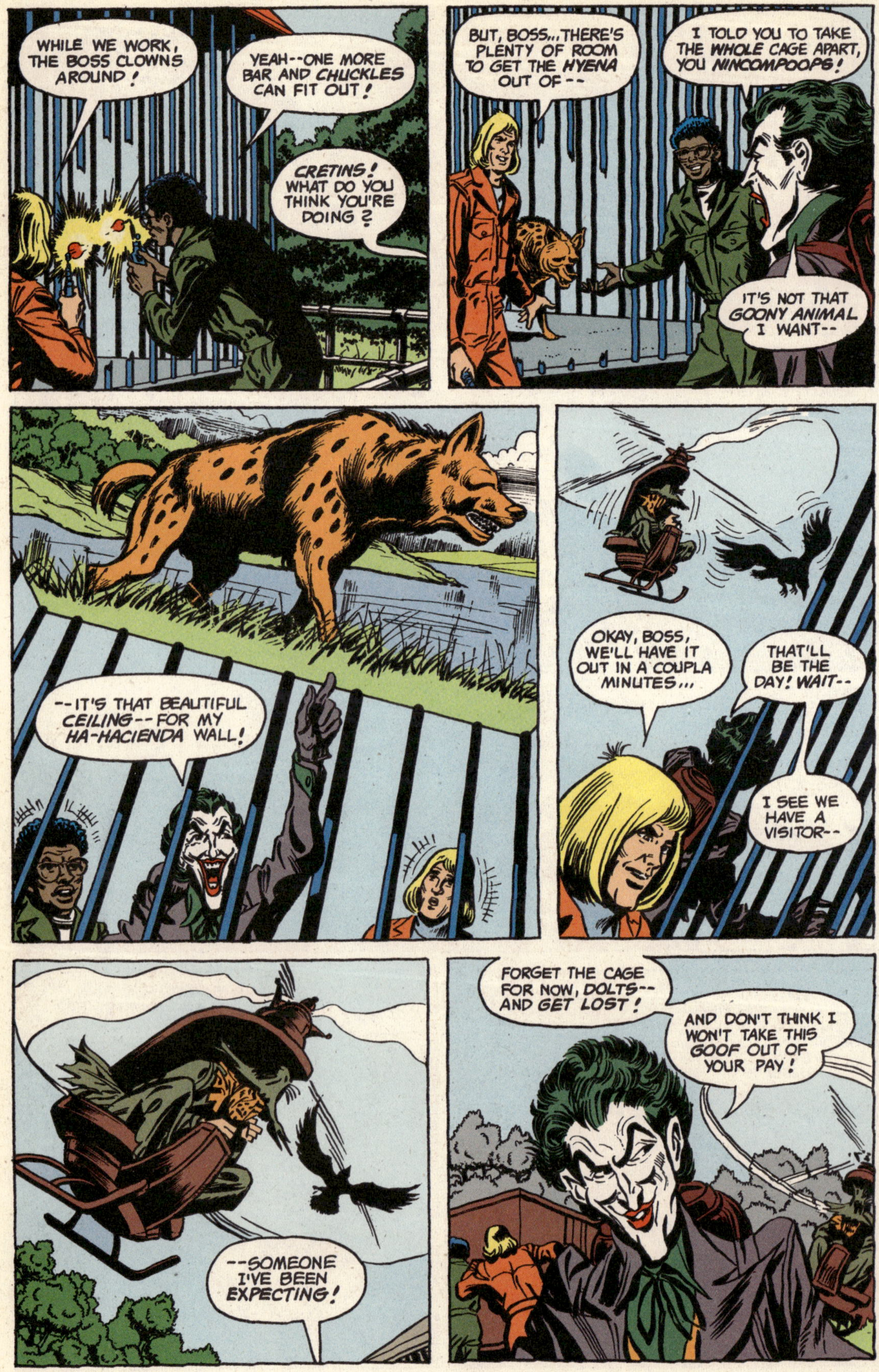
WHILE WE WORK, THE BOSS CLOWNS AROUND!
YEAH--ONE MORE BAR AND CHUCKLES CAN FIT OUT!
CRETINS! WHAT DO YOU THINK YOU'RE DOING?
BUT, BOSS...THERE'S PLENTY OF ROOM TO GET THE HYENA OUT OF--
I TOLD YOU TO TAKE THE WHOLE CAGE APART, YOU NINCOMPOOPS!
IT'S NOT THAT GOONY ANIMAL I WANT--
--IT'S THAT BEAUTIFUL CEILING--FOR MY HA-HACIENDA WALL!
OKAY, BOSS, WE'LL HAVE IT OUT IN A COUPLA MINUTES...
THAT'LL BE THE DAY! WAIT--
I SEE WE HAVE A VISITOR--
--SOMEONE I'VE BEEN EXPECTING!
FORGET THE CAGE FOR NOW, DOLTS--AND GET LOST!
AND DON'T THINK I WON'T TAKE THIS GOOF OUT OF YOUR PAY!

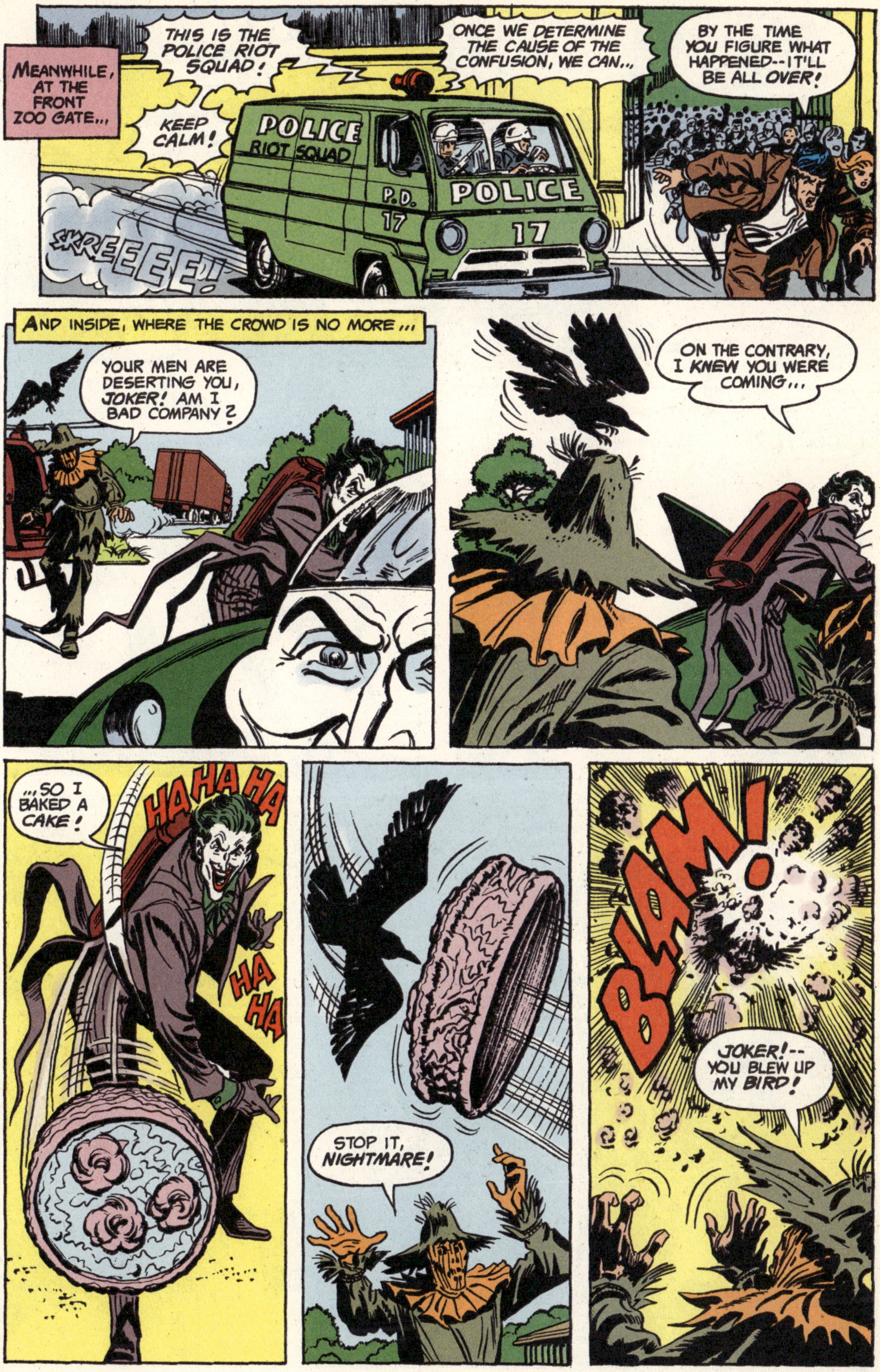
MEANWHILE, AT THE FRONT ZOO GATE...
THIS IS THE POLICE RIOT SQUAD!
KEEP CALM!
ONCE WE DETERMINE THE CAUSE OF THE CONFUSION, WE CAN...
BY THE TIME YOU FIGURE WHAT HAPPENED--IT'LL BE ALL OVER!
POLICE
RIOT SQUAD
P.D. 17
POLICE
17
SKREEEEE!!
AND INSIDE, WHERE THE CROWD IS NO MORE...
YOUR MEN ARE DESERTING YOU, JOKER! AM I BAD COMPANY?
ON THE CONTRARY, I KNEW YOU WERE COMING...
...SO I BAKED A CAKE!
HAHAHA
HA HA
STOP IT, NIGHTMARE!
BLAM!
JOKER!-- YOU BLEW UP MY BIRD!

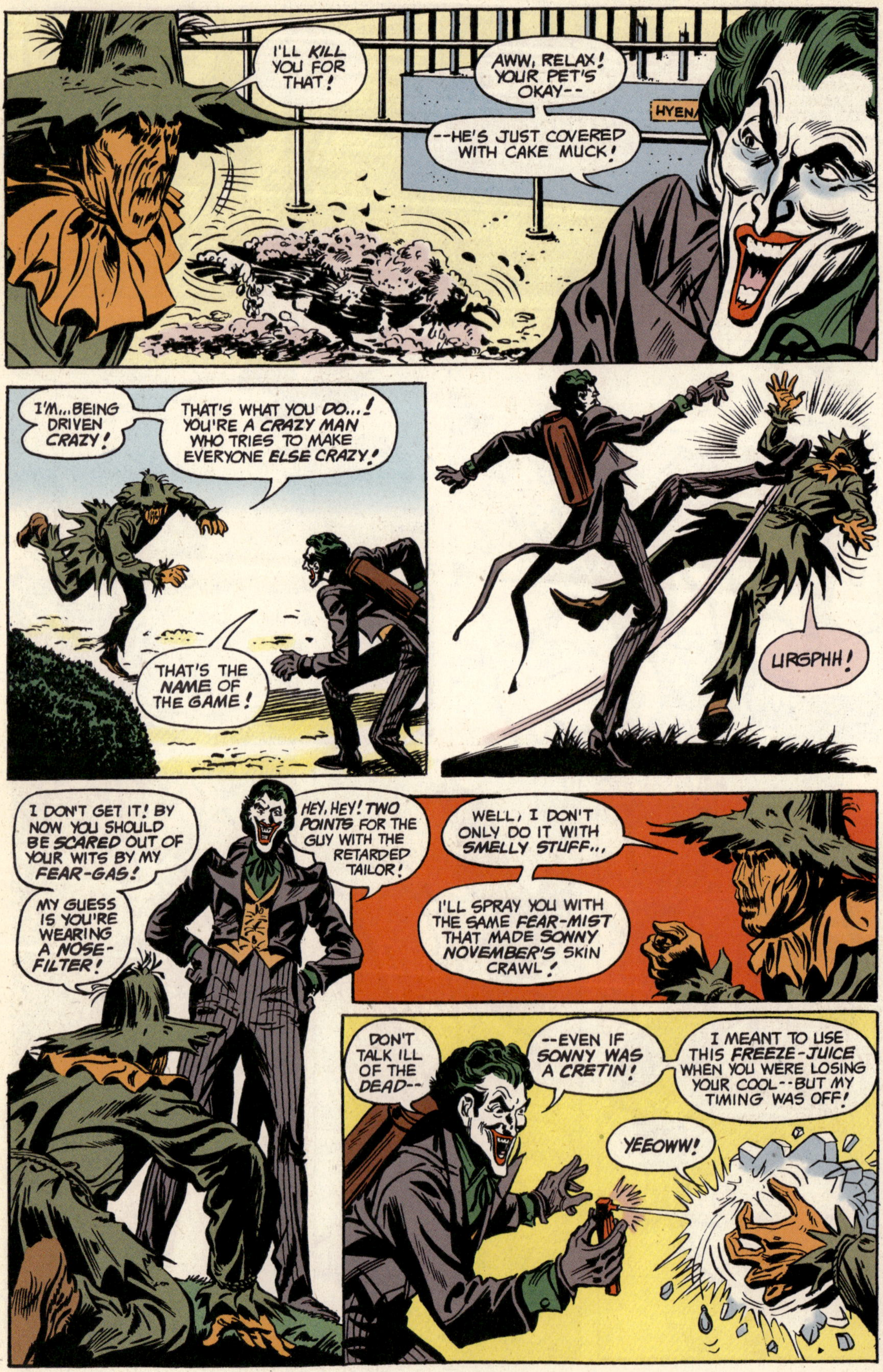
I'LL KILL YOU FOR THAT!
AWW, RELAX! YOUR PET'S OKAY--
--HE'S JUST COVERED WITH CAKE MUCK!
HYENA
I'M... BEING DRIVEN CRAZY!
THAT'S WHAT YOU DO...! YOU'RE A CRAZY MAN WHO TRIES TO MAKE EVERYONE ELSE CRAZY!
THAT'S THE NAME OF THE GAME!
URGPHH!
I DON'T GET IT! BY NOW YOU SHOULD BE SCARED OUT OF YOUR WITS BY MY FEAR-GAS!
MY GUESS IS YOU'RE WEARING A NOSE-FILTER!
HEY, HEY! TWO POINTS FOR THE GUY WITH THE RETARDED TAILOR!
WELL, I DON'T ONLY DO IT WITH SMELLY STUFF...
I'LL SPRAY YOU WITH THE SAME FEAR-MIST THAT MADE SONNY NOVEMBER'S SKIN CRAWL!
DON'T TALK ILL OF THE DEAD--
--EVEN IF SONNY WAS A CRETIN!
I MEANT TO USE THIS FREEZE-JUICE WHEN YOU WERE LOSING YOUR COOL--BUT MY TIMING WAS OFF!
YEEOWW!

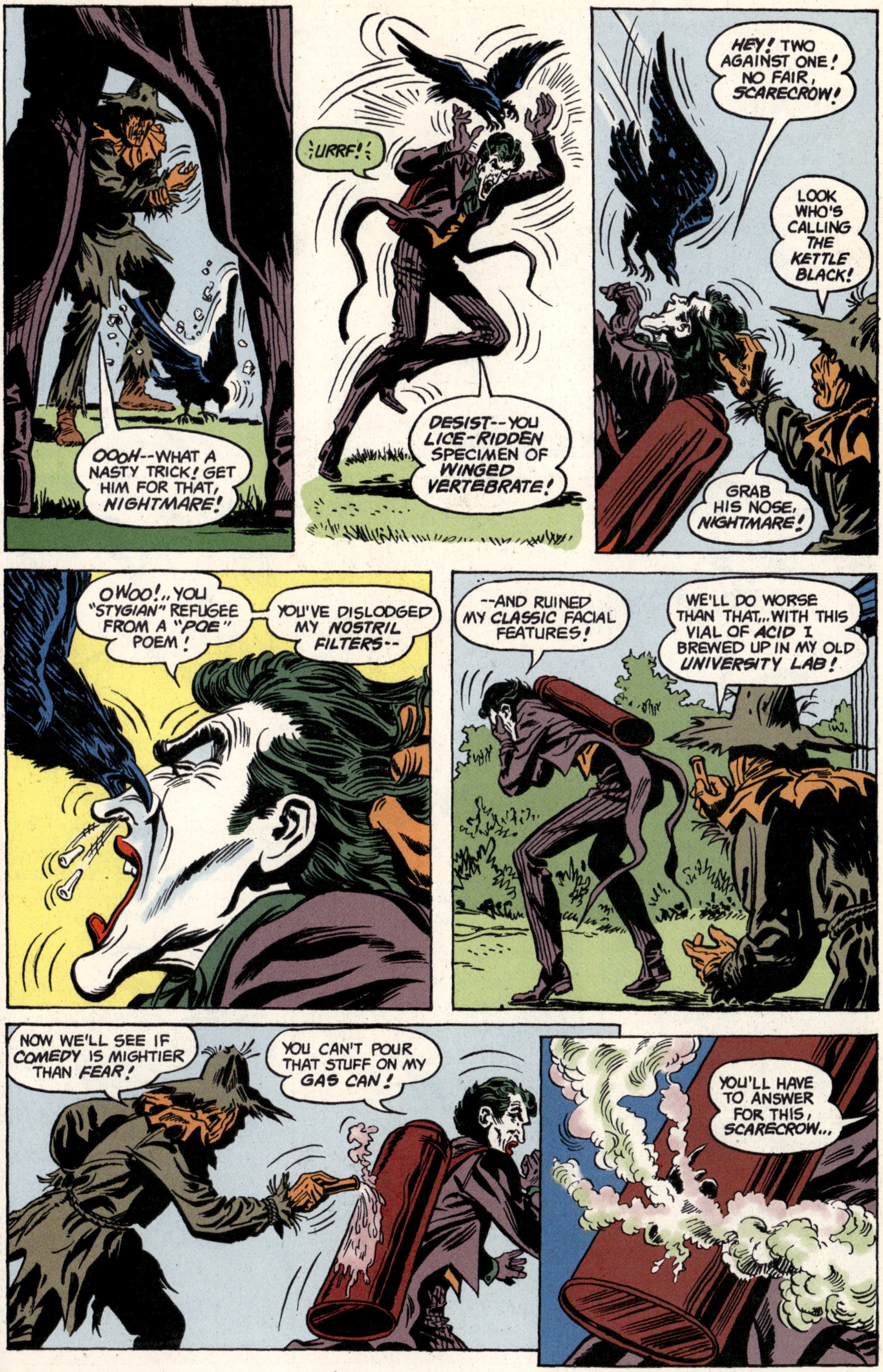
OOOH--WHAT A NASTY TRICK! GET HIM FOR THAT, NIGHTMARE!
URRF!
DESIST--YOU LICE-RIDDEN SPECIMEN OF WINGED VERTEBRATE!
HEY! TWO AGAINST ONE! NO FAIR, SCARECROW!
LOOK WHO'S CALLING THE KETTLE BLACK!
GRAB HIS NOSE, NIGHTMARE!
OWOO!..YOU "STYGIAN" REFUGEE FROM A "POE" POEM!
YOU'VE DISLODGED MY NOSTRIL FILTERS--
--AND RUINED MY CLASSIC FACIAL FEATURES!
WE'LL DO WORSE THAN THAT...WITH THIS VIAL OF ACID I BREWED UP IN MY OLD UNIVERSITY LAB!
NOW WE'LL SEE IF COMEDY IS MIGHTIER THAN FEAR!
YOU CAN'T POUR THAT STUFF ON MY GAS CAN!
YOU'LL HAVE TO ANSWER FOR THIS, SCARECROW...

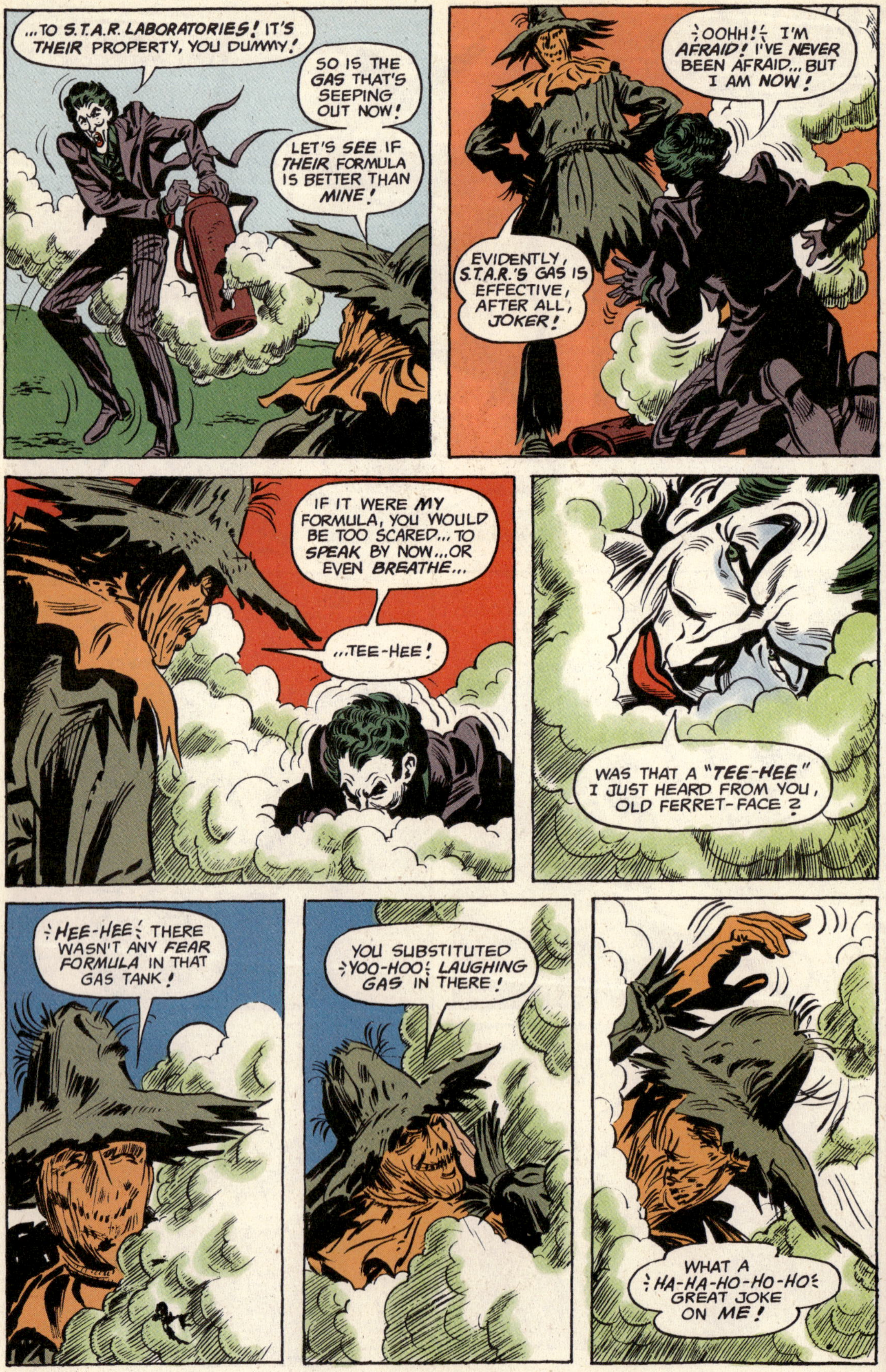
...TO S.T.A.R. LABORATORIES! IT'S THEIR PROPERTY, YOU DUMMY!
SO IS THE GAS THAT'S SEEPING OUT NOW!
LET'S SEE IF THEIR FORMULA IS BETTER THAN MINE!
OOHH! I'M AFRAID! I'VE NEVER BEEN AFRAID... BUT I AM NOW!
EVIDENTLY, S.T.A.R.'S GAS IS EFFECTIVE, AFTER ALL, JOKER!
IF IT WERE MY FORMULA, YOU WOULD BE TOO SCARED... TO SPEAK BY NOW... OR EVEN BREATHE...
...TEE-HEE!
WAS THAT A "TEE-HEE" I JUST HEARD FROM YOU, OLD FERRET-FACE?
HEE-HEE! THERE WASN'T ANY FEAR FORMULA IN THAT GAS TANK!
YOU SUBSTITUTED YOO-HOO! LAUGHING GAS IN THERE!
WHAT A HA-HA-HO-HO-HO GREAT JOKE ON ME!

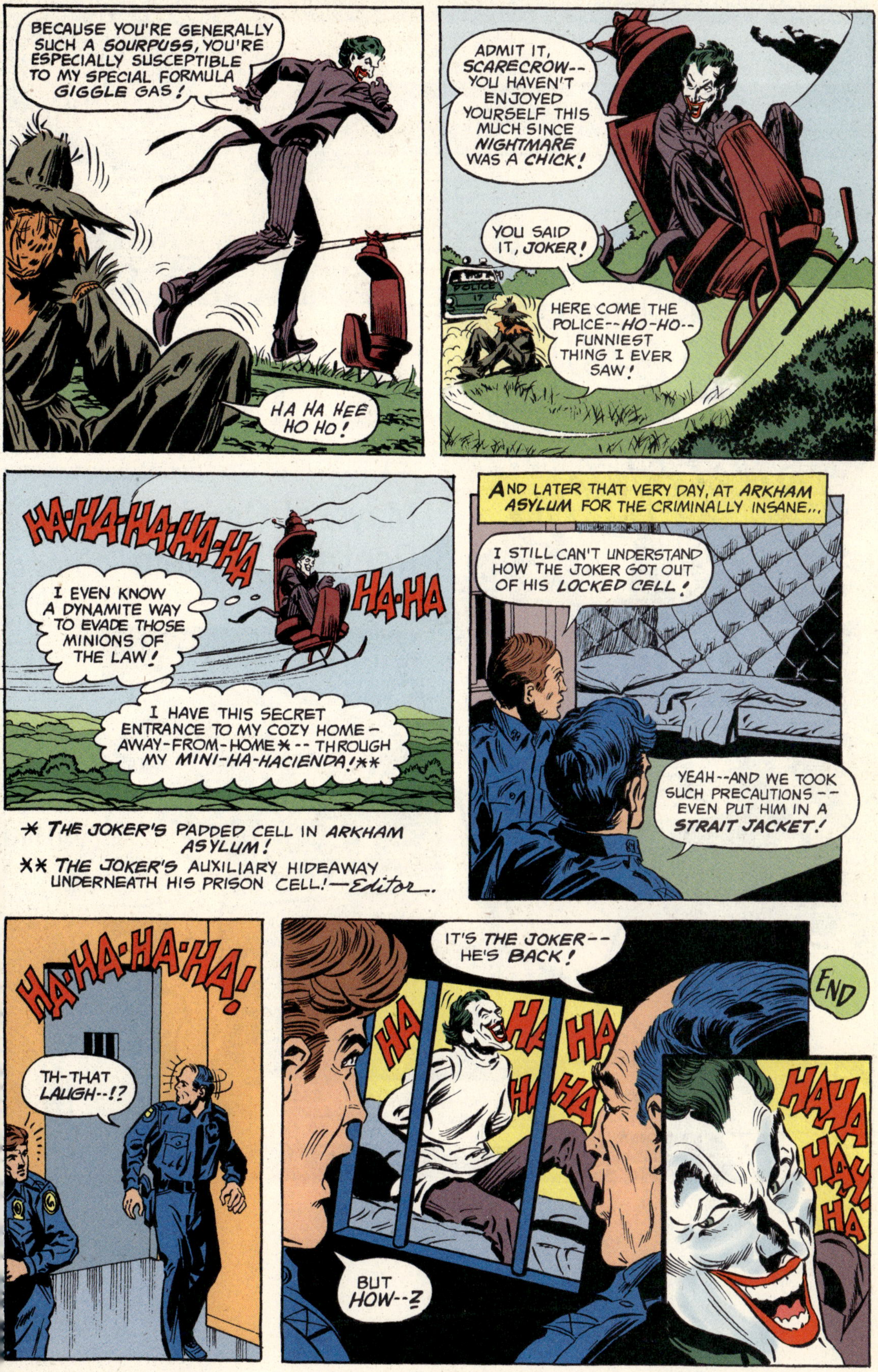
BECAUSE YOU'RE GENERALLY SUCH A SOURPUSS, YOU'RE ESPECIALLY SUSCEPTIBLE TO MY SPECIAL FORMULA GIGGLE GAS!
HA HA HEE HO HO!
ADMIT IT, SCARECROW-- YOU HAVEN'T ENJOYED YOURSELF THIS MUCH SINCE NIGHTMARE WAS A CHICK!
YOU SAID IT, JOKER!
POLICE
HERE COME THE POLICE--HO-HO-- FUNNIEST THING I EVER SAW!
HA-HA-HA-HA-HA
HA-HA
I EVEN KNOW A DYNAMITE WAY TO EVADE THOSE MINIONS OF THE LAW!
I HAVE THIS SECRET ENTRANCE TO MY COZY HOME-AWAY-FROM-HOME* -- THROUGH MY MINI-HA-HACIENDA!**
* THE JOKER'S PADDED CELL IN ARKHAM ASYLUM!
** THE JOKER'S AUXILIARY HIDEAWAY UNDERNEATH HIS PRISON CELL! —Editor.
AND LATER THAT VERY DAY, AT ARKHAM ASYLUM FOR THE CRIMINALLY INSANE...
I STILL CAN'T UNDERSTAND HOW THE JOKER GOT OUT OF HIS LOCKED CELL!
YEAH--AND WE TOOK SUCH PRECAUTIONS -- EVEN PUT HIM IN A STRAIT JACKET!
HA-HA-HA-HA!
TH-THAT LAUGH--!?
IT'S THE JOKER-- HE'S BACK!
HA HA HA HA HA
BUT HOW--?
HAHA HAHA
END

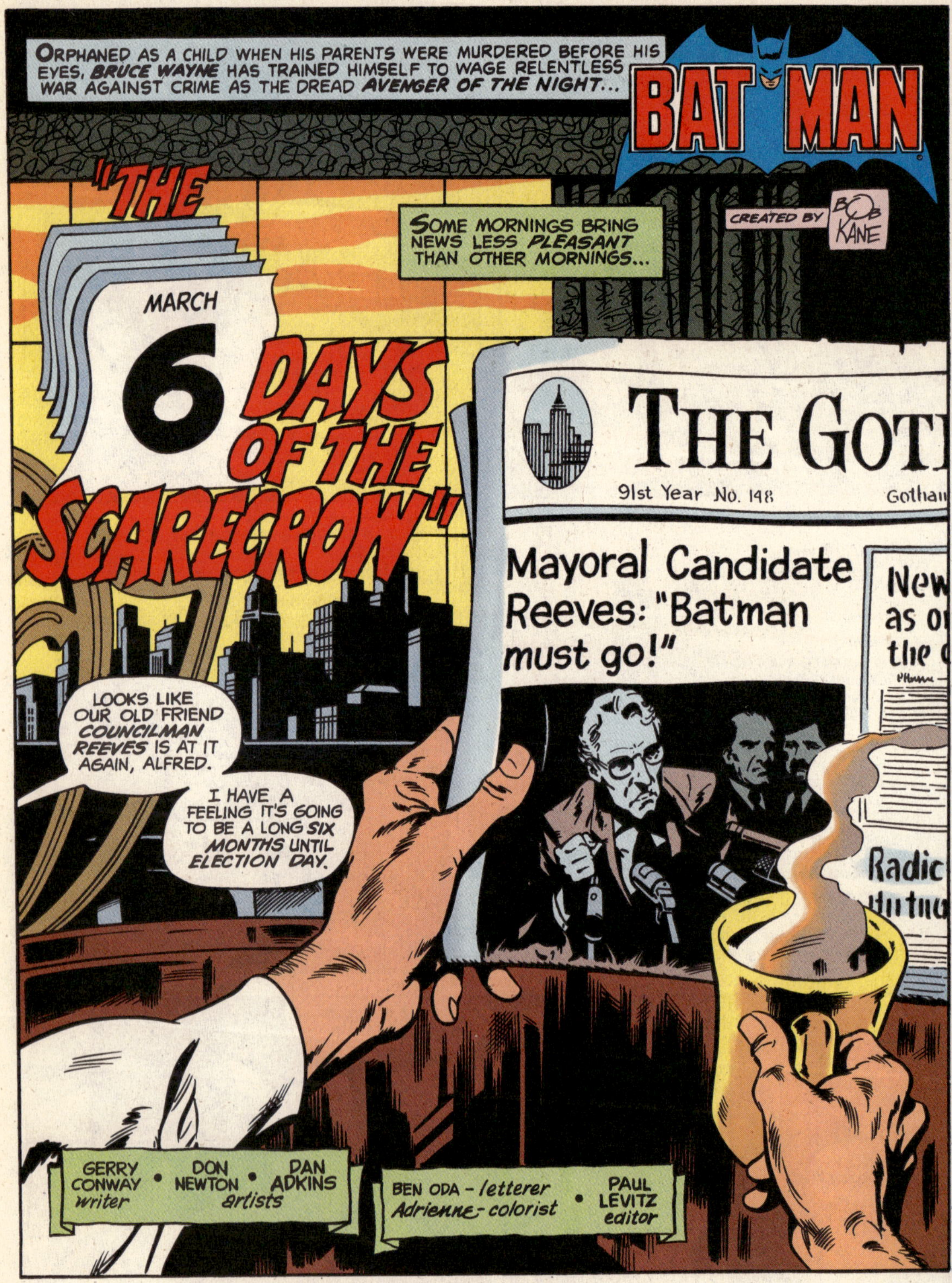
ORPHANED AS A CHILD WHEN HIS PARENTS WERE MURDERED BEFORE HIS EYES, BRUCE WAYNE HAS TRAINED HIMSELF TO WAGE RELENTLESS WAR AGAINST CRIME AS THE DREAD AVENGER OF THE NIGHT...
BATMAN
CREATED BY BOB KANE
"THE 6 DAYS OF THE SCARECROW"
MARCH
SOME MORNINGS BRING NEWS LESS PLEASANT THAN OTHER MORNINGS...
THE GOT
91st Year No. 148
Mayoral Candidate Reeves: "Batman must go!"
LOOKS LIKE OUR OLD FRIEND COUNCILMAN REEVES IS AT IT AGAIN, ALFRED.
I HAVE A FEELING IT'S GOING TO BE A LONG SIX MONTHS UNTIL ELECTION DAY.
GERRY CONWAY writer • DON NEWTON • DAN ADKINS artists
BEN ODA - letterer Adrienne - colorist • PAUL LEVITZ editor

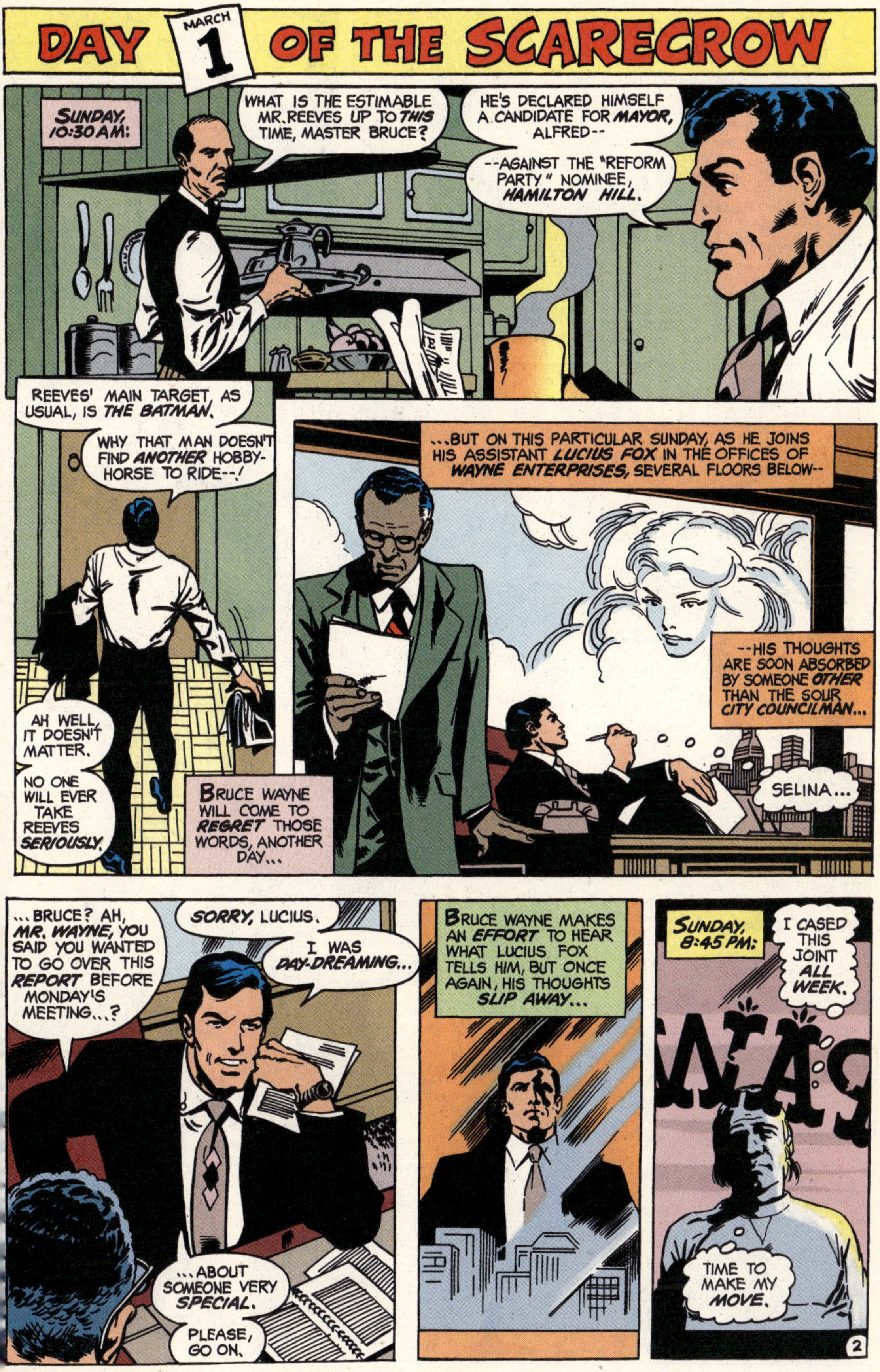
DAY MARCH 1 OF THE SCARECROW
SUNDAY, 10:30 AM:
WHAT IS THE ESTIMABLE MR. REEVES UP TO THIS TIME, MASTER BRUCE?
HE'S DECLARED HIMSELF A CANDIDATE FOR MAYOR, ALFRED--
--AGAINST THE "REFORM PARTY" NOMINEE, HAMILTON HILL.
REEVES' MAIN TARGET, AS USUAL, IS THE BATMAN.
WHY THAT MAN DOESN'T FIND ANOTHER HOBBY-HORSE TO RIDE--!
AH WELL, IT DOESN'T MATTER.
NO ONE WILL EVER TAKE REEVES SERIOUSLY.
BRUCE WAYNE WILL COME TO REGRET THOSE WORDS, ANOTHER DAY...
...BUT ON THIS PARTICULAR SUNDAY, AS HE JOINS HIS ASSISTANT LUCIUS FOX IN THE OFFICES OF WAYNE ENTERPRISES, SEVERAL FLOORS BELOW--
--HIS THOUGHTS ARE SOON ABSORBED BY SOMEONE OTHER THAN THE SOUR CITY COUNCILMAN...
SELINA...
...BRUCE? AH, MR. WAYNE, YOU SAID YOU WANTED TO GO OVER THIS REPORT BEFORE MONDAY'S MEETING...?
SORRY, LUCIUS.
I WAS DAY-DREAMING...
...ABOUT SOMEONE VERY SPECIAL.
PLEASE, GO ON.
BRUCE WAYNE MAKES AN EFFORT TO HEAR WHAT LUCIUS FOX TELLS HIM, BUT ONCE AGAIN, HIS THOUGHTS SLIP AWAY...
SUNDAY, 8:45 PM:
I CASED THIS JOINT ALL WEEK.
TIME TO MAKE MY MOVE.
2

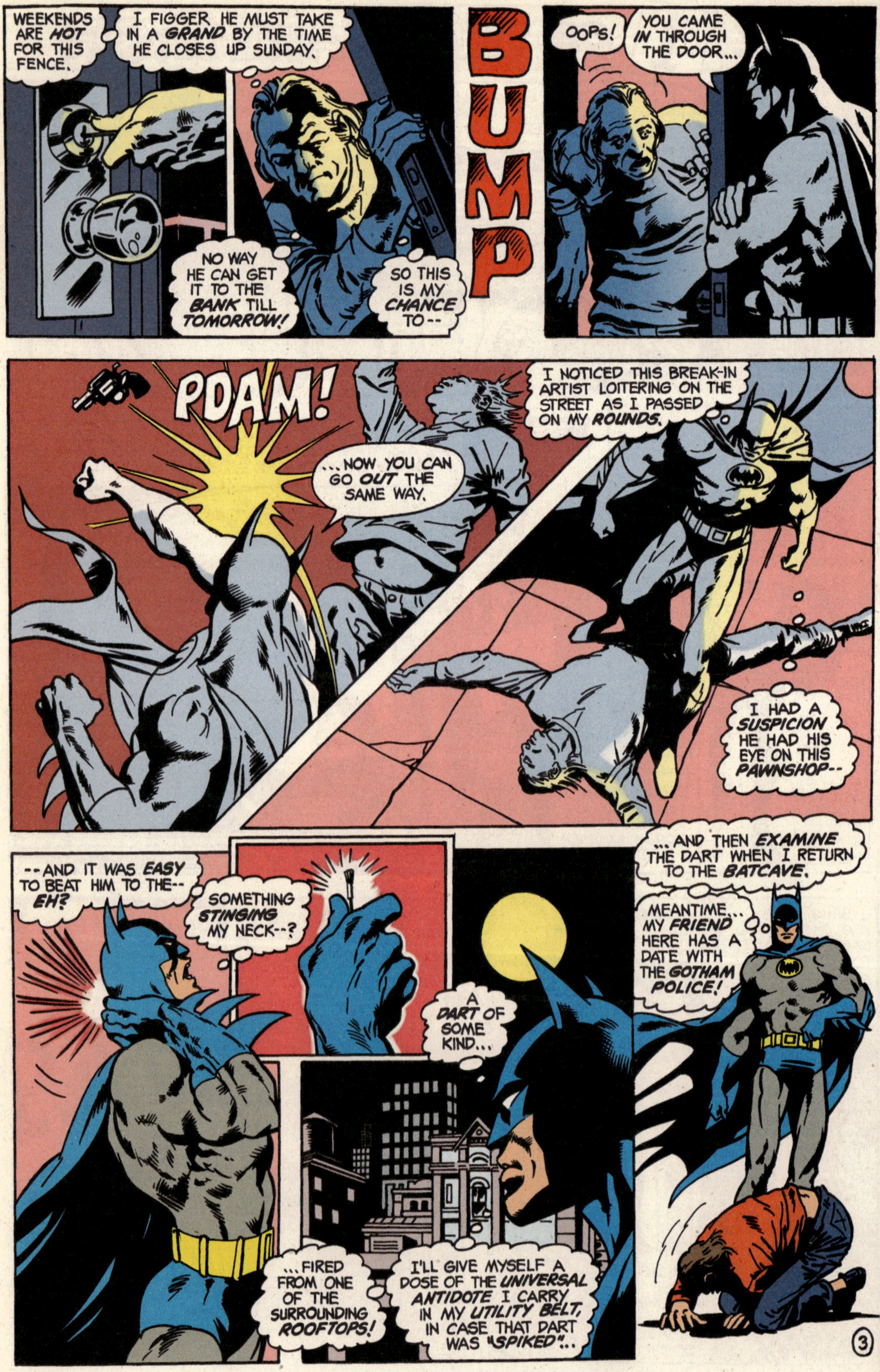
WEEKENDS ARE HOT FOR THIS FENCE.
I FIGGER HE MUST TAKE IN A GRAND BY THE TIME HE CLOSES UP SUNDAY.
NO WAY HE CAN GET IT TO THE BANK TILL TOMORROW!
SO THIS IS MY CHANCE TO--
BUMP
OOPS!
YOU CAME IN THROUGH THE DOOR...
PDAM!
...NOW YOU CAN GO OUT THE SAME WAY.
I NOTICED THIS BREAK-IN ARTIST LOITERING ON THE STREET AS I PASSED ON MY ROUNDS.
I HAD A SUSPICION HE HAD HIS EYE ON THIS PAWNSHOP--
--AND IT WAS EASY TO BEAT HIM TO THE-- EH?
SOMETHING STINGING MY NECK--?
A DART OF SOME KIND...
...FIRED FROM ONE OF THE SURROUNDING ROOFTOPS!
I'LL GIVE MYSELF A DOSE OF THE UNIVERSAL ANTIDOTE I CARRY IN MY UTILITY BELT, IN CASE THAT DART WAS "SPIKED"...
...AND THEN EXAMINE THE DART WHEN I RETURN TO THE BATCAVE.
MEANTIME... MY FRIEND HERE HAS A DATE WITH THE GOTHAM POLICE!
3

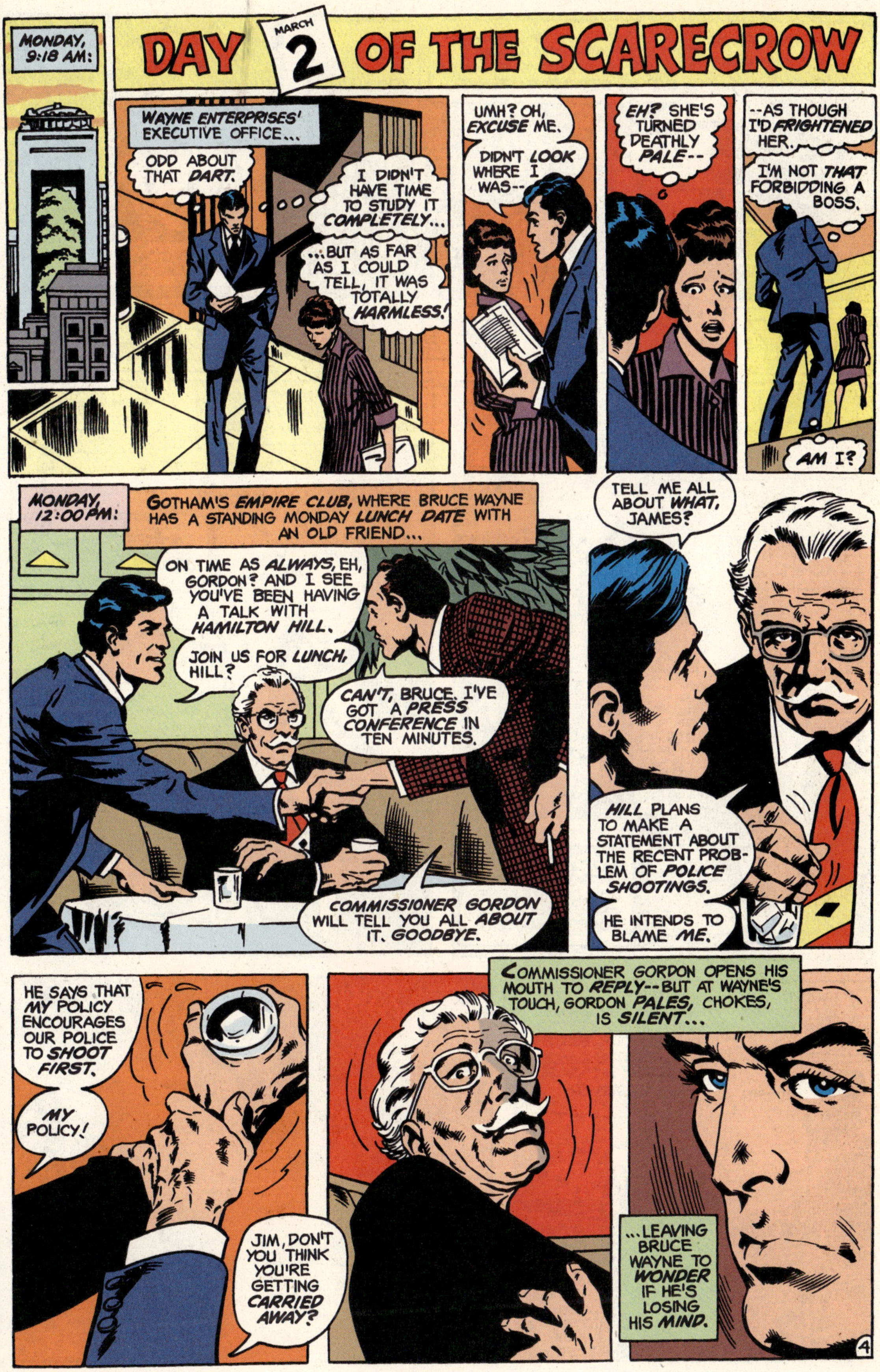
MONDAY, 9:18 AM:
DAY MARCH 2 OF THE SCARECROW
WAYNE ENTERPRISES' EXECUTIVE OFFICE...
ODD ABOUT THAT DART.
I DIDN'T HAVE TIME TO STUDY IT COMPLETELY...
...BUT AS FAR AS I COULD TELL, IT WAS TOTALLY HARMLESS!
UMH? OH, EXCUSE ME.
DIDN'T LOOK WHERE I WAS--
EH? SHE'S TURNED DEATHLY PALE--
--AS THOUGH I'D FRIGHTENED HER.
I'M NOT THAT FORBIDDING A BOSS.
AM I?
MONDAY, 12:00 PM:
GOTHAM'S EMPIRE CLUB, WHERE BRUCE WAYNE HAS A STANDING MONDAY LUNCH DATE WITH AN OLD FRIEND...
ON TIME AS ALWAYS, EH, GORDON? AND I SEE YOU'VE BEEN HAVING A TALK WITH HAMILTON HILL.
JOIN US FOR LUNCH, HILL?
CAN'T, BRUCE. I'VE GOT A PRESS CONFERENCE IN TEN MINUTES.
COMMISSIONER GORDON WILL TELL YOU ALL ABOUT IT. GOODBYE.
TELL ME ALL ABOUT WHAT, JAMES?
HILL PLANS TO MAKE A STATEMENT ABOUT THE RECENT PROB-LEM OF POLICE SHOOTINGS.
HE INTENDS TO BLAME ME.
HE SAYS THAT MY POLICY ENCOURAGES OUR POLICE TO SHOOT FIRST.
MY POLICY!
JIM, DON'T YOU THINK YOU'RE GETTING CARRIED AWAY?
COMMISSIONER GORDON OPENS HIS MOUTH TO REPLY--BUT AT WAYNE'S TOUCH, GORDON PALES, CHOKES, IS SILENT...
...LEAVING BRUCE WAYNE TO WONDER IF HE'S LOSING HIS MIND.
4

MONDAY, 9:45 PM:

THAT NIGHT, AS *THE BATMAN* PATROLS A CITY STRANGELY *QUIET*, HE PONDERS THE DAY'S EVENTS, SEEKING *PATTERNS*...

...AND THOUGH HE HAS TOO LITTLE *INFORMATION* TO BE SURE...

...A *SUSPICION* IS GROWING IN HIS MIND...

DAY [MARCH 3] OF THE SCARECROW

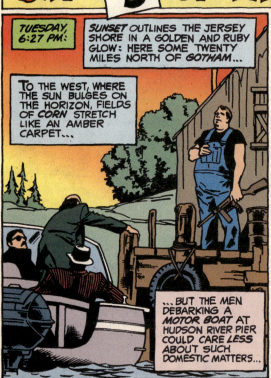

TUESDAY, 6:27 PM:

SUNSET OUTLINES THE JERSEY SHORE IN A GOLDEN AND RUBY GLOW: HERE SOME TWENTY MILES NORTH OF *GOTHAM*...

TO THE WEST, WHERE THE SUN BULGES ON THE HORIZON, FIELDS OF *CORN* STRETCH LIKE AN AMBER CARPET...

...BUT THE MEN DEBARKING A *MOTOR BOAT* AT HUDSON RIVER PIER COULD CARE *LESS* ABOUT SUCH DOMESTIC MATTERS...

...FOR THEIR EYES ARE THE HARD, GLITTERING *AGATES* OF URBAN *WOLVES*...

HE'S AWAITIN' BACK AT THE *FARM*.

THE BOSS SENT ME TO PICK YUH *UP*.

"FARM," HUH?

WHAT'S THIS ALL *ABOUT*, FATBOY?

ME AN' THE GANG GET A MESSAGE TO HUSTLE OUR BUTTS OVER TO THIS *LANDING* ...BUT THE MESSAGE AIN'T *SIGNED*.

CREAK

I WANNA KNOW WHO THINKS HE CAN BOSS *BIG FREDO* AND HIS BOYS AROUND LIKE A BUNCH'A COUNTRY HICKS.

WELL, YOU GONNA *TELL* ME?

5

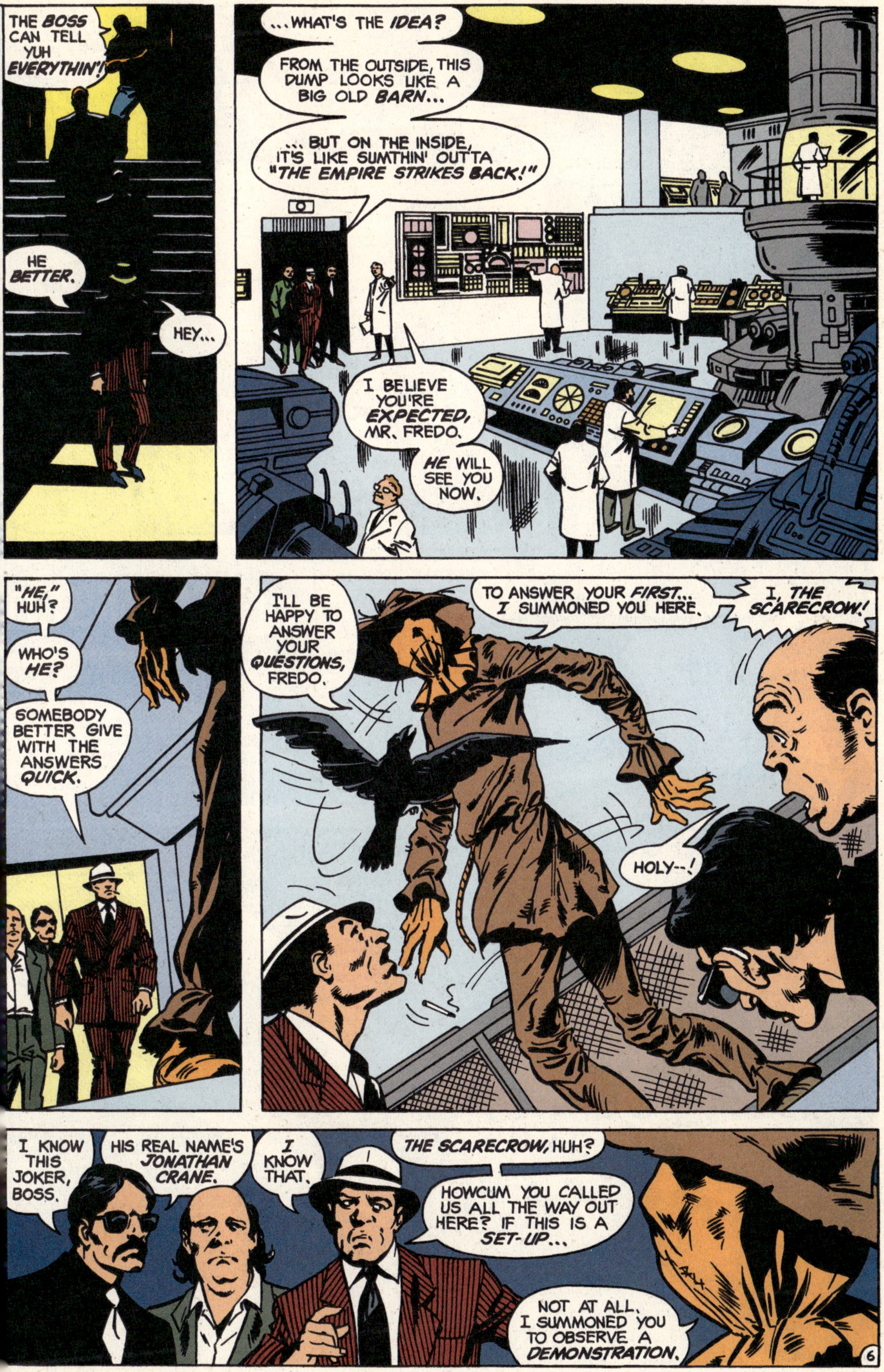
THE BOSS CAN TELL YUH EVERYTHIN'!
HE BETTER.
HEY...
...WHAT'S THE IDEA?
FROM THE OUTSIDE, THIS DUMP LOOKS LIKE A BIG OLD BARN...
...BUT ON THE INSIDE, IT'S LIKE SUMTHIN' OUTTA "THE EMPIRE STRIKES BACK!"
I BELIEVE YOU'RE EXPECTED, MR. FREDO.
HE WILL SEE YOU NOW.
"HE," HUH?
WHO'S HE?
SOMEBODY BETTER GIVE WITH THE ANSWERS QUICK.
I'LL BE HAPPY TO ANSWER YOUR QUESTIONS, FREDO.
TO ANSWER YOUR FIRST... I SUMMONED YOU HERE.
I, THE SCARECROW!
HOLY--!
I KNOW THIS JOKER, BOSS.
HIS REAL NAME'S JONATHAN CRANE.
I KNOW THAT.
THE SCARECROW, HUH?
HOWCUM YOU CALLED US ALL THE WAY OUT HERE? IF THIS IS A SET-UP...
NOT AT ALL. I SUMMONED YOU TO OBSERVE A DEMONSTRATION.
6

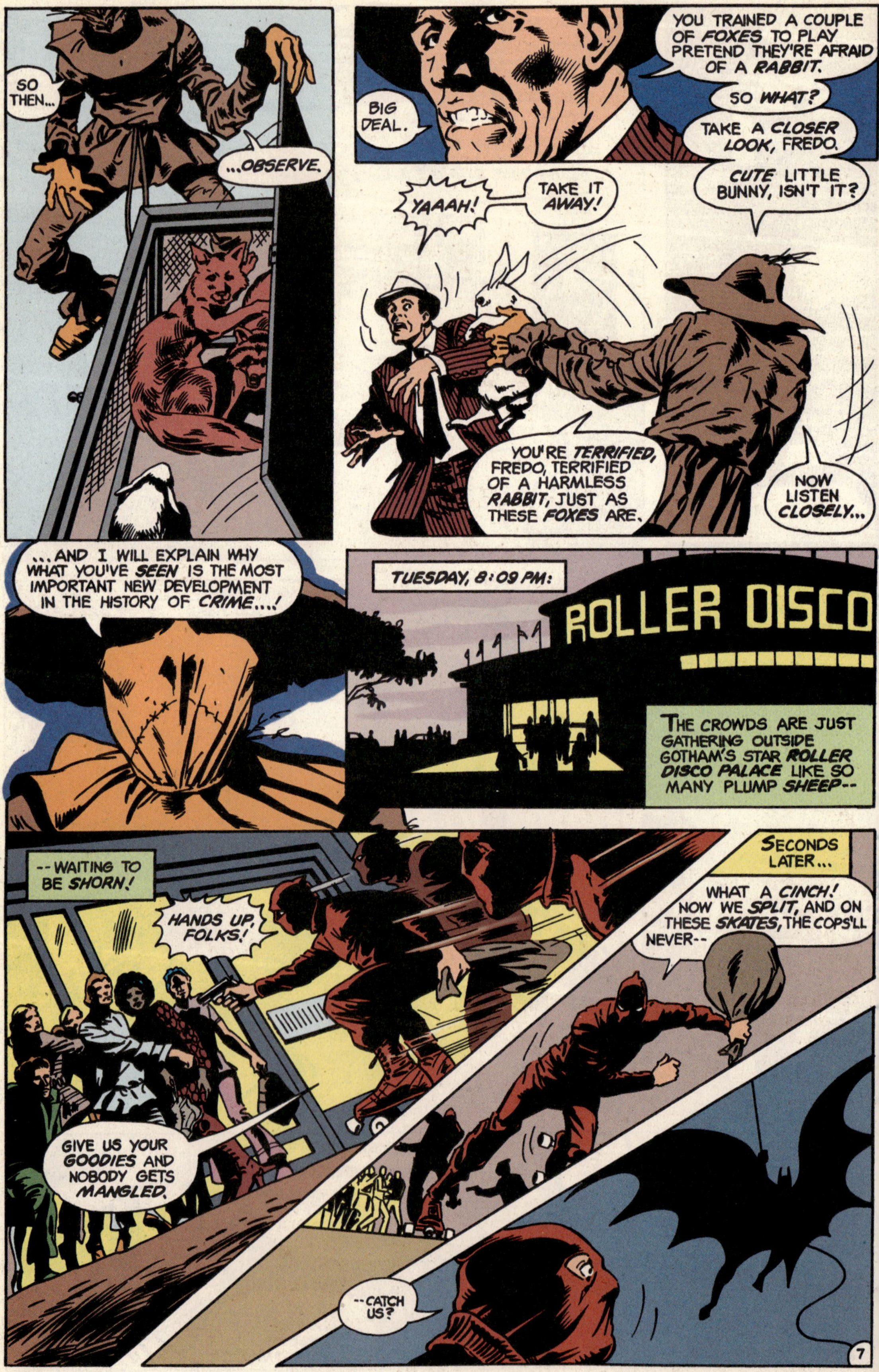
SO THEN...
...OBSERVE.
BIG DEAL.
YOU TRAINED A COUPLE OF FOXES TO PLAY PRETEND THEY'RE AFRAID OF A RABBIT.
SO WHAT?
TAKE A CLOSER LOOK, FREDO.
CUTE LITTLE BUNNY, ISN'T IT?
YAAAH!
TAKE IT AWAY!
YOU'RE TERRIFIED, FREDO, TERRIFIED OF A HARMLESS RABBIT, JUST AS THESE FOXES ARE.
NOW LISTEN CLOSELY...
...AND I WILL EXPLAIN WHY WHAT YOU'VE SEEN IS THE MOST IMPORTANT NEW DEVELOPMENT IN THE HISTORY OF CRIME...!
TUESDAY, 8:09 PM:
ROLLER DISCO
THE CROWDS ARE JUST GATHERING OUTSIDE GOTHAM'S STAR ROLLER DISCO PALACE LIKE SO MANY PLUMP SHEEP--
--WAITING TO BE SHORN!
HANDS UP, FOLKS!
GIVE US YOUR GOODIES AND NOBODY GETS MANGLED.
SECONDS LATER...
WHAT A CINCH! NOW WE SPLIT, AND ON THESE SKATES, THE COPS'LL NEVER--
--CATCH US?
7

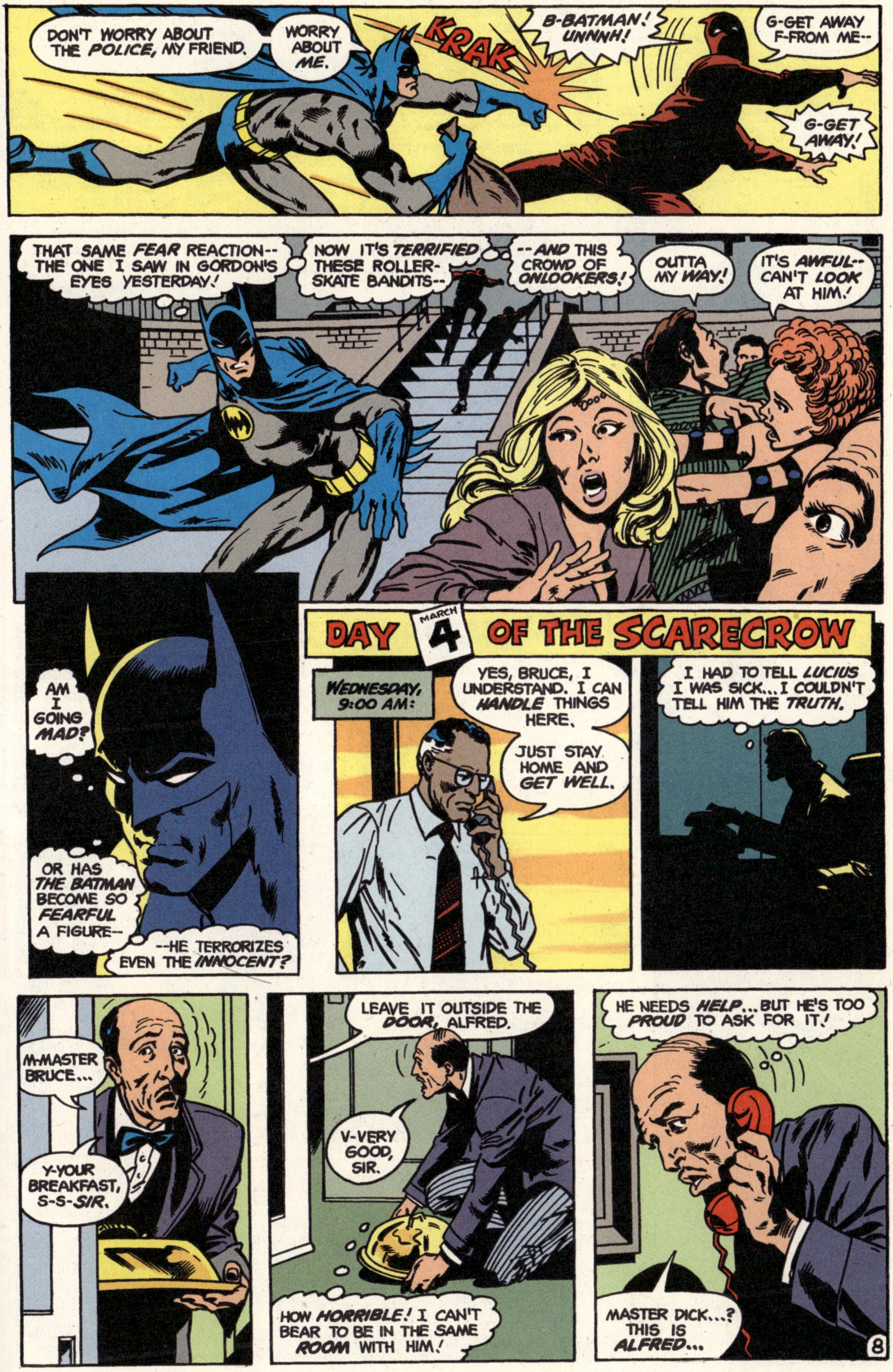

DON'T WORRY ABOUT THE POLICE, MY FRIEND.
WORRY ABOUT ME.
KRAK
B-BATMAN! UNNNH!
G-GET AWAY F-FROM ME--
G-GET AWAY!
THAT SAME FEAR REACTION-- THE ONE I SAW IN GORDON'S EYES YESTERDAY!
NOW IT'S TERRIFIED THESE ROLLER-SKATE BANDITS--
--AND THIS CROWD OF ONLOOKERS!
OUTTA MY WAY!
IT'S AWFUL-- CAN'T LOOK AT HIM!
AM I GOING MAD?
OR HAS THE BATMAN BECOME SO FEARFUL A FIGURE--
--HE TERRORIZES EVEN THE INNOCENT?
DAY MARCH 4 OF THE SCARECROW
WEDNESDAY, 9:00 AM:
YES, BRUCE, I UNDERSTAND. I CAN HANDLE THINGS HERE.
JUST STAY HOME AND GET WELL.
I HAD TO TELL LUCIUS I WAS SICK... I COULDN'T TELL HIM THE TRUTH.
M-MASTER BRUCE...
Y-YOUR BREAKFAST, S-S-SIR.
LEAVE IT OUTSIDE THE DOOR, ALFRED.
V-VERY GOOD, SIR.
HOW HORRIBLE! I CAN'T BEAR TO BE IN THE SAME ROOM WITH HIM!
HE NEEDS HELP... BUT HE'S TOO PROUD TO ASK FOR IT!
MASTER DICK...? THIS IS ALFRED...
8

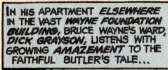

IN HIS APARTMENT *ELSEWHERE* IN THE VAST *WAYNE FOUNDATION BUILDING,* BRUCE WAYNE'S WARD, *DICK GRAYSON,* LISTENS WITH GROWING *AMAZEMENT* TO THE FAITHFUL BUTLER'S TALE...

...THEN MAKES THE ONLY *POSSIBLE* RESPONSE:

I'LL DO WHAT I *CAN,* ALFRED.

...AS *BATGIRL* AND *ROBIN.*

WEDNESDAY, 7:15 PM:

SEVERAL HUNDRED MILES SOUTH OF GOTHAM, IN *WASHINGTON, D.C.--*

--*BARBARA GORDON,* DAUGHTER OF GOTHAM'S POLICE COMMISSIONER, GIVES LAST-MINUTE INSTRUCTIONS TO HER STAFF *AIDE--*

OUR TRIP TO WASHINGTON WAS A *SUCCESS,* HARRY-- HUMANITIES RESEARCH AND *DEVELOPMENT* WILL GET A HEFTY INCREASE IN *FEDERAL FUNDING!*

--AND IS STRIDING TOWARD HER WAIT- ING *CAR* WHEN A VOICE CALLS TO HER FROM THE SHADOWS NEAR THE *CAPITOL STEPS...*

BARBARA, WE'RE *NEEDED...*

BARBARA GORDON SEES SOMETHING IN HER ERSTWHILE PARTNER'S GAZE THAT *FORESTALLS* HER QUESTIONS...

THIRTY MINUTES LATER, AFTER A HURRIED CHANGE OF *COSTUME* AND A FLIGHT TO A SECRET *NEW JERSEY* AIRFIELD...

...THE TWO HEROES ARE CROSSING THE *BRIDGE* BACK INTO GOTHAM, AS ROBIN FINISHES HIS EXPLANA- TION...

BATMAN--STRICKEN WITH SOME KIND OF AFFLICTION THAT MAKES PEOPLE *FEAR* HIM?

IT'S *FANTASTIC!*

BUT POTENTIALLY *DEADLY.* THAT'S WHY--

UH-OH!

BEEP BEEP

THE *BATMOBILE'S* LINK-UP TO THE POLICE *ROBBERY* ALARM SYSTEM--

--TELLING US THERE'S A ROBBERY IN PROGRESS AT THE *GOTHAM TRADE CENTER!*

AFRAID WE'LL HAVE TO MAKE A *DETOUR,* BATGIRL.

HANG ON!

EXIT TO DOWNTOWN GOTHAM ▼ TRADE CENTER

9

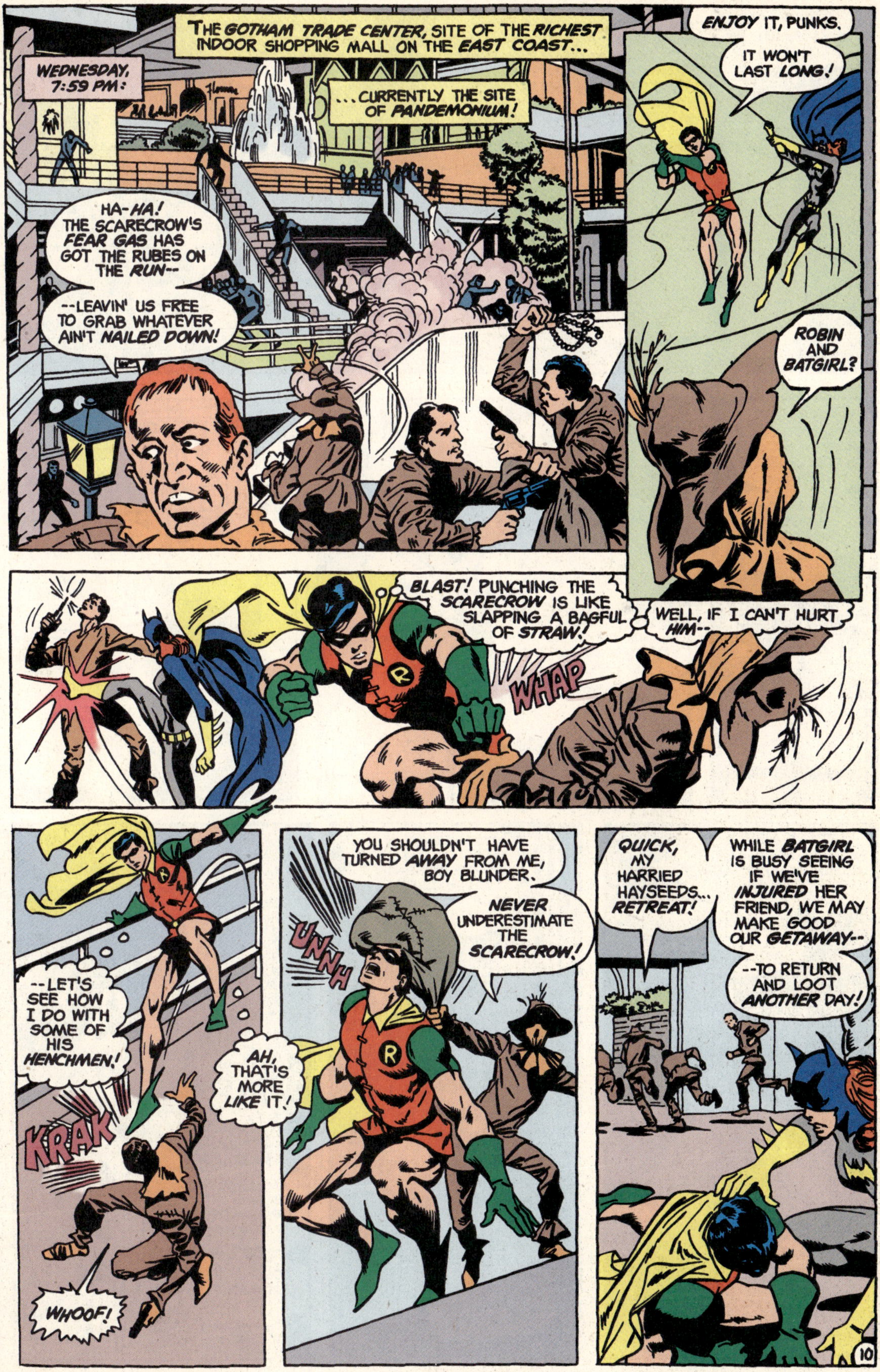
WEDNESDAY, 7:59 PM:
THE GOTHAM TRADE CENTER, SITE OF THE RICHEST INDOOR SHOPPING MALL ON THE EAST COAST...
...CURRENTLY THE SITE OF PANDEMONIUM!
HA-HA! THE SCARECROW'S FEAR GAS HAS GOT THE RUBES ON THE RUN--
--LEAVIN' US FREE TO GRAB WHATEVER AIN'T NAILED DOWN!
ENJOY IT, PUNKS.
IT WON'T LAST LONG!
ROBIN AND BATGIRL?
BLAST! PUNCHING THE SCARECROW IS LIKE SLAPPING A BAGFUL OF STRAW!
WELL, IF I CAN'T HURT HIM--
WHAP
--LET'S SEE HOW I DO WITH SOME OF HIS HENCHMEN!
AH, THAT'S MORE LIKE IT!
KRAK
WHOOF!
YOU SHOULDN'T HAVE TURNED AWAY FROM ME, BOY BLUNDER.
NEVER UNDERESTIMATE THE SCARECROW!
UNNH
QUICK, MY HARRIED HAYSEEDS... RETREAT!
WHILE BATGIRL IS BUSY SEEING IF WE'VE INJURED HER FRIEND, WE MAY MAKE GOOD OUR GETAWAY--
--TO RETURN AND LOOT ANOTHER DAY!
10

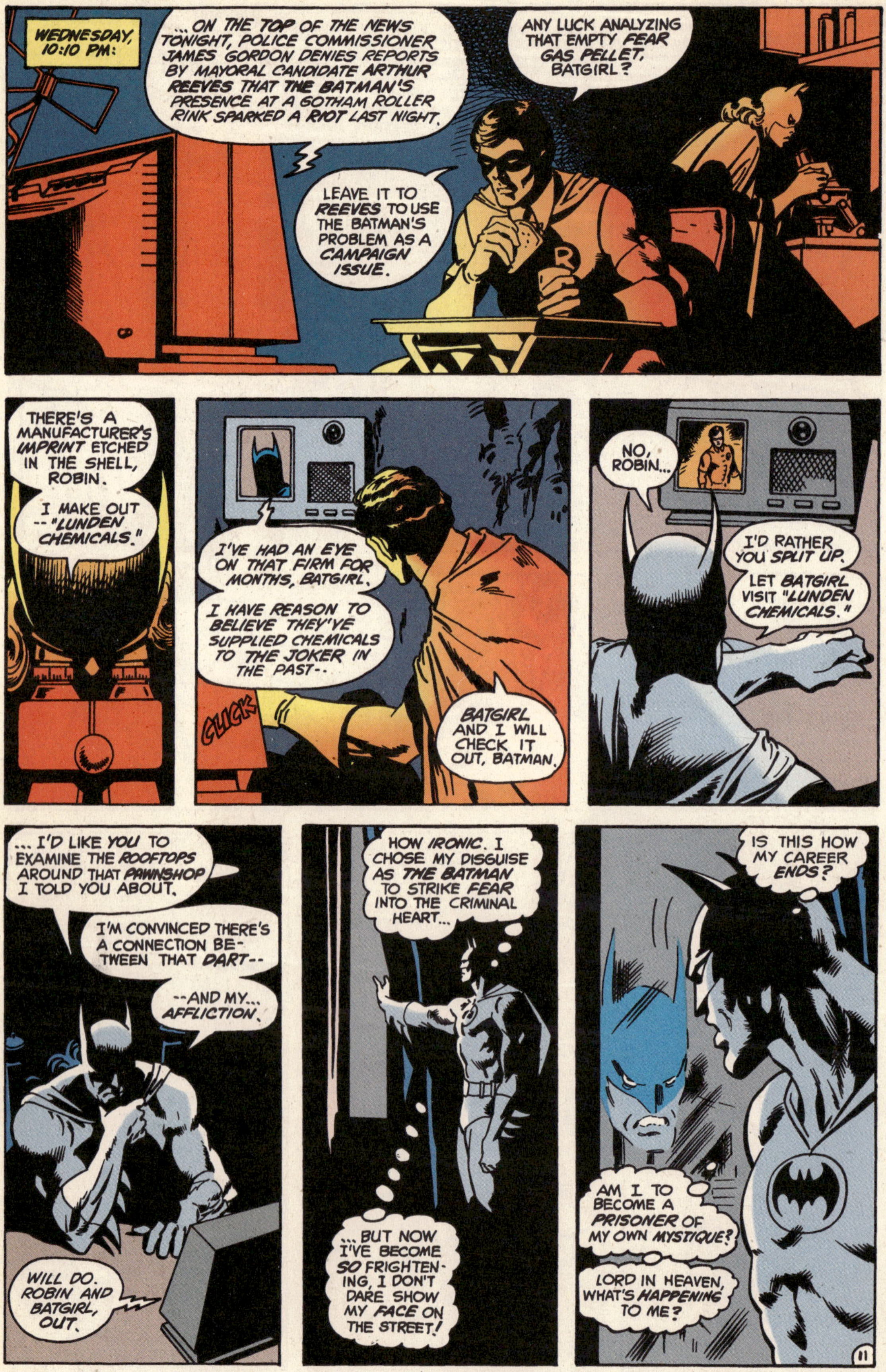
WEDNESDAY, 10:10 PM:
...ON THE TOP OF THE NEWS TONIGHT, POLICE COMMISSIONER JAMES GORDON DENIES REPORTS BY MAYORAL CANDIDATE ARTHUR REEVES THAT THE BATMAN'S PRESENCE AT A GOTHAM ROLLER RINK SPARKED A RIOT LAST NIGHT.
LEAVE IT TO REEVES TO USE THE BATMAN'S PROBLEM AS A CAMPAIGN ISSUE.
ANY LUCK ANALYZING THAT EMPTY FEAR GAS PELLET, BATGIRL?
THERE'S A MANUFACTURER'S IMPRINT ETCHED IN THE SHELL, ROBIN.
I MAKE OUT --"LUNDEN CHEMICALS."
I'VE HAD AN EYE ON THAT FIRM FOR MONTHS, BATGIRL.
I HAVE REASON TO BELIEVE THEY'VE SUPPLIED CHEMICALS TO THE JOKER IN THE PAST--
CLICK
BATGIRL AND I WILL CHECK IT OUT, BATMAN.
NO, ROBIN...
I'D RATHER YOU SPLIT UP. LET BATGIRL VISIT "LUNDEN CHEMICALS."
...I'D LIKE YOU TO EXAMINE THE ROOFTOPS AROUND THAT PAWNSHOP I TOLD YOU ABOUT.
I'M CONVINCED THERE'S A CONNECTION BETWEEN THAT DART--
--AND MY... AFFLICTION.
WILL DO. ROBIN AND BATGIRL, OUT.
HOW IRONIC. I CHOSE MY DISGUISE AS THE BATMAN TO STRIKE FEAR INTO THE CRIMINAL HEART...
...BUT NOW I'VE BECOME SO FRIGHTENING, I DON'T DARE SHOW MY FACE ON THE STREET!
IS THIS HOW MY CAREER ENDS?
AM I TO BECOME A PRISONER OF MY OWN MYSTIQUE?
LORD IN HEAVEN, WHAT'S HAPPENING TO ME?
11

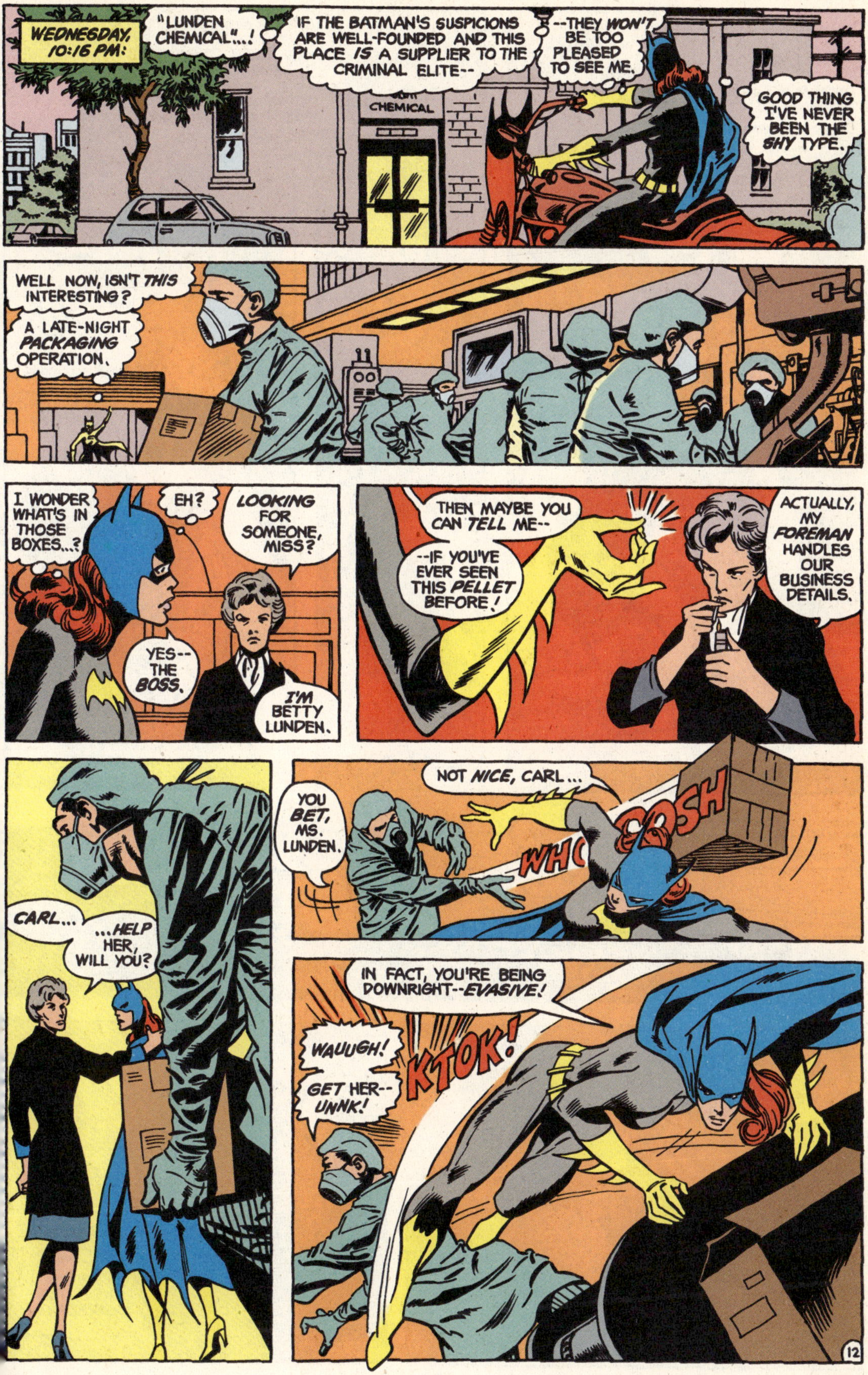

WEDNESDAY, 10:16 PM:
"LUNDEN CHEMICAL"...!
IF THE BATMAN'S SUSPICIONS ARE WELL-FOUNDED AND THIS PLACE *IS* A SUPPLIER TO THE CRIMINAL ELITE--
--THEY *WON'T* BE TOO PLEASED TO SEE ME.
GOOD THING I'VE NEVER BEEN THE *SHY* TYPE.
CHEMICAL
WELL NOW, ISN'T *THIS* INTERESTING?
A LATE-NIGHT *PACKAGING* OPERATION.
I WONDER WHAT'S IN THOSE BOXES...?
EH?
LOOKING FOR SOMEONE, MISS?
YES-- THE *BOSS*.
I'M BETTY LUNDEN.
THEN MAYBE YOU CAN *TELL* ME--
--IF YOU'VE EVER SEEN THIS *PELLET* BEFORE!
ACTUALLY, MY *FOREMAN* HANDLES OUR BUSINESS DETAILS.
CARL...
...*HELP* HER, WILL YOU?
NOT *NICE*, CARL...
YOU *BET*, MS. LUNDEN.
WHOOSH
IN FACT, YOU'RE BEING DOWNRIGHT--*EVASIVE!*
WAUUGH!
GET HER-- UNNK!
KTOK!
12

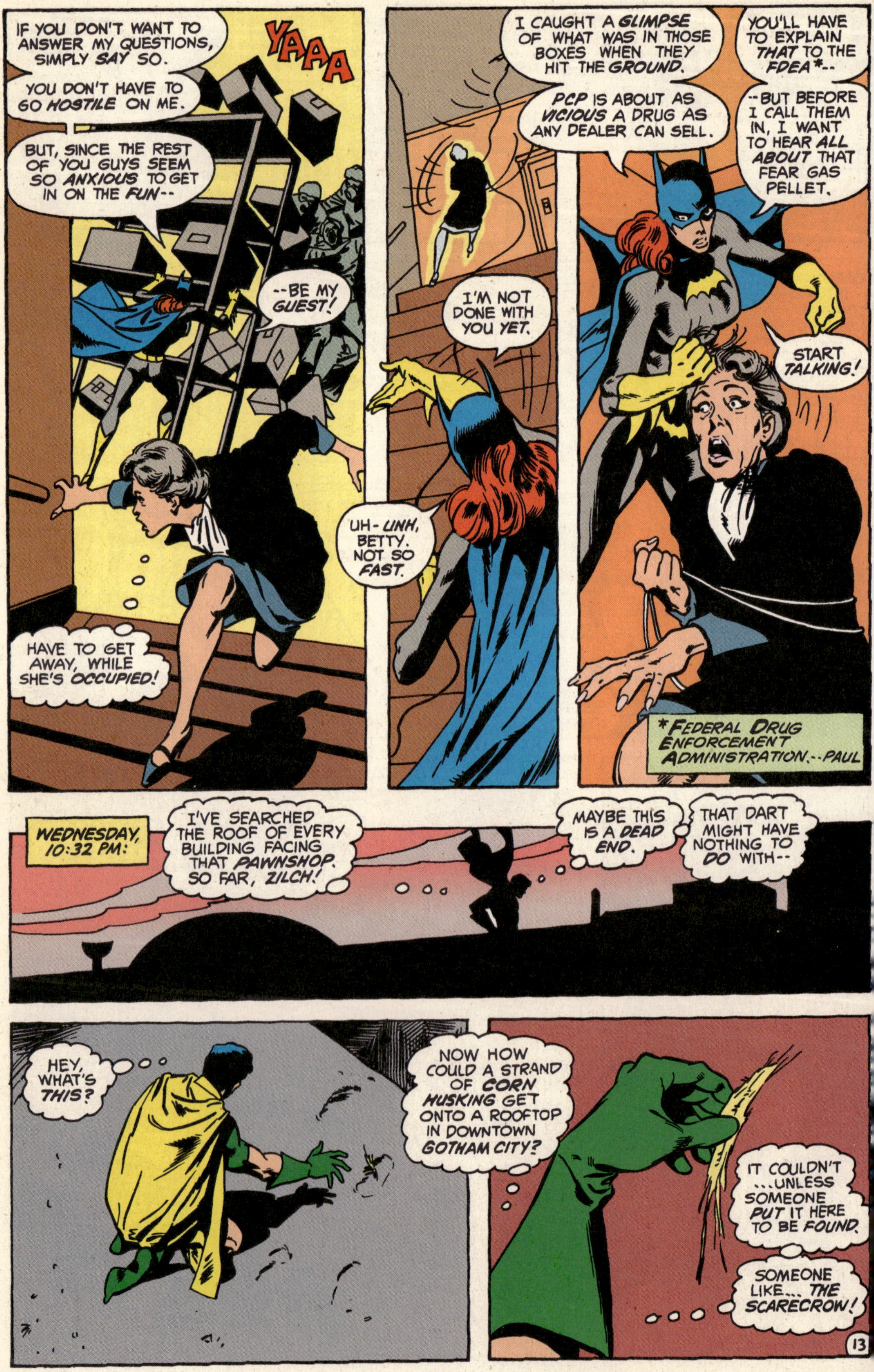
IF YOU DON'T WANT TO ANSWER MY QUESTIONS, SIMPLY SAY SO.
YOU DON'T HAVE TO GO HOSTILE ON ME.
BUT, SINCE THE REST OF YOU GUYS SEEM SO ANXIOUS TO GET IN ON THE FUN--
YAAA
--BE MY GUEST!
HAVE TO GET AWAY, WHILE SHE'S OCCUPIED!
I'M NOT DONE WITH YOU YET.
UH-UNH, BETTY. NOT SO FAST.
I CAUGHT A GLIMPSE OF WHAT WAS IN THOSE BOXES WHEN THEY HIT THE GROUND.
PCP IS ABOUT AS VICIOUS A DRUG AS ANY DEALER CAN SELL.
YOU'LL HAVE TO EXPLAIN THAT TO THE FDEA*--
--BUT BEFORE I CALL THEM IN, I WANT TO HEAR ALL ABOUT THAT FEAR GAS PELLET.
START TALKING!
*FEDERAL DRUG ENFORCEMENT ADMINISTRATION.--PAUL
WEDNESDAY, 10:32 PM:
I'VE SEARCHED THE ROOF OF EVERY BUILDING FACING THAT PAWNSHOP. SO FAR, ZILCH!
MAYBE THIS IS A DEAD END.
THAT DART MIGHT HAVE NOTHING TO DO WITH--
HEY, WHAT'S THIS?
NOW HOW COULD A STRAND OF CORN HUSKING GET ONTO A ROOFTOP IN DOWNTOWN GOTHAM CITY?
IT COULDN'T ...UNLESS SOMEONE PUT IT HERE TO BE FOUND.
SOMEONE LIKE... THE SCARECROW!
13

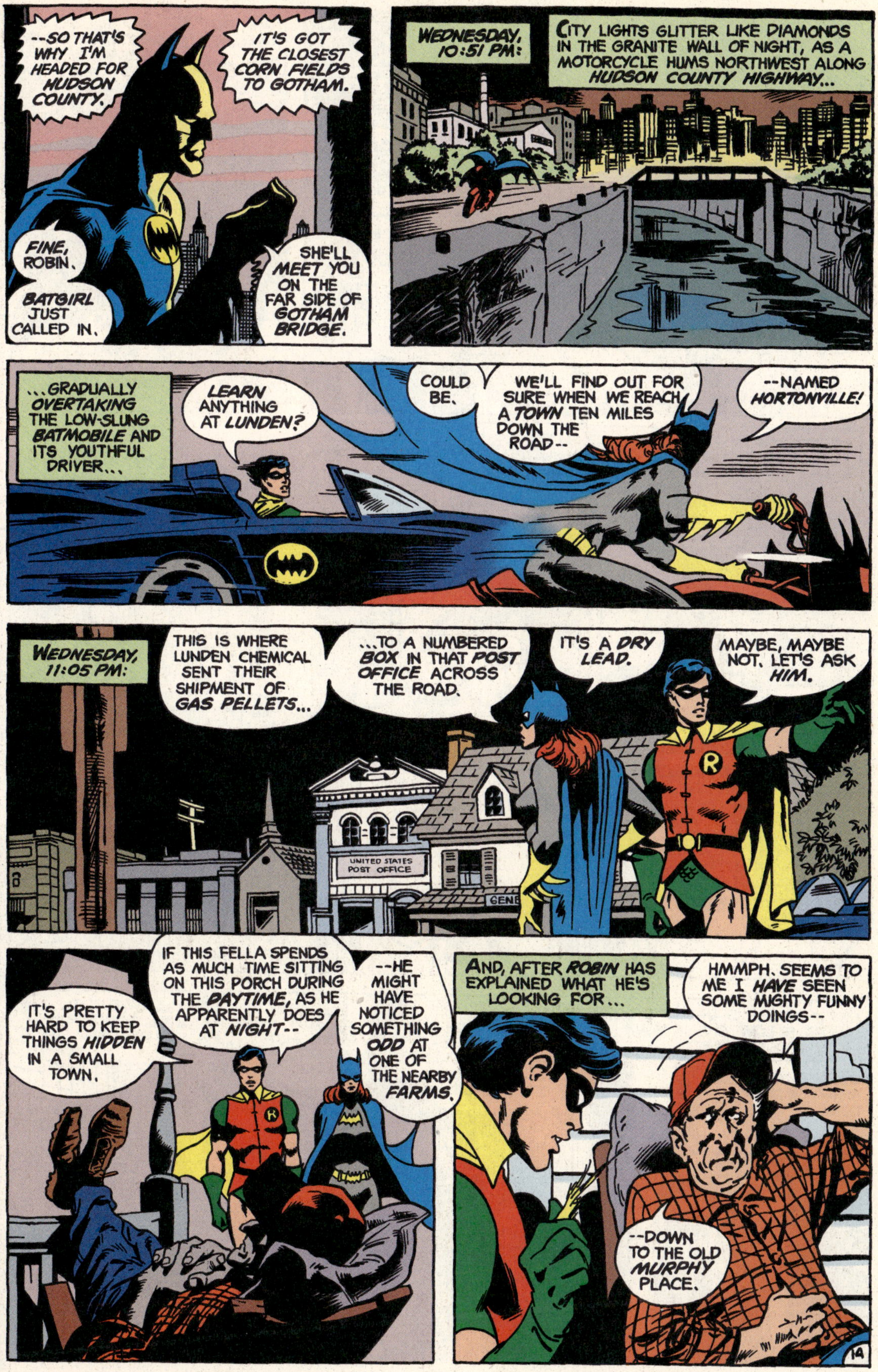
--SO THAT'S WHY I'M HEADED FOR HUDSON COUNTY.
IT'S GOT THE CLOSEST CORN FIELDS TO GOTHAM.
FINE, ROBIN.
BATGIRL JUST CALLED IN.
SHE'LL MEET YOU ON THE FAR SIDE OF GOTHAM BRIDGE.
WEDNESDAY, 10:51 PM:
CITY LIGHTS GLITTER LIKE DIAMONDS IN THE GRANITE WALL OF NIGHT, AS A MOTORCYCLE HUMS NORTHWEST ALONG HUDSON COUNTY HIGHWAY...
...GRADUALLY OVERTAKING THE LOW-SLUNG BATMOBILE AND ITS YOUTHFUL DRIVER...
LEARN ANYTHING AT LUNDEN?
COULD BE.
WE'LL FIND OUT FOR SURE WHEN WE REACH A TOWN TEN MILES DOWN THE ROAD--
--NAMED HORTONVILLE!
WEDNESDAY, 11:05 PM:
THIS IS WHERE LUNDEN CHEMICAL SENT THEIR SHIPMENT OF GAS PELLETS...
...TO A NUMBERED BOX IN THAT POST OFFICE ACROSS THE ROAD.
IT'S A DRY LEAD.
MAYBE, MAYBE NOT. LET'S ASK HIM.
UNITED STATES POST OFFICE
IT'S PRETTY HARD TO KEEP THINGS HIDDEN IN A SMALL TOWN.
IF THIS FELLA SPENDS AS MUCH TIME SITTING ON THIS PORCH DURING THE DAYTIME, AS HE APPARENTLY DOES AT NIGHT--
--HE MIGHT HAVE NOTICED SOMETHING ODD AT ONE OF THE NEARBY FARMS.
AND, AFTER ROBIN HAS EXPLAINED WHAT HE'S LOOKING FOR...
HMMPH. SEEMS TO ME I HAVE SEEN SOME MIGHTY FUNNY DOINGS--
--DOWN TO THE OLD MURPHY PLACE.
14

FOLKS COMIN' AND GOIN' AT *ALL HOURS*... A WHOLE FIELD OF RIPE WINTER *CORN* BEIN' LET TO *SPOIL*...

YOU'LL FIND THE MURPHY PLACE 'BOUT TWO MILES DOWN THE ROAD, OFF A DIRT *FORK*.

MUCH OBLIGED.

C'MON, BATGIRL, LET'S MOVE IN.

YOU *DO* THAT, BOY.

AND I'LL DO MY *BEST* TO ARRANGE A NICE *RECEPTION* FOR YA...

LOOKOUT TO *SCARECROW*, BOSS, THEY'S ON THEIR *WAY!*

WEDNESDAY, 11:45 PM:

AND, IN GOTHAM CITY, ANOTHER MAN TRIES TO MAKE RADIO CONTACT WITH *HIS* ALLIES--

--TO NO *AVAIL*.

ALFRED, BRING THE PRIVATE ELEVATOR UP FROM THE *BATCAVE*.

THEN STEP AWAY FROM THE *DOOR*--

--I'M GOING *DOWNSTAIRS*.

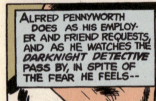

ALFRED PENNYWORTH DOES AS HIS EMPLOY-ER AND FRIEND REQUESTS, AND AS HE WATCHES THE *DARKNIGHT DETECTIVE* PASS BY, IN SPITE OF THE FEAR HE FEELS--

--IT IS ALL HE CAN DO TO KEEP A *TEAR* FROM HIS EYE.

THE BATCAVE IS AN UNSUSPECTED CAVERN BELOW THE *WAYNE FOUNDATION*...

SOMETHING IS JAM-MING COMMUNICA-TIONS ON THE RADIO FREQUEN-CY ROBIN AND I USE.

BEFORE I *RISK* GOING OUTSIDE-- WHICH COULD HAVE FATAL CONSEQUENCES FOR INNOCENT *BYSTANDERS*--

--I'LL NEED TO *REVIEW* WHAT ROBIN AND BATGIRL LEARNED.

I'LL GIVE THEM UNTIL TOMORROW TO RETURN.

THEN I'LL HAVE TO MAKE MY OWN PLANS...

15

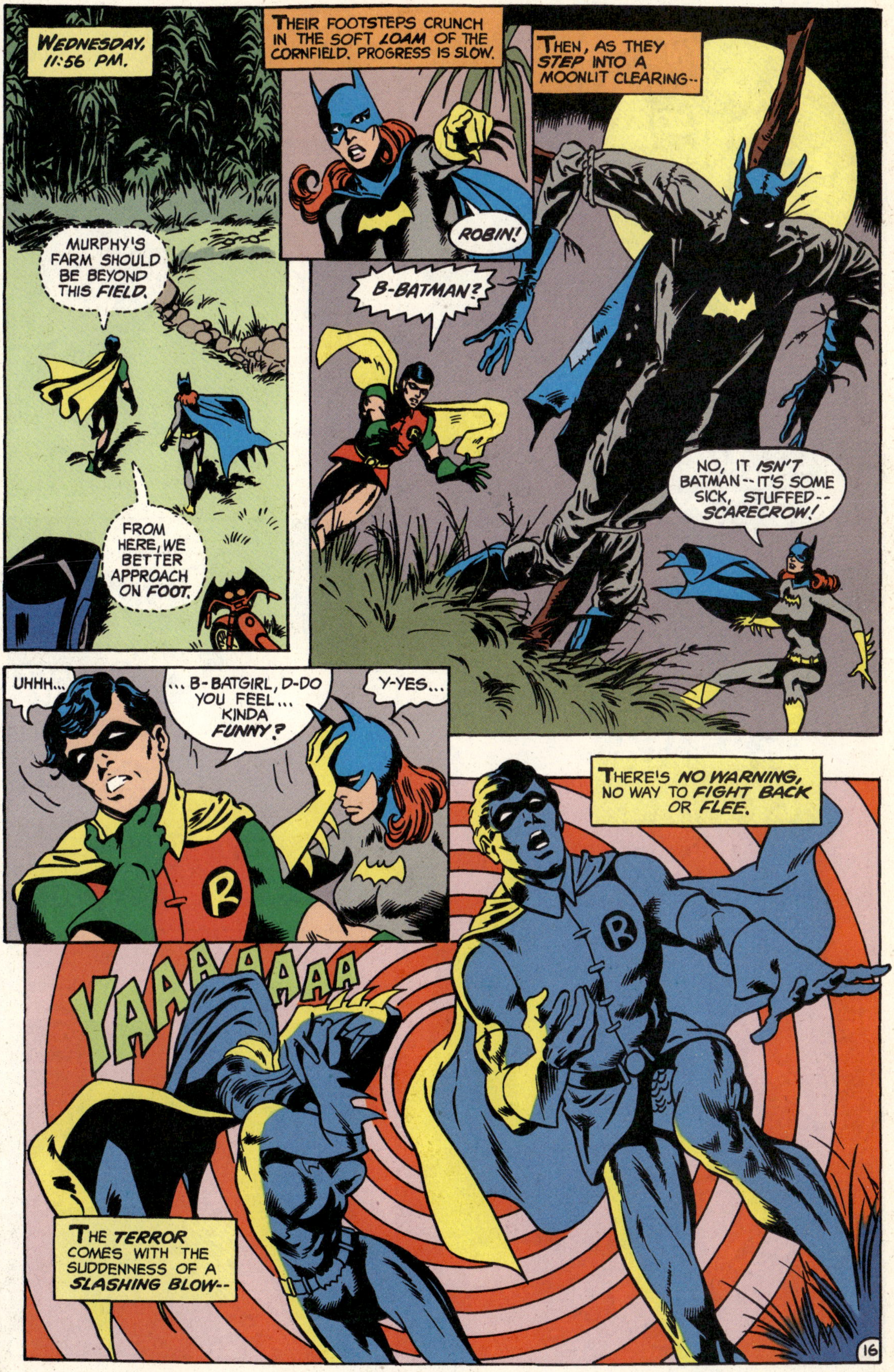
WEDNESDAY, 11:56 PM.
MURPHY'S FARM SHOULD BE BEYOND THIS FIELD.
FROM HERE, WE BETTER APPROACH ON FOOT.
THEIR FOOTSTEPS CRUNCH IN THE SOFT LOAM OF THE CORNFIELD. PROGRESS IS SLOW.
ROBIN!
THEN, AS THEY STEP INTO A MOONLIT CLEARING--
B-BATMAN?
NO, IT ISN'T BATMAN--IT'S SOME SICK, STUFFED--SCARECROW!
UHHH...
...B-BATGIRL, D-DO YOU FEEL... KINDA FUNNY?
Y-YES...
THERE'S NO WARNING, NO WAY TO FIGHT BACK OR FLEE.
YAAAAAAA
THE TERROR COMES WITH THE SUDDENNESS OF A SLASHING BLOW--
16

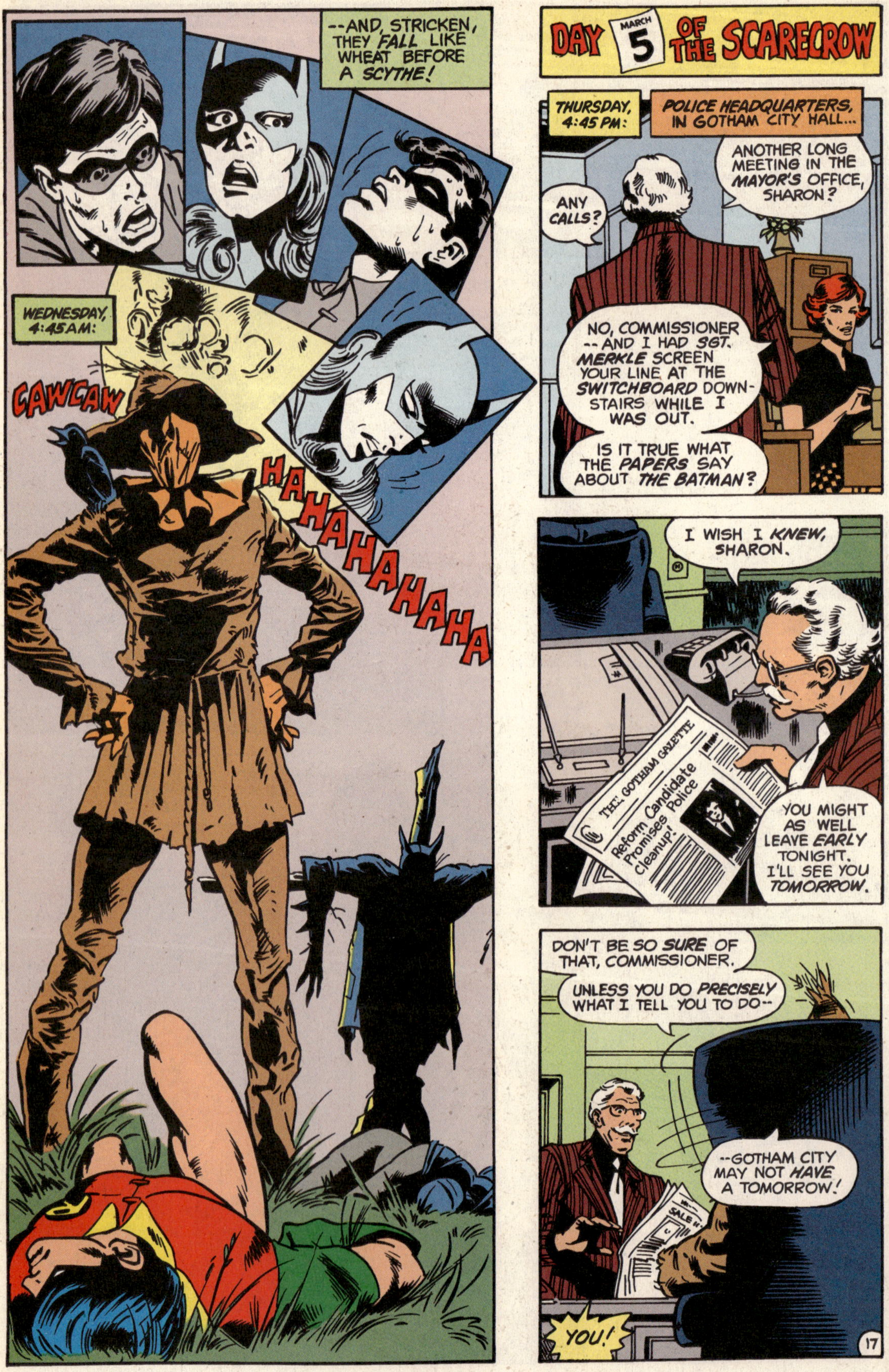
--AND, STRICKEN, THEY FALL LIKE WHEAT BEFORE A SCYTHE!
WEDNESDAY, 4:45 AM:
CAWCAW
HAHAHAHAHAHAHA
DAY MARCH 5 OF THE SCARECROW
THURSDAY, 4:45 PM:
POLICE HEADQUARTERS, IN GOTHAM CITY HALL...
ANY CALLS?
ANOTHER LONG MEETING IN THE MAYOR'S OFFICE, SHARON?
NO, COMMISSIONER --AND I HAD SGT. MERKLE SCREEN YOUR LINE AT THE SWITCHBOARD DOWN-STAIRS WHILE I WAS OUT.
IS IT TRUE WHAT THE PAPERS SAY ABOUT THE BATMAN?
I WISH I KNEW, SHARON.
THE GOTHAM GAZETTE
Reform Candidate Promises Police Cleanup!
YOU MIGHT AS WELL LEAVE EARLY TONIGHT. I'LL SEE YOU TOMORROW.
DON'T BE SO SURE OF THAT, COMMISSIONER.
UNLESS YOU DO PRECISELY WHAT I TELL YOU TO DO--
--GOTHAM CITY MAY NOT HAVE A TOMORROW!
YOU!
17

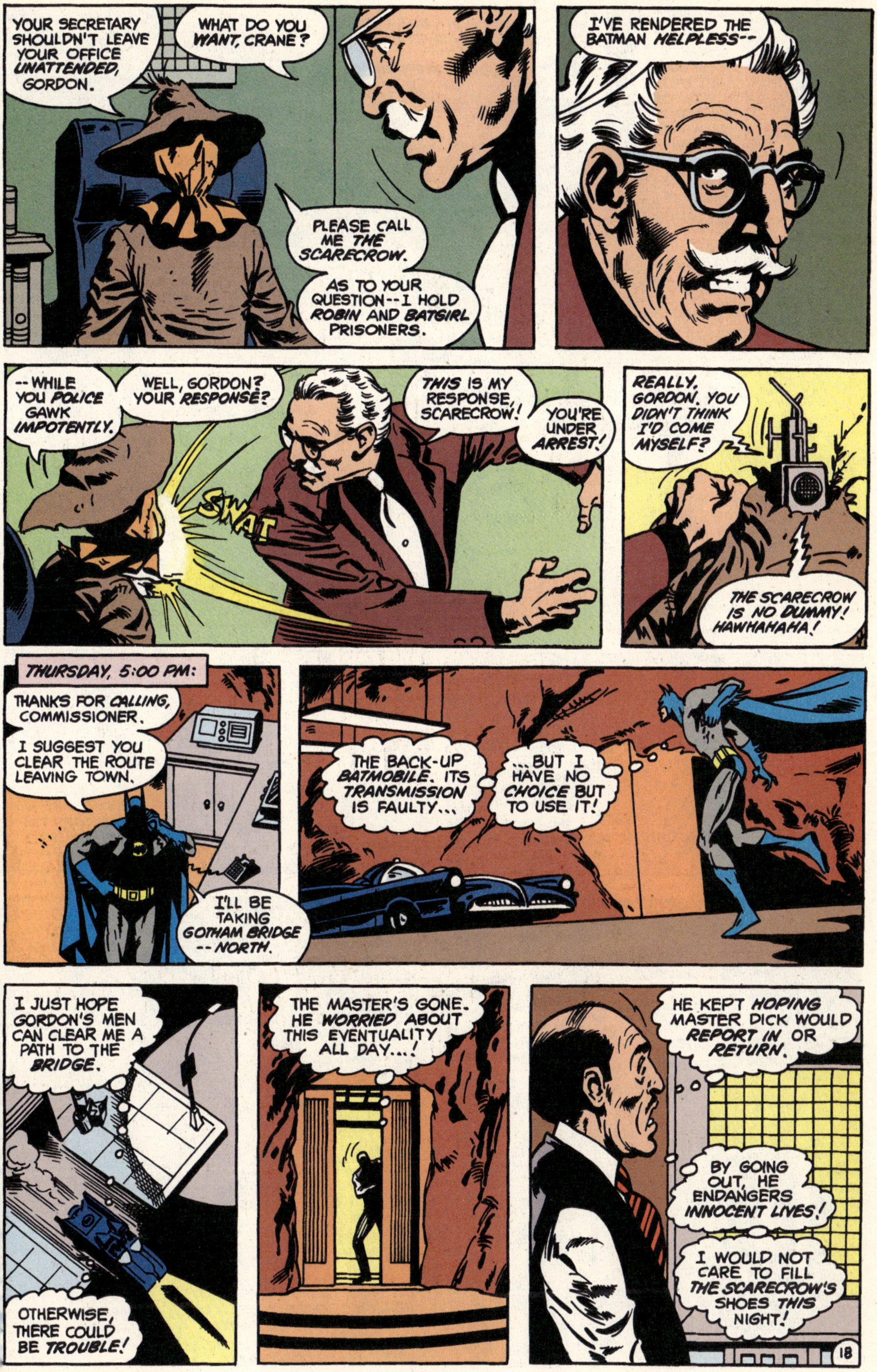
YOUR SECRETARY SHOULDN'T LEAVE YOUR OFFICE UNATTENDED, GORDON.
WHAT DO YOU WANT, CRANE?
PLEASE CALL ME THE SCARECROW.
AS TO YOUR QUESTION--I HOLD ROBIN AND BATGIRL PRISONERS.
I'VE RENDERED THE BATMAN HELPLESS--
--WHILE YOU POLICE GAWK IMPOTENTLY.
WELL, GORDON? YOUR RESPONSE?
THIS IS MY RESPONSE, SCARECROW!
YOU'RE UNDER ARREST!
SWAT
REALLY, GORDON. YOU DIDN'T THINK I'D COME MYSELF?
THE SCARECROW IS NO DUMMY! HAWHAHAHA!
THURSDAY, 5:00 PM:
THANKS FOR CALLING, COMMISSIONER.
I SUGGEST YOU CLEAR THE ROUTE LEAVING TOWN.
I'LL BE TAKING GOTHAM BRIDGE --NORTH.
THE BACK-UP BATMOBILE. ITS TRANSMISSION IS FAULTY...
...BUT I HAVE NO CHOICE BUT TO USE IT!
I JUST HOPE GORDON'S MEN CAN CLEAR ME A PATH TO THE BRIDGE.
OTHERWISE, THERE COULD BE TROUBLE!
THE MASTER'S GONE. HE WORRIED ABOUT THIS EVENTUALITY ALL DAY...!
HE KEPT HOPING MASTER DICK WOULD REPORT IN OR RETURN.
BY GOING OUT, HE ENDANGERS INNOCENT LIVES!
I WOULD NOT CARE TO FILL THE SCARECROW'S SHOES THIS NIGHT!
18

THURSDAY, 5:14 PM: **HUDSON COUNTY HIGHWAY, EIGHT MILES NORTH OF GOTHAM'S GLOWING SKYLINE...**

GORDON WAS AS GOOD AS HIS *WORD*--POLICE ROADBLOCKS GAVE ME A CLEAR PATH TO THE BRIDGE.

SO FAR, THE HIGHWAY'S BEEN *DESERTED*...

...BUT I'M AFRAID THAT SITUATION'S JUST *CHANGED.*

DON'T GET SO *CLOSE* TO ME, YOU *FOOL!*

TOO LATE! THIS IS WHAT I WAS AFRAID MIGHT HAPPEN... HE'S *PANICKING* AT THE VERY *SIGHT* OF ME...

...LOSING CONTROL OF HIS *CAR!*

FORTUNATELY, THERE'S A SOFT *EMBANKMENT* AT THIS POINT OF THE HIGHWAY.

HE'S CLIMBING OUT-- HE'S *ALL RIGHT.*

IF THIS HAD HAPPENED IN THE *CITY,* THOUGH...

...THAT DRIVER COULD HAVE BEEN *KILLED!*

I *PRAY* THERE ARE NO MORE CARS ON THE ROAD TO *HORTONVILLE!*

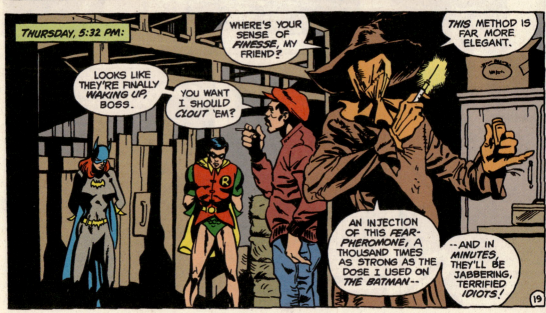

THURSDAY, 5:32 PM:

WHERE'S YOUR SENSE OF *FINESSE,* MY FRIEND?

THIS METHOD IS FAR MORE *ELEGANT.*

LOOKS LIKE THEY'RE FINALLY *WAKING UP,* BOSS.

YOU WANT I SHOULD *CLOUT* 'EM?

AN INJECTION OF THIS *FEAR-PHEROMONE,* A THOUSAND TIMES AS STRONG AS THE DOSE I USED ON *THE BATMAN*--

--AND IN *MINUTES,* THEY'LL BE JABBERING, TERRIFIED IDIOTS!

19

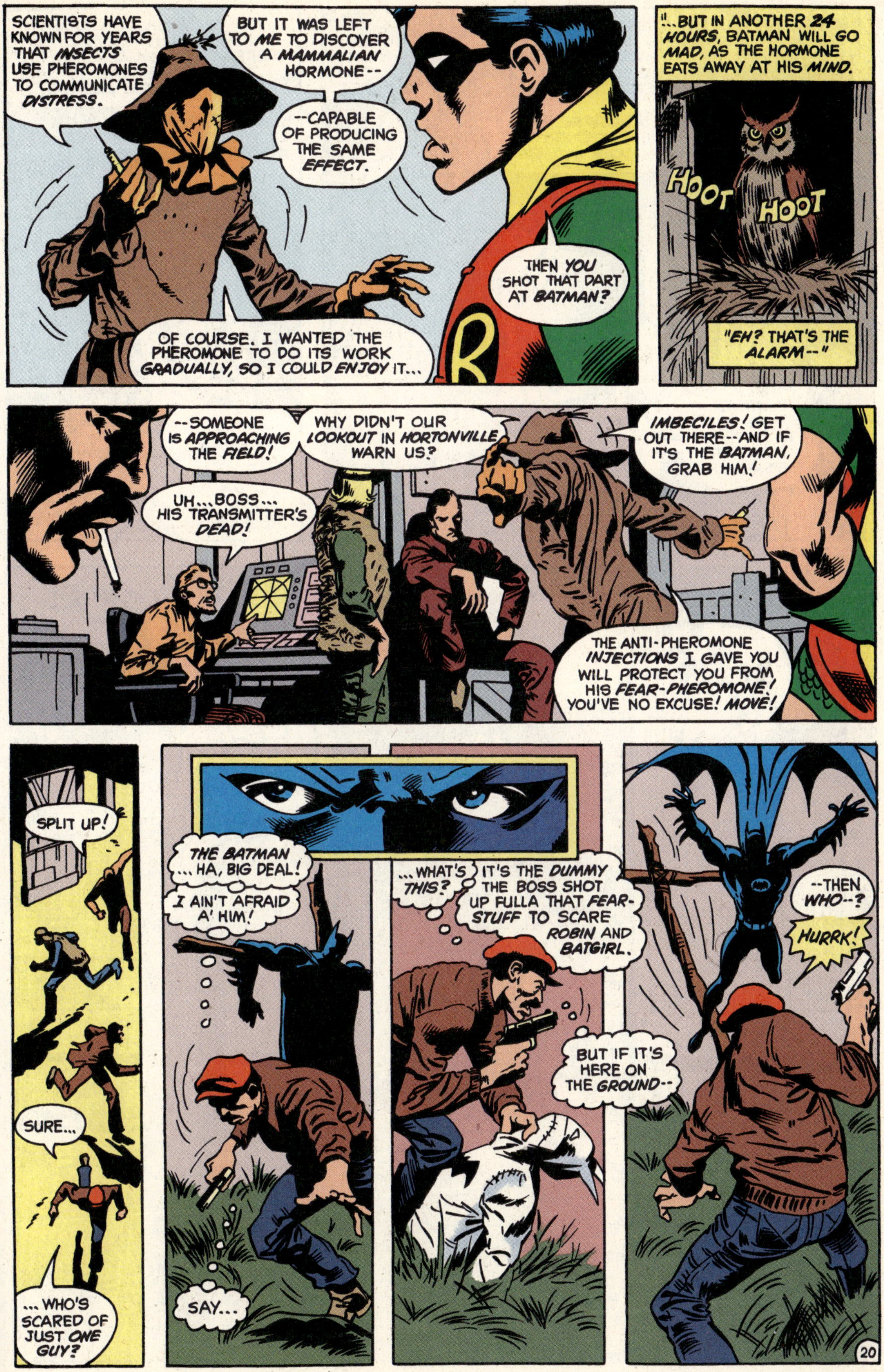
SCIENTISTS HAVE KNOWN FOR YEARS THAT *INSECTS* USE PHEROMONES TO COMMUNICATE *DISTRESS*.
BUT IT WAS LEFT TO *ME* TO DISCOVER A *MAMMALIAN* HORMONE--
--CAPABLE OF PRODUCING THE SAME *EFFECT*.
THEN *YOU* SHOT THAT DART AT *BATMAN?*
OF COURSE. I WANTED THE PHEROMONE TO DO ITS WORK *GRADUALLY*, SO I COULD *ENJOY* IT...
"...BUT IN ANOTHER *24 HOURS*, BATMAN WILL GO *MAD*, AS THE HORMONE EATS AWAY AT HIS *MIND*.
HOOT
HOOT
"*EH?* THAT'S THE *ALARM*--"
--SOMEONE IS *APPROACHING* THE *FIELD!*
WHY DIDN'T OUR *LOOKOUT* IN *HORTONVILLE* WARN US?
UH...BOSS... HIS TRANSMITTER'S *DEAD!*
IMBECILES! GET OUT THERE--AND IF IT'S THE *BATMAN*, GRAB HIM!
THE ANTI-PHEROMONE *INJECTIONS* I GAVE YOU WILL PROTECT YOU FROM HIS *FEAR-PHEROMONE!* YOU'VE NO EXCUSE! *MOVE!*
SPLIT UP!
SURE...
...WHO'S SCARED OF JUST *ONE* GUY?
THE BATMAN ...HA, BIG DEAL!
I AIN'T AFRAID A' HIM!
SAY...
...WHAT'S *THIS?*
IT'S THE *DUMMY* THE BOSS SHOT UP FULLA THAT *FEAR-STUFF* TO SCARE *ROBIN* AND *BATGIRL*.
BUT IF IT'S HERE ON THE *GROUND*--
--THEN *WHO*--?
HURRK!
20

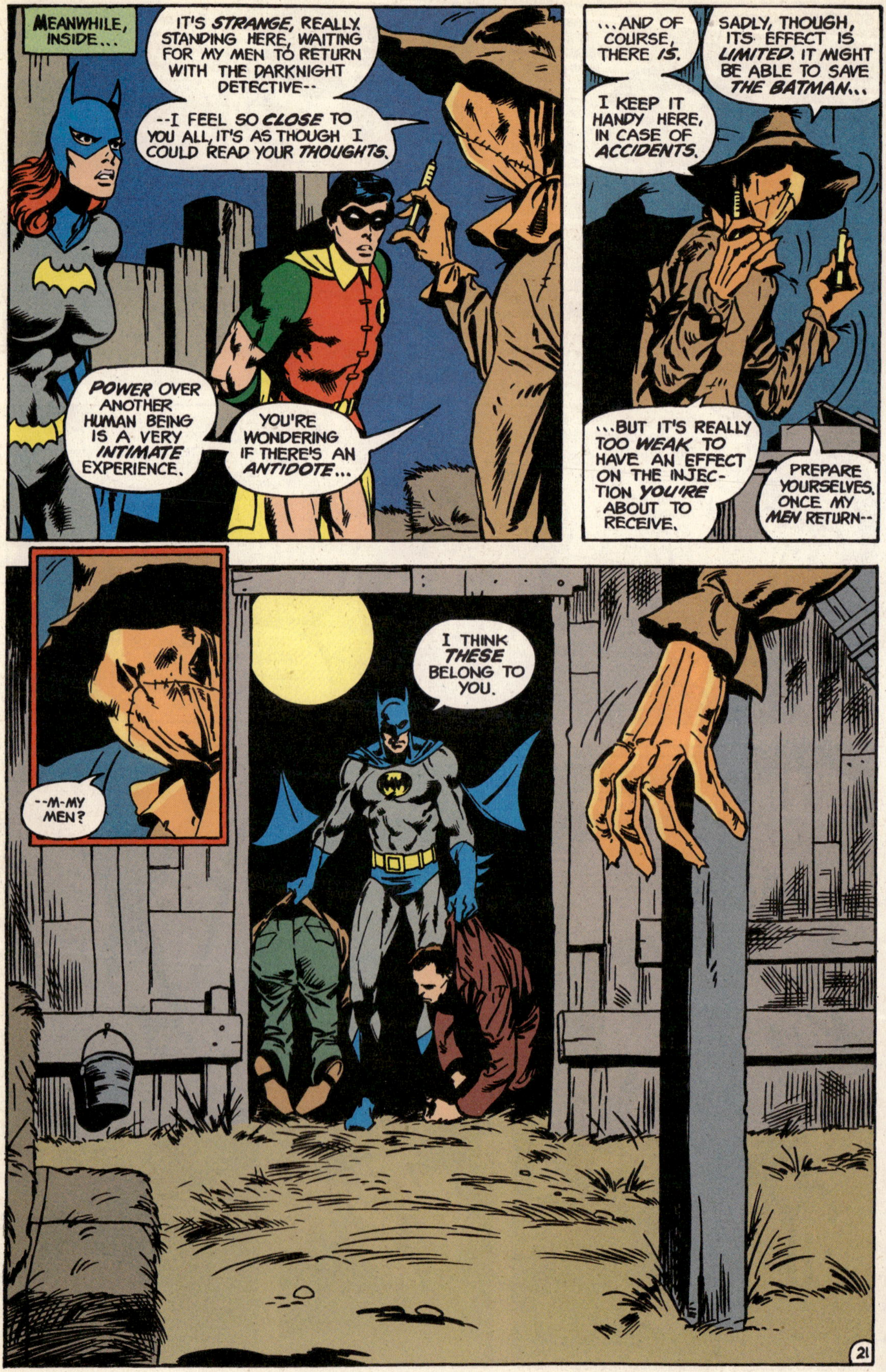
MEANWHILE, INSIDE...
IT'S STRANGE, REALLY. STANDING HERE, WAITING FOR MY MEN TO RETURN WITH THE DARKNIGHT DETECTIVE--
--I FEEL SO CLOSE TO YOU ALL, IT'S AS THOUGH I COULD READ YOUR THOUGHTS.
POWER OVER ANOTHER HUMAN BEING IS A VERY INTIMATE EXPERIENCE.
YOU'RE WONDERING IF THERE'S AN ANTIDOTE...
...AND OF COURSE, THERE IS.
I KEEP IT HANDY HERE, IN CASE OF ACCIDENTS.
SADLY, THOUGH, ITS EFFECT IS LIMITED. IT MIGHT BE ABLE TO SAVE THE BATMAN...
...BUT IT'S REALLY TOO WEAK TO HAVE AN EFFECT ON THE INJECTION YOU'RE ABOUT TO RECEIVE.
PREPARE YOURSELVES, ONCE MY MEN RETURN--
--M-MY MEN?
I THINK THESE BELONG TO YOU.
21

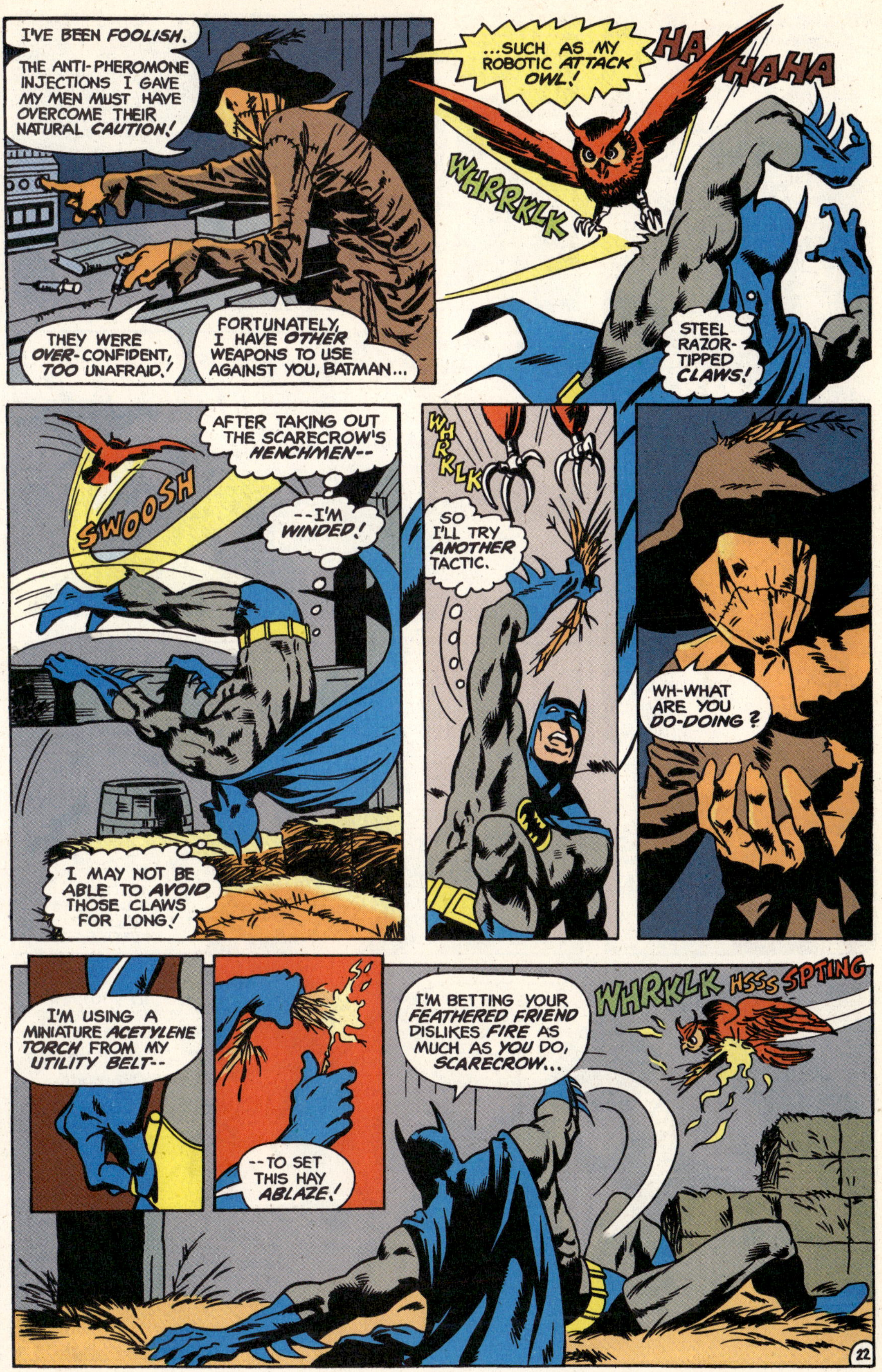
I'VE BEEN FOOLISH.
THE ANTI-PHEROMONE INJECTIONS I GAVE MY MEN MUST HAVE OVERCOME THEIR NATURAL CAUTION!
THEY WERE OVER-CONFIDENT, TOO UNAFRAID!
FORTUNATELY, I HAVE OTHER WEAPONS TO USE AGAINST YOU, BATMAN...
...SUCH AS MY ROBOTIC ATTACK OWL!
HA HA HAHA
WHRRKLK
STEEL RAZOR-TIPPED CLAWS!
AFTER TAKING OUT THE SCARECROW'S HENCHMEN--
SWOOSH
--I'M WINDED!
I MAY NOT BE ABLE TO AVOID THOSE CLAWS FOR LONG!
WHRKLK
SO I'LL TRY ANOTHER TACTIC.
WH-WHAT ARE YOU DO-DOING?
I'M USING A MINIATURE ACETYLENE TORCH FROM MY UTILITY BELT--
--TO SET THIS HAY ABLAZE!
I'M BETTING YOUR FEATHERED FRIEND DISLIKES FIRE AS MUCH AS YOU DO, SCARECROW...
WHRKLK HSSS SPTING
22

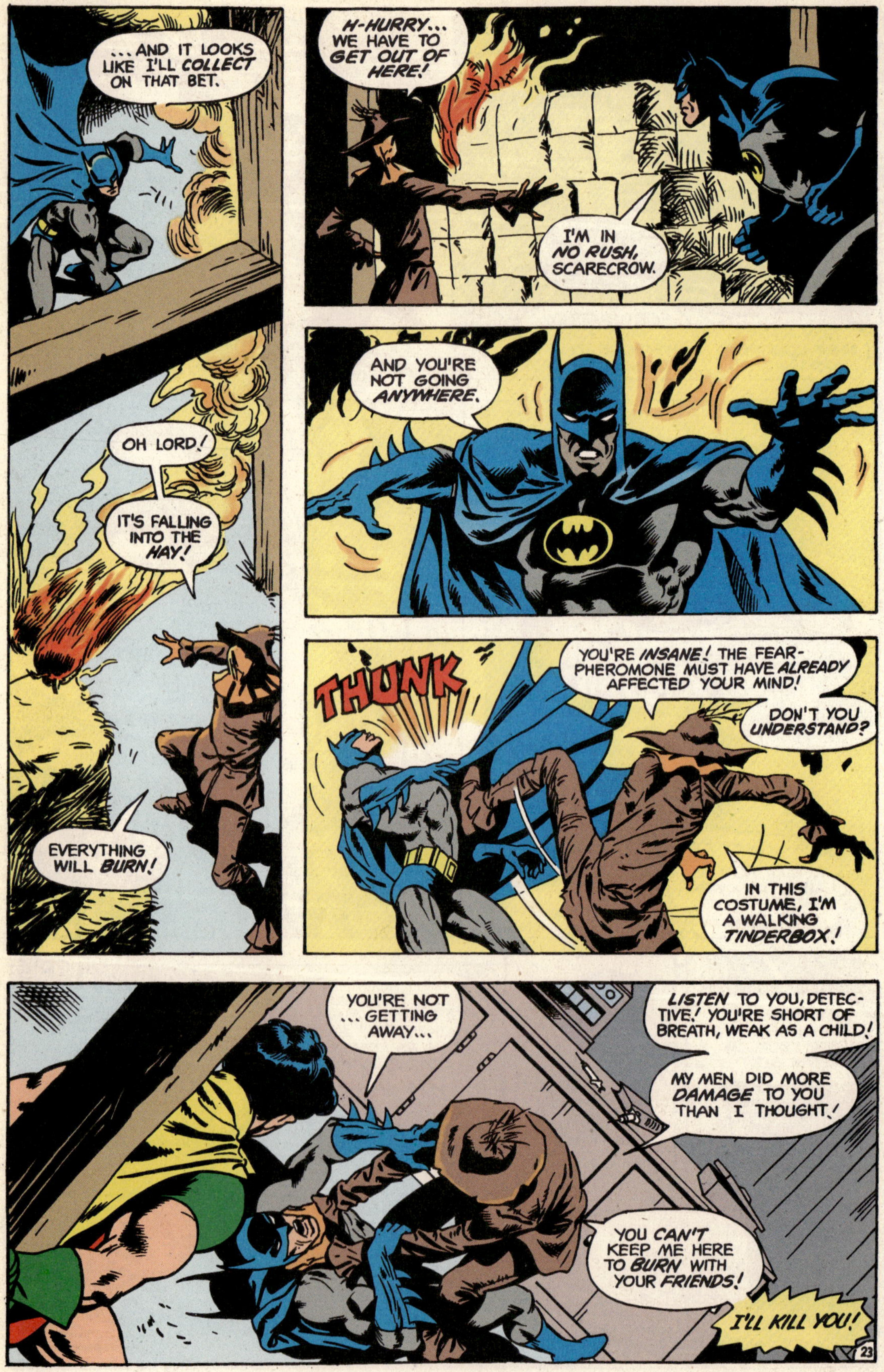

...AND IT LOOKS LIKE I'LL COLLECT ON THAT BET.
H-HURRY... WE HAVE TO GET OUT OF HERE!
I'M IN NO RUSH, SCARECROW.
OH LORD!
IT'S FALLING INTO THE HAY!
EVERYTHING WILL BURN!
AND YOU'RE NOT GOING ANYWHERE.
THUNK
YOU'RE INSANE! THE FEAR-PHEROMONE MUST HAVE ALREADY AFFECTED YOUR MIND!
DON'T YOU UNDERSTAND?
IN THIS COSTUME, I'M A WALKING TINDERBOX!
YOU'RE NOT ...GETTING AWAY...
LISTEN TO YOU, DETECTIVE! YOU'RE SHORT OF BREATH, WEAK AS A CHILD!
MY MEN DID MORE DAMAGE TO YOU THAN I THOUGHT!
YOU CAN'T KEEP ME HERE TO BURN WITH YOUR FRIENDS!
I'LL KILL YOU!
23

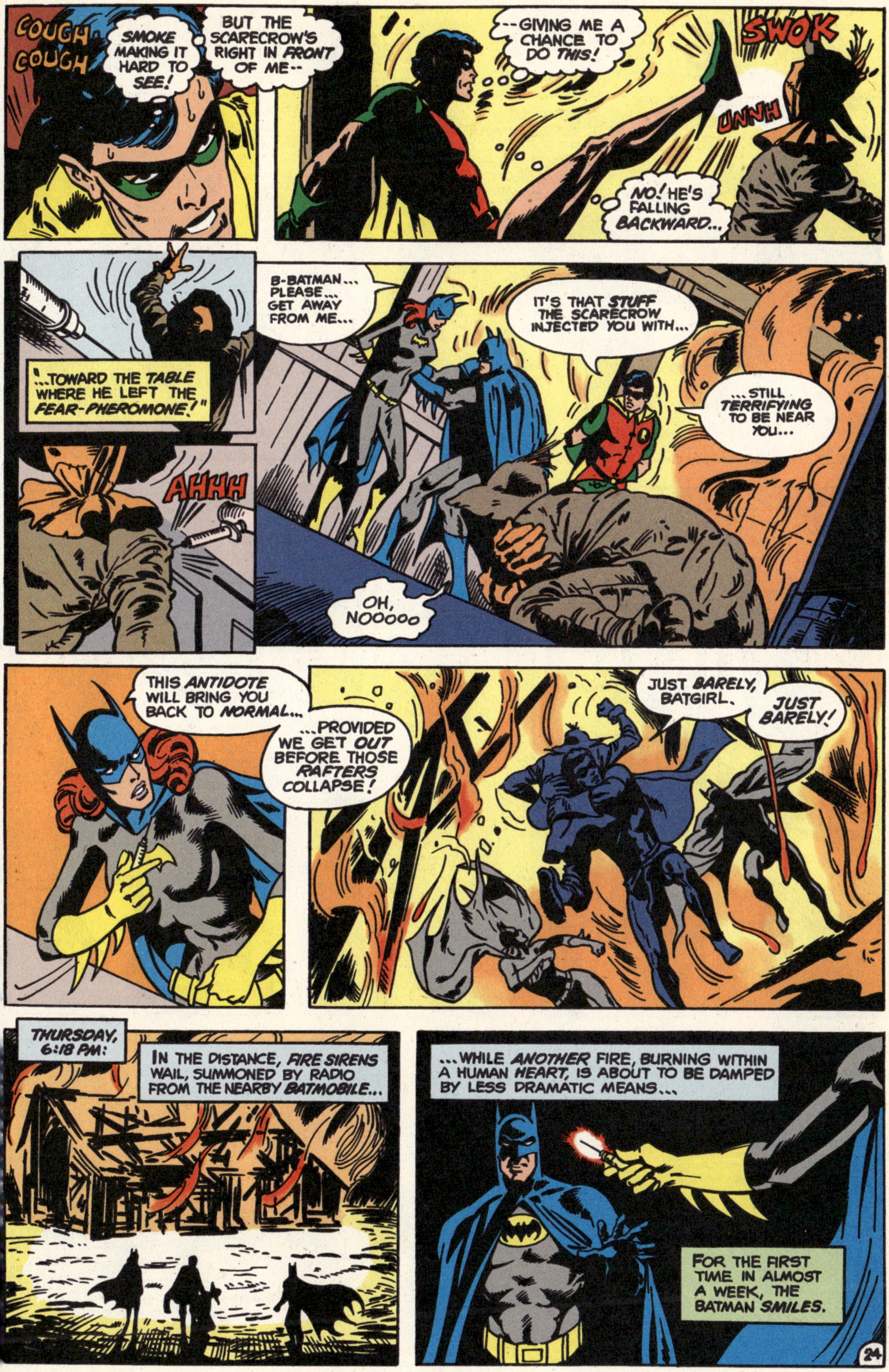
COUGH COUGH
SMOKE MAKING IT HARD TO SEE!
BUT THE SCARECROW'S RIGHT IN FRONT OF ME--
--GIVING ME A CHANCE TO DO THIS!
SWOK
UNNH
NO! HE'S FALLING BACKWARD...
"...TOWARD THE TABLE WHERE HE LEFT THE FEAR-PHEROMONE!"
AHHH
B-BATMAN... PLEASE... GET AWAY FROM ME...
IT'S THAT STUFF THE SCARECROW INJECTED YOU WITH...
...STILL TERRIFYING TO BE NEAR YOU...
OH, NOOOOO
THIS ANTIDOTE WILL BRING YOU BACK TO NORMAL...
...PROVIDED WE GET OUT BEFORE THOSE RAFTERS COLLAPSE!
JUST BARELY, BATGIRL.
JUST BARELY!
THURSDAY, 6:18 PM:
IN THE DISTANCE, FIRE SIRENS WAIL, SUMMONED BY RADIO FROM THE NEARBY BATMOBILE...
...WHILE ANOTHER FIRE, BURNING WITHIN A HUMAN HEART, IS ABOUT TO BE DAMPED BY LESS DRAMATIC MEANS...
FOR THE FIRST TIME IN ALMOST A WEEK, THE BATMAN SMILES.
24

DAY [MARCH 6] OF THE SCARECROW

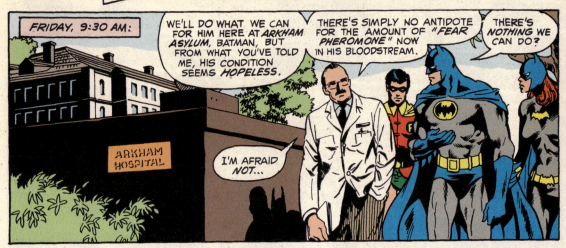

FRIDAY, 9:30 AM:

WE'LL DO WHAT WE CAN FOR HIM HERE AT *ARKHAM ASYLUM,* BATMAN, BUT FROM WHAT YOU'VE TOLD ME, HIS CONDITION SEEMS *HOPELESS.*

THERE'S SIMPLY NO ANTIDOTE FOR THE AMOUNT OF *"FEAR PHEROMONE"* NOW IN HIS BLOODSTREAM.

THERE'S *NOTHING* WE CAN DO?

ARKHAM HOSPITAL

I'M AFRAID *NOT...*

"JONATHAN CRANE, THE MAN YOU CALL *THE SCARECROW,* IS NOW SO *PHOBIC...*

B-18

"...HE'S EVEN AFRAID OF *HIMSELF.*

"SO *END* THE SIX DAYS OF THE *SCARECROW."*

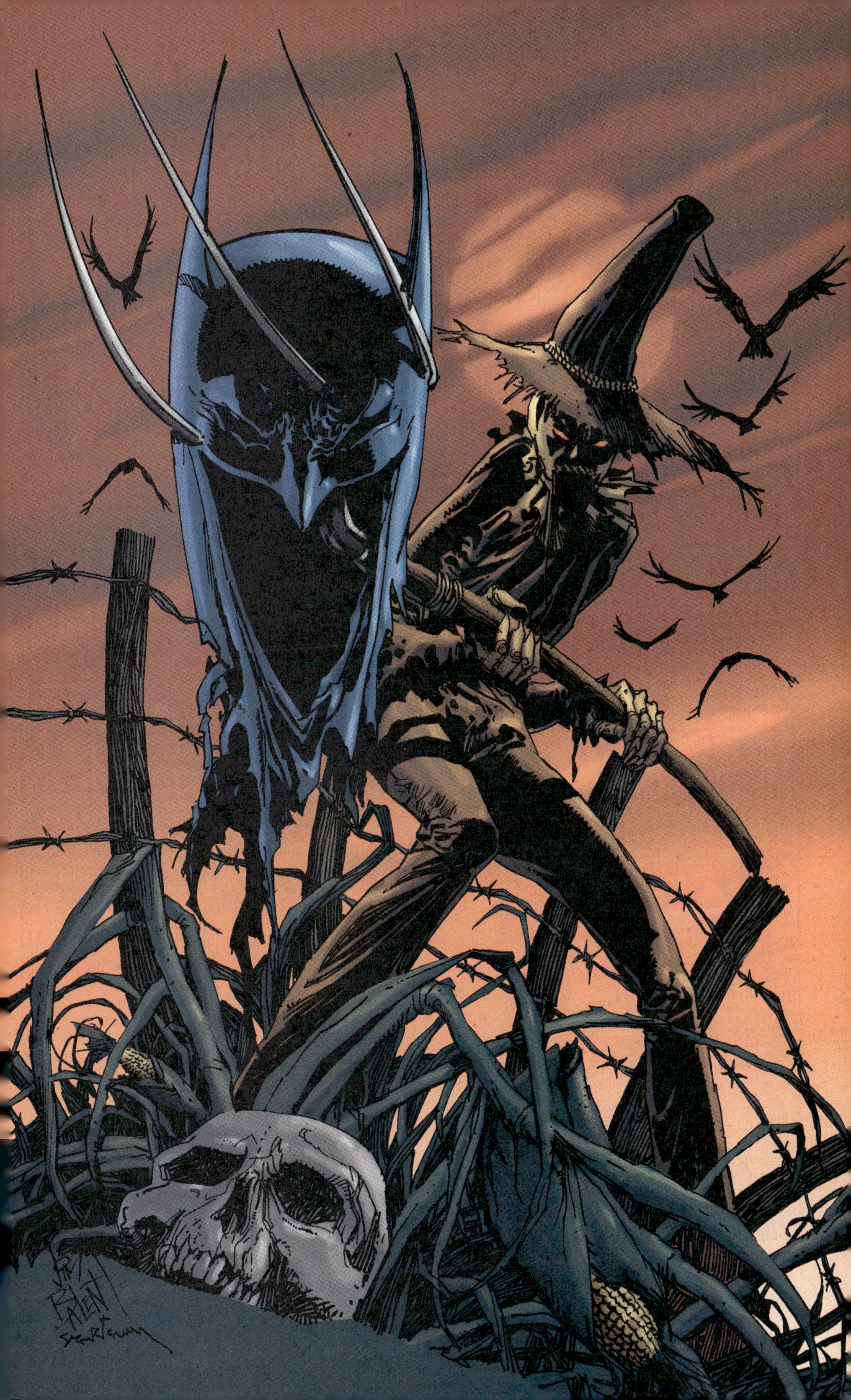

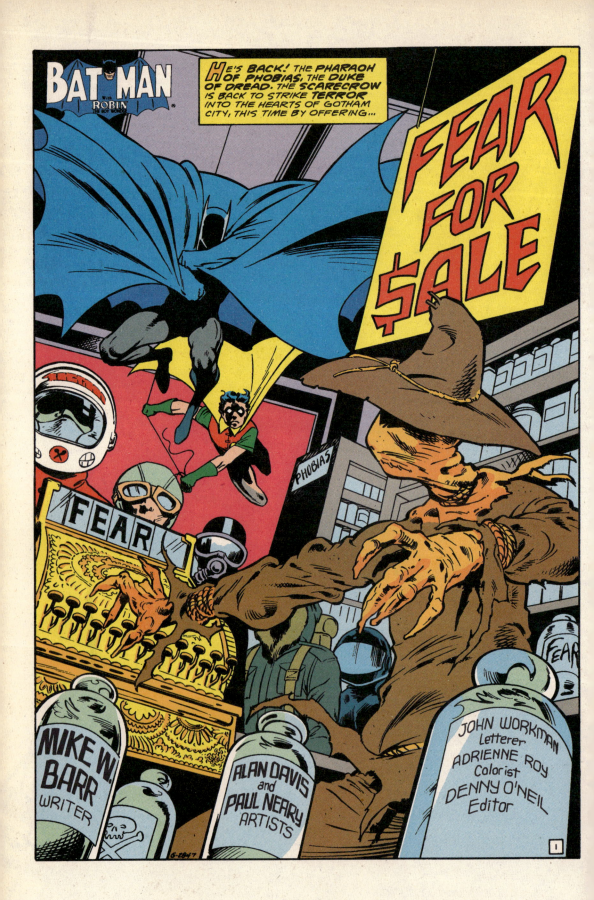

BATMAN with ROBIN THE BOY WONDER

He's back! The Pharaoh of phobias, the Duke of dread. The Scarecrow is back to strike terror into the hearts of Gotham City, this time by offering...

FEAR FOR SALE

FEAR

PHOBIAS

MIKE W. BARR Writer

ALAN DAVIS and PAUL NEARY Artists

JOHN WORKMAN Letterer
ADRIENNE ROY Colorist
DENNY O'NEIL Editor

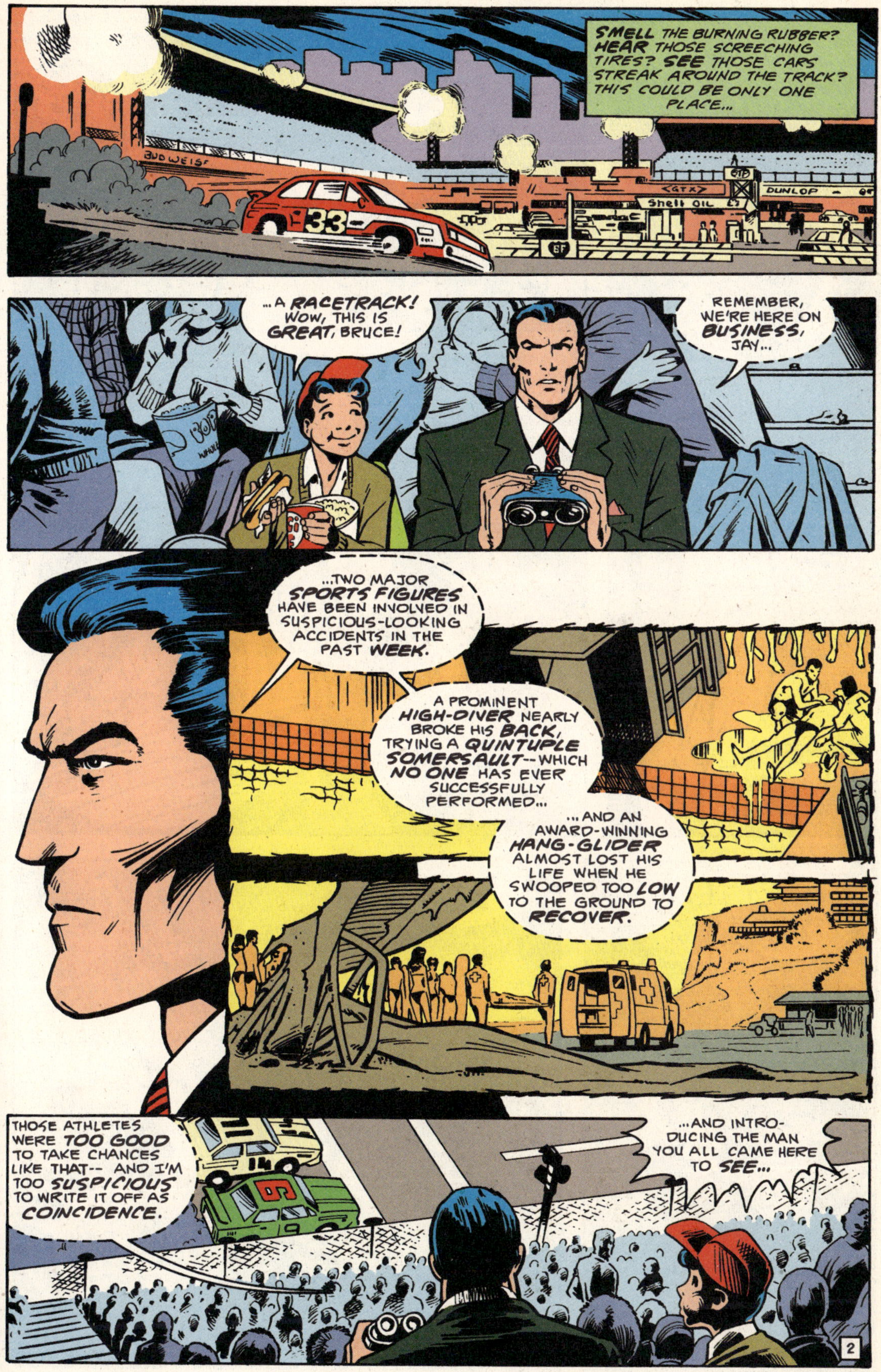
SMELL THE BURNING RUBBER? HEAR THOSE SCREECHING TIRES? SEE THOSE CARS STREAK AROUND THE TRACK? THIS COULD BE ONLY ONE PLACE...
BUDWEISER
GTX
DUNLOP
Shell OIL
33
...A RACETRACK! WOW, THIS IS GREAT, BRUCE!
REMEMBER, WE'RE HERE ON BUSINESS, JAY...
...TWO MAJOR SPORTS FIGURES HAVE BEEN INVOLVED IN SUSPICIOUS-LOOKING ACCIDENTS IN THE PAST WEEK.
A PROMINENT HIGH-DIVER NEARLY BROKE HIS BACK, TRYING A QUINTUPLE SOMERSAULT--WHICH NO ONE HAS EVER SUCCESSFULLY PERFORMED...
...AND AN AWARD-WINNING HANG-GLIDER ALMOST LOST HIS LIFE WHEN HE SWOOPED TOO LOW TO THE GROUND TO RECOVER.
THOSE ATHLETES WERE TOO GOOD TO TAKE CHANCES LIKE THAT-- AND I'M TOO SUSPICIOUS TO WRITE IT OFF AS COINCIDENCE.
...AND INTRODUCING THE MAN YOU ALL CAME HERE TO SEE...
2

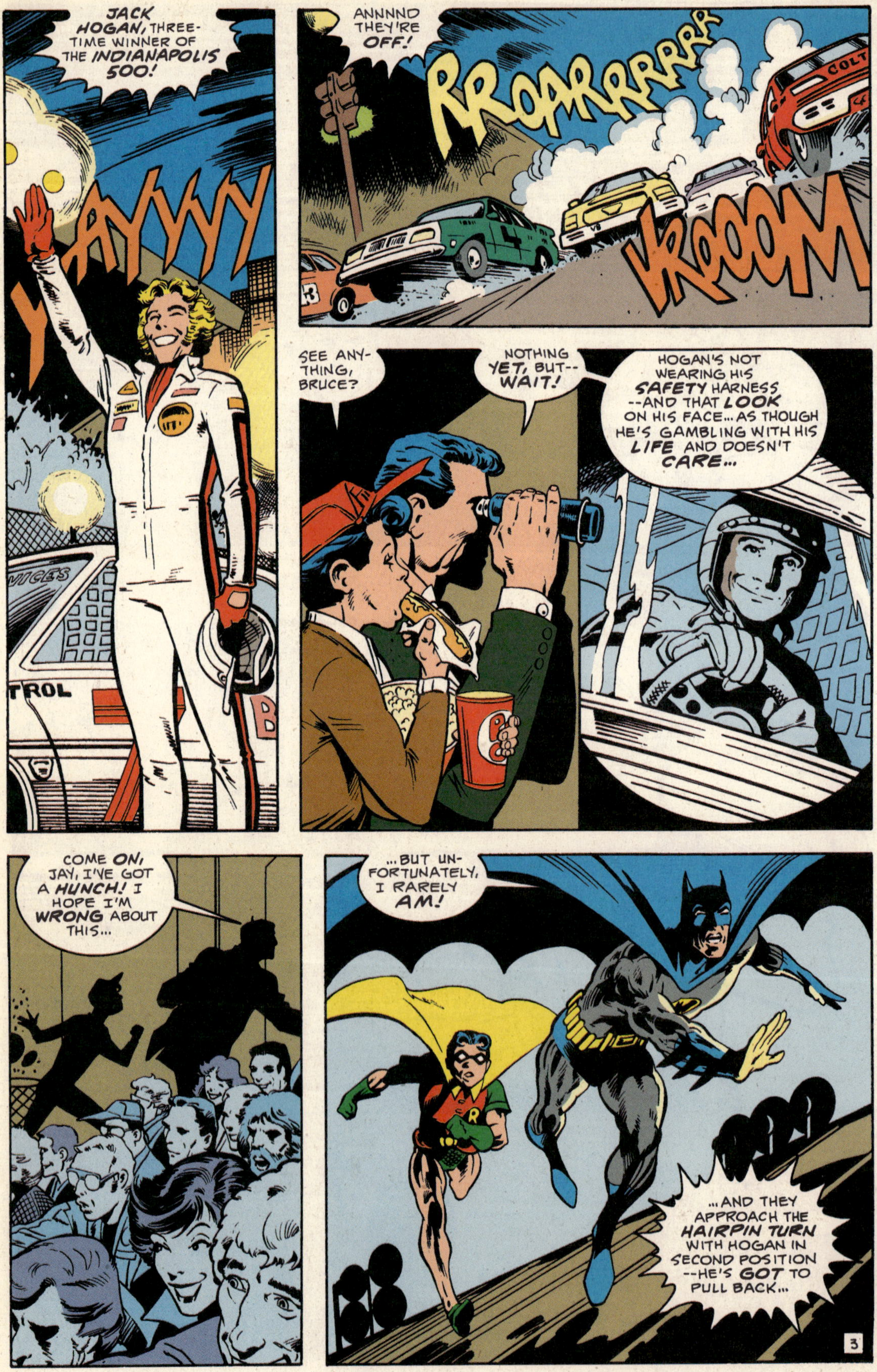

JACK HOGAN, THREE-TIME WINNER OF THE INDIANAPOLIS 500!
YAYYYY
ANNNND THEY'RE OFF!
RROARRRRRR
VROOOM
COLT
SEE ANY-THING, BRUCE?
NOTHING YET, BUT-- WAIT!
HOGAN'S NOT WEARING HIS SAFETY HARNESS --AND THAT LOOK ON HIS FACE... AS THOUGH HE'S GAMBLING WITH HIS LIFE AND DOESN'T CARE...
COME ON, JAY, I'VE GOT A HUNCH! I HOPE I'M WRONG ABOUT THIS...
...BUT UN-FORTUNATELY, I RARELY AM!
...AND THEY APPROACH THE HAIRPIN TURN WITH HOGAN IN SECOND POSITION --HE'S GOT TO PULL BACK...
3

...BUT *NO,* HE'S *POURING IT ON!* TWO CARS CAN'T TAKE THAT TURN AT THE SAME TIME! SOMETHING'S GOT TO--

BDUNT

SKREEEEEGH

WHOOOM

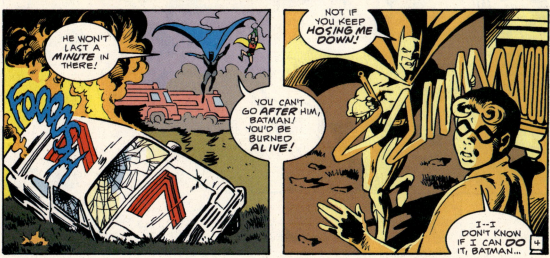

HE WON'T LAST A *MINUTE* IN THERE!

FOOOSH

NOT IF YOU KEEP *HOSING* ME *DOWN!*

YOU CAN'T GO *AFTER* HIM, BATMAN! YOU'D BE BURNED *ALIVE!*

I--I DON'T KNOW IF I CAN *DO* IT, BATMAN...

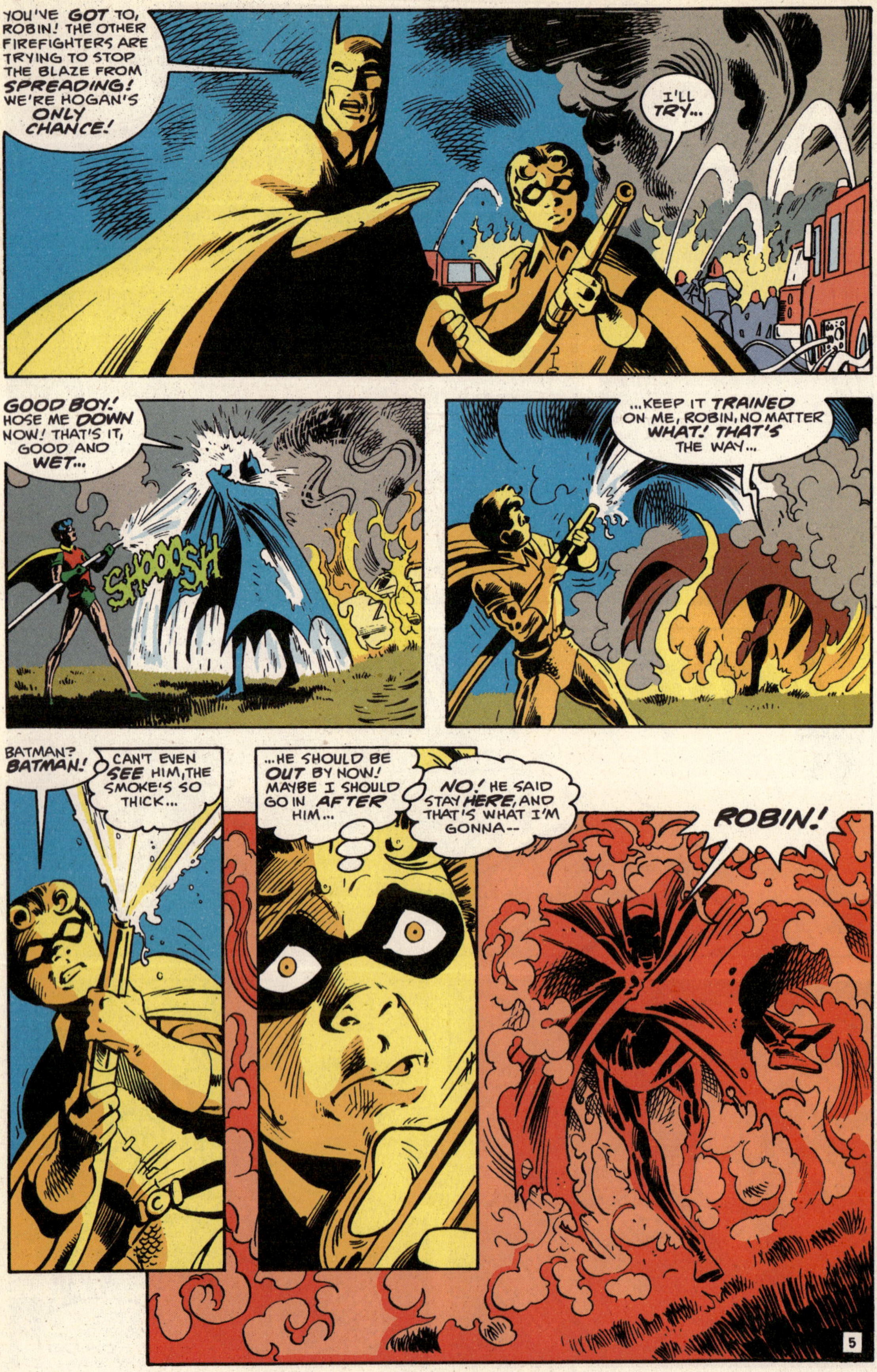

YOU'VE GOT TO, ROBIN! THE OTHER FIREFIGHTERS ARE TRYING TO STOP THE BLAZE FROM SPREADING! WE'RE HOGAN'S ONLY CHANCE!
I'LL TRY...
GOOD BOY! HOSE ME DOWN NOW! THAT'S IT, GOOD AND WET...
SHOOOSH
...KEEP IT TRAINED ON ME, ROBIN, NO MATTER WHAT! THAT'S THE WAY...
BATMAN? BATMAN!
CAN'T EVEN SEE HIM, THE SMOKE'S SO THICK...
...HE SHOULD BE OUT BY NOW! MAYBE I SHOULD GO IN AFTER HIM...
NO! HE SAID STAY HERE, AND THAT'S WHAT I'M GONNA--
ROBIN!
5

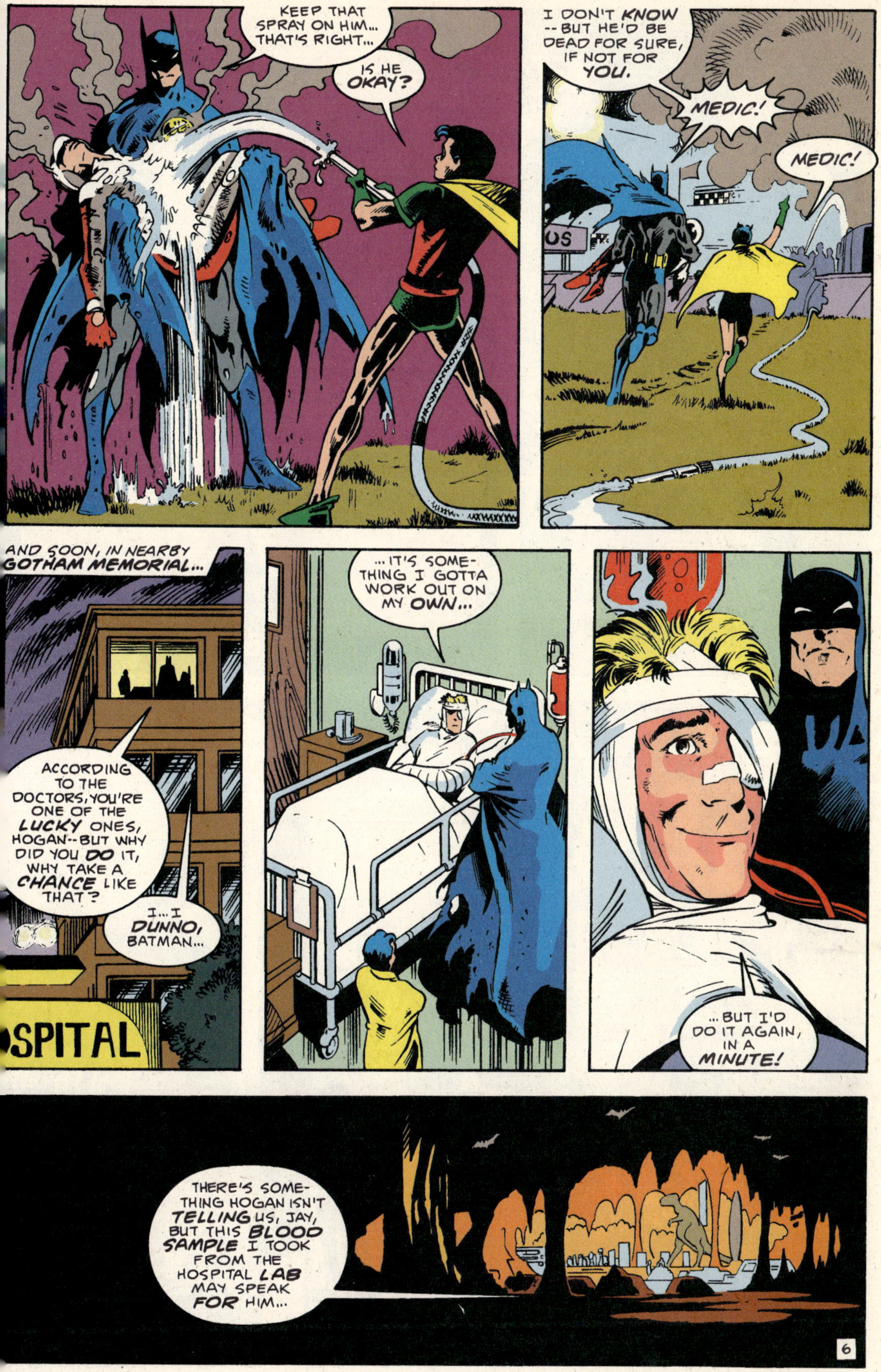

KEEP THAT SPRAY ON HIM... THAT'S RIGHT...
IS HE OKAY?
I DON'T KNOW --BUT HE'D BE DEAD FOR SURE, IF NOT FOR YOU.
MEDIC!
MEDIC!
AND SOON, IN NEARBY GOTHAM MEMORIAL...
ACCORDING TO THE DOCTORS, YOU'RE ONE OF THE LUCKY ONES, HOGAN--BUT WHY DID YOU DO IT, WHY TAKE A CHANCE LIKE THAT?
I...I DUNNO, BATMAN...
SPITAL
...IT'S SOMETHING I GOTTA WORK OUT ON MY OWN...
...BUT I'D DO IT AGAIN, IN A MINUTE!
THERE'S SOMETHING HOGAN ISN'T TELLING US, JAY, BUT THIS BLOOD SAMPLE I TOOK FROM THE HOSPITAL LAB MAY SPEAK FOR HIM...
6

...I THINK I DETECT A PSYCHO-ACTIVE CHEMICAL I'VE ENCOUNTERED *BEFORE*...

...BUT ONCE I'VE COMPARED IT TO OUR *FILE SLIDE*...

..."I'LL KNOW FOR *SURE*.

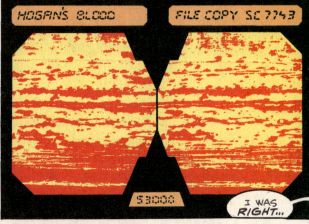

HOGAN'S BLOOD

FILE COPY SC 7743

53000

I WAS *RIGHT*...

...THIS IS A CHEMICAL EXCLUSIVELY BY THE *SCARECROW*. BACKGROUND ON HIM, JAY?

Uh... LET'S SEE... REAL NAME'S *CRAIG*... NO, *CRANE*... *JONATHAN CRANE*...

"...HE WAS A *PSYCHOLOGY PROFESSOR*... TALENTED, BUT DIDN'T HAVE A LOTTA *FRIENDS*..."

THERE'S THAT FUNNY PROFESSOR *CRANE* AGAIN...

..."HE'S SO *FUNNY LOOKING*... LIKE A *SCARE-CROW*..."

THEY LAUGH AT ME BECAUSE I'D RATHER SPEND MONEY ON *BOOKS* THAN ON FANCY *CLOTHES*, OR STUPID *PARTIES*...

...BUT IF I COULD USE MY *BOOKS* TO *GET MONEY*... *THEN* THEY WOULDN'T LAUGH AT ME... THEY'D *FEAR* ME...

THE PSYCHOLOGY OF FEAR

7

"...AND CRANE'S BEEN AT IT EVER *SINCE.* BUT I FEEL KINDA *SORRY* FOR HIM, BRUCE..."

"...I MEAN, NOBODY LIKES TO BE *LAUGHED* AT..."

I *KNOW,* JAY--BUT I CAN'T ALLOW HIM TO TAKE HIS *HUMILIATION* OUT ON *SOCIETY.*

YOUR NEW COSTUME, MASTER BRUCE... I'M AFRAID THE OLD ONE WAS PAST SAVING.

FORTUNES OF *WAR,* ALFRED.

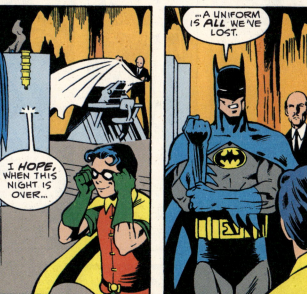

I *HOPE,* WHEN THIS NIGHT IS OVER...

...A UNIFORM IS *ALL* WE'VE LOST.

"IT MIGHT BE A *LONG* NIGHT, ALFRED--DON'T *WAIT UP.*"

8

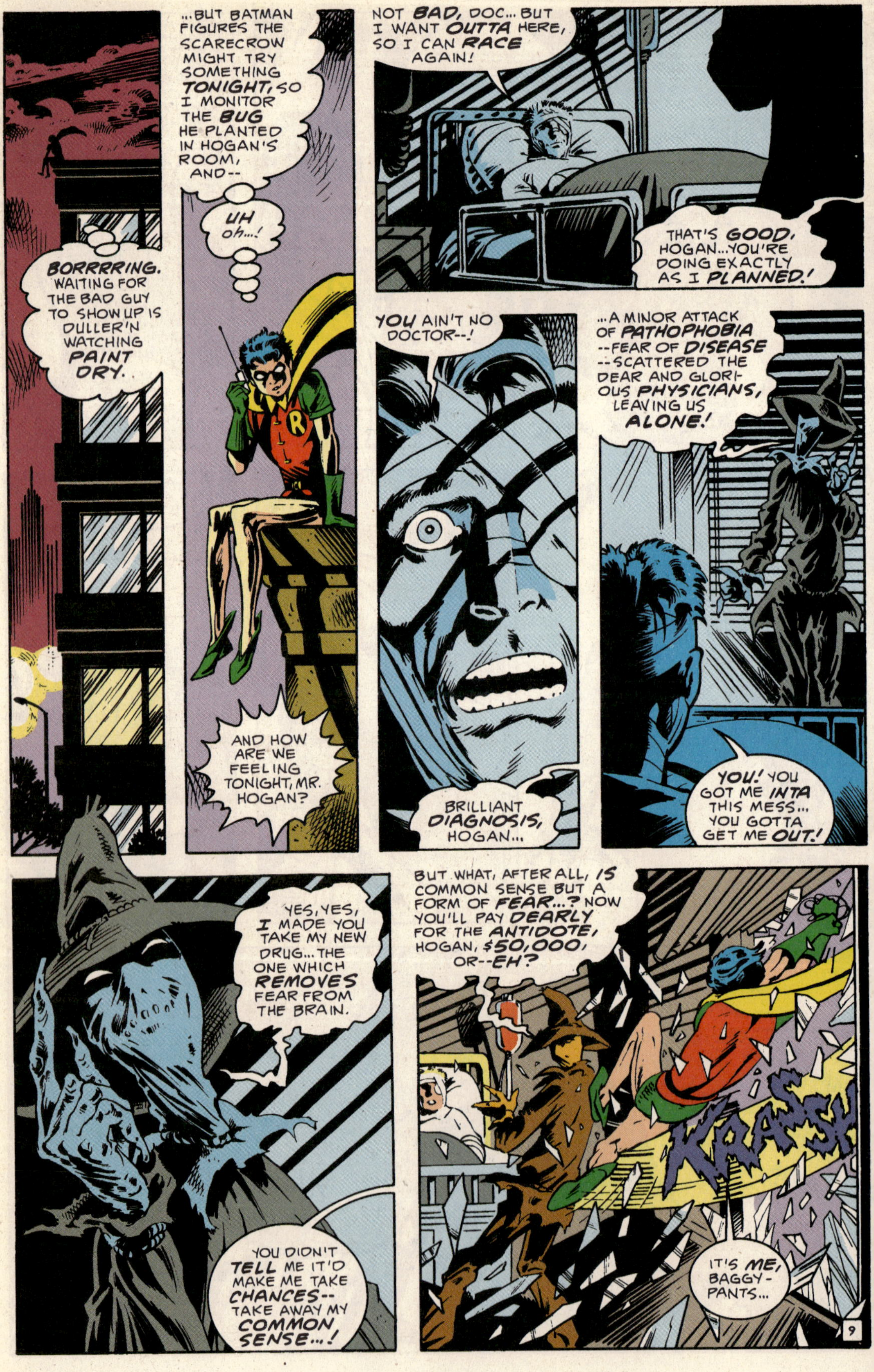
...BUT BATMAN FIGURES THE SCARECROW MIGHT TRY SOMETHING TONIGHT, SO I MONITOR THE BUG HE PLANTED IN HOGAN'S ROOM, AND--
UH oh...!
BORRRRING. WAITING FOR THE BAD GUY TO SHOW UP IS DULLER'N WATCHING PAINT DRY.
AND HOW ARE WE FEELING TONIGHT, MR. HOGAN?
NOT BAD, DOC... BUT I WANT OUTTA HERE, SO I CAN RACE AGAIN!
THAT'S GOOD, HOGAN... YOU'RE DOING EXACTLY AS I PLANNED!
YOU AIN'T NO DOCTOR--!
BRILLIANT DIAGNOSIS, HOGAN...
...A MINOR ATTACK OF PATHOPHOBIA --FEAR OF DISEASE --SCATTERED THE DEAR AND GLORIOUS PHYSICIANS, LEAVING US ALONE!
YOU! YOU GOT ME INTA THIS MESS... YOU GOTTA GET ME OUT!
YES, YES, I MADE YOU TAKE MY NEW DRUG... THE ONE WHICH REMOVES FEAR FROM THE BRAIN.
YOU DIDN'T TELL ME IT'D MAKE ME TAKE CHANCES-- TAKE AWAY MY COMMON SENSE...!
BUT WHAT, AFTER ALL, IS COMMON SENSE BUT A FORM OF FEAR...? NOW YOU'LL PAY DEARLY FOR THE ANTIDOTE, HOGAN, $50,000, OR--EH?
KRASSH
IT'S ME, BAGGY-PANTS...
9

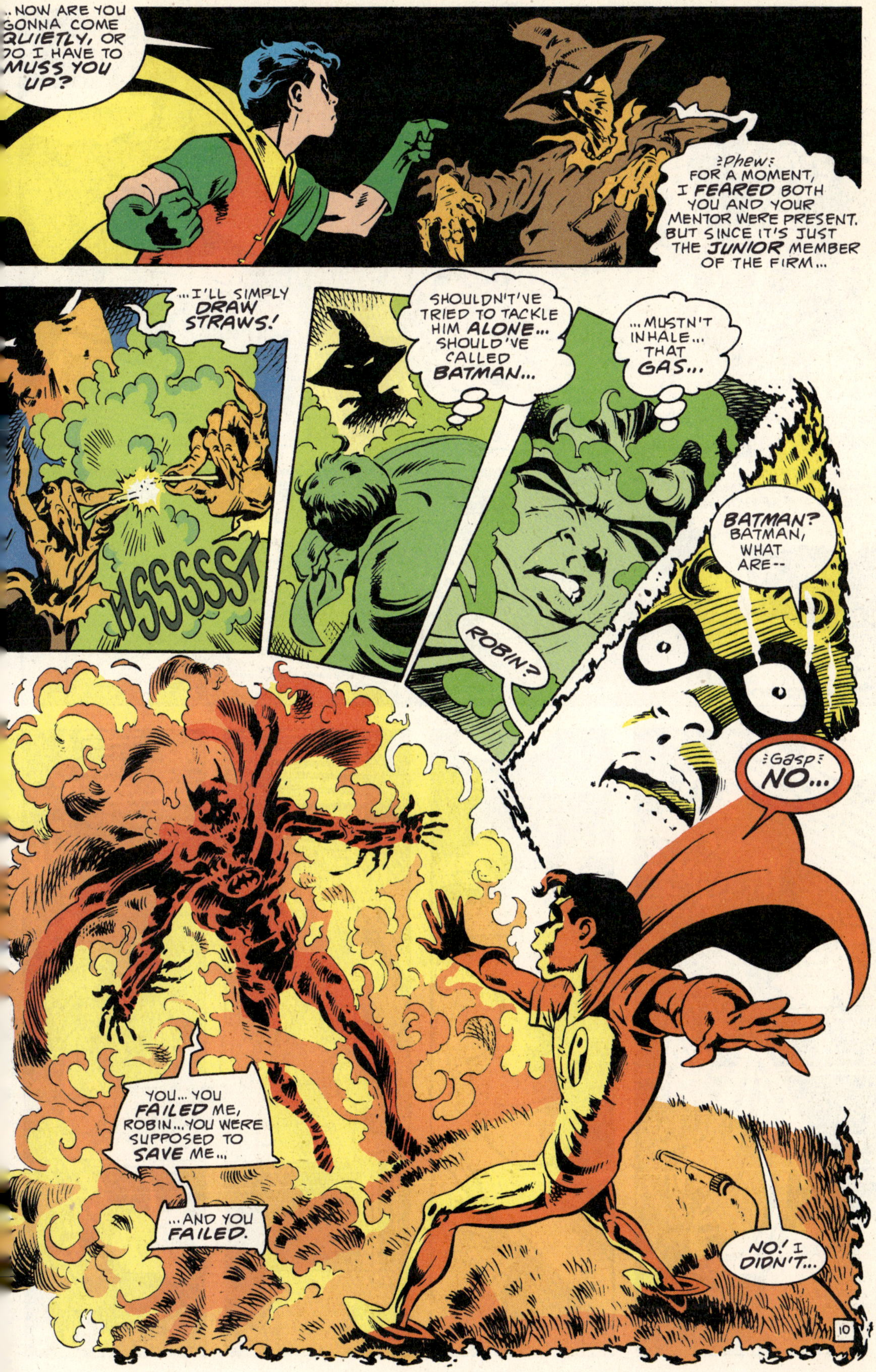
..NOW ARE YOU GONNA COME QUIETLY, OR DO I HAVE TO MUSS YOU UP?
Phew: FOR A MOMENT, I FEARED BOTH YOU AND YOUR MENTOR WERE PRESENT. BUT SINCE IT'S JUST THE JUNIOR MEMBER OF THE FIRM...
...I'LL SIMPLY DRAW STRAWS!
HSSSSST
SHOULDN'T'VE TRIED TO TACKLE HIM ALONE... SHOULD'VE CALLED BATMAN...
...MUSTN'T INHALE... THAT GAS...
ROBIN?
BATMAN? BATMAN, WHAT ARE--
Gasp: NO...
YOU... YOU FAILED ME, ROBIN... YOU WERE SUPPOSED TO SAVE ME...
...AND YOU FAILED.
NO! I DIDN'T...
10

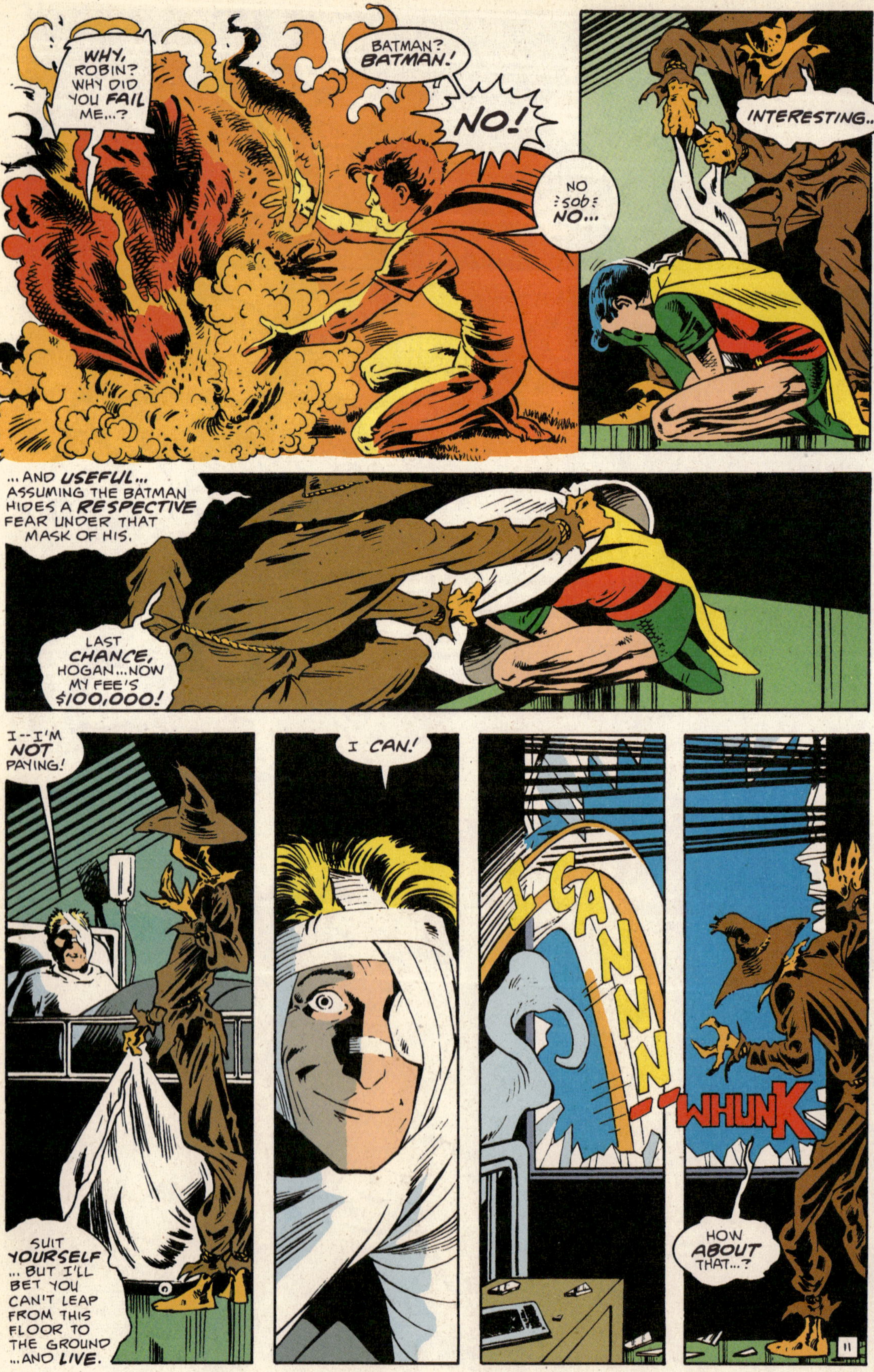
WHY, ROBIN? WHY DID YOU FAIL ME...?
BATMAN? BATMAN!
NO!
NO sob NO...
INTERESTING...
...AND USEFUL... ASSUMING THE BATMAN HIDES A RESPECTIVE FEAR UNDER THAT MASK OF HIS.
LAST CHANCE, HOGAN...NOW MY FEE'S $100,000!
I--I'M NOT PAYING!
SUIT YOURSELF ...BUT I'LL BET YOU CAN'T LEAP FROM THIS FLOOR TO THE GROUND ...AND LIVE.
I CAN!
I CANNN--
WHUNK
HOW ABOUT THAT...?
11

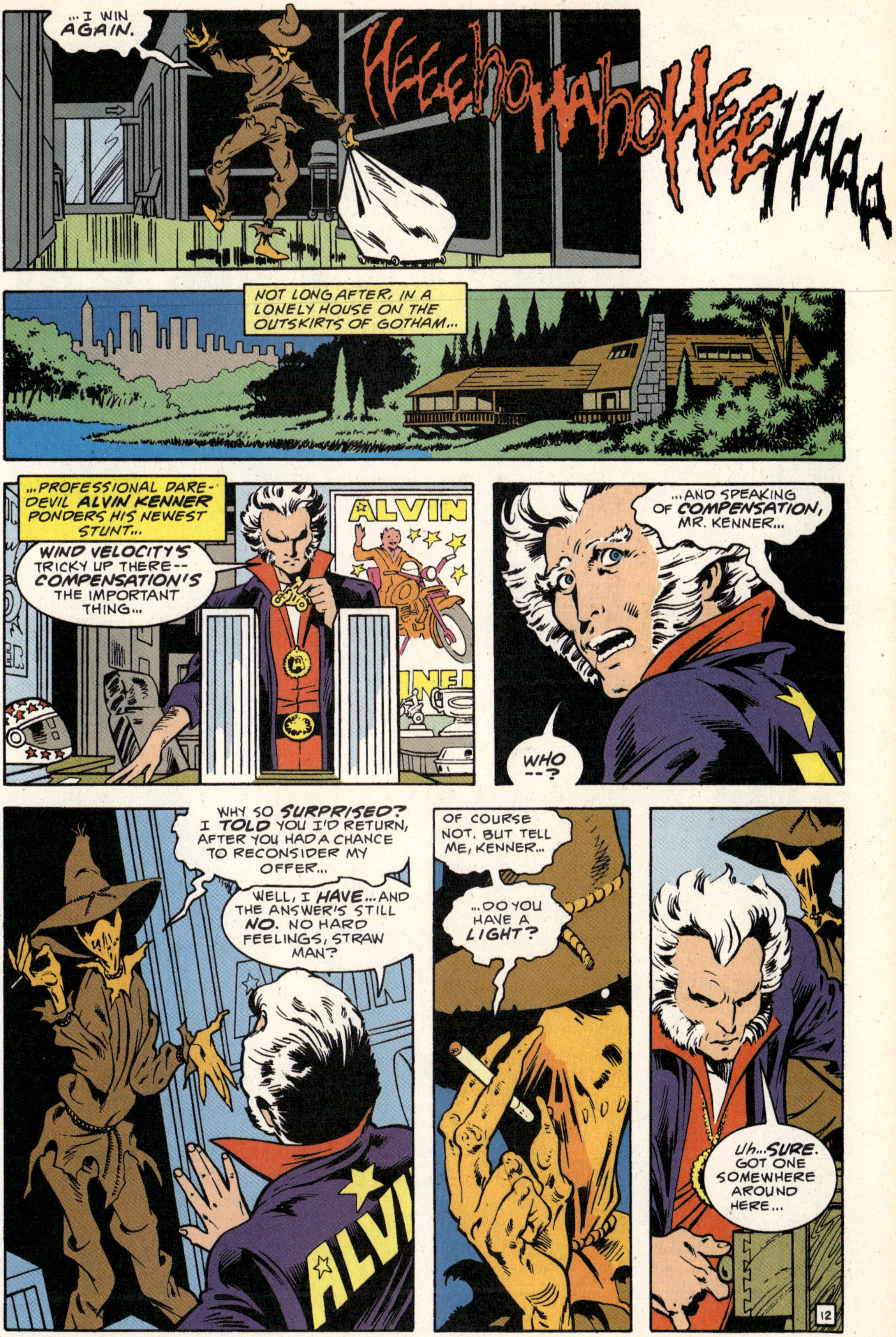
...I WIN AGAIN.
HEEEHOHAHOHEEHAAA
NOT LONG AFTER, IN A LONELY HOUSE ON THE OUTSKIRTS OF GOTHAM...
...PROFESSIONAL DARE-DEVIL ALVIN KENNER PONDERS HIS NEWEST STUNT...
WIND VELOCITY'S TRICKY UP THERE-- COMPENSATION'S THE IMPORTANT THING...
ALVIN
...AND SPEAKING OF COMPENSATION, MR. KENNER...
WHO --?
WHY SO SURPRISED? I TOLD YOU I'D RETURN, AFTER YOU HAD A CHANCE TO RECONSIDER MY OFFER...
WELL, I HAVE... AND THE ANSWER'S STILL NO. NO HARD FEELINGS, STRAW MAN?
OF COURSE NOT. BUT TELL ME, KENNER...
...DO YOU HAVE A LIGHT?
Uh... SURE. GOT ONE SOMEWHERE AROUND HERE...
12

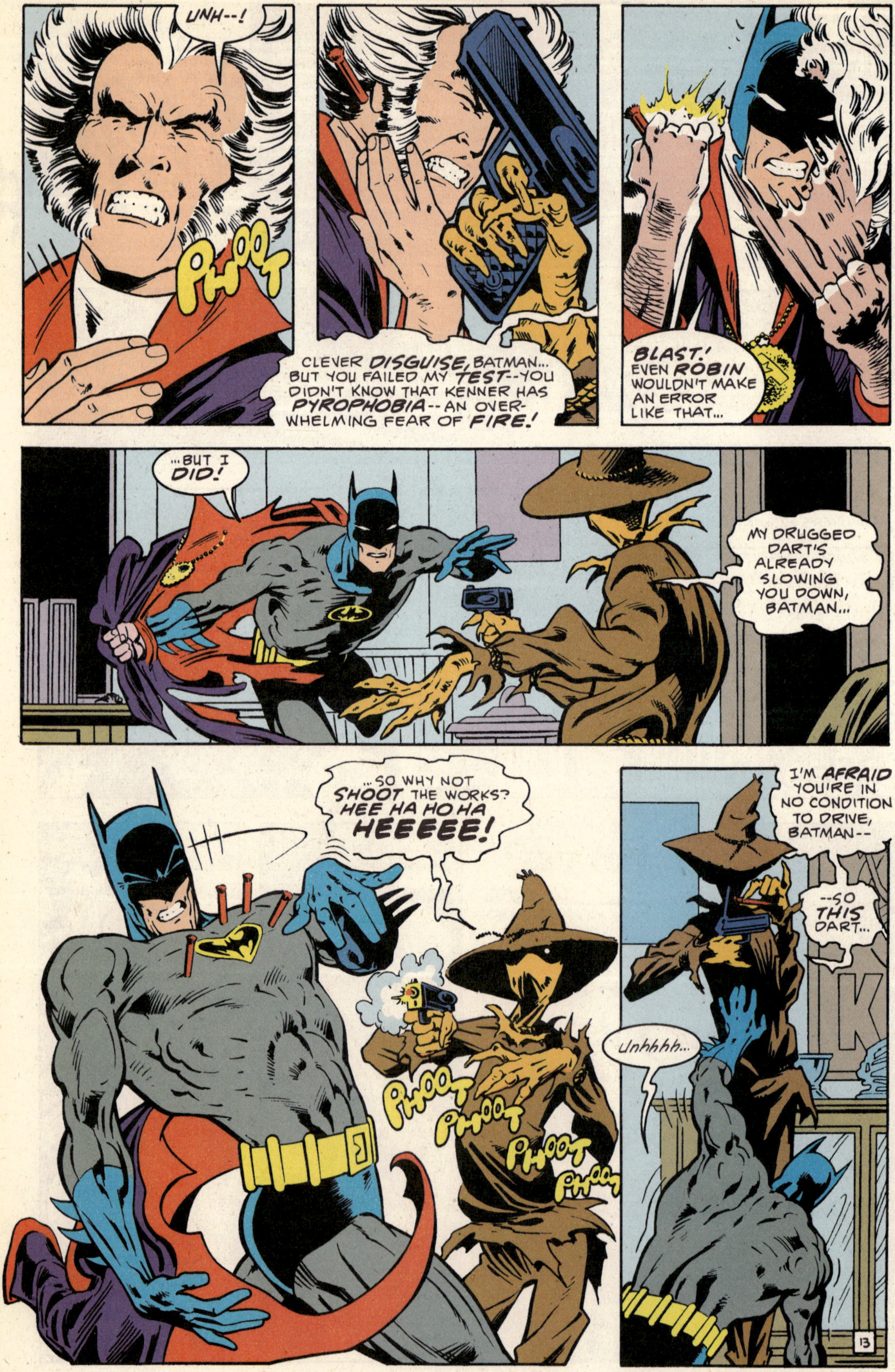
UNH--!
PHOOT
CLEVER DISGUISE, BATMAN... BUT YOU FAILED MY TEST--YOU DIDN'T KNOW THAT KENNER HAS PYROPHOBIA--AN OVER-WHELMING FEAR OF FIRE!
BLAST! EVEN ROBIN WOULDN'T MAKE AN ERROR LIKE THAT...
...BUT I DID!
MY DRUGGED DART'S ALREADY SLOWING YOU DOWN, BATMAN...
...SO WHY NOT SHOOT THE WORKS? HEE HA HO HA HEEEEEE!
PHOOT
PHOOT
PHOOT
PHOOT
I'M AFRAID YOU'RE IN NO CONDITION TO DRIVE, BATMAN--
--SO THIS DART...
Unhhhh...
13

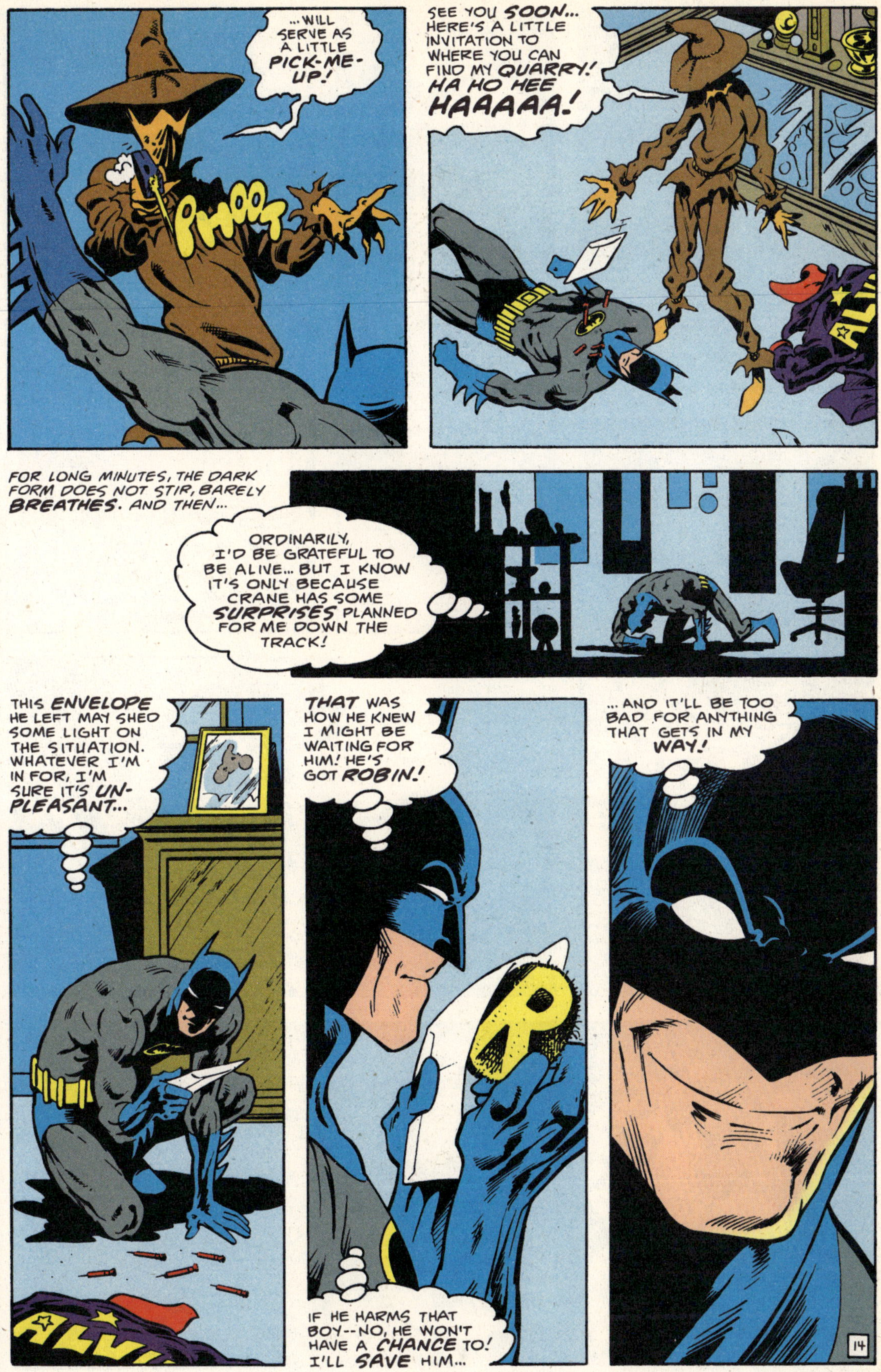
...WILL SERVE AS A LITTLE PICK-ME-UP!
PHOOT
SEE YOU SOON... HERE'S A LITTLE INVITATION TO WHERE YOU CAN FIND MY QUARRY! HA HO HEE HAAAAA!
FOR LONG MINUTES, THE DARK FORM DOES NOT STIR, BARELY BREATHES. AND THEN...
ORDINARILY, I'D BE GRATEFUL TO BE ALIVE... BUT I KNOW IT'S ONLY BECAUSE CRANE HAS SOME SURPRISES PLANNED FOR ME DOWN THE TRACK!
THIS ENVELOPE HE LEFT MAY SHED SOME LIGHT ON THE SITUATION. WHATEVER I'M IN FOR, I'M SURE IT'S UN-PLEASANT...
THAT WAS HOW HE KNEW I MIGHT BE WAITING FOR HIM! HE'S GOT ROBIN!
IF HE HARMS THAT BOY--NO, HE WON'T HAVE A CHANCE TO! I'LL SAVE HIM...
...AND IT'LL BE TOO BAD FOR ANYTHING THAT GETS IN MY WAY!
14

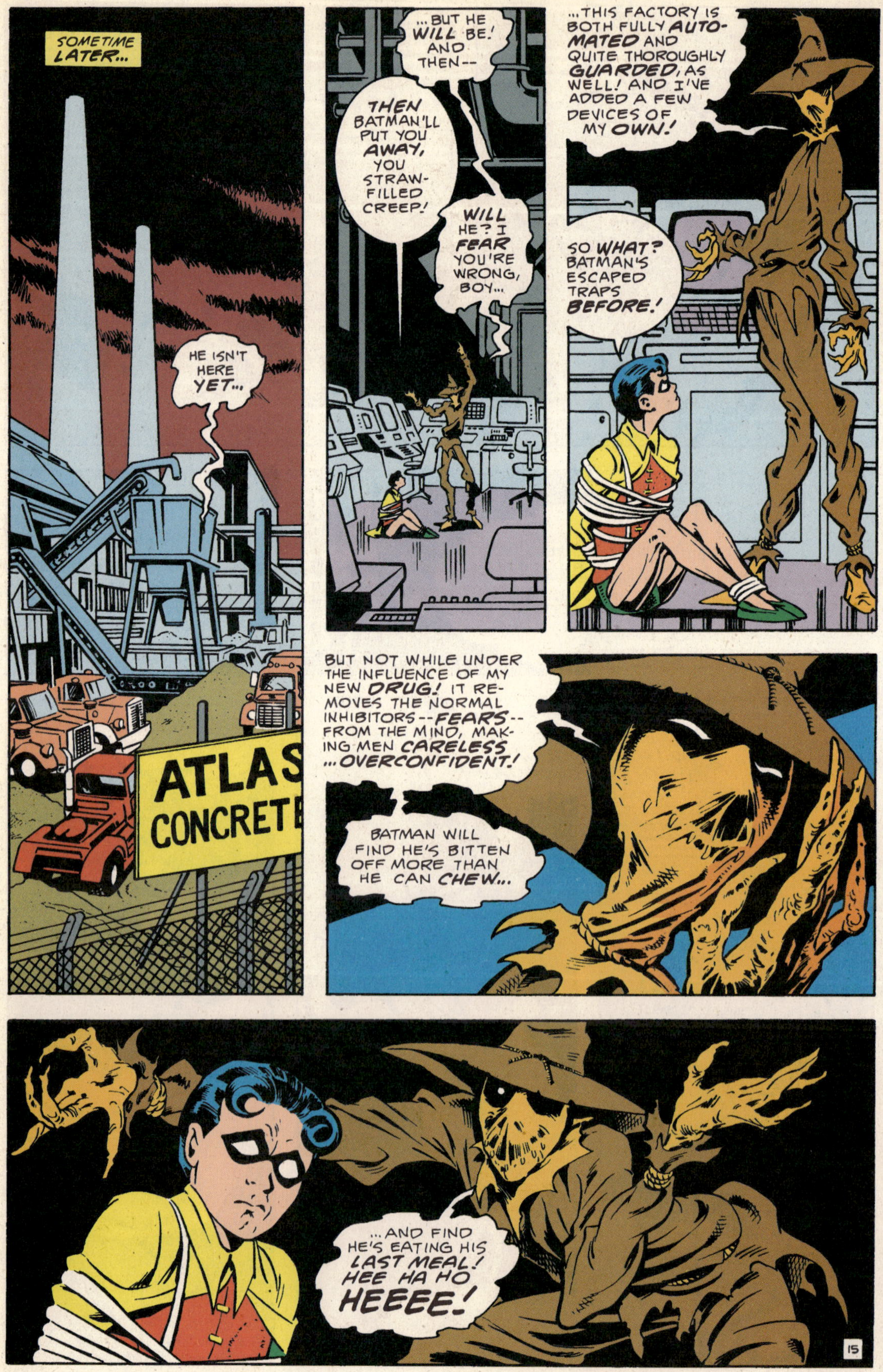
SOMETIME LATER...
HE ISN'T HERE YET...
ATLAS CONCRETE
...BUT HE WILL BE! AND THEN--
THEN BATMAN'LL PUT YOU AWAY, YOU STRAW-FILLED CREEP!
WILL HE? I FEAR YOU'RE WRONG, BOY...
...THIS FACTORY IS BOTH FULLY AUTO-MATED AND QUITE THOROUGHLY GUARDED, AS WELL! AND I'VE ADDED A FEW DEVICES OF MY OWN!
SO WHAT? BATMAN'S ESCAPED TRAPS BEFORE!
BUT NOT WHILE UNDER THE INFLUENCE OF MY NEW DRUG! IT RE-MOVES THE NORMAL INHIBITORS--FEARS--FROM THE MIND, MAK-ING MEN CARELESS ...OVERCONFIDENT!
BATMAN WILL FIND HE'S BITTEN OFF MORE THAN HE CAN CHEW...
...AND FIND HE'S EATING HIS LAST MEAL! HEE HA HO HEEEE!
15

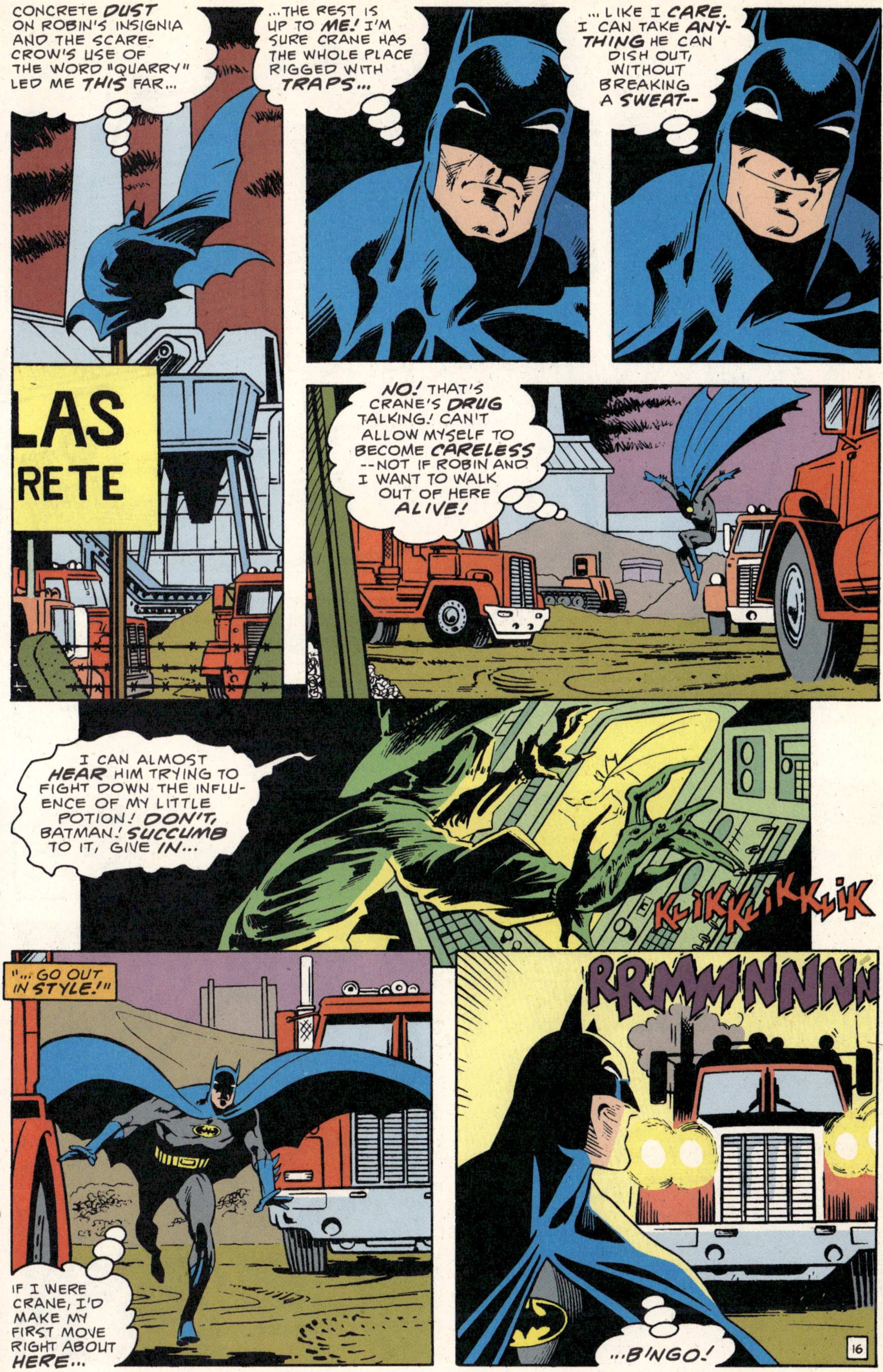
CONCRETE DUST ON ROBIN'S INSIGNIA AND THE SCARE-CROW'S USE OF THE WORD "QUARRY" LED ME THIS FAR...
LAS
RETE
...THE REST IS UP TO ME! I'M SURE CRANE HAS THE WHOLE PLACE RIGGED WITH TRAPS...
...LIKE I CARE. I CAN TAKE ANY-THING HE CAN DISH OUT, WITHOUT BREAKING A SWEAT--
NO! THAT'S CRANE'S DRUG TALKING! CAN'T ALLOW MYSELF TO BECOME CARELESS --NOT IF ROBIN AND I WANT TO WALK OUT OF HERE ALIVE!
I CAN ALMOST HEAR HIM TRYING TO FIGHT DOWN THE INFLU-ENCE OF MY LITTLE POTION! DON'T, BATMAN! SUCCUMB TO IT, GIVE IN...
KLIKKLIKKLIK
"...GO OUT IN STYLE!"
IF I WERE CRANE, I'D MAKE MY FIRST MOVE RIGHT ABOUT HERE...
RRMMNNNN
...BINGO!
16

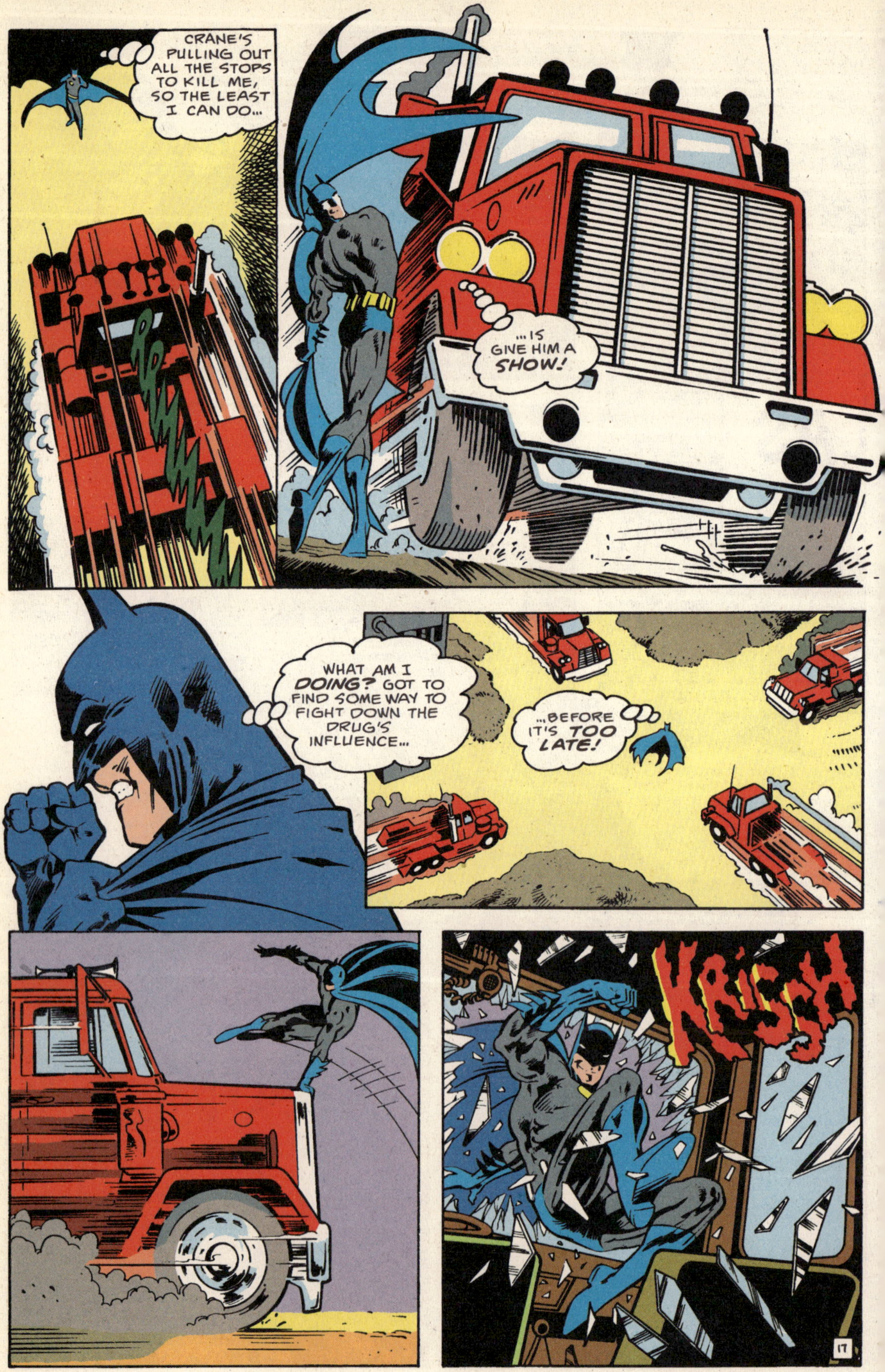
CRANE'S PULLING OUT ALL THE STOPS TO KILL ME, SO THE LEAST I CAN DO...
...IS GIVE HIM A SHOW!
WHAT AM I DOING? GOT TO FIND SOME WAY TO FIGHT DOWN THE DRUG'S INFLUENCE...
...BEFORE IT'S TOO LATE!
KRSSH
17

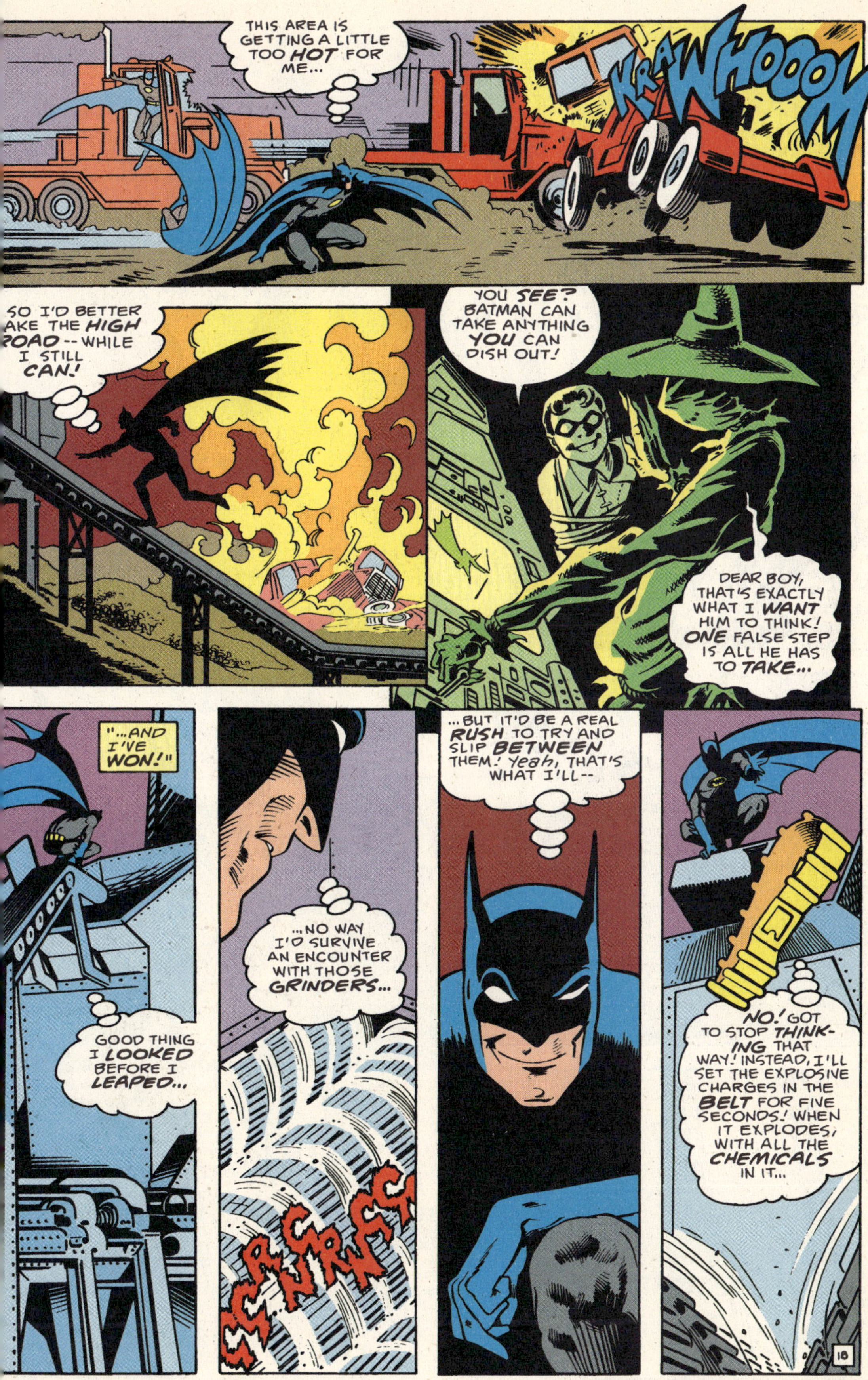

THIS AREA IS GETTING A LITTLE TOO HOT FOR ME...
KRAWHOOOOM
SO I'D BETTER TAKE THE HIGH ROAD -- WHILE I STILL CAN!
YOU SEE? BATMAN CAN TAKE ANYTHING YOU CAN DISH OUT!
DEAR BOY, THAT'S EXACTLY WHAT I WANT HIM TO THINK! ONE FALSE STEP IS ALL HE HAS TO TAKE...
"...AND I'VE WON!"
GOOD THING I LOOKED BEFORE I LEAPED...
...NO WAY I'D SURVIVE AN ENCOUNTER WITH THOSE GRINDERS...
...BUT IT'D BE A REAL RUSH TO TRY AND SLIP BETWEEN THEM! Yeah, THAT'S WHAT I'LL--
NO! GOT TO STOP THINKING THAT WAY! INSTEAD, I'LL SET THE EXPLOSIVE CHARGES IN THE BELT FOR FIVE SECONDS! WHEN IT EXPLODES, WITH ALL THE CHEMICALS IN IT...
10

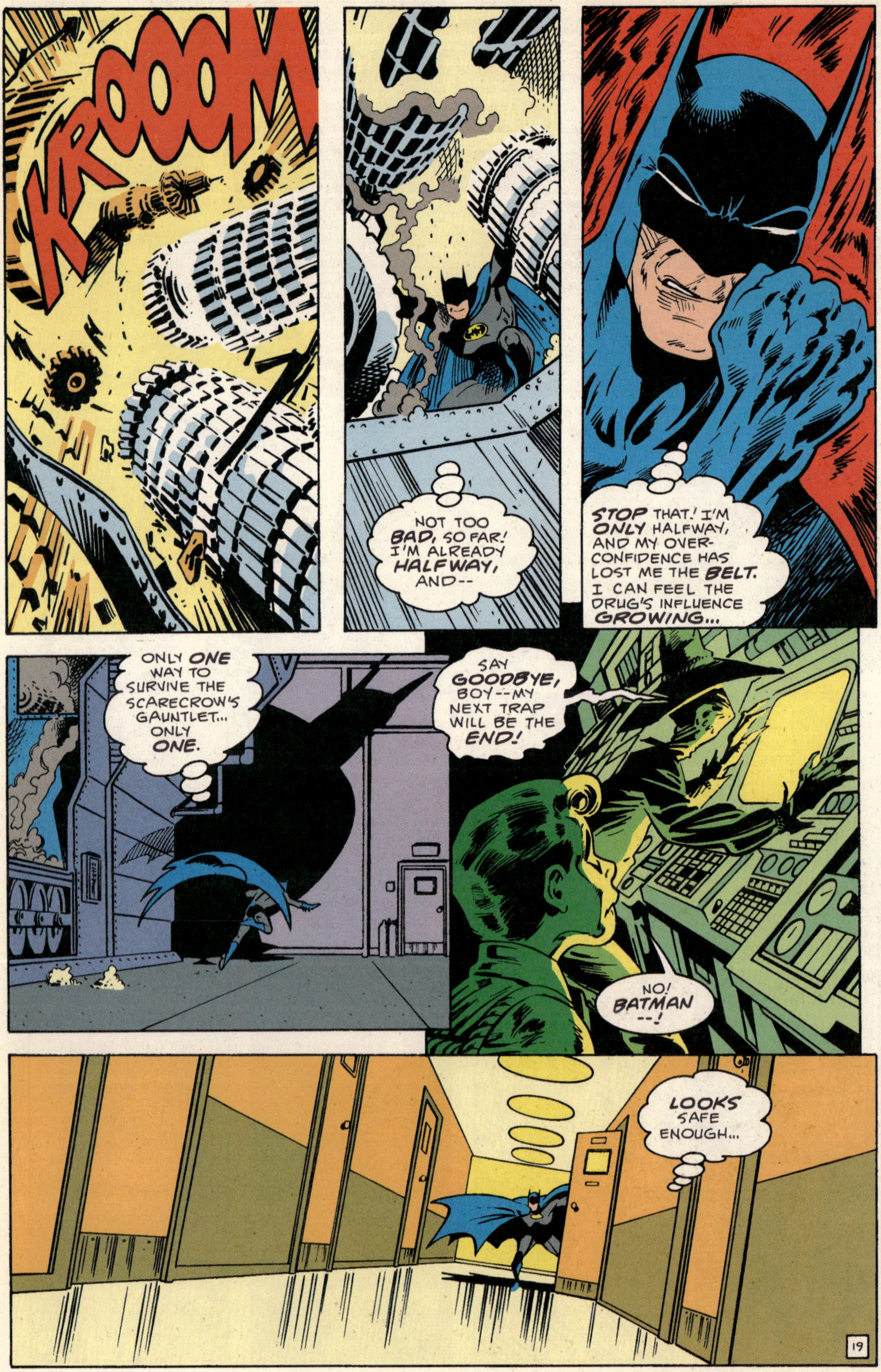
KROOOM
NOT TOO BAD, SO FAR! I'M ALREADY HALFWAY, AND--
STOP THAT! I'M ONLY HALFWAY, AND MY OVER-CONFIDENCE HAS LOST ME THE BELT. I CAN FEEL THE DRUG'S INFLUENCE GROWING...
ONLY ONE WAY TO SURVIVE THE SCARECROW'S GAUNTLET... ONLY ONE.
SAY GOODBYE, BOY--MY NEXT TRAP WILL BE THE END!
NO! BATMAN--!
LOOKS SAFE ENOUGH...
19

...SO *THAT'S* THE *CATCH!* LOOKS LIKE CRANE WANTS ME TO GO *FORWARD*...

...AND IT WOULD BE RUDE TO *REFUSE.*

? A *PIT,* OPENING AHEAD. PROBABLY TOO WIDE TO *LEAP*...

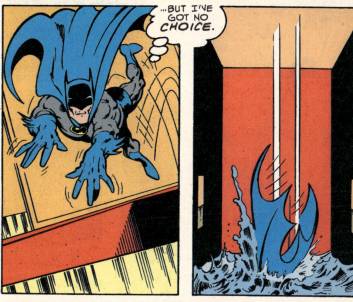

...BUT I'VE GOT NO *CHOICE.*

BRRRRRRTTTTT

ZINNG

SPWEEE

FOR FULLY *TEN* MINUTES, THE PUNISHING BARRAGE CONTINUES...

20

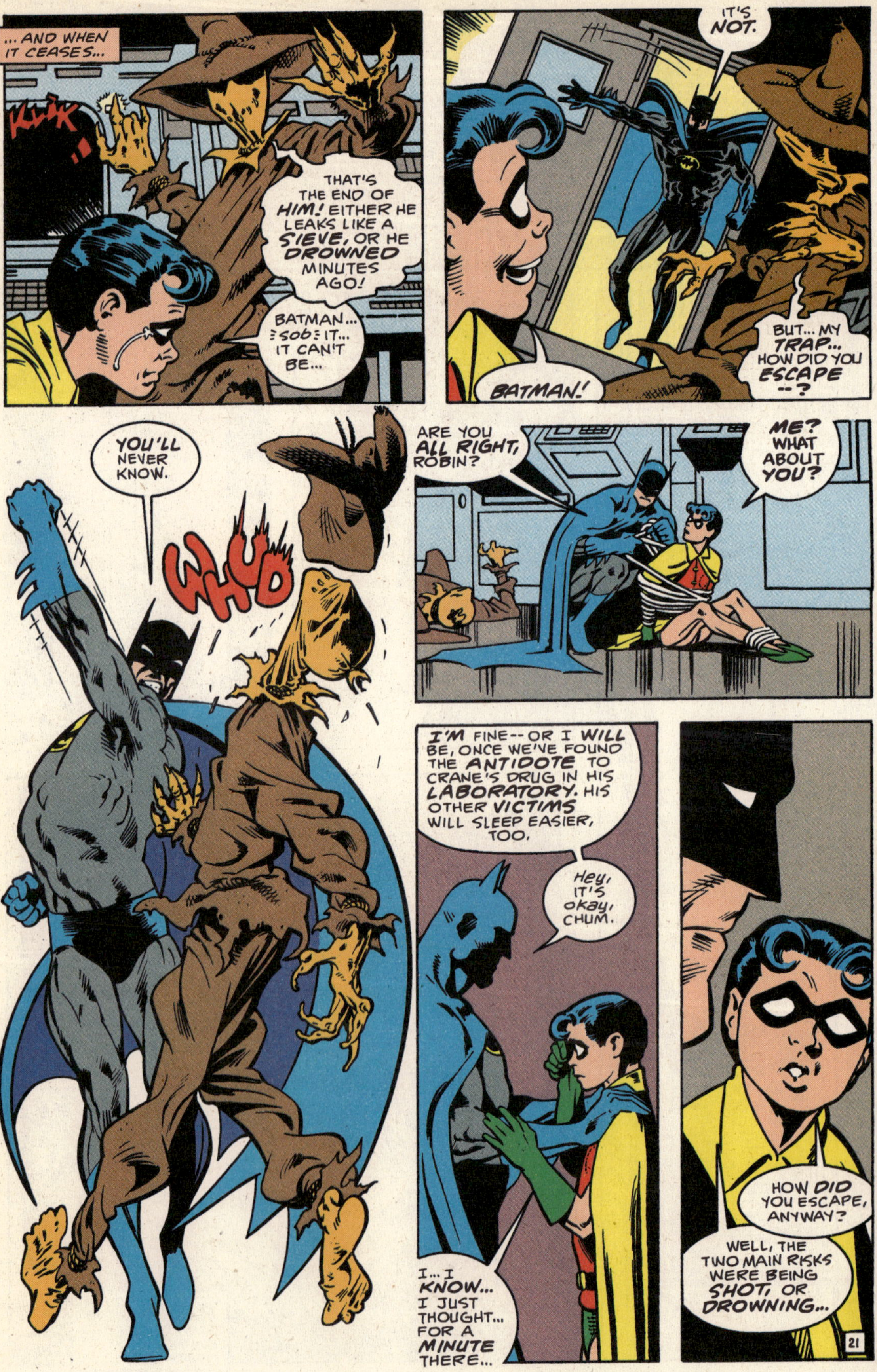
...AND WHEN IT CEASES...
KLIK
THAT'S THE END OF HIM! EITHER HE LEAKS LIKE A SIEVE, OR HE DROWNED MINUTES AGO!
BATMAN... sob IT... IT CAN'T BE...
IT'S NOT.
BATMAN!
BUT... MY TRAP... HOW DID YOU ESCAPE --?
YOU'LL NEVER KNOW.
WHUD
ARE YOU ALL RIGHT, ROBIN?
ME? WHAT ABOUT YOU?
I'M FINE-- OR I WILL BE, ONCE WE'VE FOUND THE ANTIDOTE TO CRANE'S DRUG IN HIS LABORATORY. HIS OTHER VICTIMS WILL SLEEP EASIER, TOO.
Hey, it's okay, CHUM.
I... I KNOW... I JUST THOUGHT... FOR A MINUTE THERE...
HOW DID YOU ESCAPE, ANYWAY?
WELL, THE TWO MAIN RISKS WERE BEING SHOT, OR DROWNING...
21

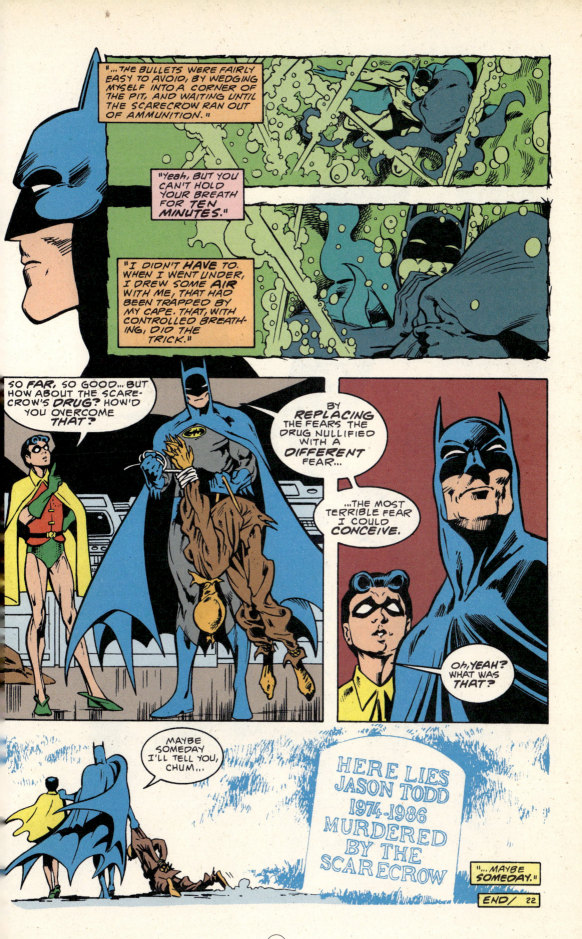

"...THE BULLETS WERE FAIRLY EASY TO AVOID, BY WEDGING MYSELF INTO A CORNER OF THE PIT, AND WAITING UNTIL THE SCARECROW RAN OUT OF AMMUNITION."

"YEAH, BUT YOU CAN'T HOLD YOUR BREATH FOR TEN MINUTES."

"I DIDN'T HAVE TO. WHEN I WENT UNDER, I DREW SOME AIR WITH ME, THAT HAD BEEN TRAPPED BY MY CAPE. THAT, WITH CONTROLLED BREATHING, DID THE TRICK."

SO FAR, SO GOOD... BUT HOW ABOUT THE SCARE-CROW'S DRUG? HOW'D YOU OVERCOME THAT?

BY REPLACING THE FEARS THE DRUG NULLIFIED WITH A DIFFERENT FEAR...

...THE MOST TERRIBLE FEAR I COULD CONCEIVE.

OH, YEAH? WHAT WAS THAT?

MAYBE SOMEDAY I'LL TELL YOU, CHUM...

HERE LIES JASON TODD 1974-1986 MURDERED BY THE SCARECROW

"...MAYBE SOMEDAY."

END/ 22

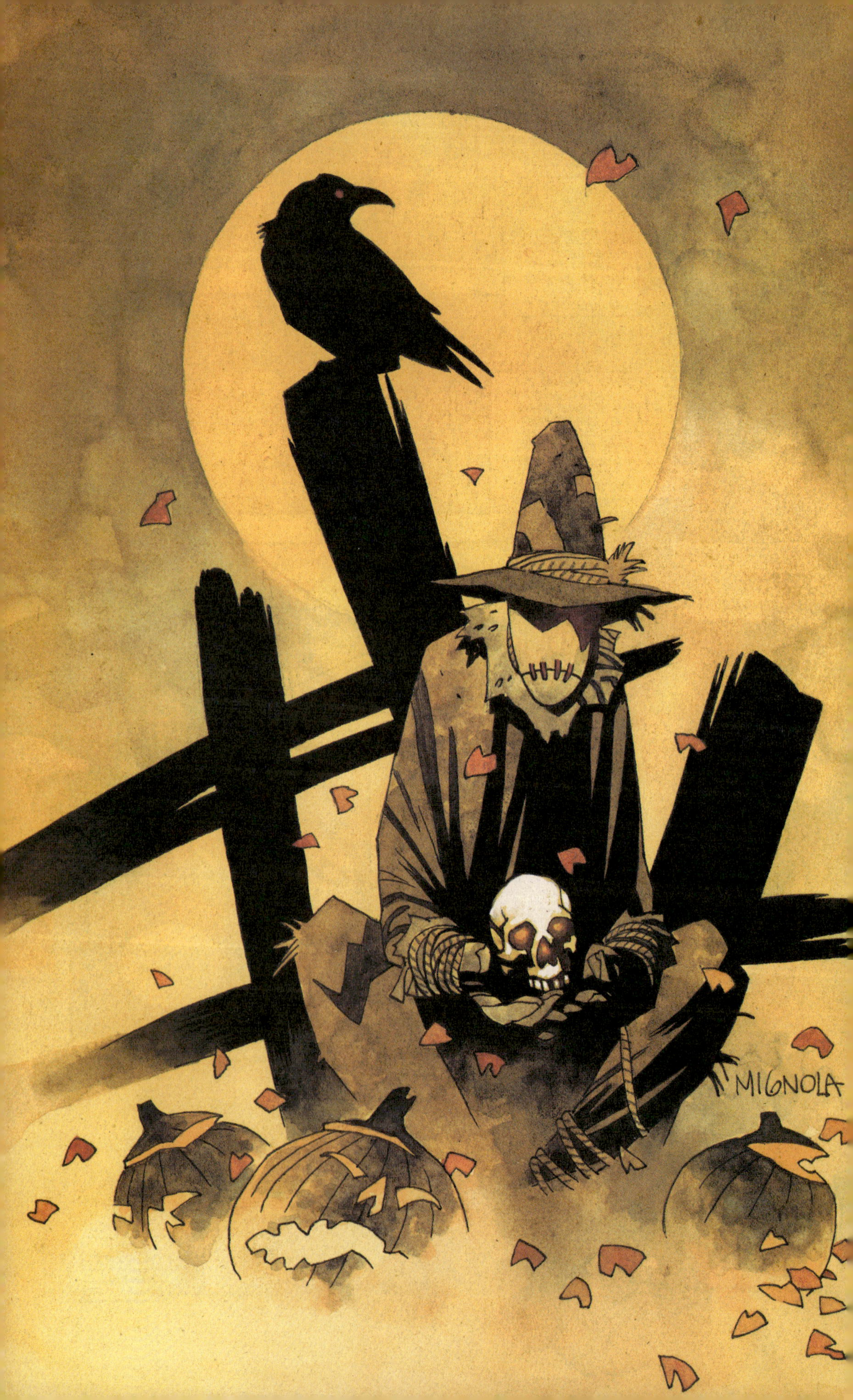
MIGNOLA

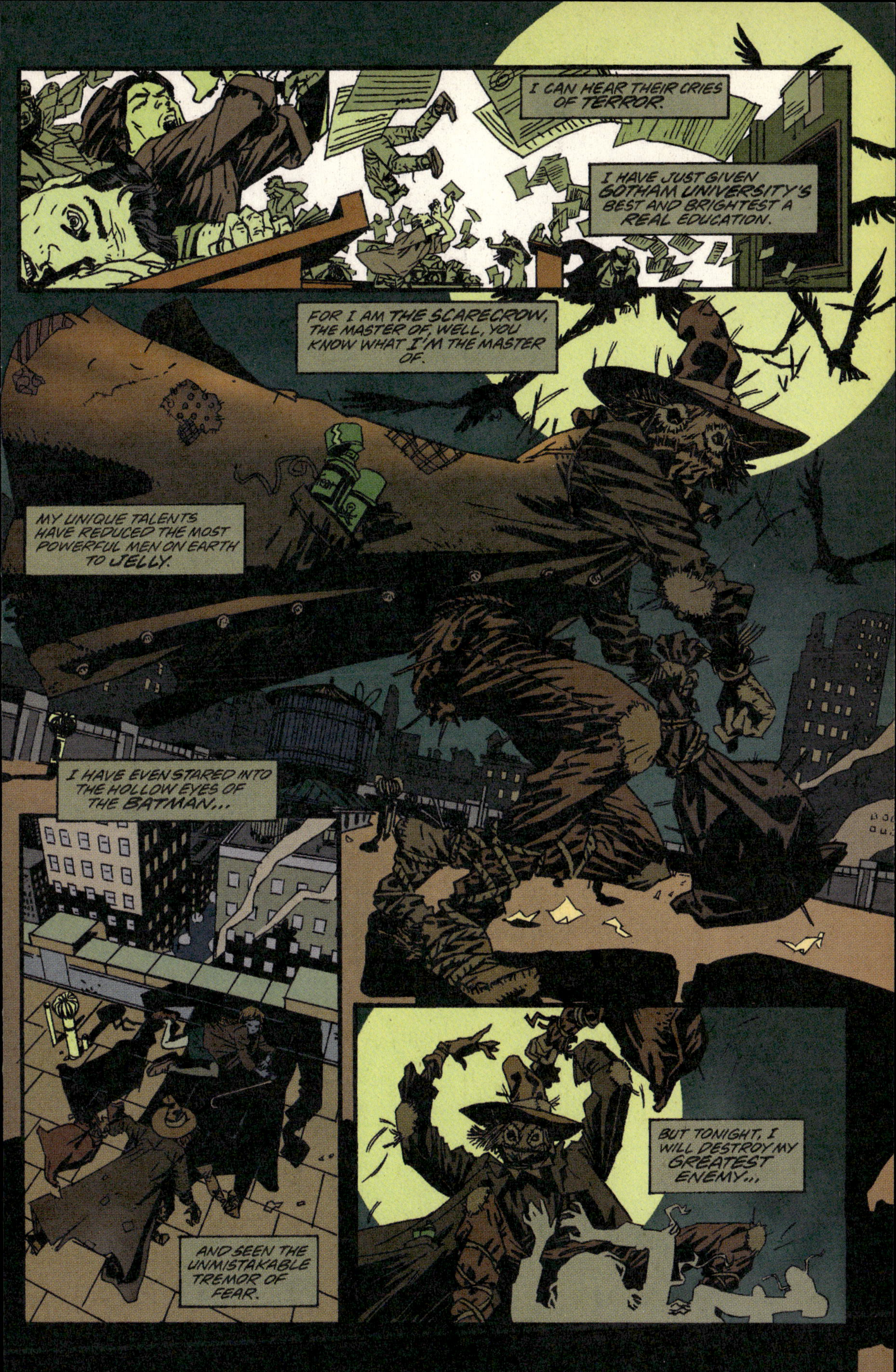
I CAN HEAR THEIR CRIES OF TERROR.
I HAVE JUST GIVEN GOTHAM UNIVERSITY'S BEST AND BRIGHTEST A REAL EDUCATION.
FOR I AM THE SCARECROW, THE MASTER OF, WELL, YOU KNOW WHAT I'M THE MASTER OF.
MY UNIQUE TALENTS HAVE REDUCED THE MOST POWERFUL MEN ON EARTH TO JELLY.
I HAVE EVEN STARED INTO THE HOLLOW EYES OF THE BATMAN...
AND SEEN THE UNMISTAKABLE TREMOR OF FEAR.
BUT TONIGHT, I WILL DESTROY MY GREATEST ENEMY...

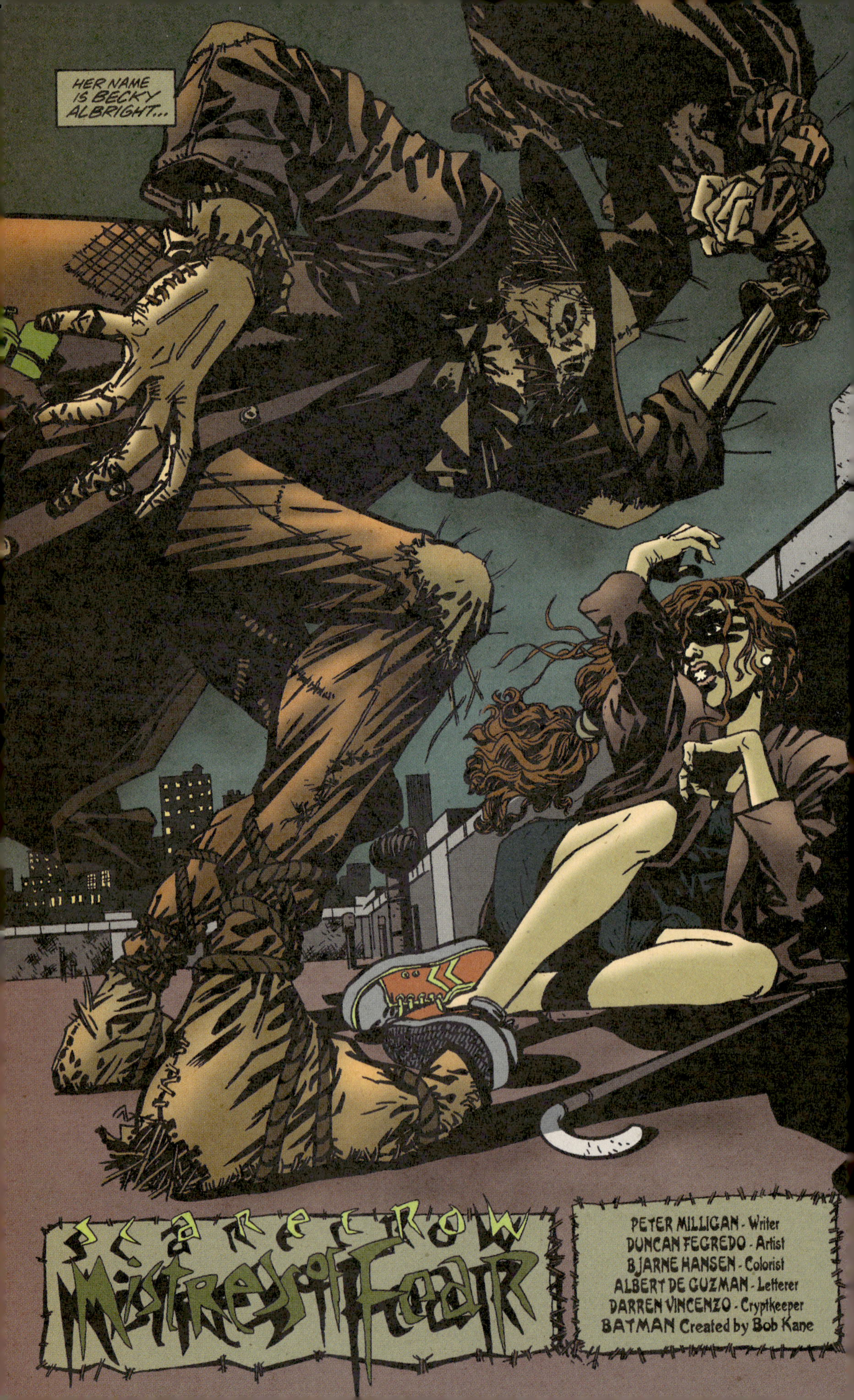
HER NAME IS BECKY ALBRIGHT...
SCARECROW
Mistress of Fear
PETER MILLIGAN - Writer
DUNCAN FEGREDO - Artist
BJARNE HANSEN - Colorist
ALBERT DE GUZMAN - Letterer
DARREN VINCENZO - Cryptkeeper
BATMAN Created by Bob Kane

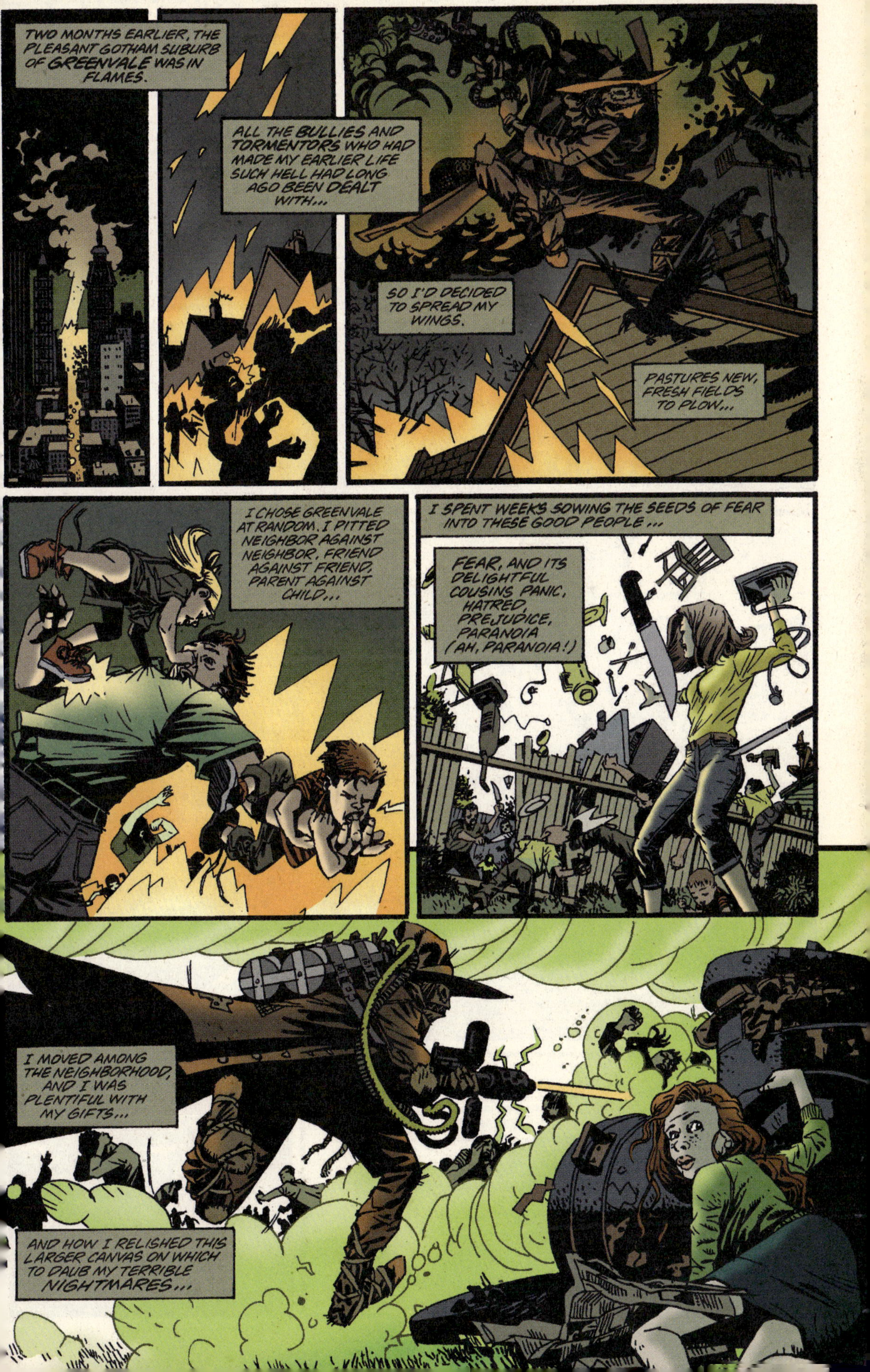

TWO MONTHS EARLIER, THE PLEASANT GOTHAM SUBURB OF GREENVALE WAS IN FLAMES.
ALL THE BULLIES AND TORMENTORS WHO HAD MADE MY EARLIER LIFE SUCH HELL HAD LONG AGO BEEN DEALT WITH...
SO I'D DECIDED TO SPREAD MY WINGS.
PASTURES NEW, FRESH FIELDS TO PLOW...
I CHOSE GREENVALE AT RANDOM. I PITTED NEIGHBOR AGAINST NEIGHBOR, FRIEND AGAINST FRIEND, PARENT AGAINST CHILD...
I SPENT WEEKS SOWING THE SEEDS OF FEAR INTO THESE GOOD PEOPLE...
FEAR, AND ITS DELIGHTFUL COUSINS PANIC, HATRED, PREJUDICE, PARANOIA (AH, PARANOIA!)
I MOVED AMONG THE NEIGHBORHOOD, AND I WAS PLENTIFUL WITH MY GIFTS...
AND HOW I RELISHED THIS LARGER CANVAS ON WHICH TO DAUB MY TERRIBLE NIGHTMARES...

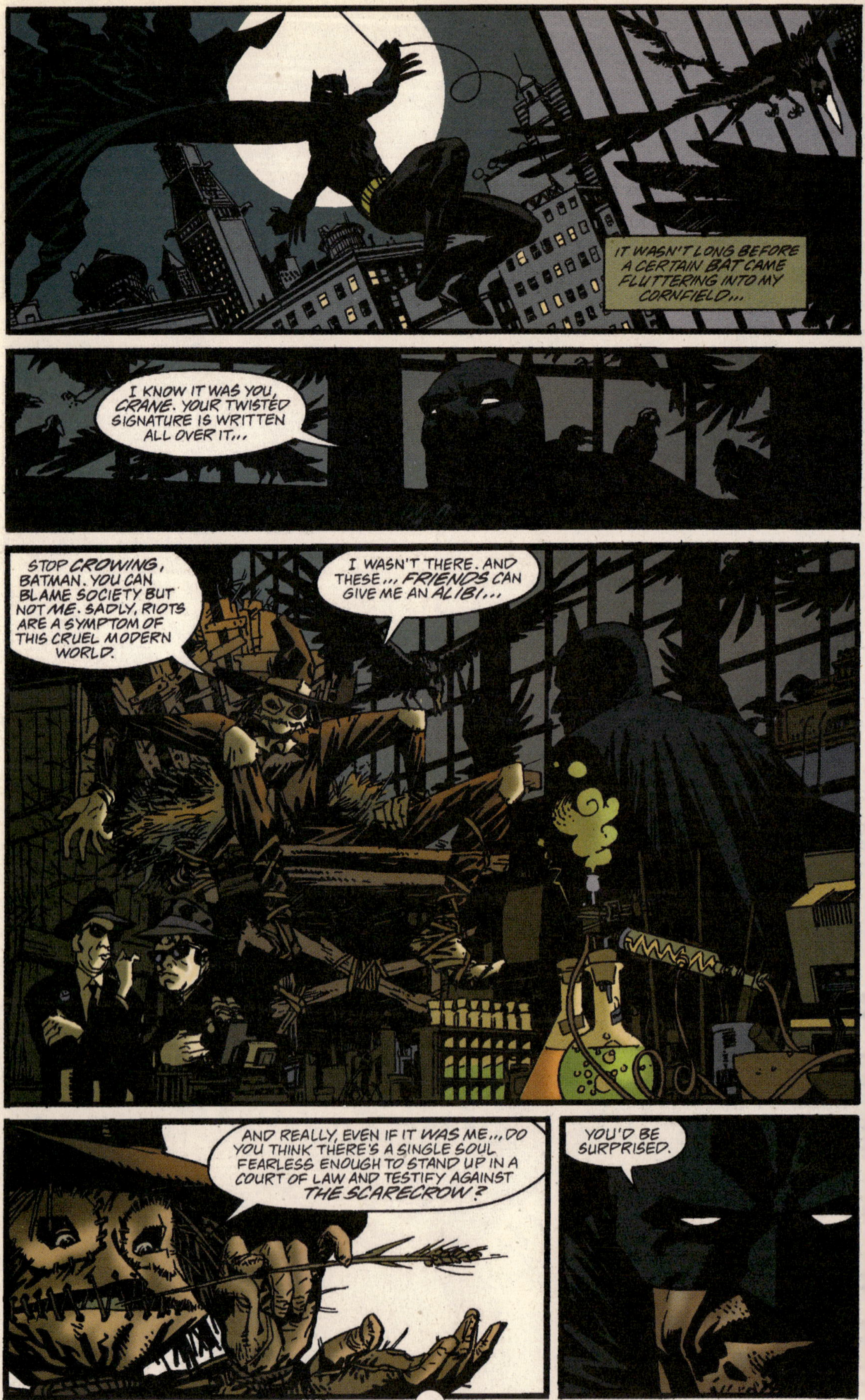
IT WASN'T LONG BEFORE A CERTAIN BAT CAME FLUTTERING INTO MY CORNFIELD...
I KNOW IT WAS YOU, CRANE. YOUR TWISTED SIGNATURE IS WRITTEN ALL OVER IT...
STOP CROWING, BATMAN. YOU CAN BLAME SOCIETY BUT NOT ME. SADLY, RIOTS ARE A SYMPTOM OF THIS CRUEL MODERN WORLD.
I WASN'T THERE. AND THESE... FRIENDS CAN GIVE ME AN ALIBI...
AND REALLY, EVEN IF IT WAS ME... DO YOU THINK THERE'S A SINGLE SOUL FEARLESS ENOUGH TO STAND UP IN A COURT OF LAW AND TESTIFY AGAINST THE SCARECROW?
YOU'D BE SURPRISED.

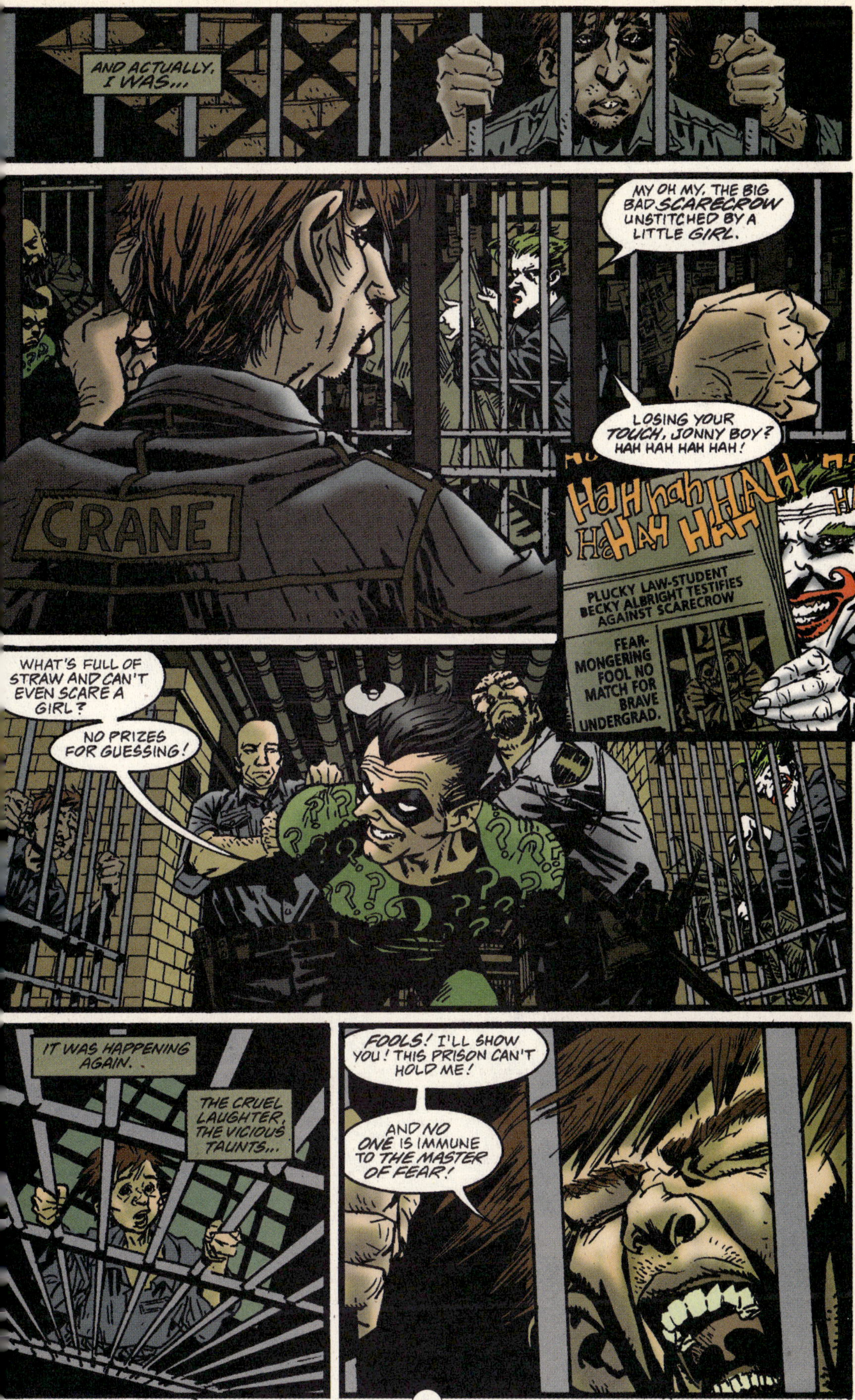

AND ACTUALLY, I WAS...
MY OH MY, THE BIG BAD SCARECROW UNSTITCHED BY A LITTLE GIRL.
CRANE
LOSING YOUR TOUCH, JONNY BOY? HAH HAH HAH HAH!
HaH hah HAH HaHAH HAH
PLUCKY LAW-STUDENT BECKY ALBRIGHT TESTIFIES AGAINST SCARECROW
FEAR-MONGERING FOOL NO MATCH FOR BRAVE UNDERGRAD.
WHAT'S FULL OF STRAW AND CAN'T EVEN SCARE A GIRL?
NO PRIZES FOR GUESSING!
IT WAS HAPPENING AGAIN.
THE CRUEL LAUGHTER, THE VICIOUS TAUNTS...
FOOLS! I'LL SHOW YOU! THIS PRISON CAN'T HOLD ME!
AND NO ONE IS IMMUNE TO THE MASTER OF FEAR!

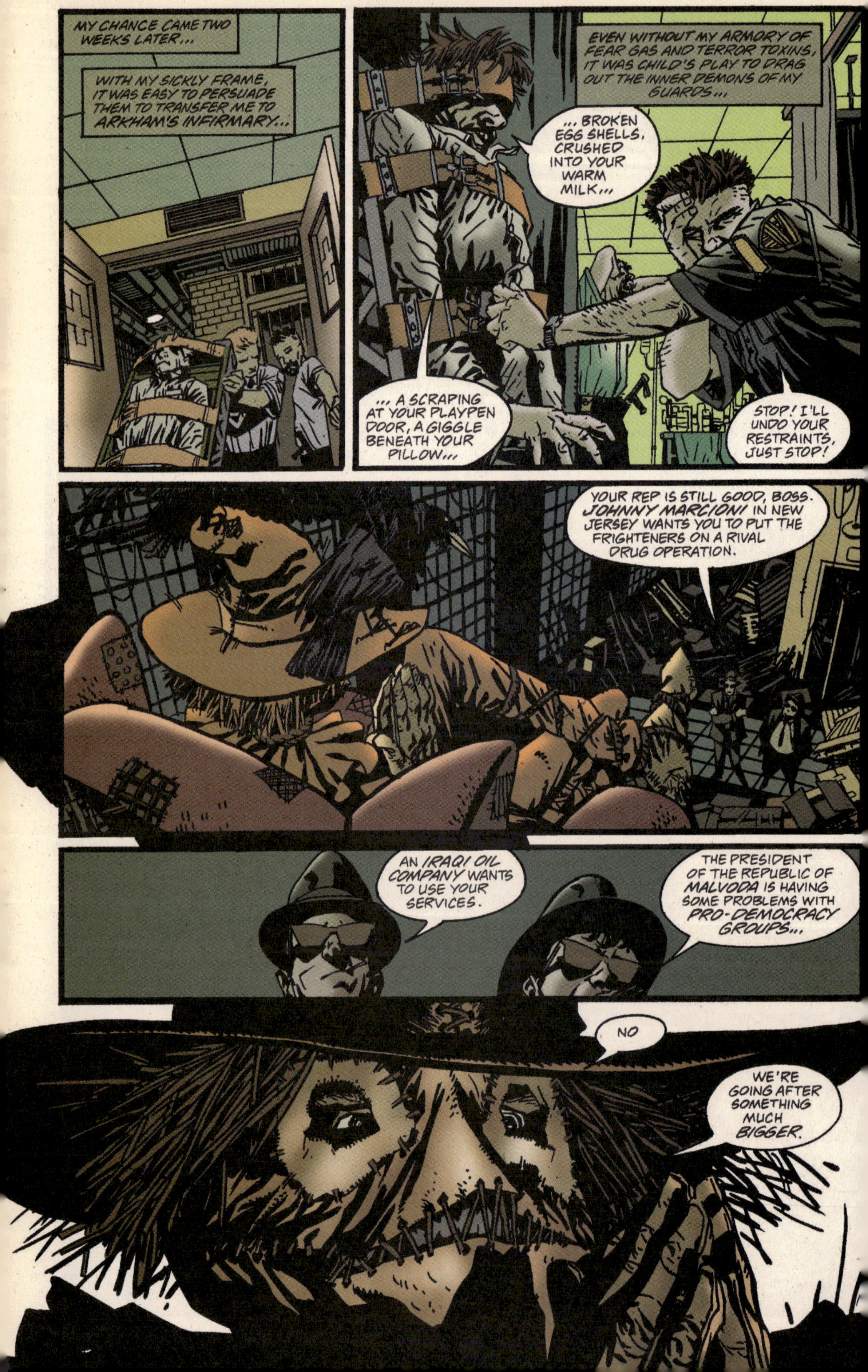
MY CHANCE CAME TWO WEEKS LATER...
WITH MY SICKLY FRAME, IT WAS EASY TO PERSUADE THEM TO TRANSFER ME TO ARKHAM'S INFIRMARY...
EVEN WITHOUT MY ARMORY OF FEAR GAS AND TERROR TOXINS, IT WAS CHILD'S PLAY TO DRAG OUT THE INNER DEMONS OF MY GUARDS...
...BROKEN EGG SHELLS, CRUSHED INTO YOUR WARM MILK...
...A SCRAPING AT YOUR PLAYPEN DOOR, A GIGGLE BENEATH YOUR PILLOW...
STOP! I'LL UNDO YOUR RESTRAINTS, JUST STOP!
YOUR REP IS STILL GOOD, BOSS. JOHNNY MARCIONI IN NEW JERSEY WANTS YOU TO PUT THE FRIGHTENERS ON A RIVAL DRUG OPERATION.
AN IRAQI OIL COMPANY WANTS TO USE YOUR SERVICES.
THE PRESIDENT OF THE REPUBLIC OF MALVODA IS HAVING SOME PROBLEMS WITH PRO-DEMOCRACY GROUPS...
NO
WE'RE GOING AFTER SOMETHING MUCH BIGGER.

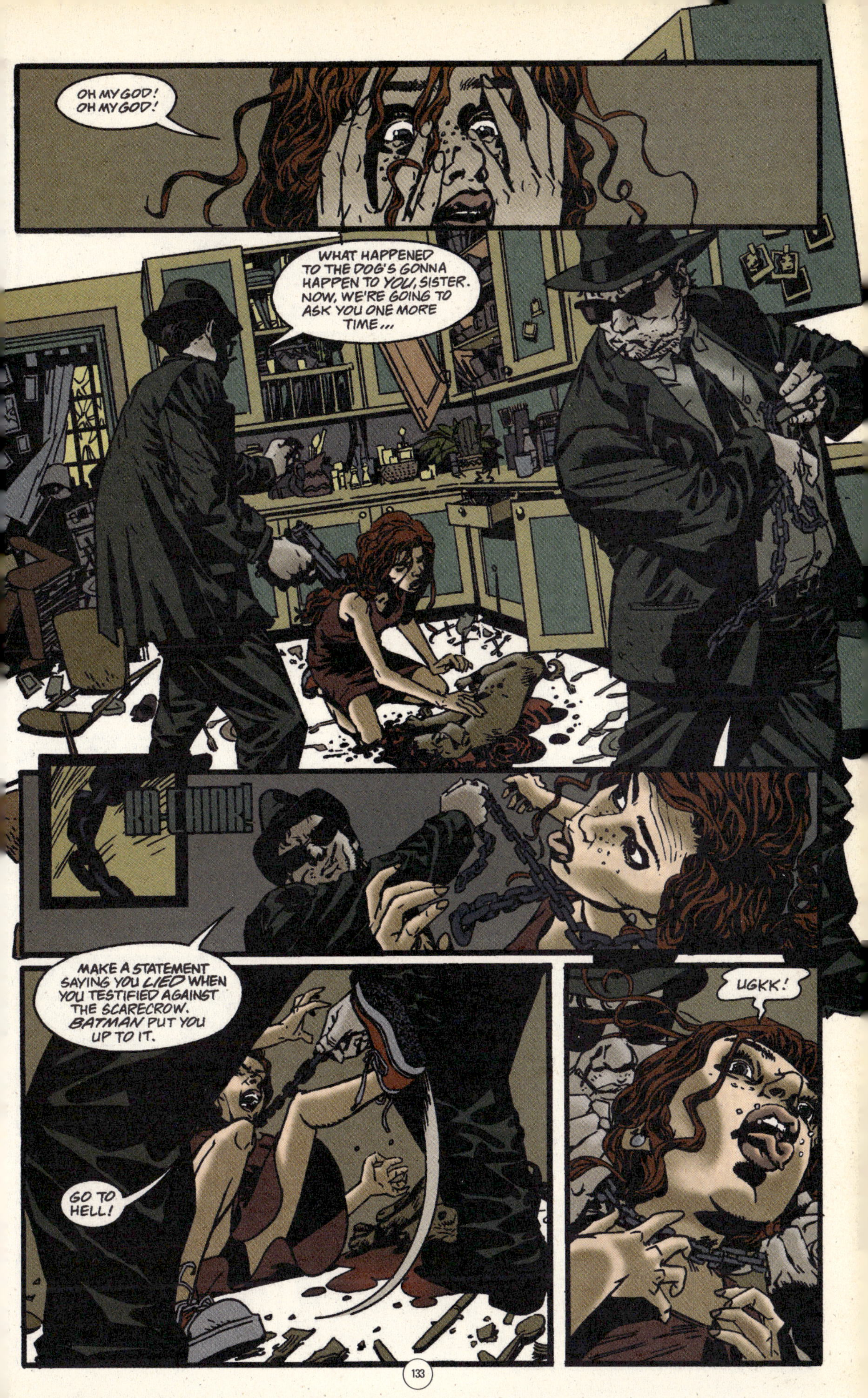

OH MY GOD! OH MY GOD!
WHAT HAPPENED TO THE DOG'S GONNA HAPPEN TO YOU, SISTER. NOW, WE'RE GOING TO ASK YOU ONE MORE TIME...
KA-CHINK!
MAKE A STATEMENT SAYING YOU LIED WHEN YOU TESTIFIED AGAINST THE SCARECROW. BATMAN PUT YOU UP TO IT.
GO TO HELL!
UGKK!

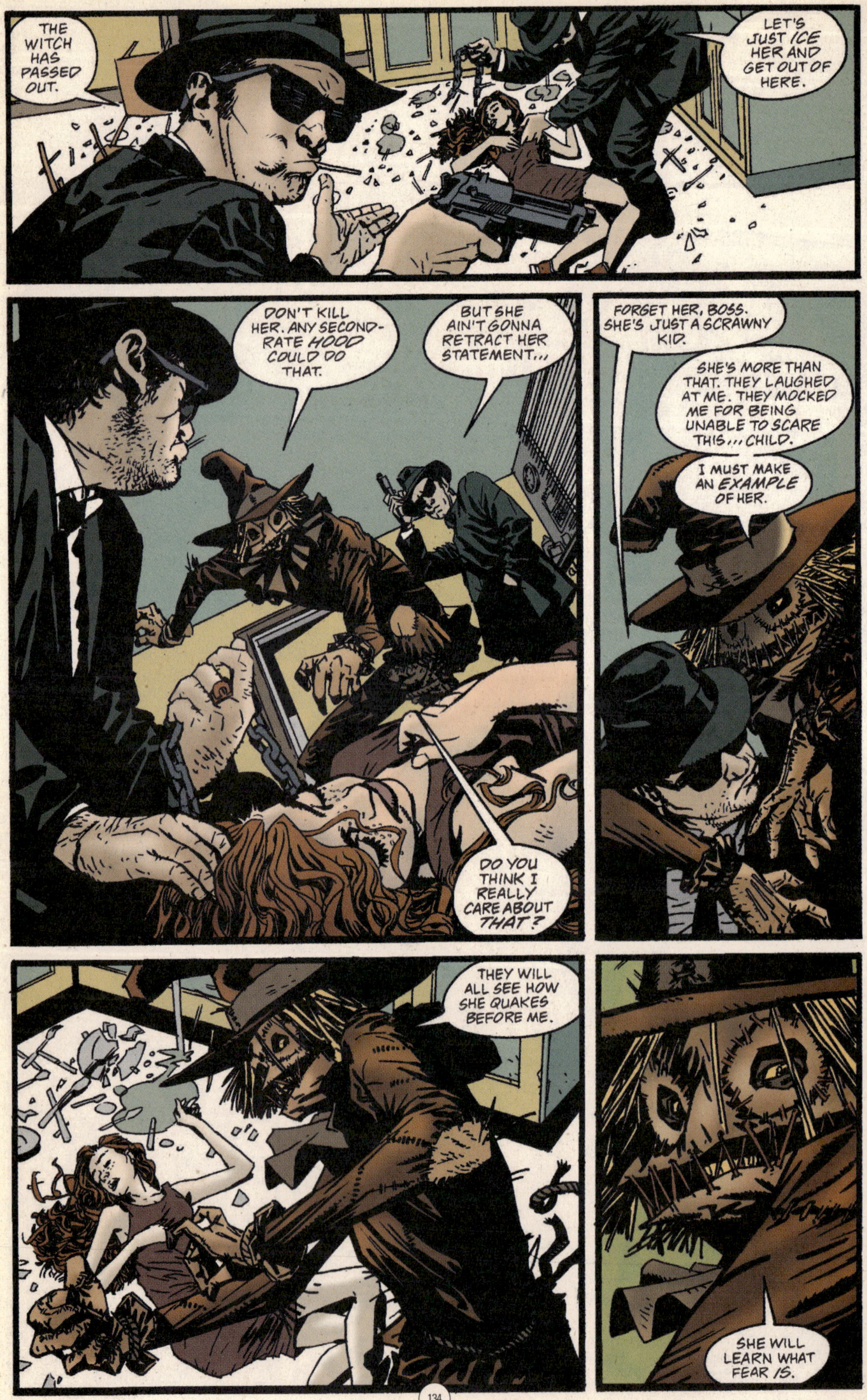
THE WITCH HAS PASSED OUT.
LET'S JUST ICE HER AND GET OUT OF HERE.
DON'T KILL HER. ANY SECOND-RATE HOOD COULD DO THAT.
BUT SHE AIN'T GONNA RETRACT HER STATEMENT...
DO YOU THINK I REALLY CARE ABOUT THAT?
FORGET HER, BOSS. SHE'S JUST A SCRAWNY KID.
SHE'S MORE THAN THAT. THEY LAUGHED AT ME. THEY MOCKED ME FOR BEING UNABLE TO SCARE THIS... CHILD.
I MUST MAKE AN EXAMPLE OF HER.
THEY WILL ALL SEE HOW SHE QUAKES BEFORE ME.
SHE WILL LEARN WHAT FEAR IS.

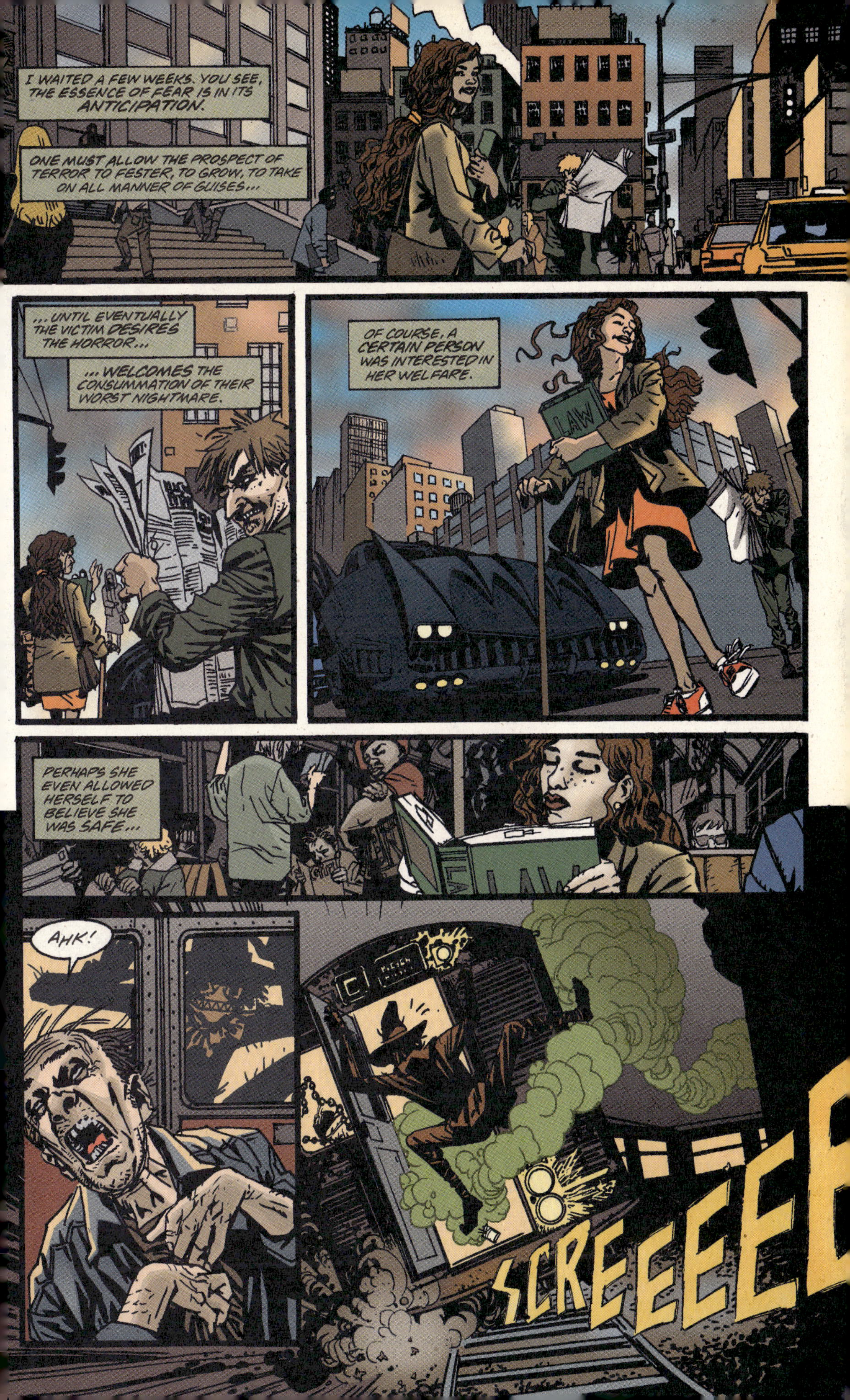
I WAITED A FEW WEEKS. YOU SEE, THE ESSENCE OF FEAR IS IN ITS ANTICIPATION.
ONE MUST ALLOW THE PROSPECT OF TERROR TO FESTER, TO GROW, TO TAKE ON ALL MANNER OF GUISES...
...UNTIL EVENTUALLY THE VICTIM DESIRES THE HORROR...
...WELCOMES THE CONSUMMATION OF THEIR WORST NIGHTMARE.
OF COURSE, A CERTAIN PERSON WAS INTERESTED IN HER WELFARE.
LAW
PERHAPS SHE EVEN ALLOWED HERSELF TO BELIEVE SHE WAS SAFE...
AHK!
SCREEEEE

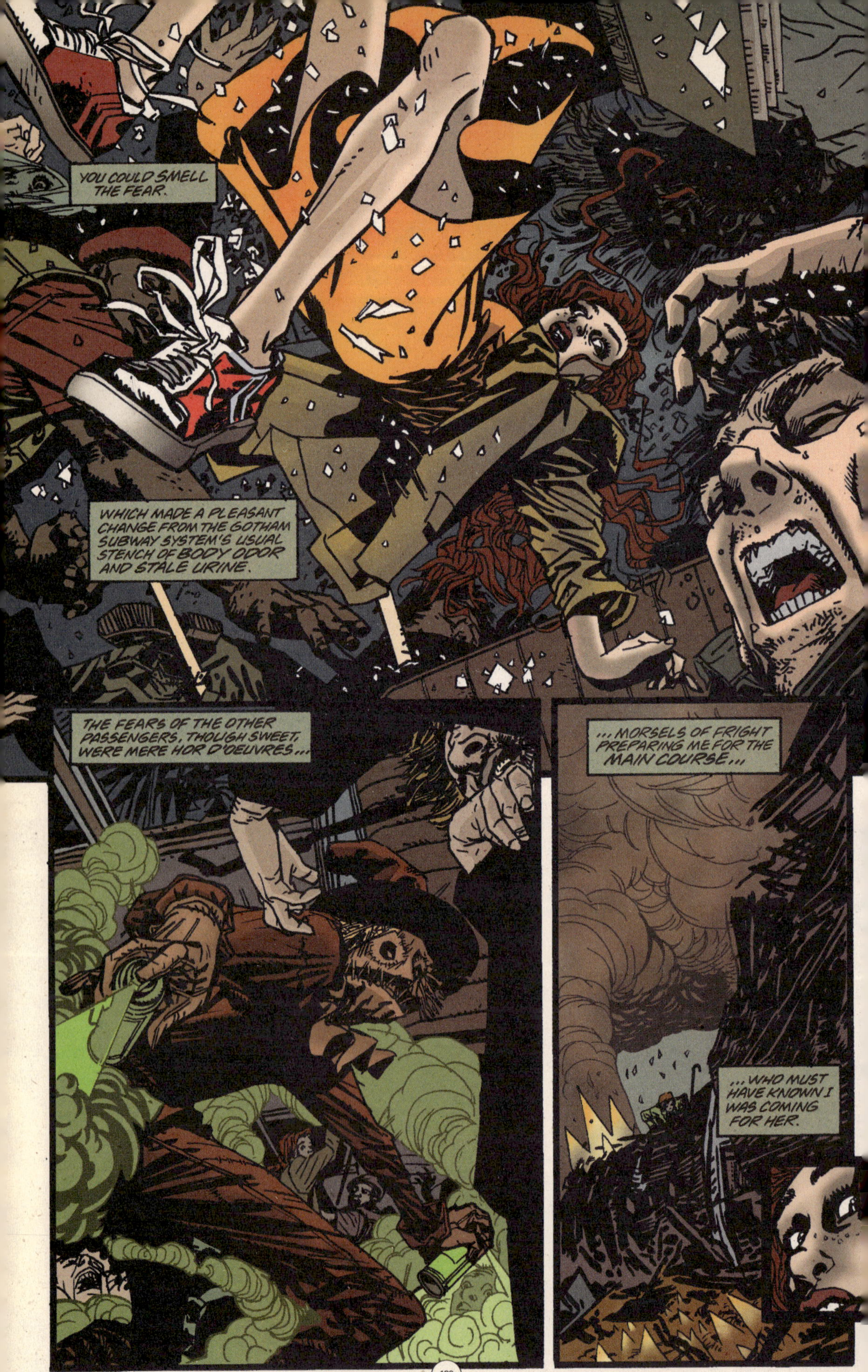
YOU COULD SMELL THE FEAR.
WHICH MADE A PLEASANT CHANGE FROM THE GOTHAM SUBWAY SYSTEM'S USUAL STENCH OF BODY ODOR AND STALE URINE.
THE FEARS OF THE OTHER PASSENGERS, THOUGH SWEET, WERE MERE HOR D'OEUVRES...
...MORSELS OF FRIGHT PREPARING ME FOR THE MAIN COURSE...
...WHO MUST HAVE KNOWN I WAS COMING FOR HER.

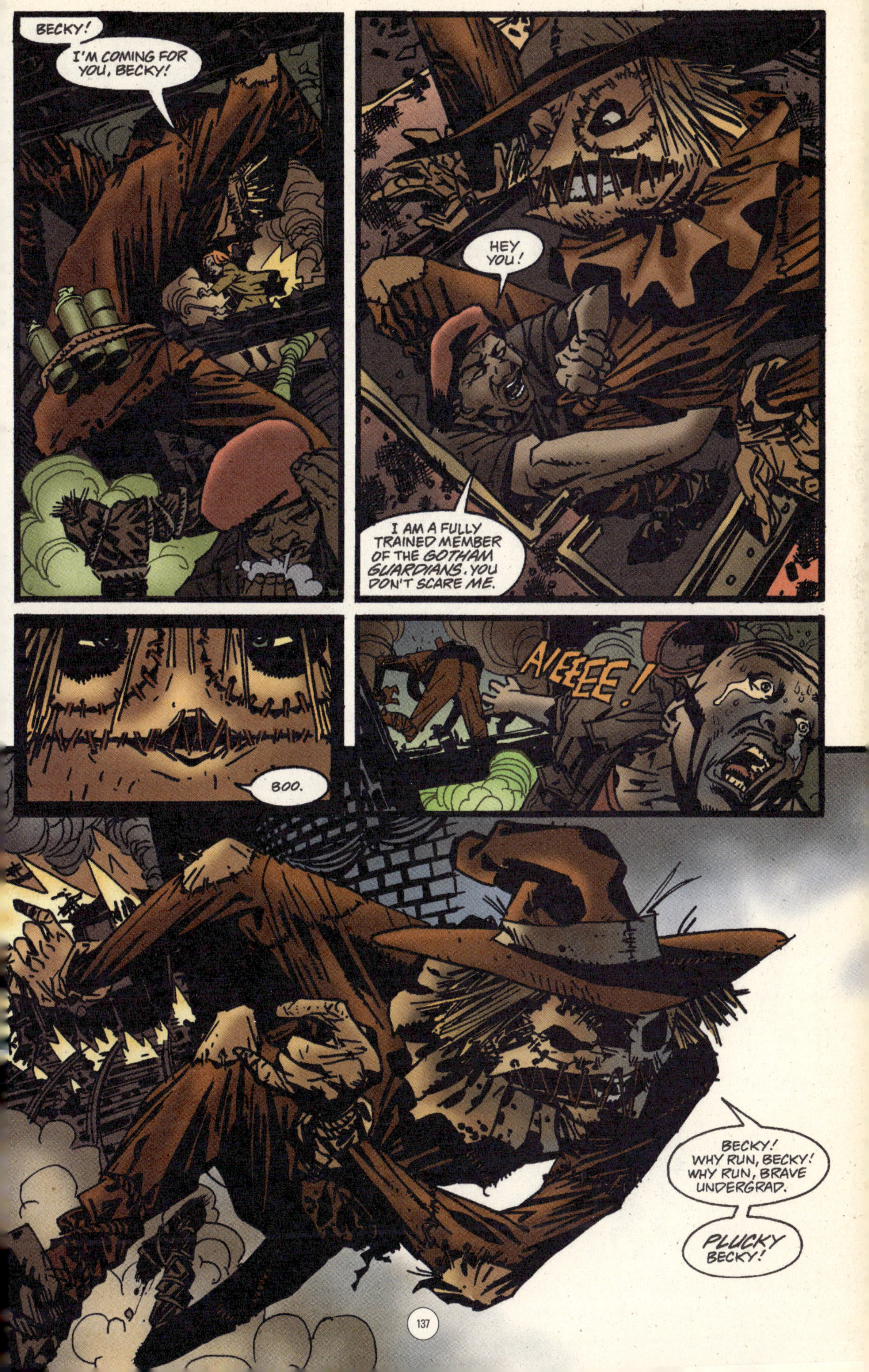
BECKY!
I'M COMING FOR YOU, BECKY!
HEY YOU!
I AM A FULLY TRAINED MEMBER OF THE GOTHAM GUARDIANS. YOU DON'T SCARE ME.
BOO.
AIEEEEE!
BECKY! WHY RUN, BECKY! WHY RUN, BRAVE UNDERGRAD.
PLUCKY BECKY!

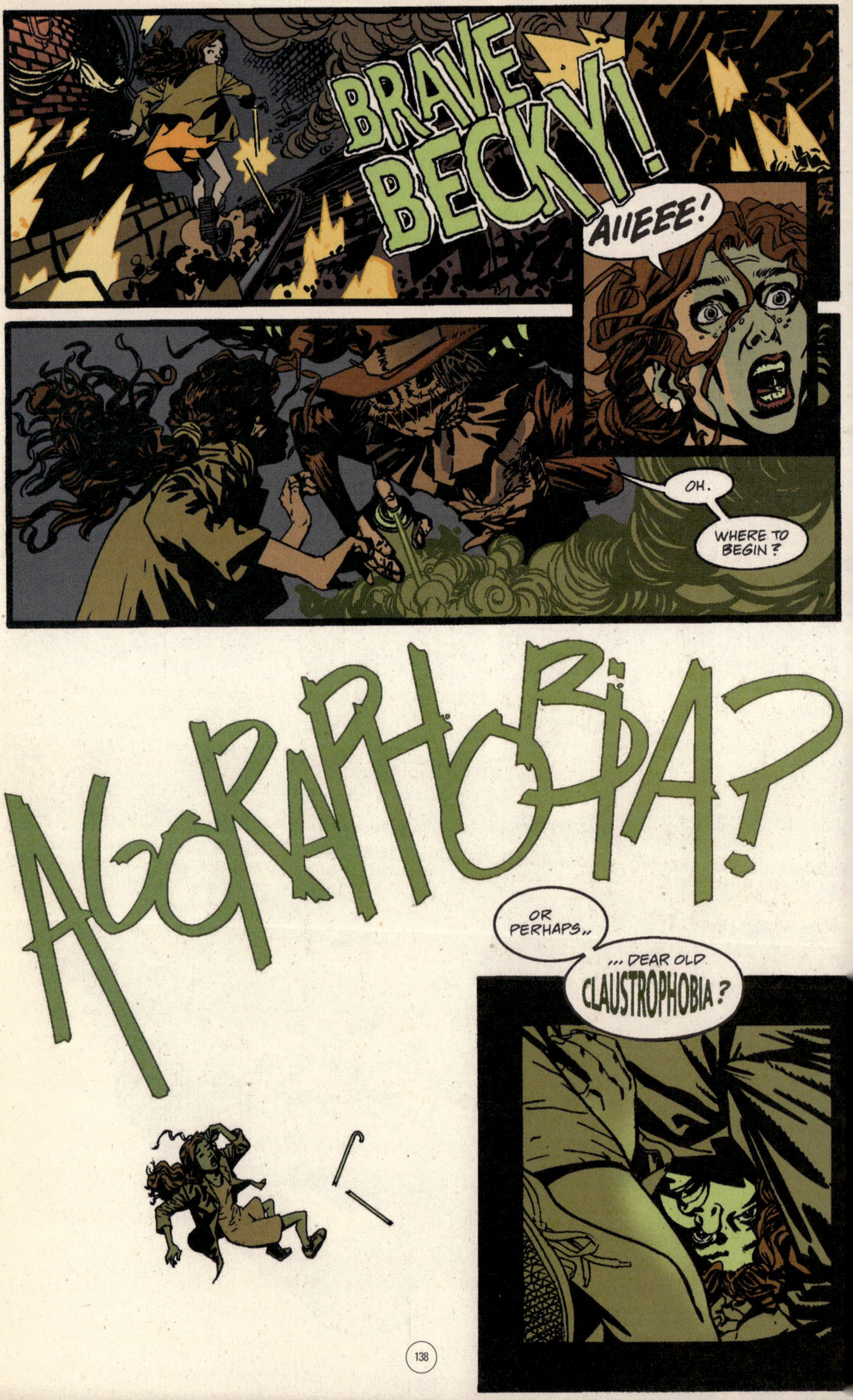
BRAVE BECKY!
AIIEEE!
OH.
WHERE TO BEGIN?
AGORAPHOBIA?
OR PERHAPS..
...DEAR OLD CLAUSTROPHOBIA?

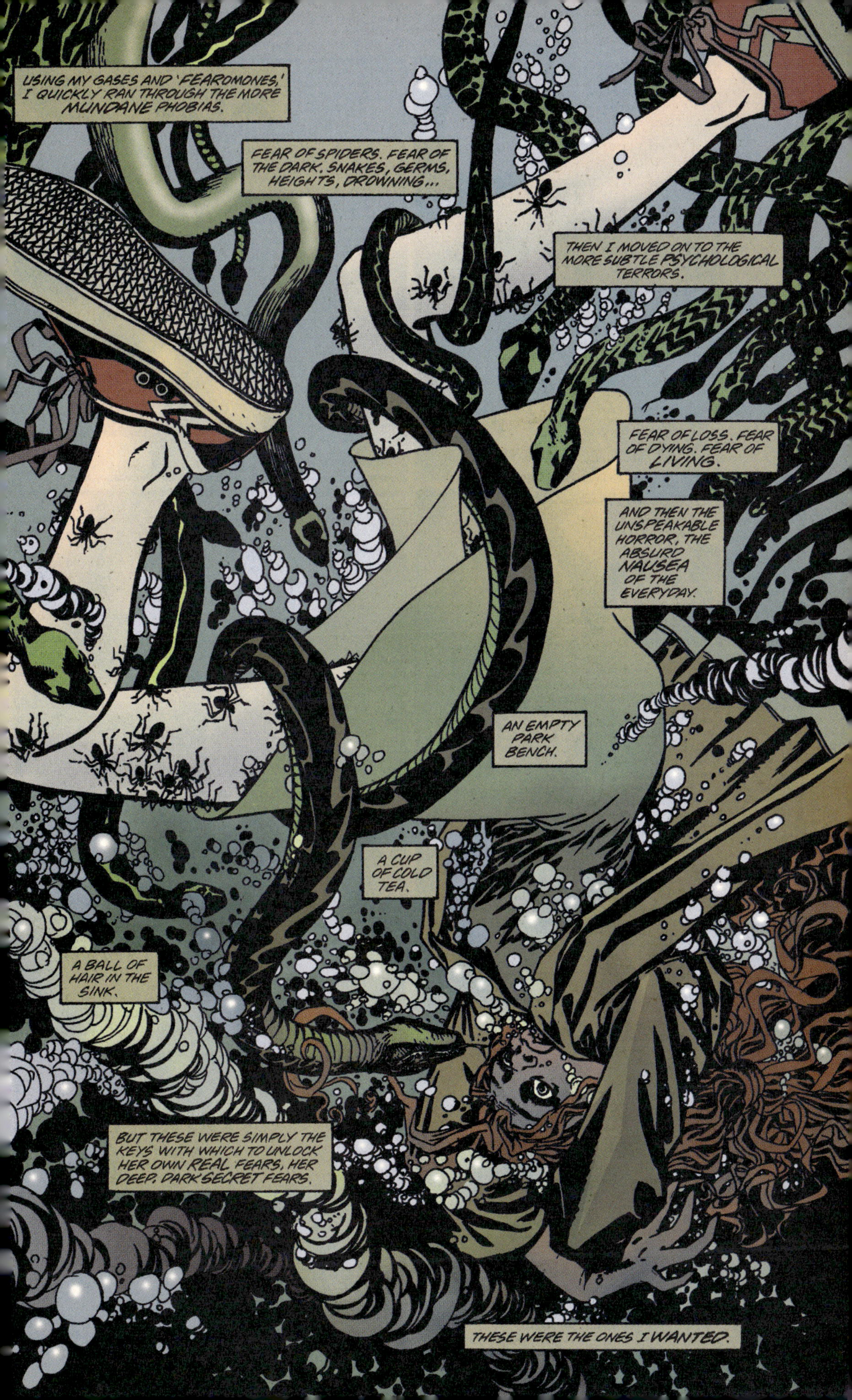

USING MY GASES AND 'FEAROMONES,' I QUICKLY RAN THROUGH THE MORE MUNDANE PHOBIAS.
FEAR OF SPIDERS. FEAR OF THE DARK. SNAKES, GERMS, HEIGHTS, DROWNING...
THEN I MOVED ON TO THE MORE SUBTLE PSYCHOLOGICAL TERRORS.
FEAR OF LOSS. FEAR OF DYING. FEAR OF LIVING.
AND THEN THE UNSPEAKABLE HORROR, THE ABSURD NAUSEA OF THE EVERYDAY.
AN EMPTY PARK BENCH.
A CUP OF COLD TEA.
A BALL OF HAIR IN THE SINK.
BUT THESE WERE SIMPLY THE KEYS WITH WHICH TO UNLOCK HER OWN REAL FEARS. HER DEEP, DARK SECRET FEARS.
THESE WERE THE ONES I WANTED.

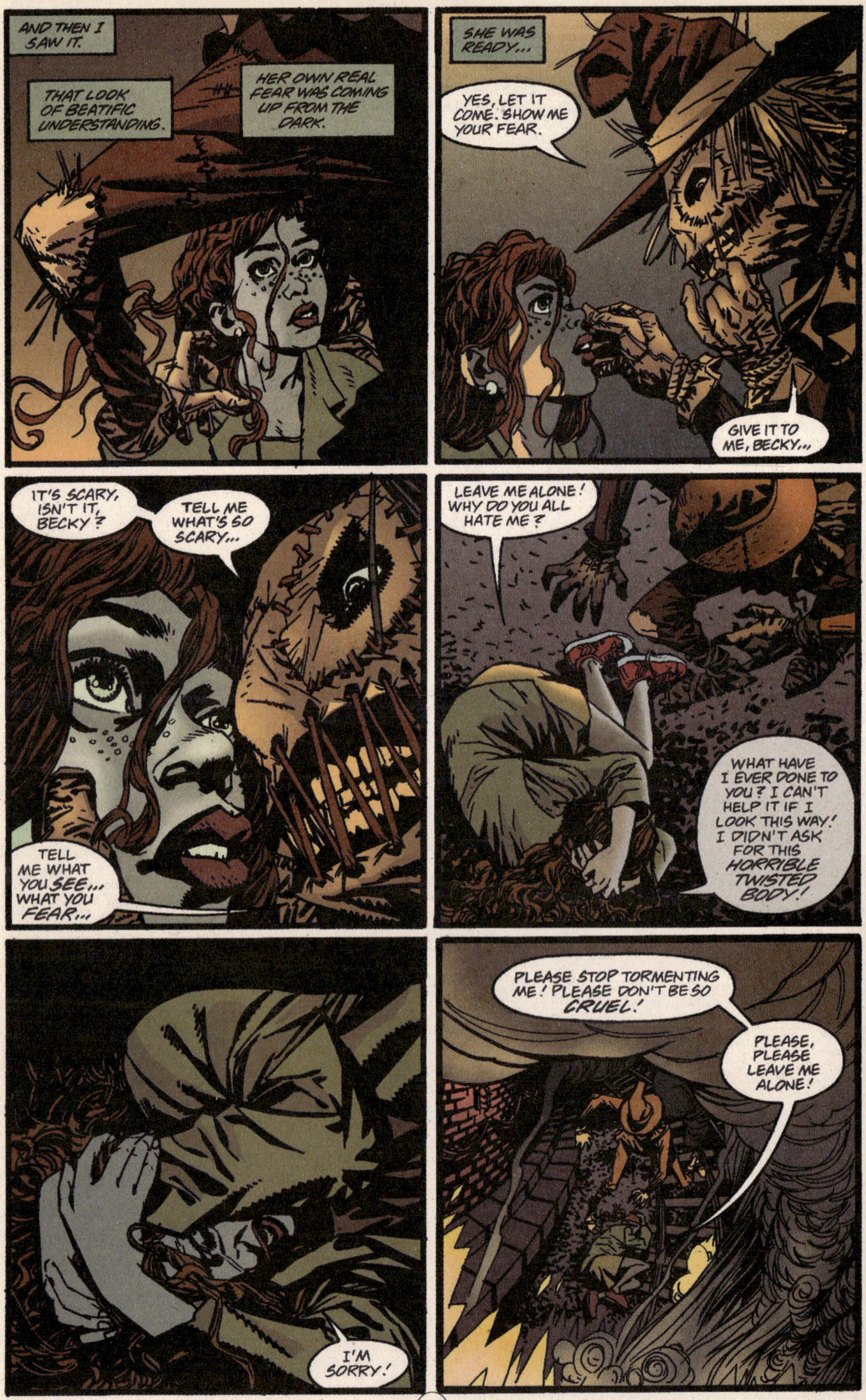
AND THEN I SAW IT.
THAT LOOK OF BEATIFIC UNDERSTANDING.
HER OWN REAL FEAR WAS COMING UP FROM THE DARK.
SHE WAS READY...
YES, LET IT COME. SHOW ME YOUR FEAR.
GIVE IT TO ME, BECKY...
IT'S SCARY, ISN'T IT, BECKY?
TELL ME WHAT'S SO SCARY...
TELL ME WHAT YOU SEE... WHAT YOU FEAR...
LEAVE ME ALONE! WHY DO YOU ALL HATE ME?
WHAT HAVE I EVER DONE TO YOU? I CAN'T HELP IT IF I LOOK THIS WAY! I DIDN'T ASK FOR THIS HORRIBLE TWISTED BODY!
I'M SORRY!
PLEASE STOP TORMENTING ME! PLEASE DON'T BE SO CRUEL!
PLEASE, PLEASE LEAVE ME ALONE!

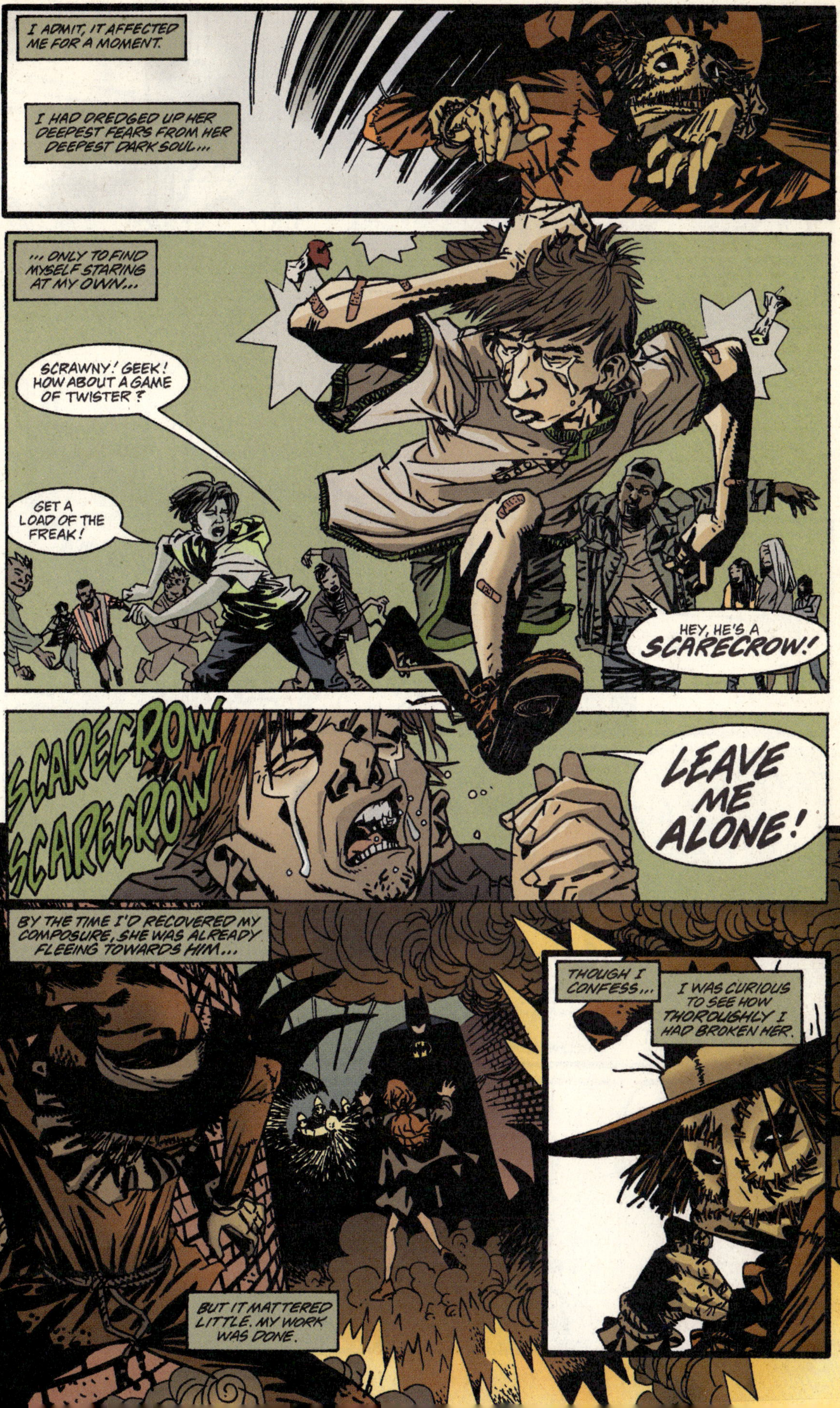

I ADMIT, IT AFFECTED ME FOR A MOMENT.
I HAD DREDGED UP HER DEEPEST FEARS FROM HER DEEPEST DARK SOUL...
...ONLY TO FIND MYSELF STARING AT MY OWN...
SCRAWNY! GEEK! HOW ABOUT A GAME OF TWISTER?
GET A LOAD OF THE FREAK!
HEY, HE'S A SCARECROW!
SCARECROW SCARECROW
LEAVE ME ALONE!
BY THE TIME I'D RECOVERED MY COMPOSURE, SHE WAS ALREADY FLEEING TOWARDS HIM...
THOUGH I CONFESS...
I WAS CURIOUS TO SEE HOW THOROUGHLY I HAD BROKEN HER.
BUT IT MATTERED LITTLE. MY WORK WAS DONE.

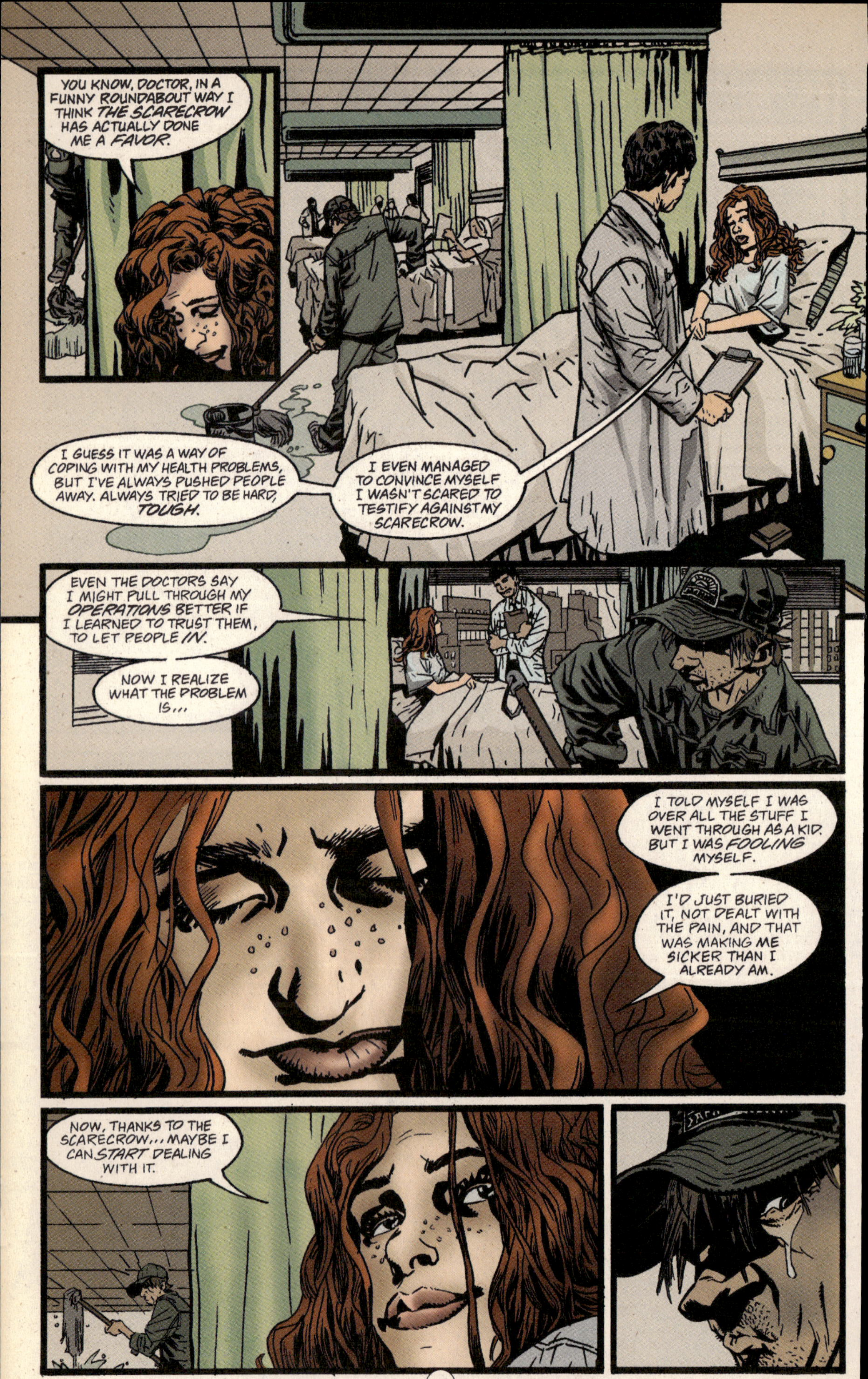
YOU KNOW, DOCTOR, IN A FUNNY ROUNDABOUT WAY I THINK THE SCARECROW HAS ACTUALLY DONE ME A FAVOR.
I GUESS IT WAS A WAY OF COPING WITH MY HEALTH PROBLEMS, BUT I'VE ALWAYS PUSHED PEOPLE AWAY. ALWAYS TRIED TO BE HARD, TOUGH.
I EVEN MANAGED TO CONVINCE MYSELF I WASN'T SCARED TO TESTIFY AGAINST MY SCARECROW.
EVEN THE DOCTORS SAY I MIGHT PULL THROUGH MY OPERATIONS BETTER IF I LEARNED TO TRUST THEM, TO LET PEOPLE IN.
NOW I REALIZE WHAT THE PROBLEM IS...
I TOLD MYSELF I WAS OVER ALL THE STUFF I WENT THROUGH AS A KID. BUT I WAS FOOLING MYSELF.
I'D JUST BURIED IT, NOT DEALT WITH THE PAIN, AND THAT WAS MAKING ME SICKER THAN I ALREADY AM.
NOW, THANKS TO THE SCARECROW... MAYBE I CAN START DEALING WITH IT.

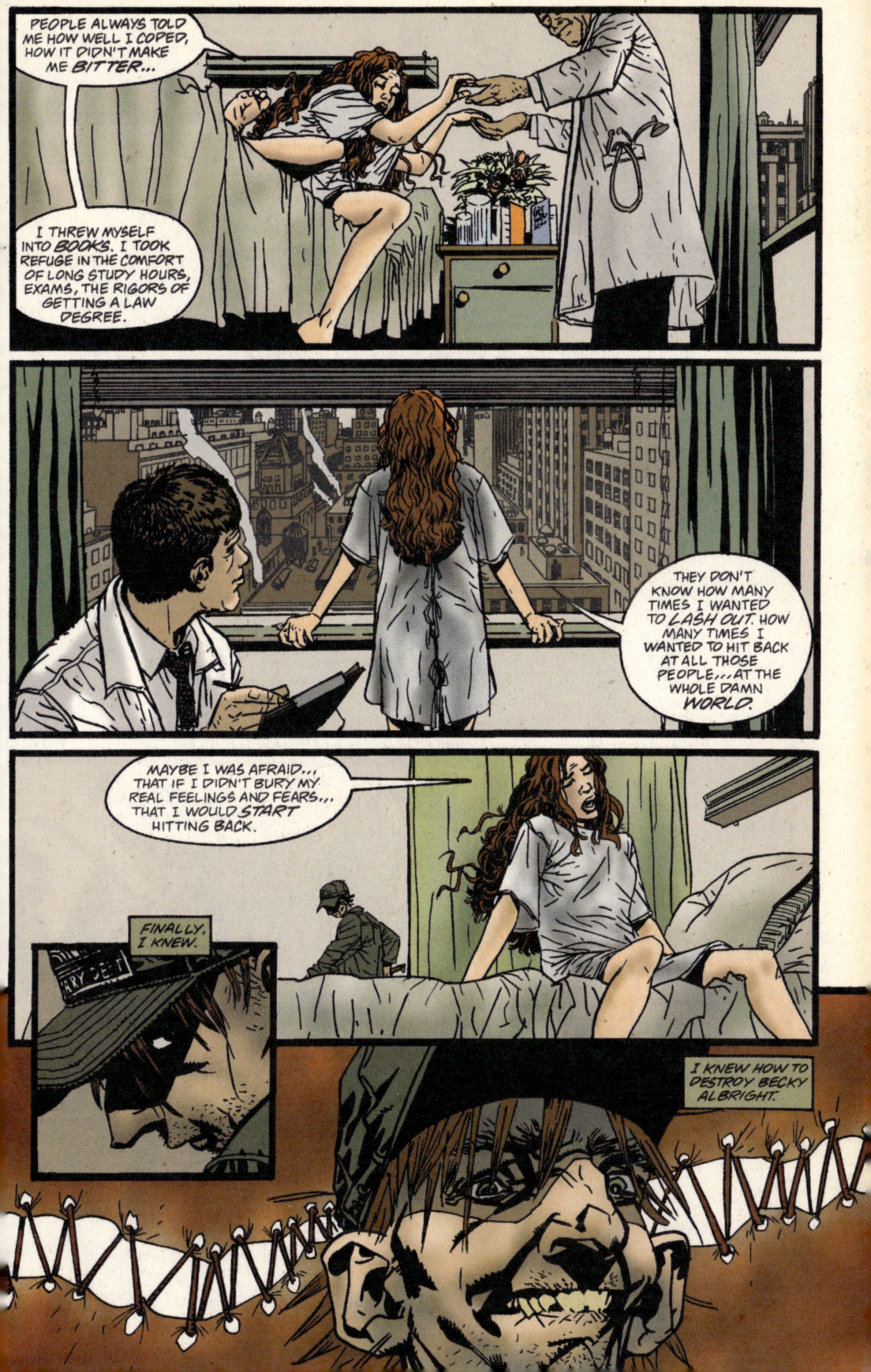
PEOPLE ALWAYS TOLD ME HOW WELL I COPED, HOW IT DIDN'T MAKE ME BITTER...
I THREW MYSELF INTO BOOKS. I TOOK REFUGE IN THE COMFORT OF LONG STUDY HOURS, EXAMS, THE RIGORS OF GETTING A LAW DEGREE.
THEY DON'T KNOW HOW MANY TIMES I WANTED TO LASH OUT. HOW MANY TIMES I WANTED TO HIT BACK AT ALL THOSE PEOPLE... AT THE WHOLE DAMN WORLD.
MAYBE I WAS AFRAID... THAT IF I DIDN'T BURY MY REAL FEELINGS AND FEARS... THAT I WOULD START HITTING BACK.
FINALLY. I KNEW.
I KNEW HOW TO DESTROY BECKY ALBRIGHT.

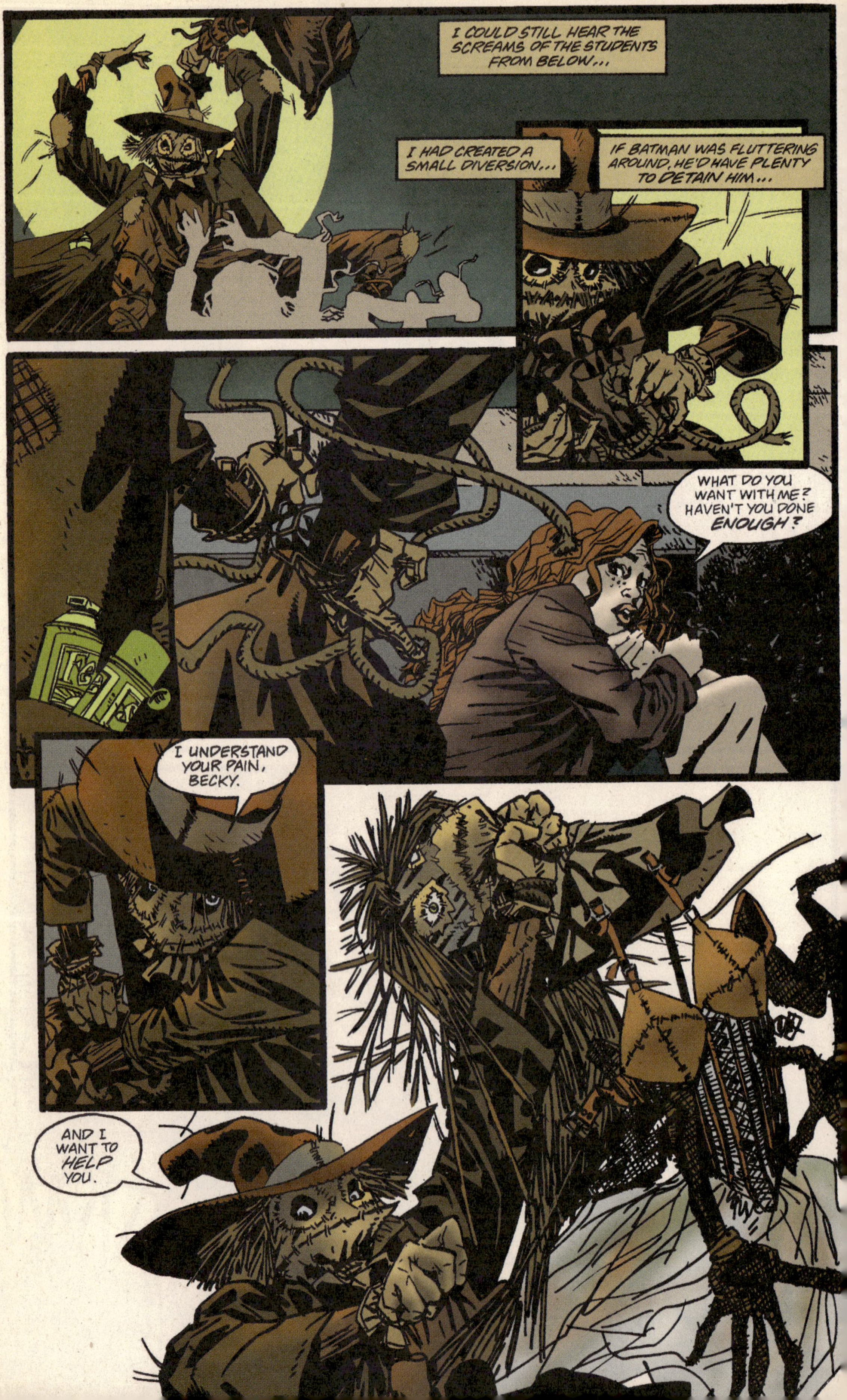
I COULD STILL HEAR THE SCREAMS OF THE STUDENTS FROM BELOW...
I HAD CREATED A SMALL DIVERSION...
IF BATMAN WAS FLUTTERING AROUND, HE'D HAVE PLENTY TO DETAIN HIM...
WHAT DO YOU WANT WITH ME? HAVEN'T YOU DONE ENOUGH?
I UNDERSTAND YOUR PAIN, BECKY.
AND I WANT TO HELP YOU.

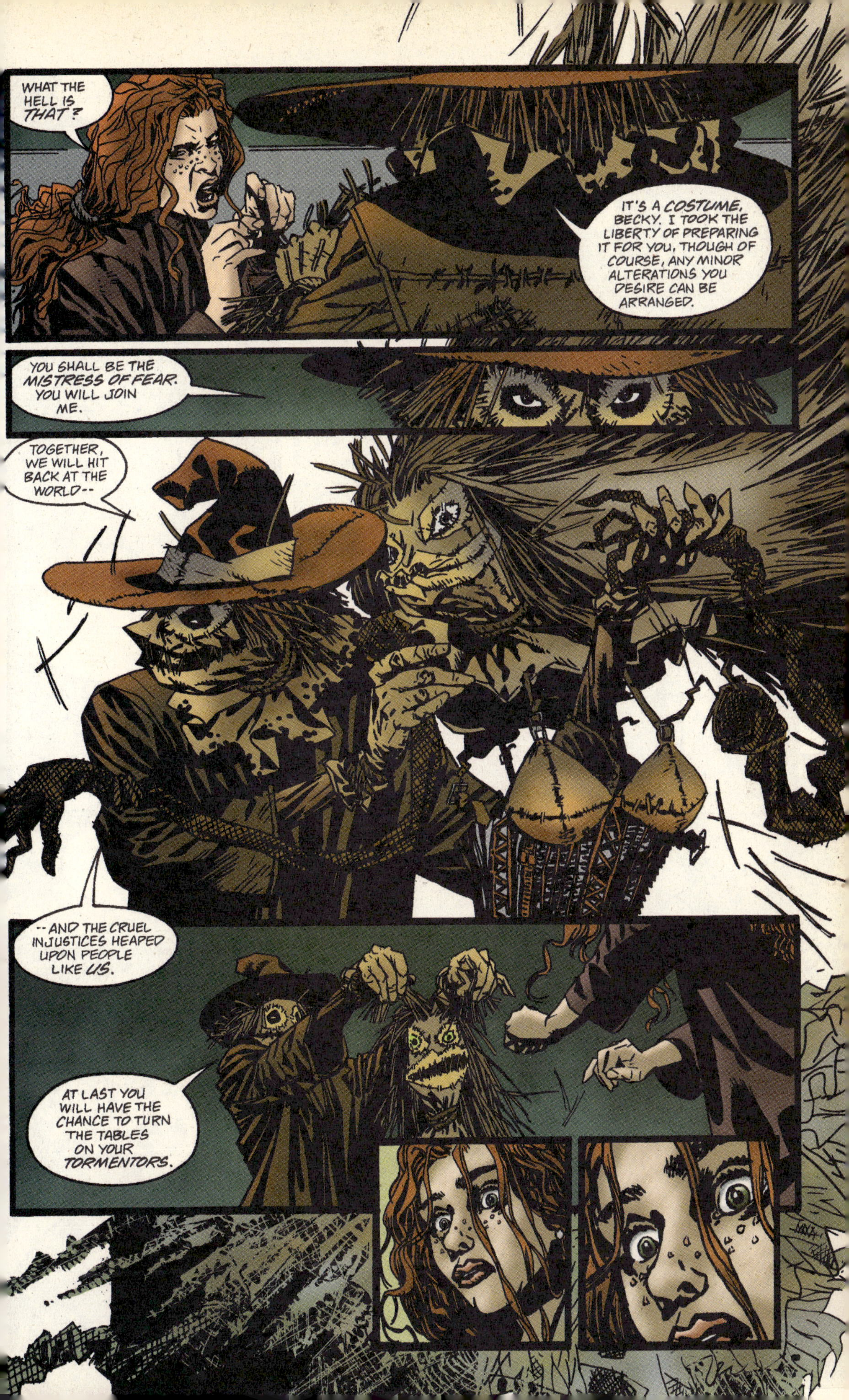
WHAT THE HELL IS *THAT*?
IT'S A *COSTUME*, BECKY. I TOOK THE LIBERTY OF PREPARING IT FOR YOU, THOUGH OF COURSE, ANY MINOR ALTERATIONS YOU DESIRE CAN BE ARRANGED.
YOU SHALL BE THE *MISTRESS OF FEAR*. YOU WILL JOIN ME.
TOGETHER, WE WILL HIT BACK AT THE WORLD--
--AND THE CRUEL INJUSTICES HEAPED UPON PEOPLE LIKE *US*.
AT LAST YOU WILL HAVE THE CHANCE TO TURN THE TABLES ON YOUR *TORMENTORS*.

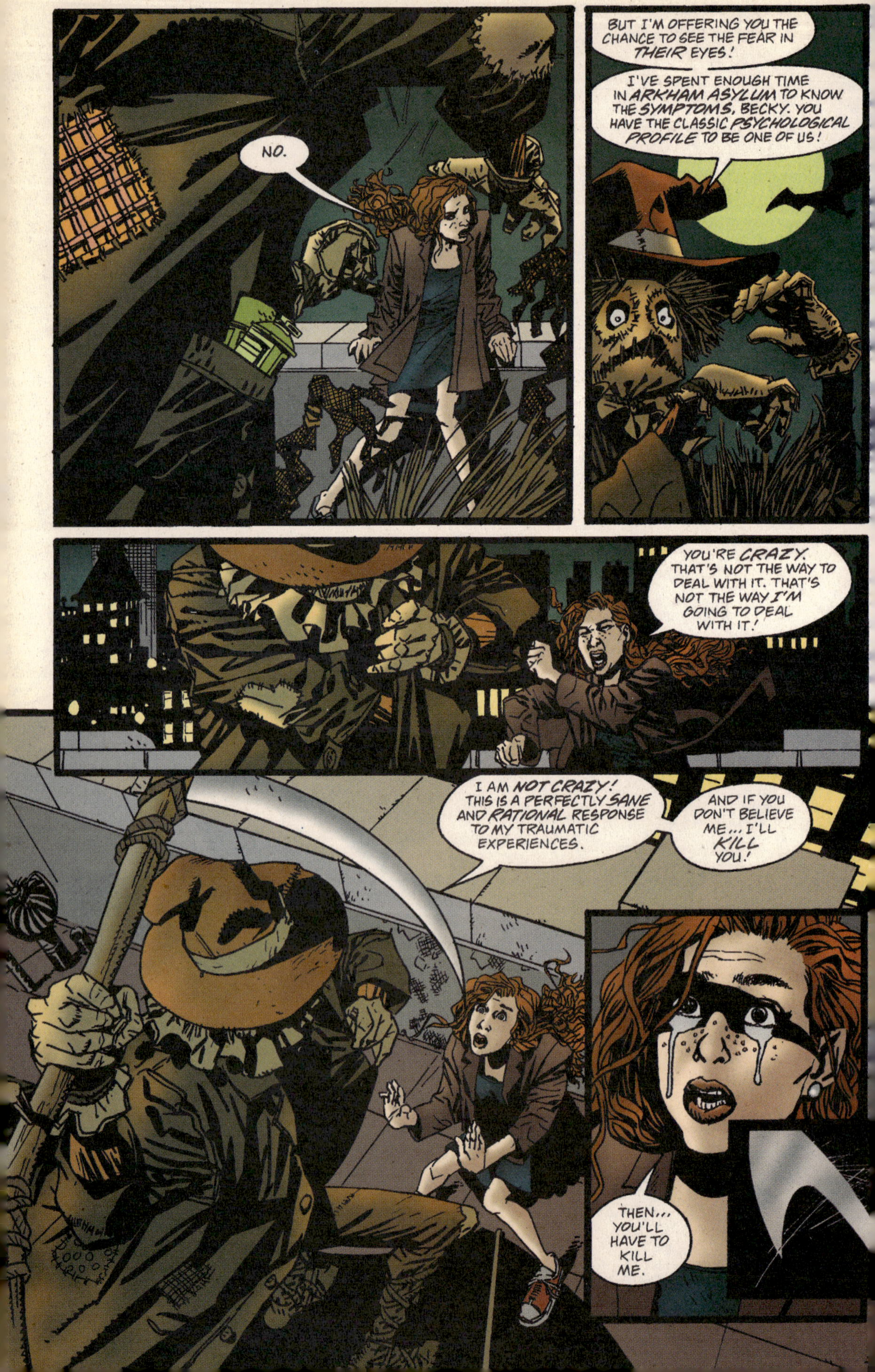
NO.
BUT I'M OFFERING YOU THE CHANCE TO SEE THE FEAR IN THEIR EYES!
I'VE SPENT ENOUGH TIME IN ARKHAM ASYLUM TO KNOW THE SYMPTOMS, BECKY. YOU HAVE THE CLASSIC PSYCHOLOGICAL PROFILE TO BE ONE OF US!
YOU'RE CRAZY. THAT'S NOT THE WAY TO DEAL WITH IT. THAT'S NOT THE WAY I'M GOING TO DEAL WITH IT!
I AM NOT CRAZY! THIS IS A PERFECTLY SANE AND RATIONAL RESPONSE TO MY TRAUMATIC EXPERIENCES.
AND IF YOU DON'T BELIEVE ME... I'LL KILL YOU!
THEN... YOU'LL HAVE TO KILL ME.

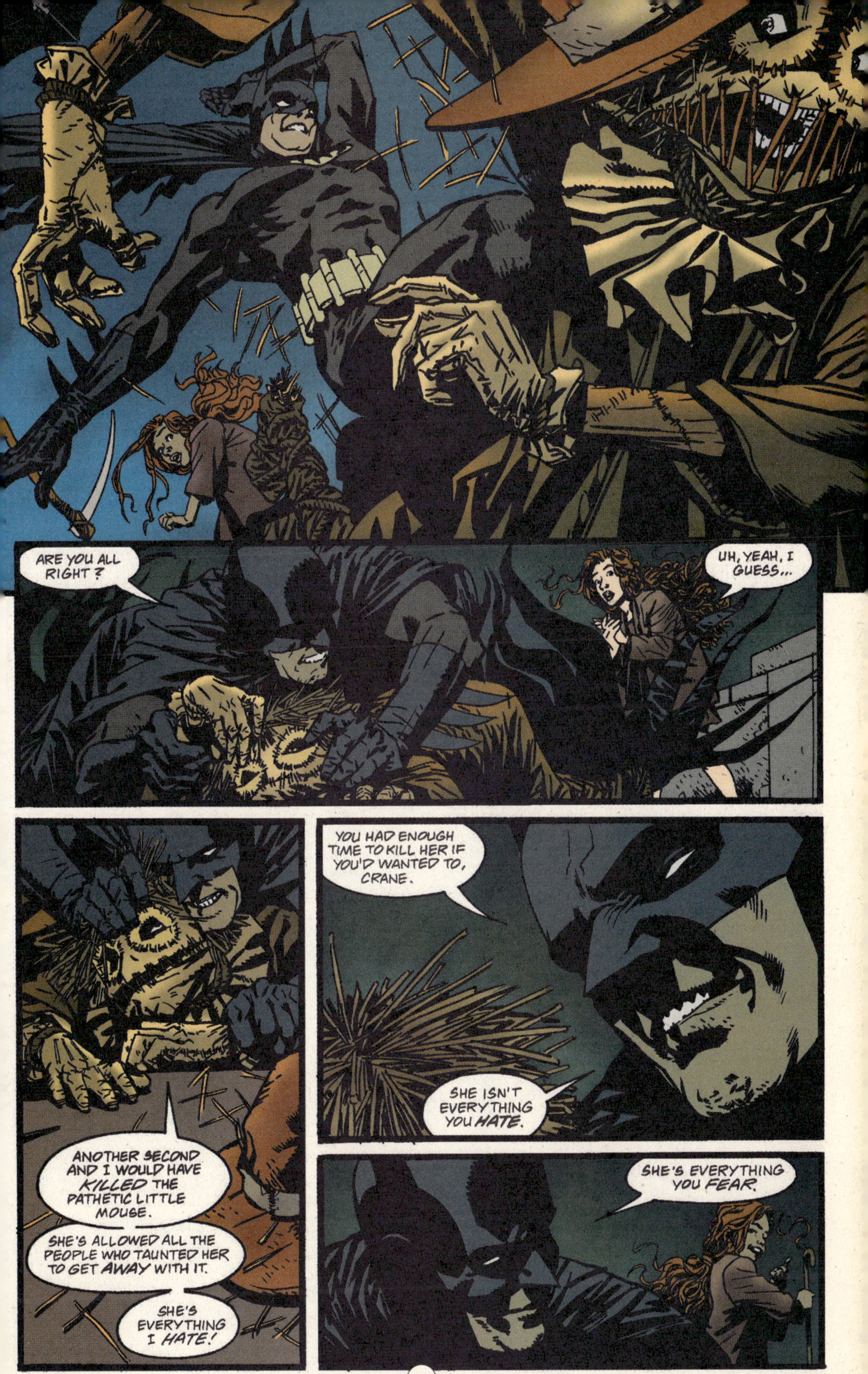
ARE YOU ALL RIGHT?
UH, YEAH. I GUESS...
ANOTHER SECOND AND I WOULD HAVE KILLED THE PATHETIC LITTLE MOUSE.
SHE'S ALLOWED ALL THE PEOPLE WHO TAUNTED HER TO GET AWAY WITH IT.
SHE'S EVERYTHING I HATE!
YOU HAD ENOUGH TIME TO KILL HER IF YOU'D WANTED TO, CRANE.
SHE ISN'T EVERYTHING YOU HATE.
SHE'S EVERYTHING YOU FEAR.

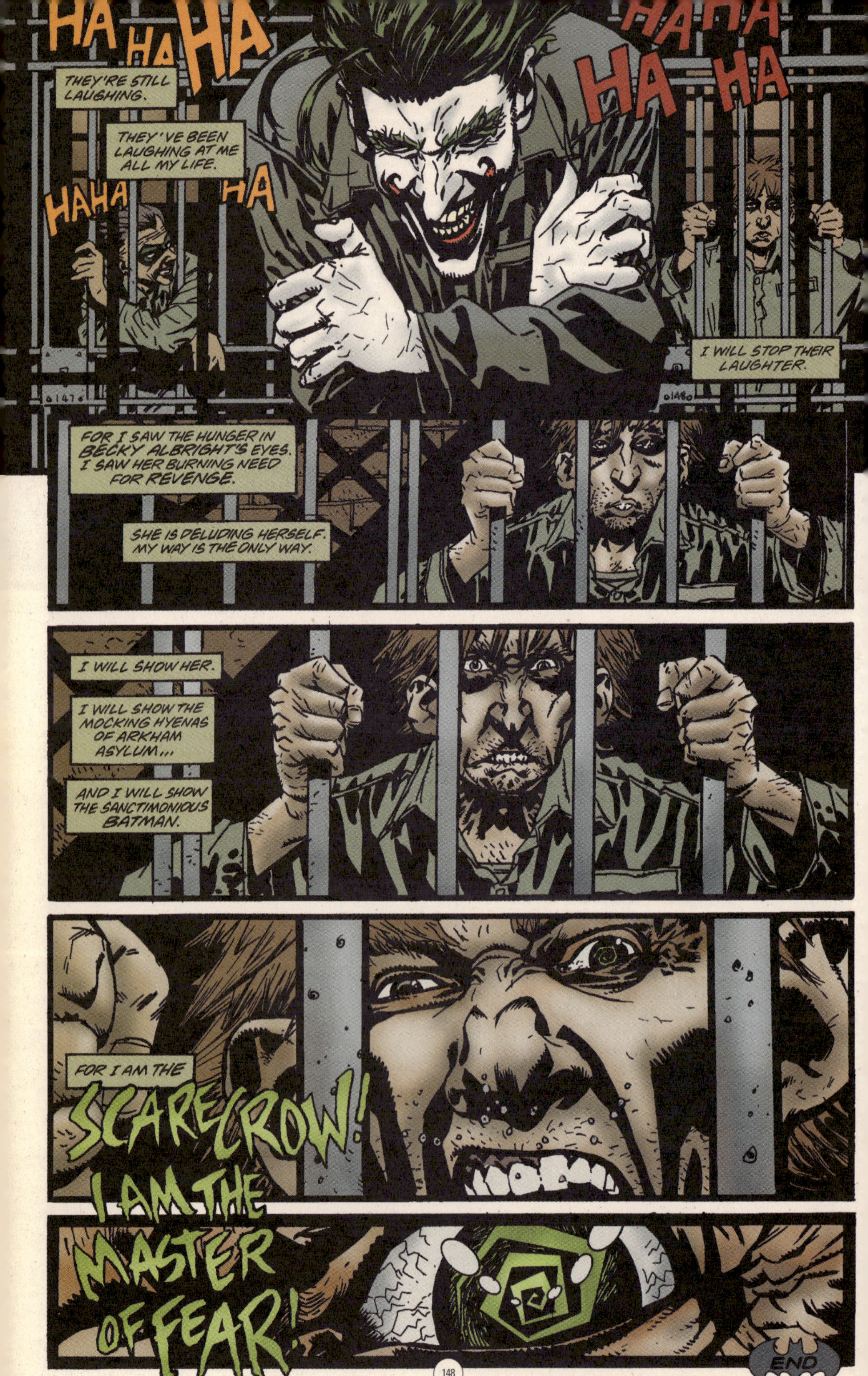
HA HA HA
HA HA HA HA
THEY'RE STILL LAUGHING.
THEY'VE BEEN LAUGHING AT ME ALL MY LIFE.
HAHA HA
I WILL STOP THEIR LAUGHTER.
FOR I SAW THE HUNGER IN BECKY ALBRIGHT'S EYES. I SAW HER BURNING NEED FOR REVENGE.
SHE IS DELUDING HERSELF. MY WAY IS THE ONLY WAY.
I WILL SHOW HER.
I WILL SHOW THE MOCKING HYENAS OF ARKHAM ASYLUM...
AND I WILL SHOW THE SANCTIMONIOUS BATMAN.
FOR I AM THE
SCARECROW!
I AM THE MASTER OF FEAR!
END

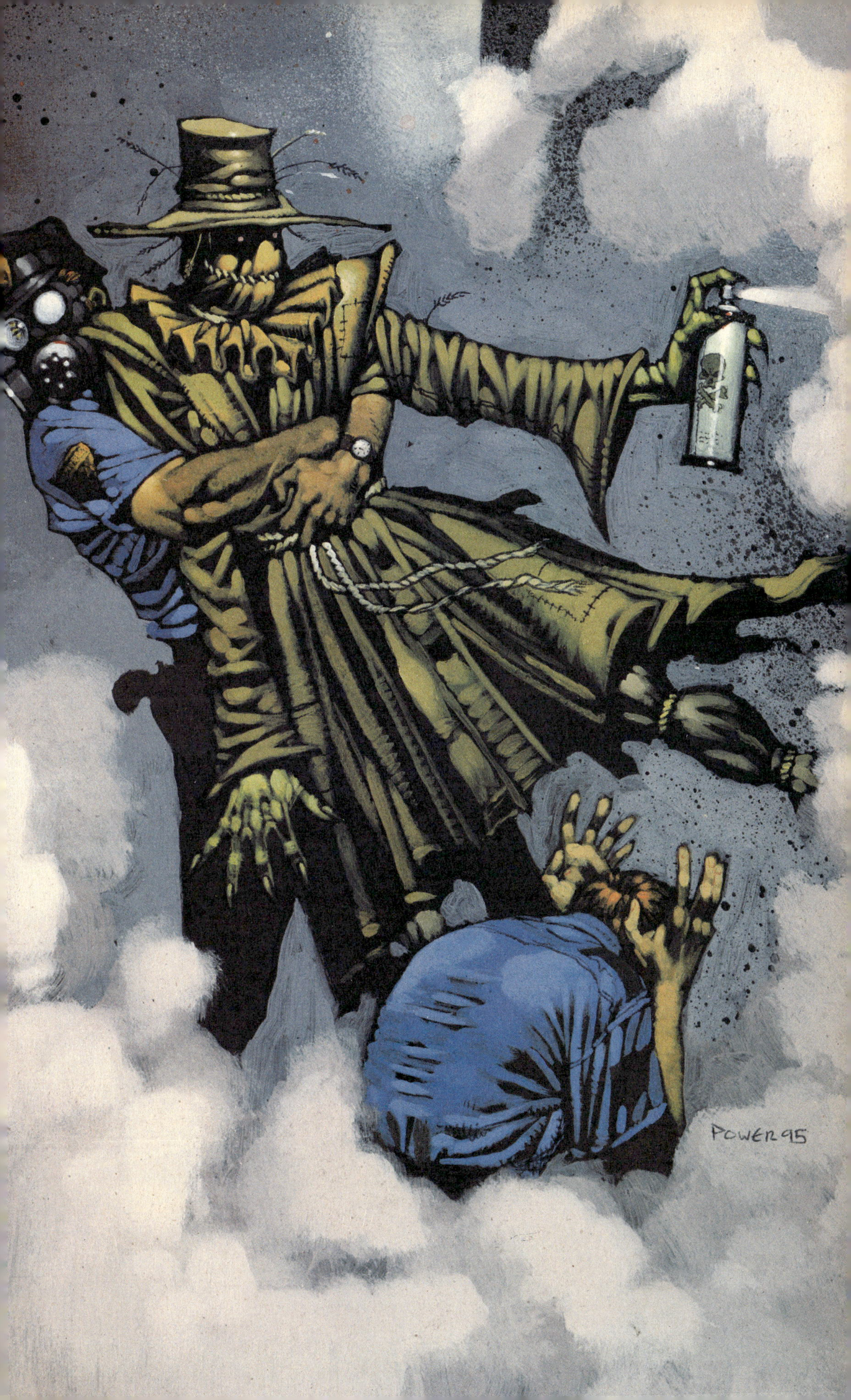
POWER95

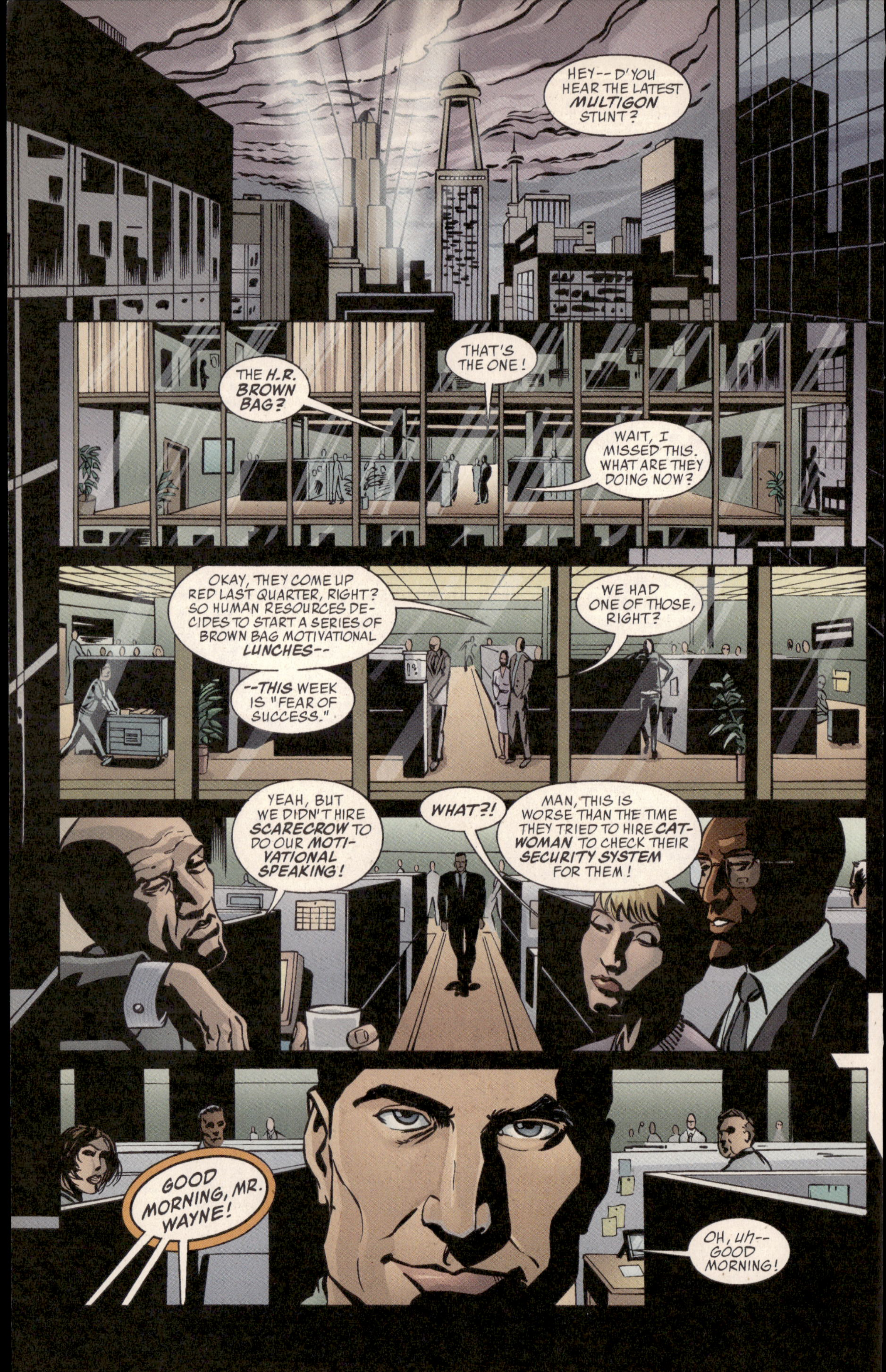
HEY-- D'YOU HEAR THE LATEST MULTIGON STUNT?
THE H.R. BROWN BAG?
THAT'S THE ONE!
WAIT, I MISSED THIS. WHAT ARE THEY DOING NOW?
OKAY, THEY COME UP RED LAST QUARTER, RIGHT? SO HUMAN RESOURCES DECIDES TO START A SERIES OF BROWN BAG MOTIVATIONAL LUNCHES--
--THIS WEEK IS "FEAR OF SUCCESS."
WE HAD ONE OF THOSE, RIGHT?
YEAH, BUT WE DIDN'T HIRE SCARECROW TO DO OUR MOTIVATIONAL SPEAKING!
WHAT?!
MAN, THIS IS WORSE THAN THE TIME THEY TRIED TO HIRE CATWOMAN TO CHECK THEIR SECURITY SYSTEM FOR THEM!
GOOD MORNING, MR. WAYNE!
OH, UH-- GOOD MORNING!

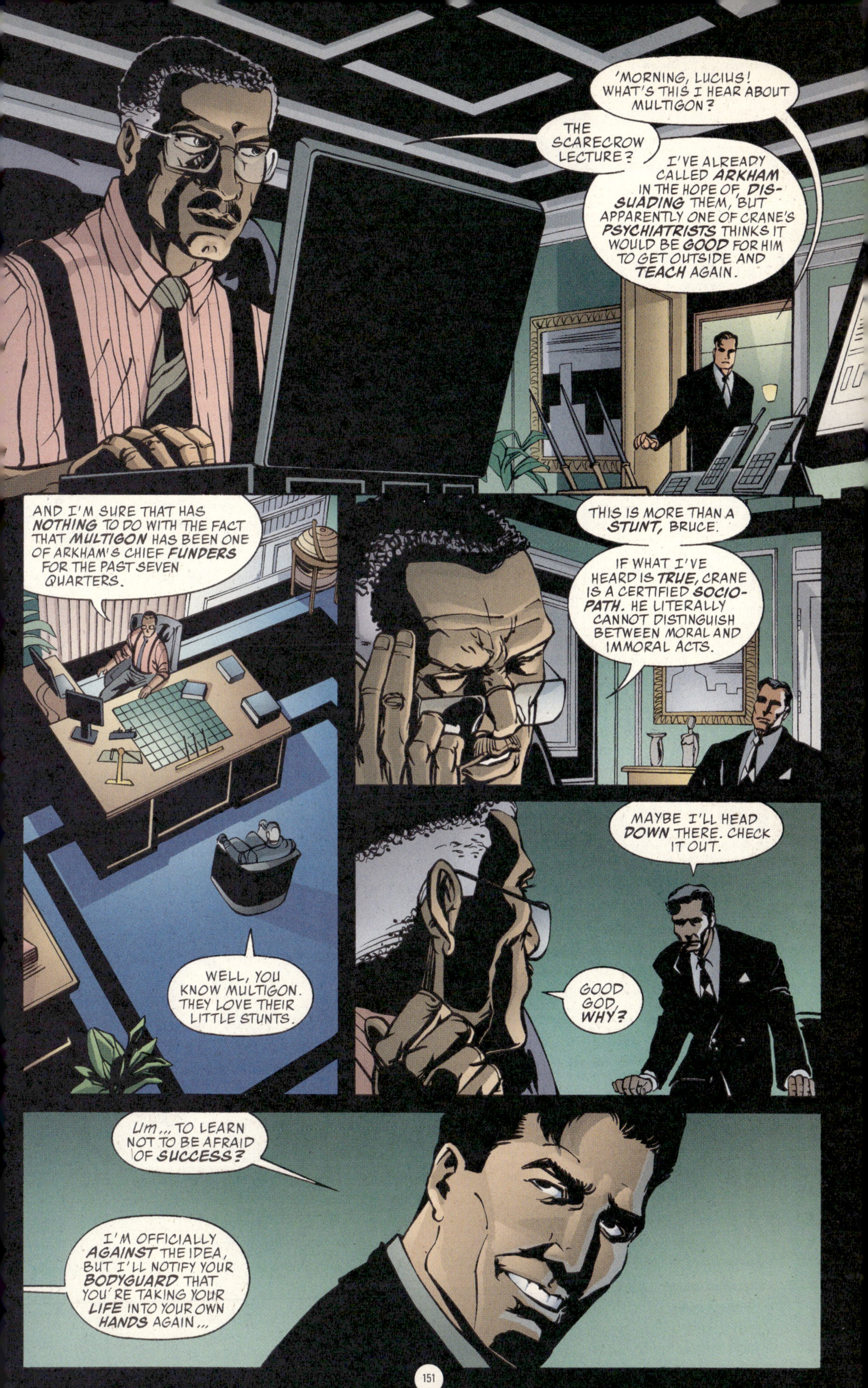
'MORNING, LUCIUS! WHAT'S THIS I HEAR ABOUT MULTIGON?
THE SCARECROW LECTURE?
I'VE ALREADY CALLED ARKHAM IN THE HOPE OF DISSUADING THEM, BUT APPARENTLY ONE OF CRANE'S PSYCHIATRISTS THINKS IT WOULD BE GOOD FOR HIM TO GET OUTSIDE AND TEACH AGAIN.
AND I'M SURE THAT HAS NOTHING TO DO WITH THE FACT THAT MULTIGON HAS BEEN ONE OF ARKHAM'S CHIEF FUNDERS FOR THE PAST SEVEN QUARTERS.
WELL, YOU KNOW MULTIGON. THEY LOVE THEIR LITTLE STUNTS.
THIS IS MORE THAN A STUNT, BRUCE.
IF WHAT I'VE HEARD IS TRUE, CRANE IS A CERTIFIED SOCIOPATH. HE LITERALLY CANNOT DISTINGUISH BETWEEN MORAL AND IMMORAL ACTS.
MAYBE I'LL HEAD DOWN THERE. CHECK IT OUT.
GOOD GOD, WHY?
UM... TO LEARN NOT TO BE AFRAID OF SUCCESS?
I'M OFFICIALLY AGAINST THE IDEA, BUT I'LL NOTIFY YOUR BODYGUARD THAT YOU'RE TAKING YOUR LIFE INTO YOUR OWN HANDS AGAIN...

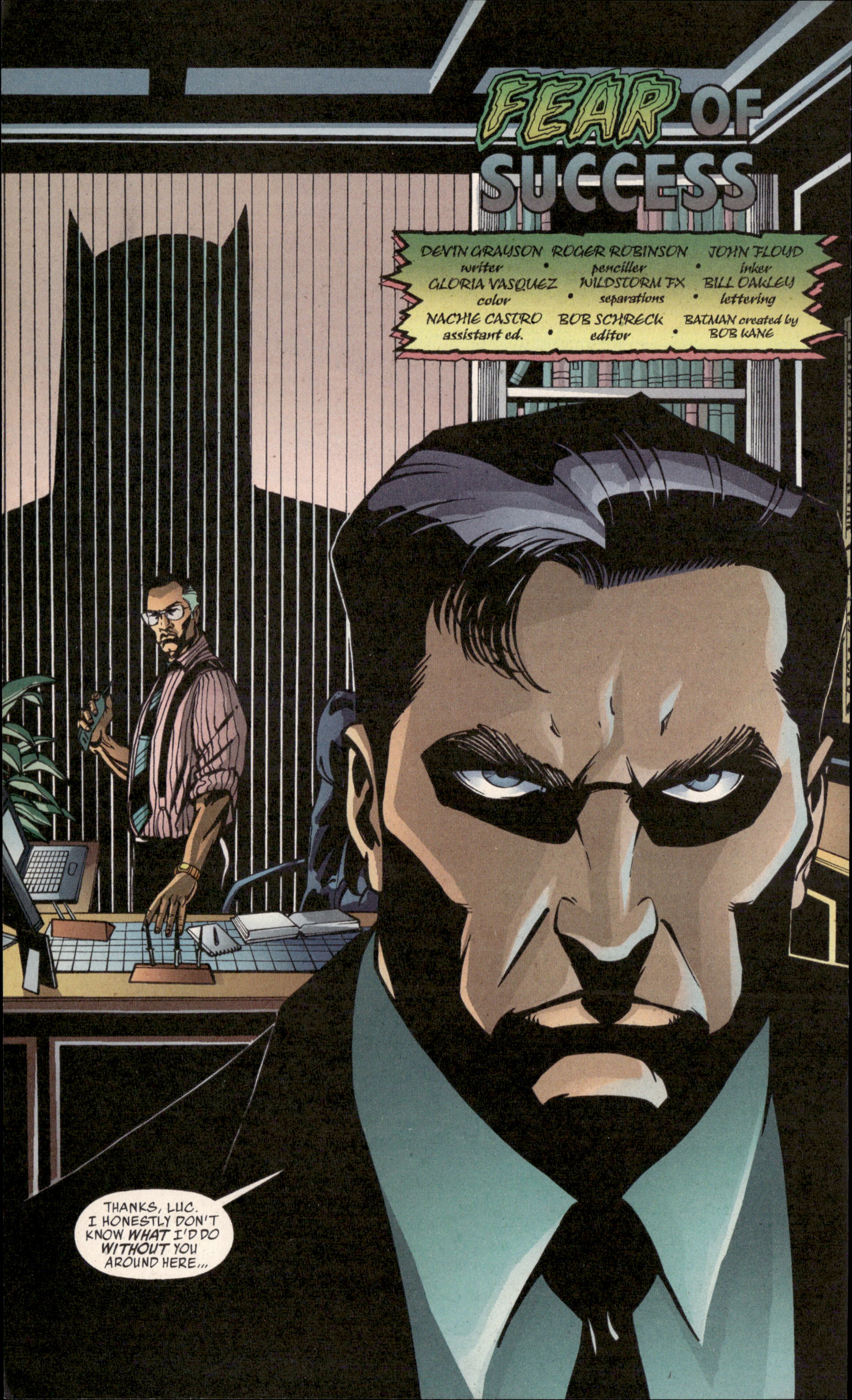
FEAR OF SUCCESS
DEVIN GRAYSON writer • ROGER ROBINSON penciller • JOHN FLOYD inker
GLORIA VASQUEZ color • WILDSTORM FX separations • BILL OAKLEY lettering
NACHIE CASTRO assistant ed. • BOB SCHRECK editor • BATMAN created by BOB KANE
THANKS, LUC. I HONESTLY DON'T KNOW WHAT I'D DO WITHOUT YOU AROUND HERE...

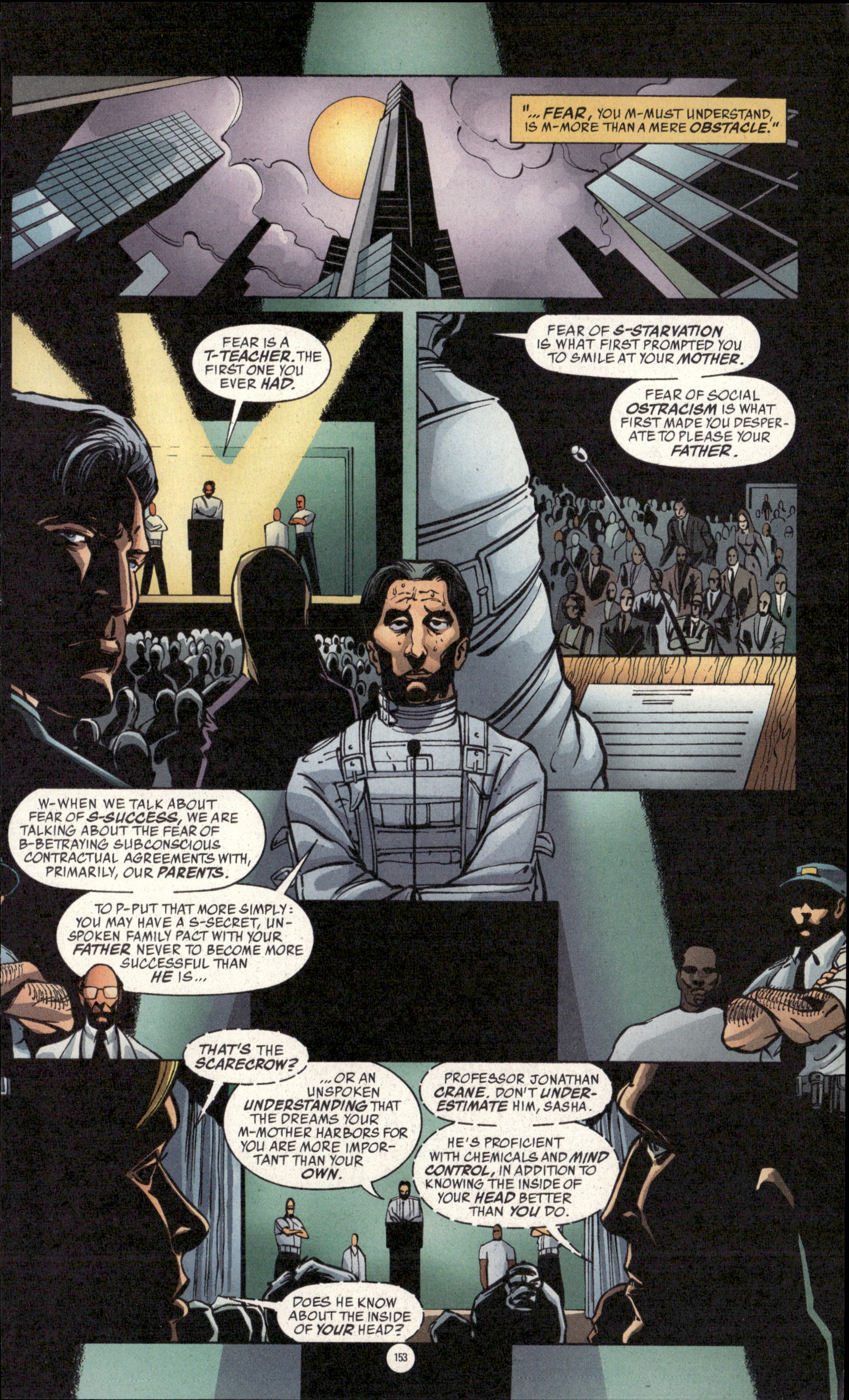
"...FEAR, YOU M-MUST UNDERSTAND, IS M-MORE THAN A MERE OBSTACLE."
FEAR IS A T-TEACHER. THE FIRST ONE YOU EVER HAD.
FEAR OF S-STARVATION IS WHAT FIRST PROMPTED YOU TO SMILE AT YOUR MOTHER.
FEAR OF SOCIAL OSTRACISM IS WHAT FIRST MADE YOU DESPERATE TO PLEASE YOUR FATHER.
W-WHEN WE TALK ABOUT FEAR OF S-SUCCESS, WE ARE TALKING ABOUT THE FEAR OF B-BETRAYING SUBCONSCIOUS CONTRACTUAL AGREEMENTS WITH, PRIMARILY, OUR PARENTS.
TO P-PUT THAT MORE SIMPLY: YOU MAY HAVE A S-SECRET, UNSPOKEN FAMILY PACT WITH YOUR FATHER NEVER TO BECOME MORE SUCCESSFUL THAN HE IS...
THAT'S THE SCARECROW?
...OR AN UNSPOKEN UNDERSTANDING THAT THE DREAMS YOUR M-MOTHER HARBORS FOR YOU ARE MORE IMPORTANT THAN YOUR OWN.
PROFESSOR JONATHAN CRANE. DON'T UNDERESTIMATE HIM, SASHA.
HE'S PROFICIENT WITH CHEMICALS AND MIND CONTROL, IN ADDITION TO KNOWING THE INSIDE OF YOUR HEAD BETTER THAN YOU DO.
DOES HE KNOW ABOUT THE INSIDE OF YOUR HEAD?

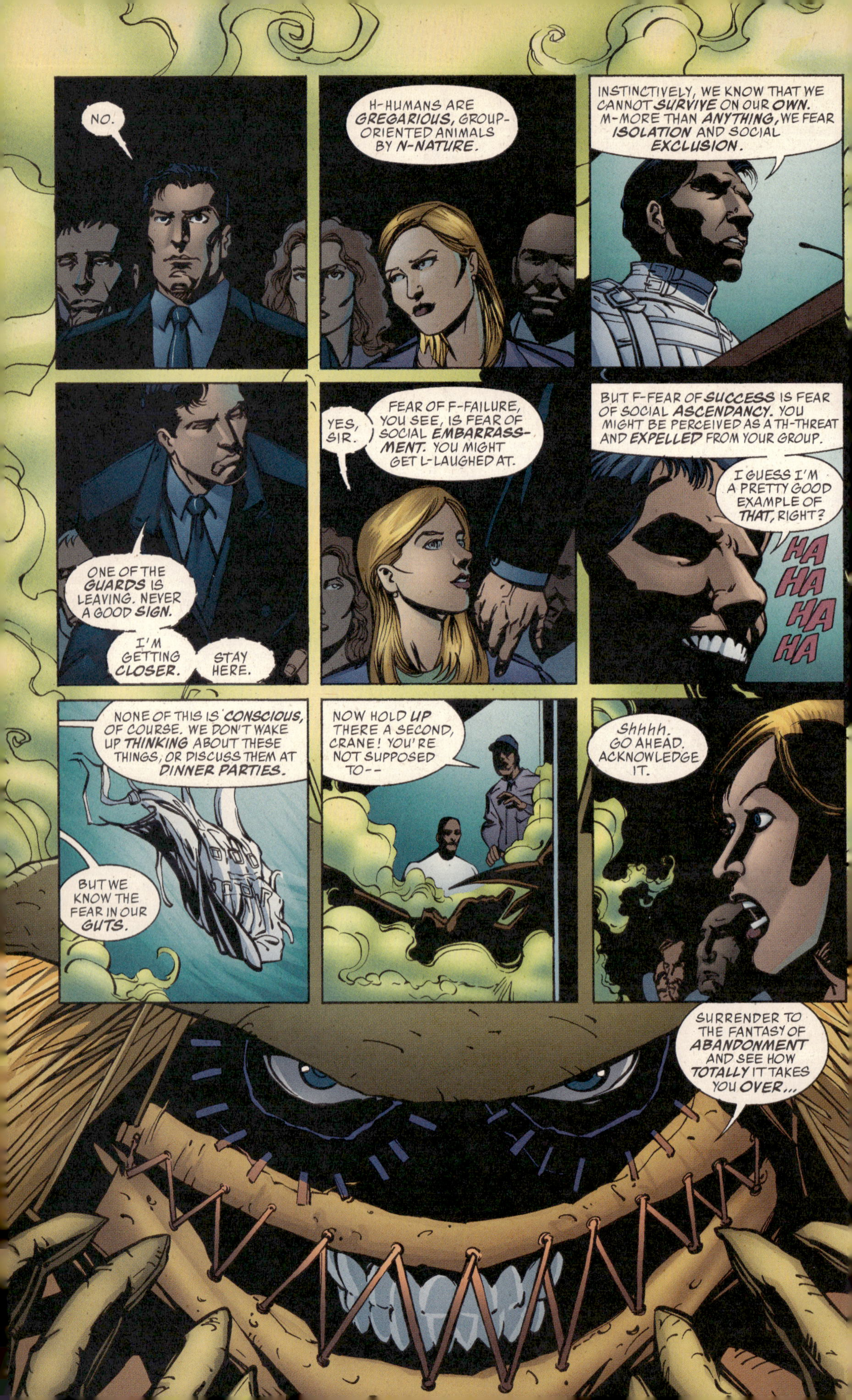
NO.
H-HUMANS ARE GREGARIOUS, GROUP-ORIENTED ANIMALS BY N-NATURE.
INSTINCTIVELY, WE KNOW THAT WE CANNOT SURVIVE ON OUR OWN. M-MORE THAN ANYTHING, WE FEAR ISOLATION AND SOCIAL EXCLUSION.
ONE OF THE GUARDS IS LEAVING. NEVER A GOOD SIGN.
I'M GETTING CLOSER.
STAY HERE.
YES, SIR.
FEAR OF F-FAILURE, YOU SEE, IS FEAR OF SOCIAL EMBARRASS-MENT. YOU MIGHT GET L-LAUGHED AT.
BUT F-FEAR OF SUCCESS IS FEAR OF SOCIAL ASCENDANCY. YOU MIGHT BE PERCEIVED AS A TH-THREAT AND EXPELLED FROM YOUR GROUP.
I GUESS I'M A PRETTY GOOD EXAMPLE OF THAT, RIGHT?
HA HA HA HA
NONE OF THIS IS CONSCIOUS, OF COURSE. WE DON'T WAKE UP THINKING ABOUT THESE THINGS, OR DISCUSS THEM AT DINNER PARTIES.
BUT WE KNOW THE FEAR IN OUR GUTS.
NOW HOLD UP THERE A SECOND, CRANE! YOU'RE NOT SUPPOSED TO--
Shhhh. GO AHEAD. ACKNOWLEDGE IT.
SURRENDER TO THE FANTASY OF ABANDONMENT AND SEE HOW TOTALLY IT TAKES YOU OVER...

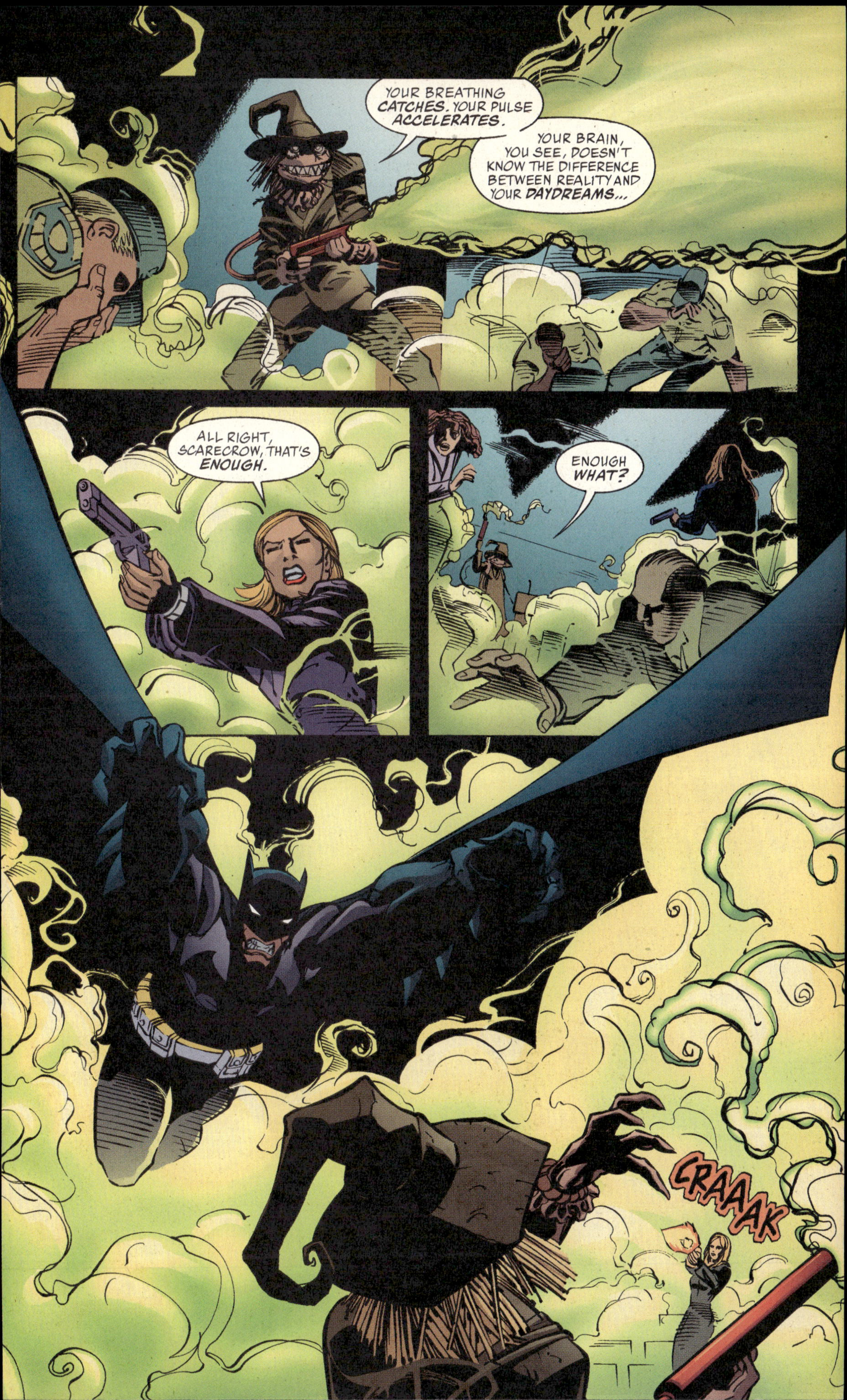
YOUR BREATHING CATCHES. YOUR PULSE ACCELERATES.
YOUR BRAIN, YOU SEE, DOESN'T KNOW THE DIFFERENCE BETWEEN REALITY AND YOUR DAYDREAMS...
ALL RIGHT, SCARECROW, THAT'S ENOUGH.
ENOUGH WHAT?
CRAAAK

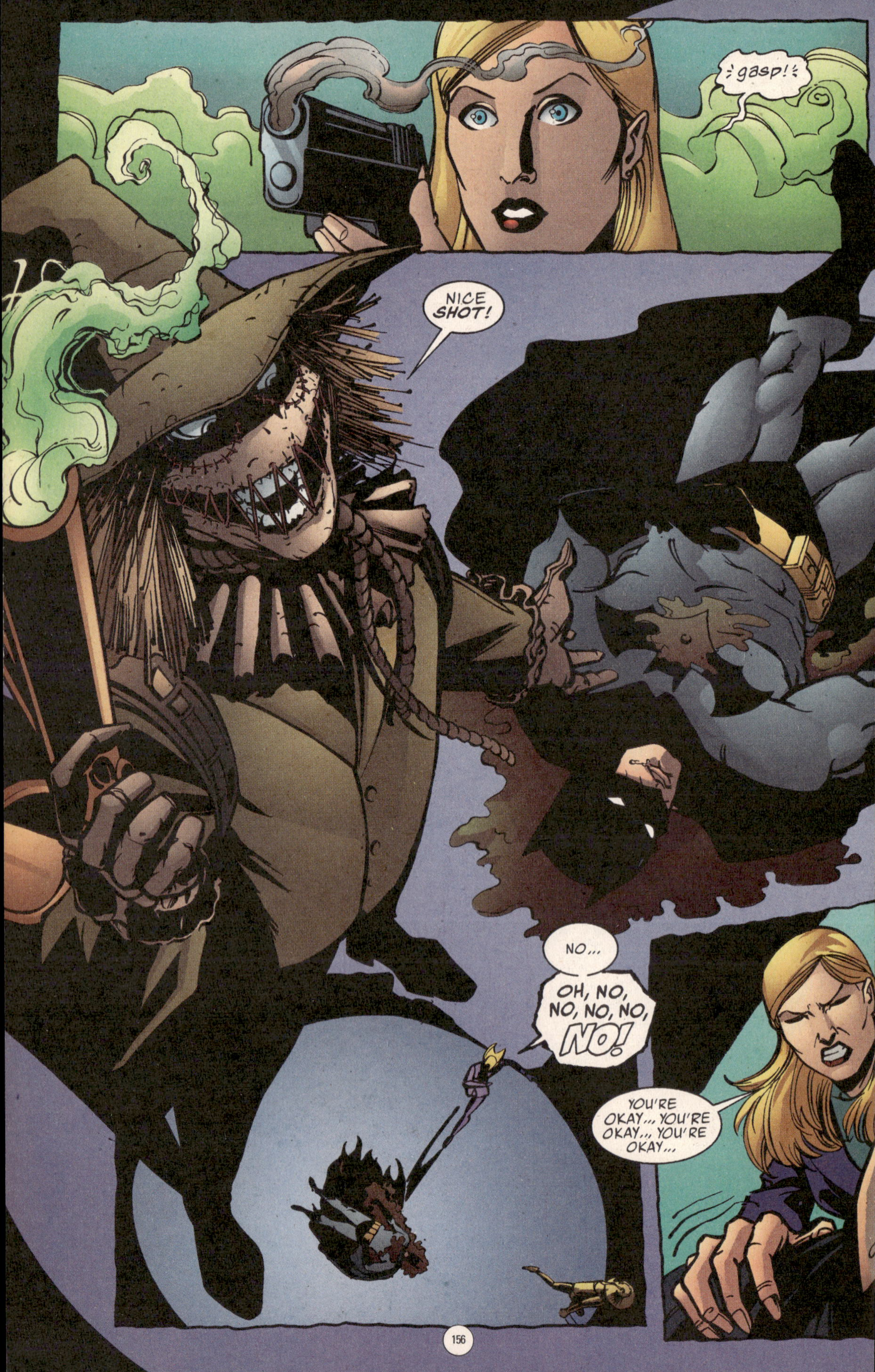
gasp!
NICE SHOT!
NO...
OH, NO, NO, NO, NO, NO!
YOU'RE OKAY... YOU'RE OKAY... YOU'RE OKAY...

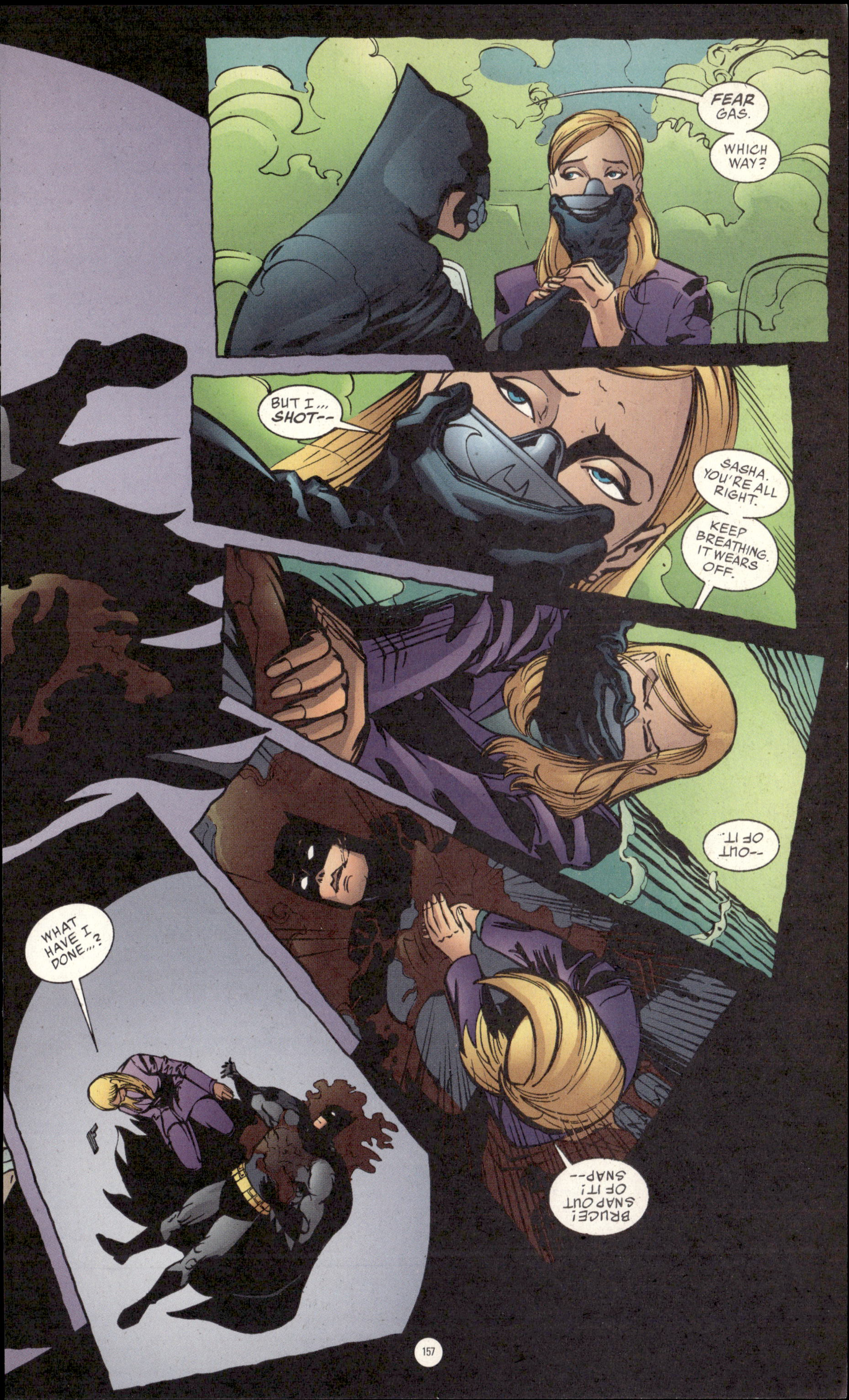
FEAR GAS.
WHICH WAY?
BUT I... SHOT--
SASHA. YOU'RE ALL RIGHT.
KEEP BREATHING. IT WEARS OFF.
BRUCE! SNAP OUT OF IT! SNAP--
--OUT OF IT.
WHAT HAVE I DONE...?

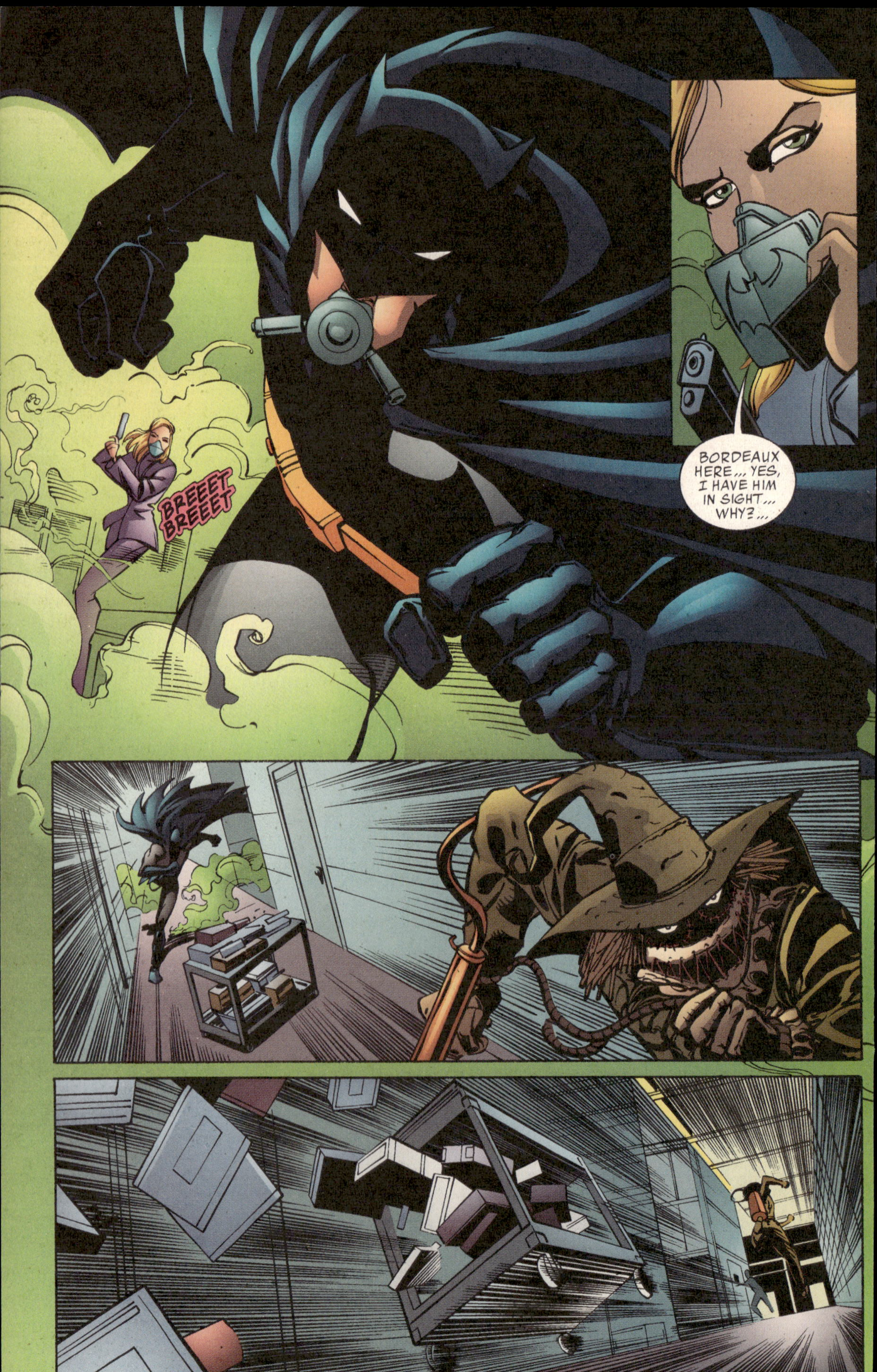
BREEEET BREEEET
BORDEAUX HERE... YES, I HAVE HIM IN SIGHT... WHY?...

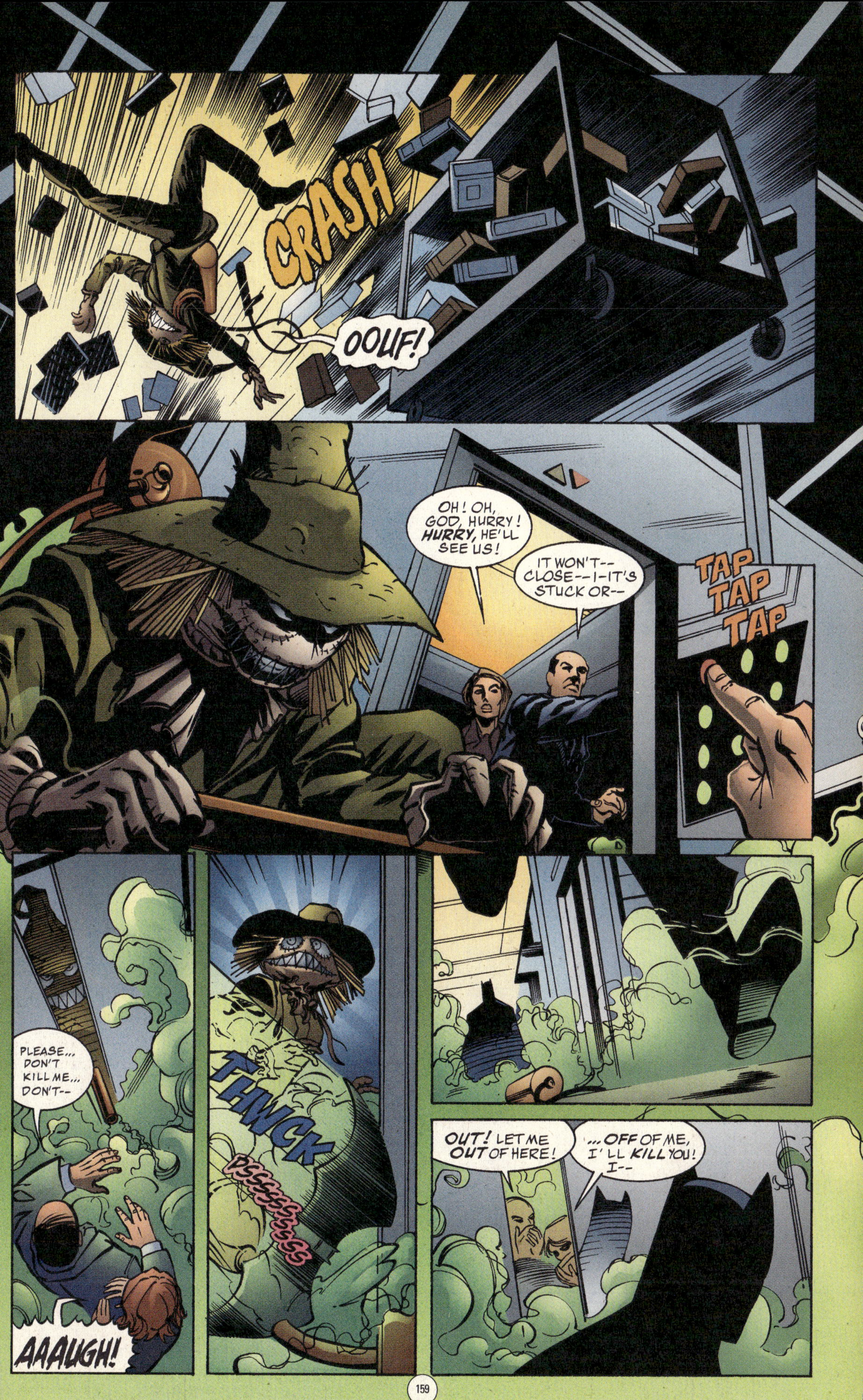
CRASH
OOUF!
OH! OH, GOD, HURRY! HURRY, HE'LL SEE US!
IT WON'T-- CLOSE--I-IT'S STUCK OR--
TAP TAP TAP
PLEASE... DON'T KILL ME... DON'T--
AAAUGH!
THWCK
PSSSSSSSSSS
OUT! LET ME OUT OF HERE!
...OFF OF ME, I'LL KILL YOU! I--

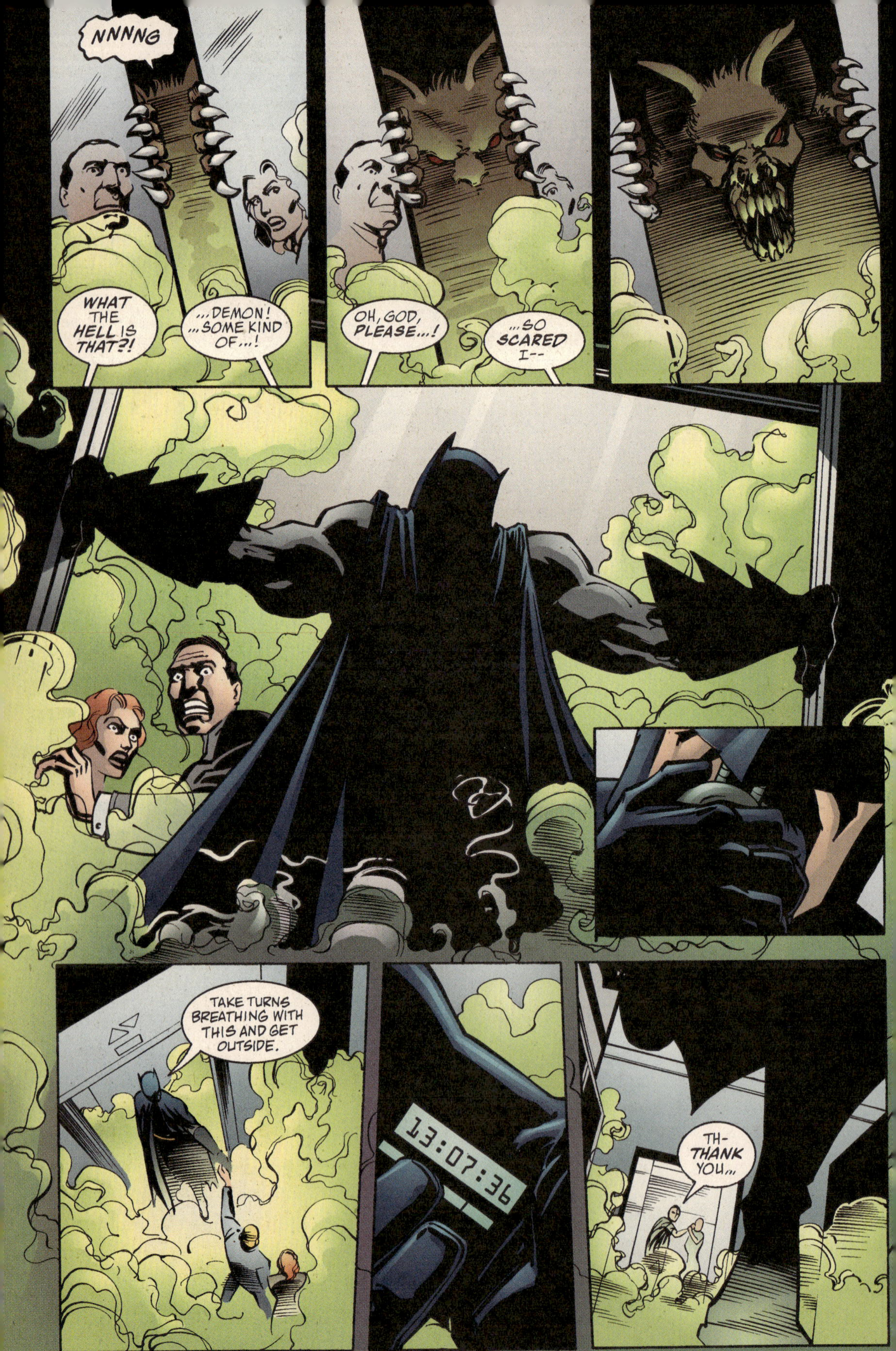
NNNNG
WHAT THE HELL IS THAT?!
...DEMON! ...SOME KIND OF...!
OH, GOD, PLEASE...!
...SO SCARED I--
TAKE TURNS BREATHING WITH THIS AND GET OUTSIDE.
13:07:36
TH- THANK YOU...

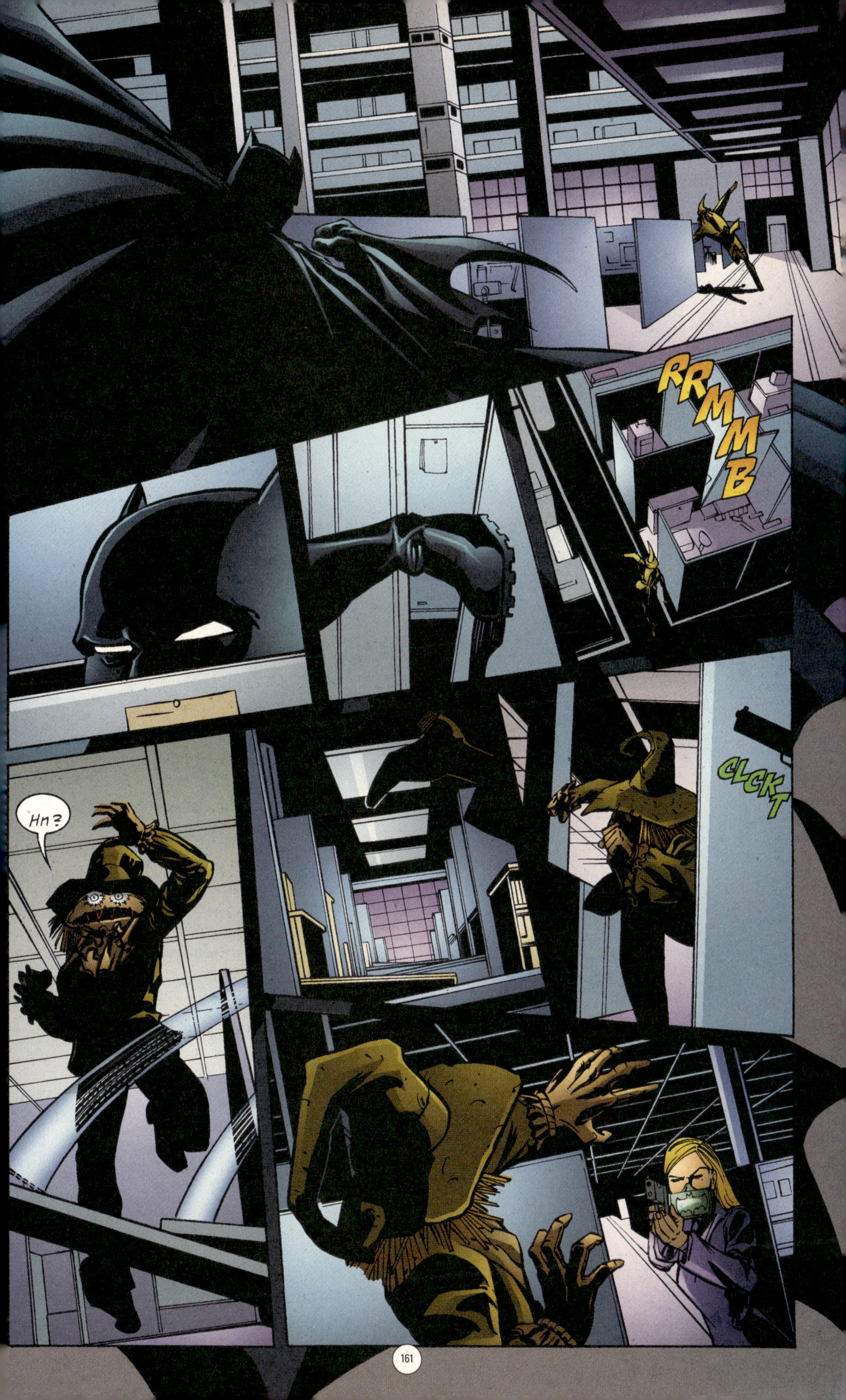
RRMMB
CLCKT
Hn?

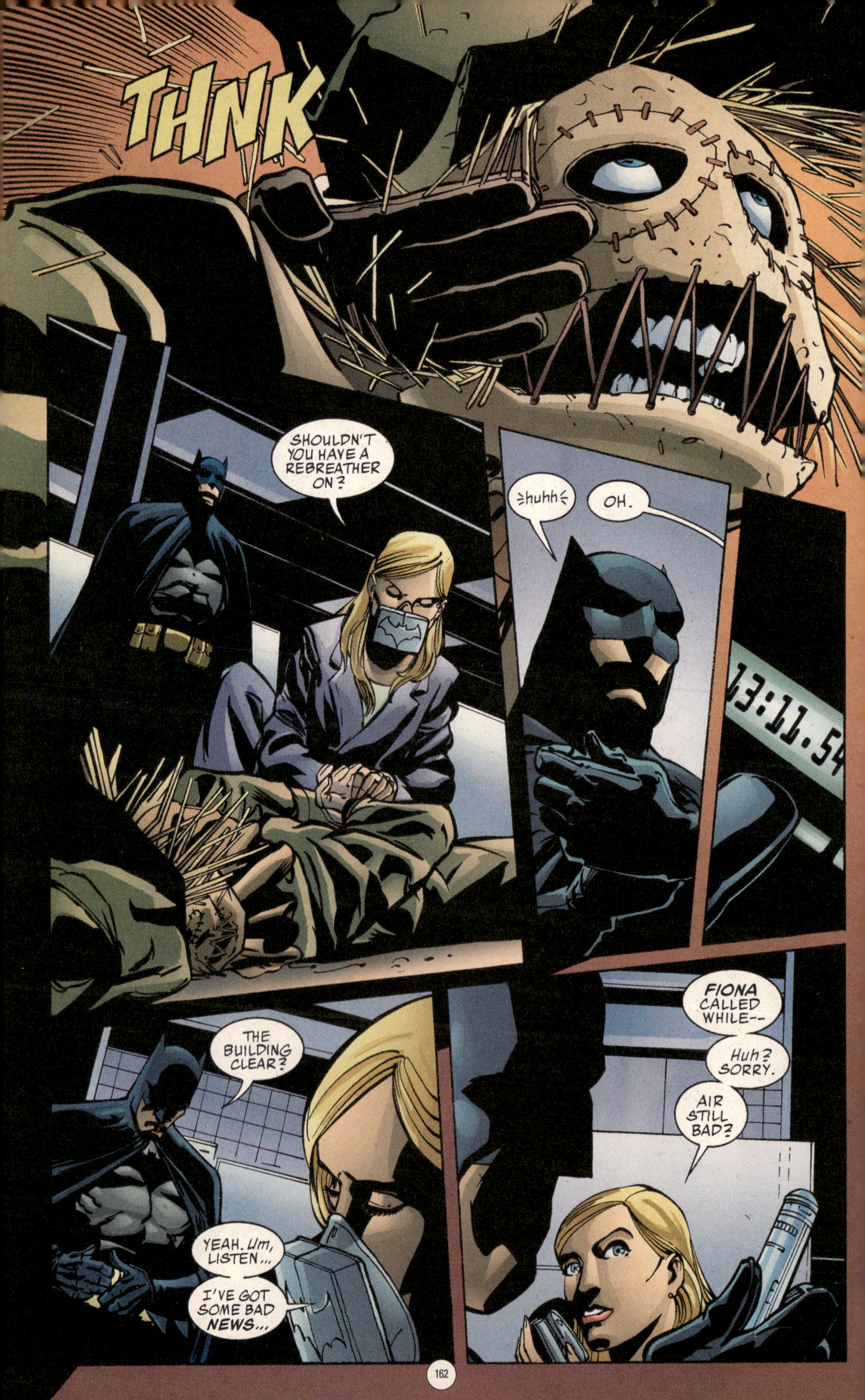
THNK
SHOULDN'T YOU HAVE A REBREATHER ON?
huhh
OH.
13:11.54
THE BUILDING CLEAR?
YEAH. Um, LISTEN...
I'VE GOT SOME BAD NEWS...
FIONA CALLED WHILE--
Huh? SORRY.
AIR STILL BAD?

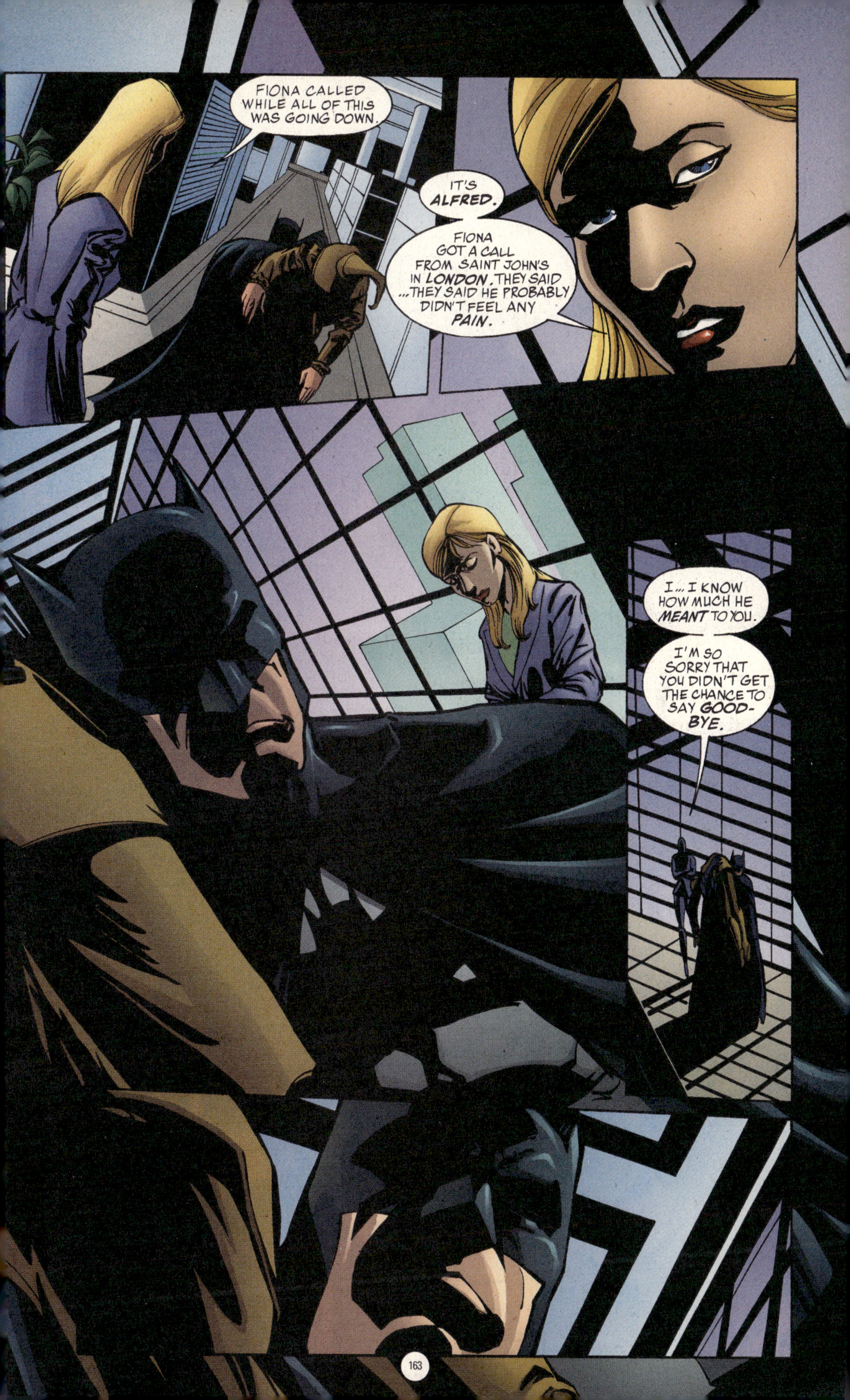
FIONA CALLED WHILE ALL OF THIS WAS GOING DOWN.
IT'S ALFRED.
FIONA GOT A CALL FROM SAINT JOHN'S IN LONDON. THEY SAID ...THEY SAID HE PROBABLY DIDN'T FEEL ANY PAIN.
I... I KNOW HOW MUCH HE MEANT TO YOU.
I'M SO SORRY THAT YOU DIDN'T GET THE CHANCE TO SAY GOOD-BYE.

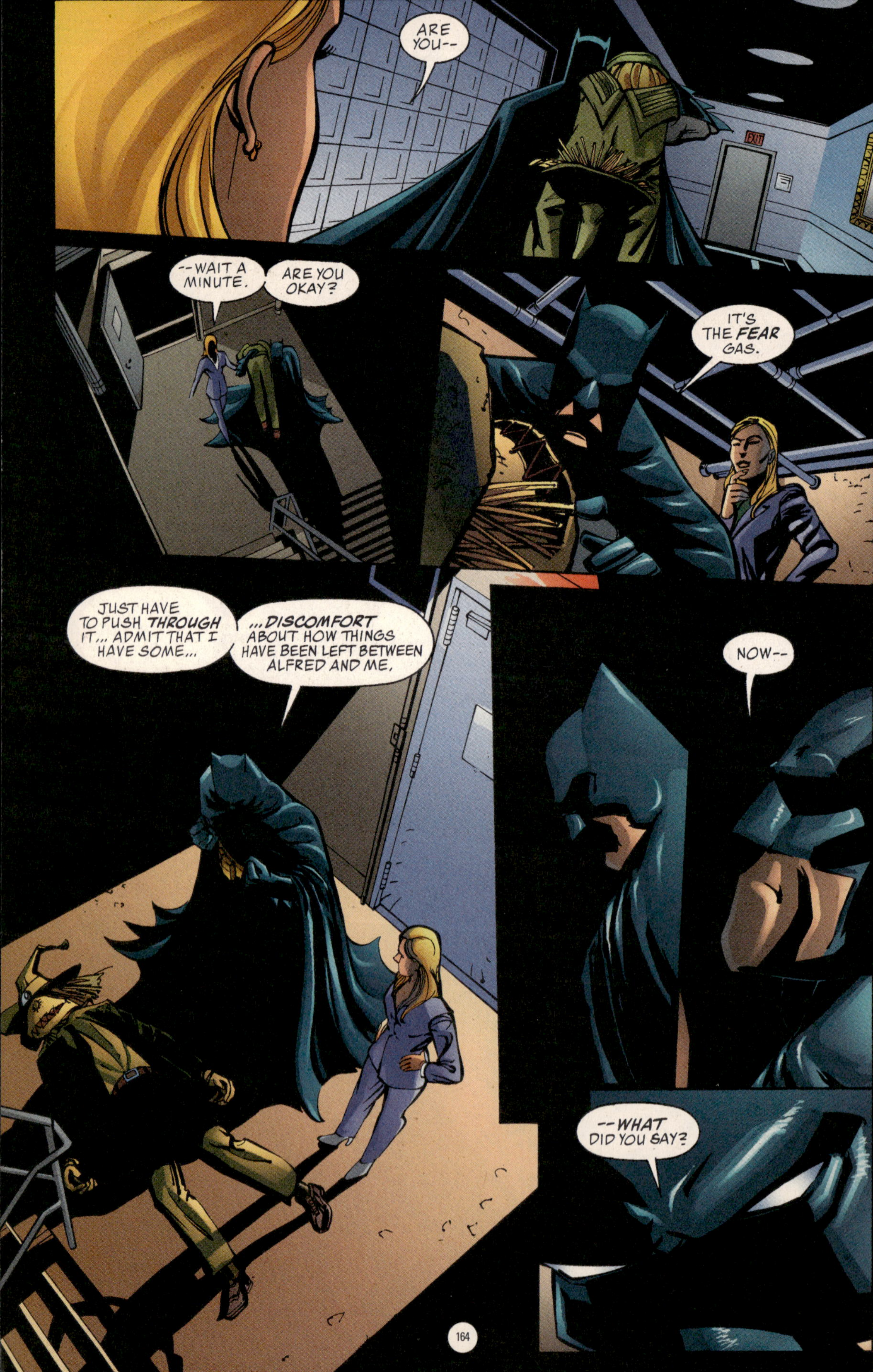
ARE YOU--
--WAIT A MINUTE.
ARE YOU OKAY?
IT'S THE FEAR GAS.
JUST HAVE TO PUSH THROUGH IT... ADMIT THAT I HAVE SOME...
...DISCOMFORT ABOUT HOW THINGS HAVE BEEN LEFT BETWEEN ALFRED AND ME.
NOW--
--WHAT DID YOU SAY?

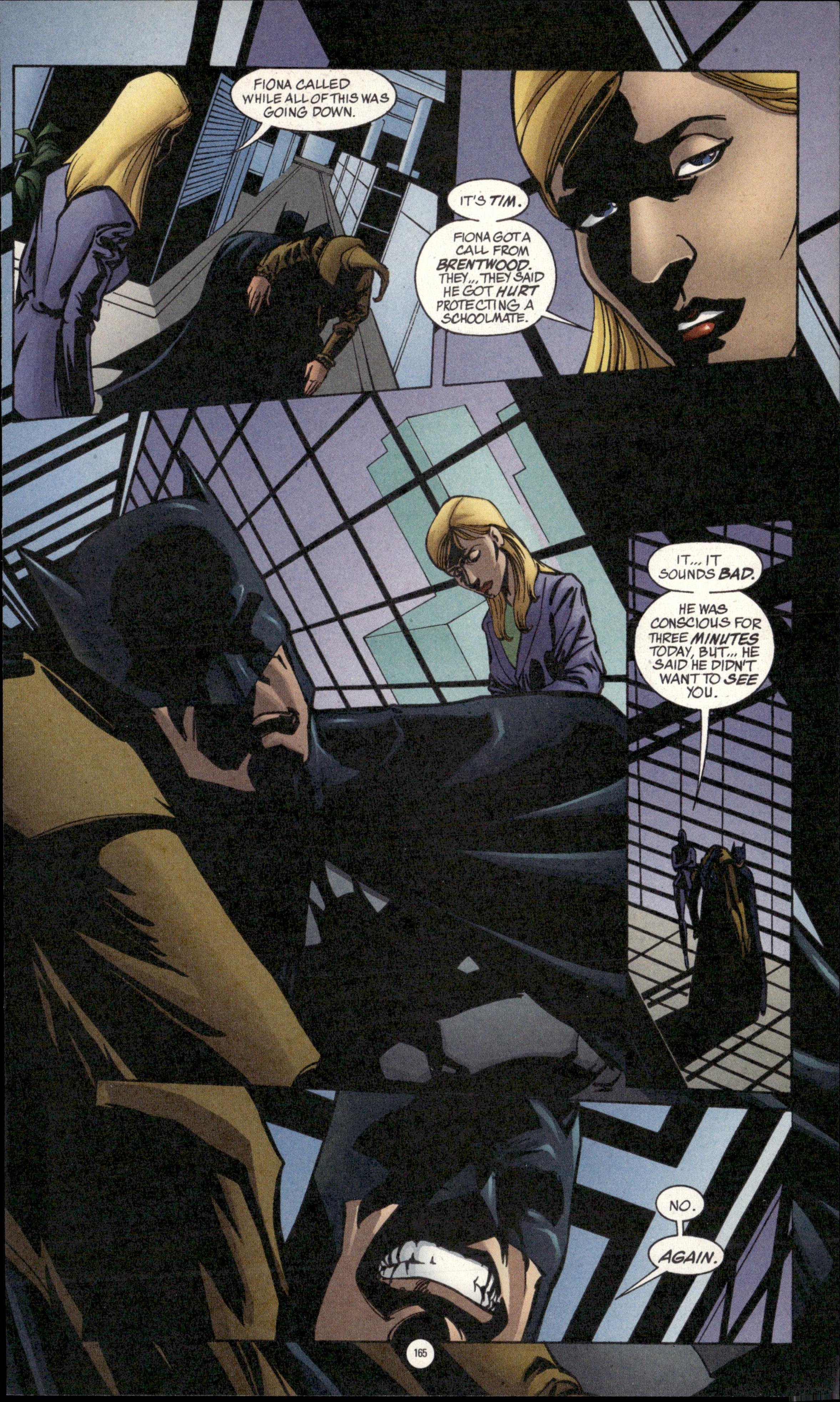
FIONA CALLED WHILE ALL OF THIS WAS GOING DOWN.
IT'S TIM.
FIONA GOT A CALL FROM BRENTWOOD. THEY... THEY SAID HE GOT HURT PROTECTING A SCHOOLMATE.
IT... IT SOUNDS BAD.
HE WAS CONSCIOUS FOR THREE MINUTES TODAY, BUT... HE SAID HE DIDN'T WANT TO SEE YOU.
NO.
AGAIN.

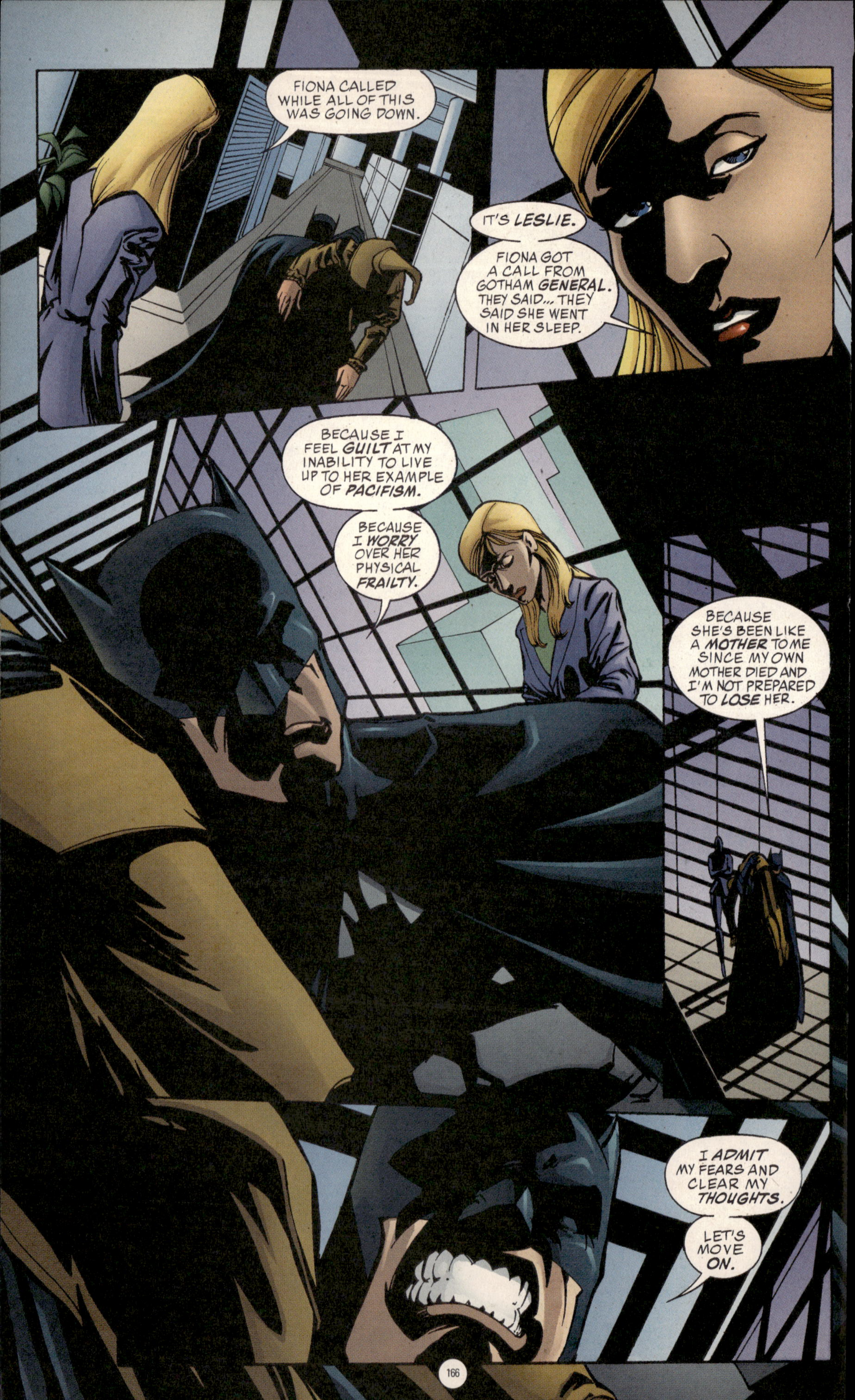
FIONA CALLED WHILE ALL OF THIS WAS GOING DOWN.
IT'S LESLIE.
FIONA GOT A CALL FROM GOTHAM GENERAL. THEY SAID... THEY SAID SHE WENT IN HER SLEEP.
BECAUSE I FEEL GUILT AT MY INABILITY TO LIVE UP TO HER EXAMPLE OF PACIFISM.
BECAUSE I WORRY OVER HER PHYSICAL FRAILTY.
BECAUSE SHE'S BEEN LIKE A MOTHER TO ME SINCE MY OWN MOTHER DIED AND I'M NOT PREPARED TO LOSE HER.
I ADMIT MY FEARS AND CLEAR MY THOUGHTS.
LET'S MOVE ON.

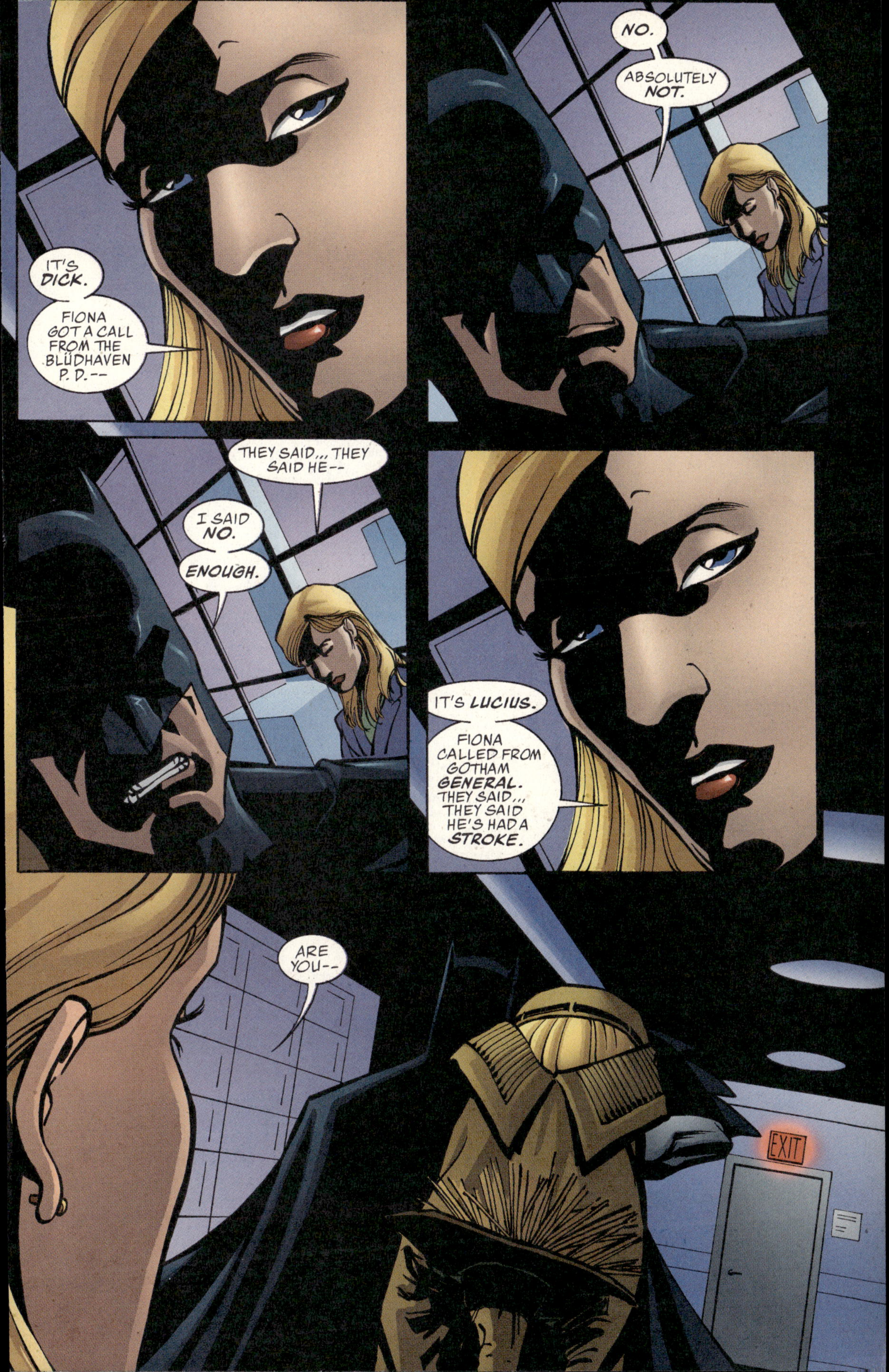
IT'S DICK.
FIONA GOT A CALL FROM THE BLÜDHAVEN P.D.--
NO.
ABSOLUTELY NOT.
THEY SAID... THEY SAID HE--
I SAID NO.
ENOUGH.
IT'S LUCIUS.
FIONA CALLED FROM GOTHAM GENERAL. THEY SAID... THEY SAID HE'S HAD A STROKE.
ARE YOU--
EXIT

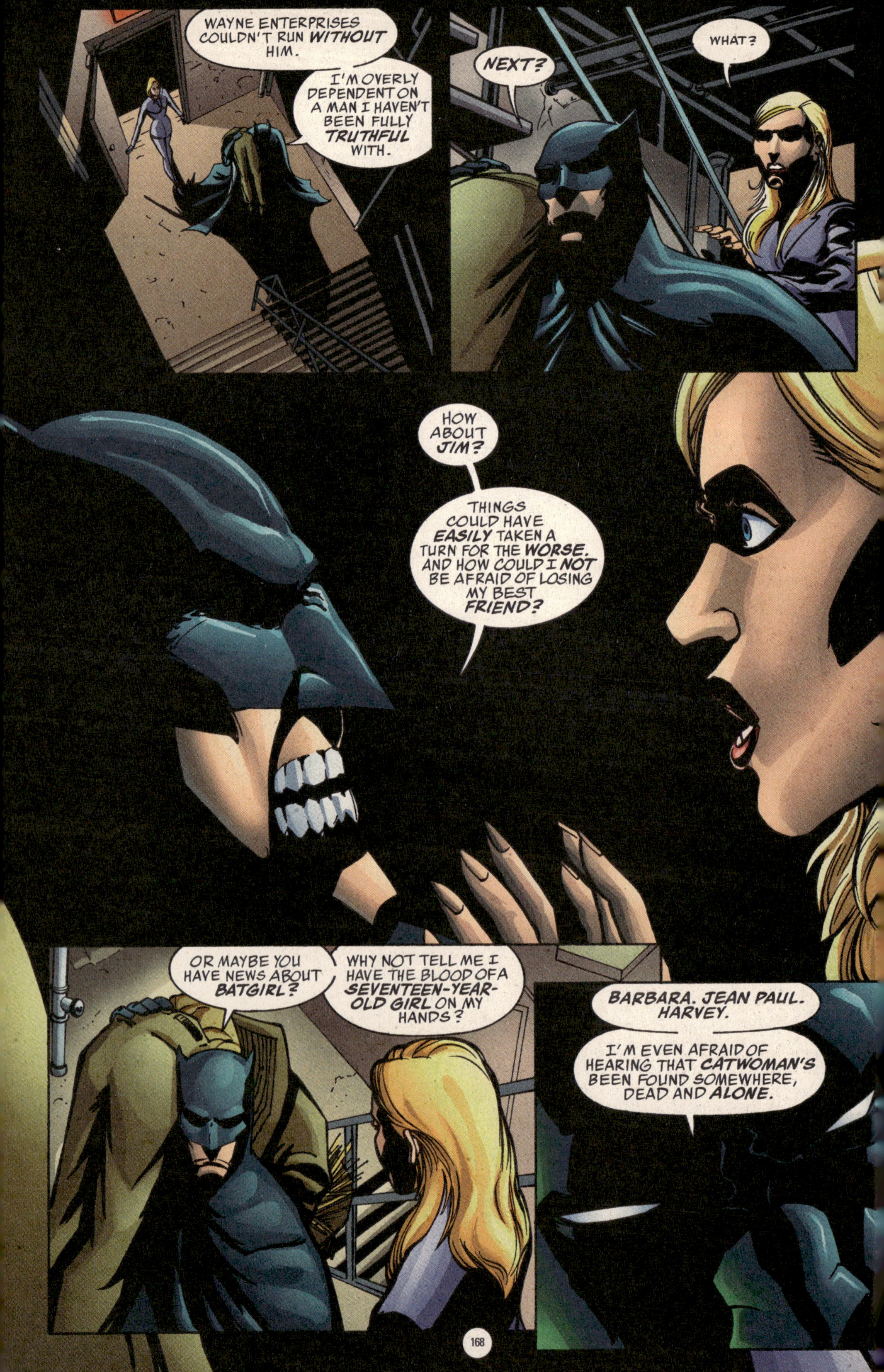
WAYNE ENTERPRISES COULDN'T RUN WITHOUT HIM.
I'M OVERLY DEPENDENT ON A MAN I HAVEN'T BEEN FULLY TRUTHFUL WITH.
NEXT?
WHAT?
HOW ABOUT JIM?
THINGS COULD HAVE EASILY TAKEN A TURN FOR THE WORSE. AND HOW COULD I NOT BE AFRAID OF LOSING MY BEST FRIEND?
OR MAYBE YOU HAVE NEWS ABOUT BATGIRL?
WHY NOT TELL ME I HAVE THE BLOOD OF A SEVENTEEN-YEAR-OLD GIRL ON MY HANDS?
BARBARA. JEAN PAUL. HARVEY.
I'M EVEN AFRAID OF HEARING THAT CATWOMAN'S BEEN FOUND SOMEWHERE, DEAD AND ALONE.

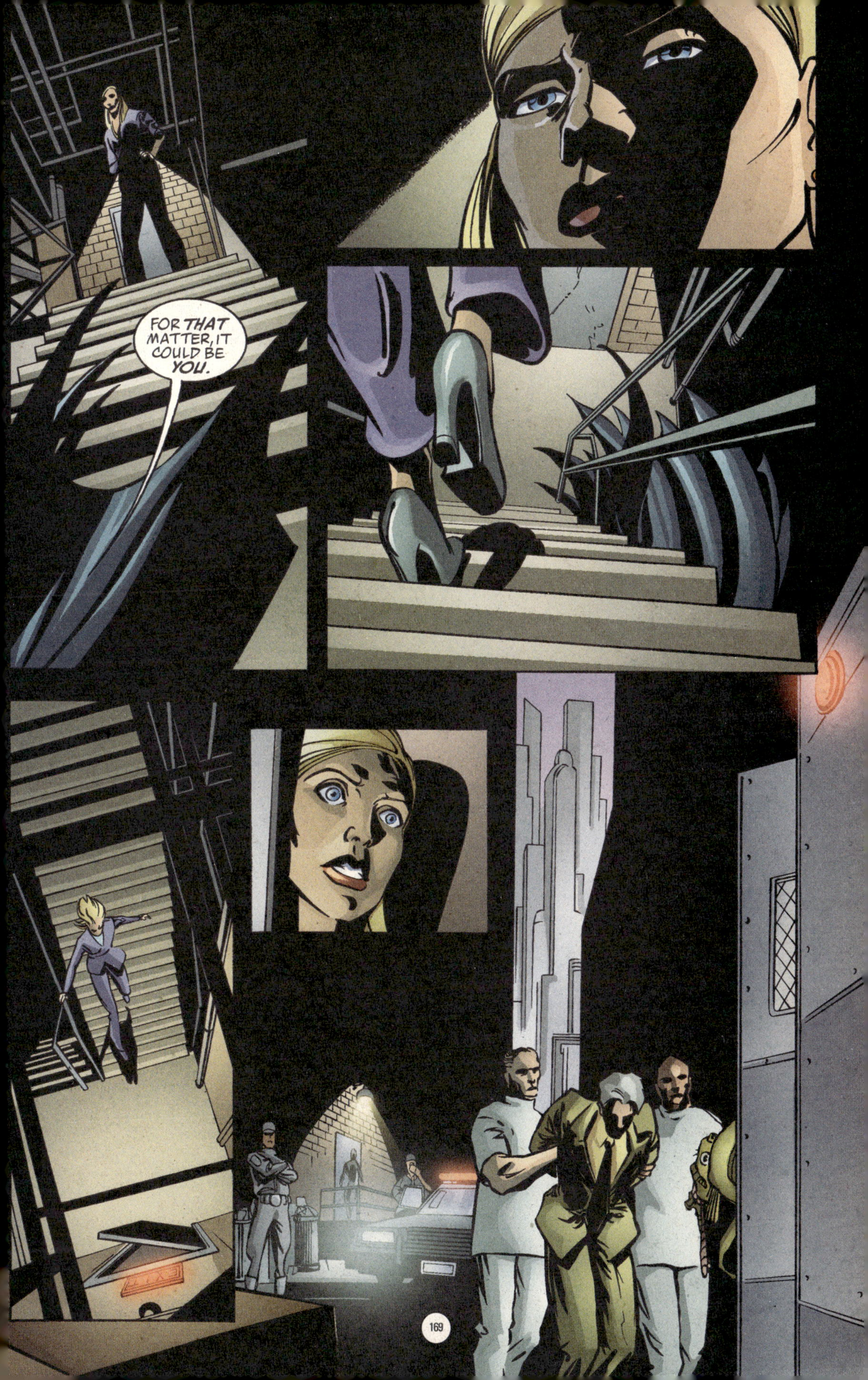
FOR THAT MATTER, IT COULD BE YOU.

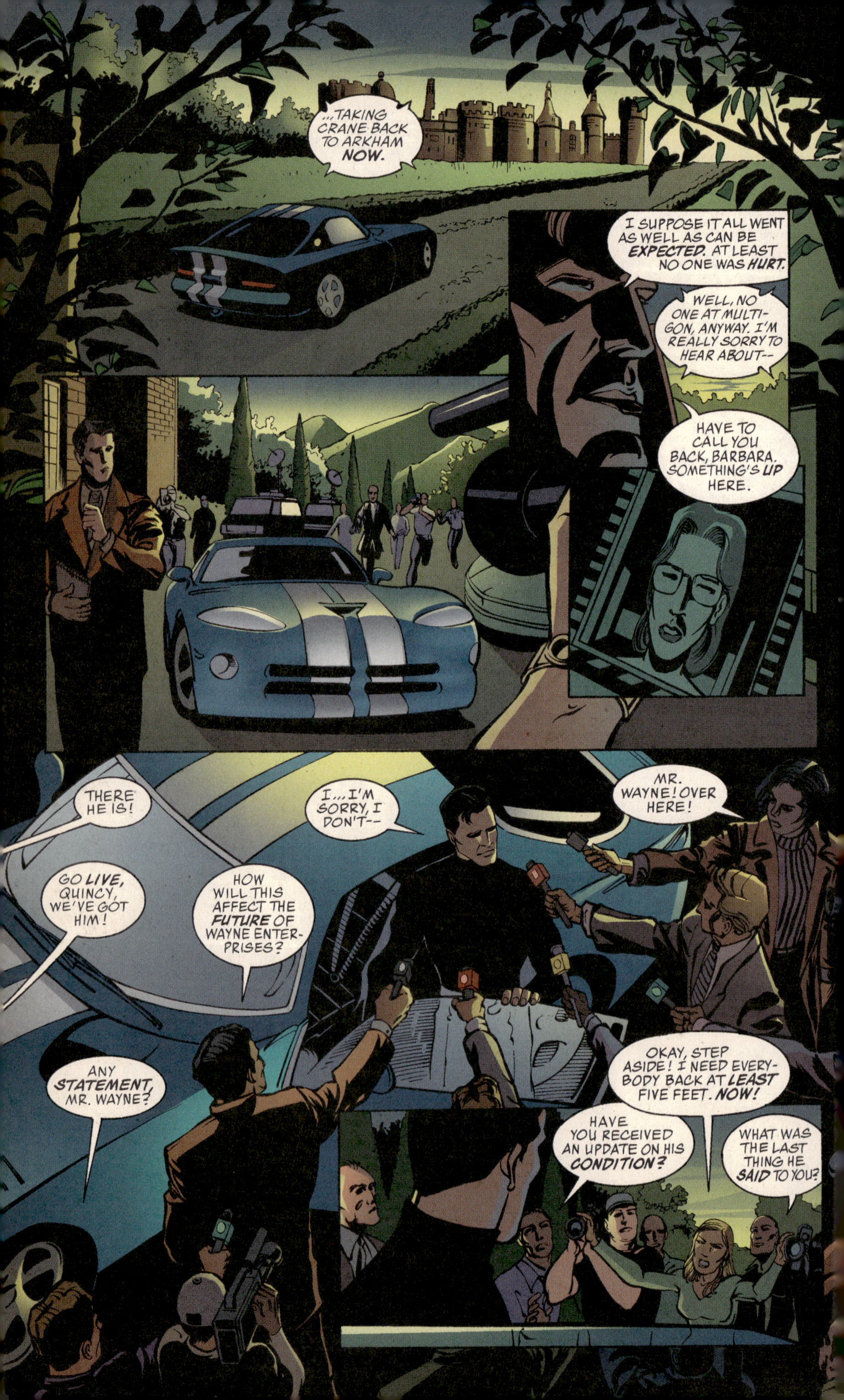
...TAKING CRANE BACK TO ARKHAM NOW.
I SUPPOSE IT ALL WENT AS WELL AS CAN BE EXPECTED. AT LEAST NO ONE WAS HURT.
WELL, NO ONE AT MULTI-GON, ANYWAY. I'M REALLY SORRY TO HEAR ABOUT--
HAVE TO CALL YOU BACK, BARBARA. SOMETHING'S UP HERE.
THERE HE IS!
I... I'M SORRY, I DON'T--
MR. WAYNE! OVER HERE!
GO LIVE, QUINCY, WE'VE GOT HIM!
HOW WILL THIS AFFECT THE FUTURE OF WAYNE ENTERPRISES?
ANY STATEMENT, MR. WAYNE?
OKAY, STEP ASIDE! I NEED EVERYBODY BACK AT LEAST FIVE FEET. NOW!
HAVE YOU RECEIVED AN UPDATE ON HIS CONDITION?
WHAT WAS THE LAST THING HE SAID TO YOU?

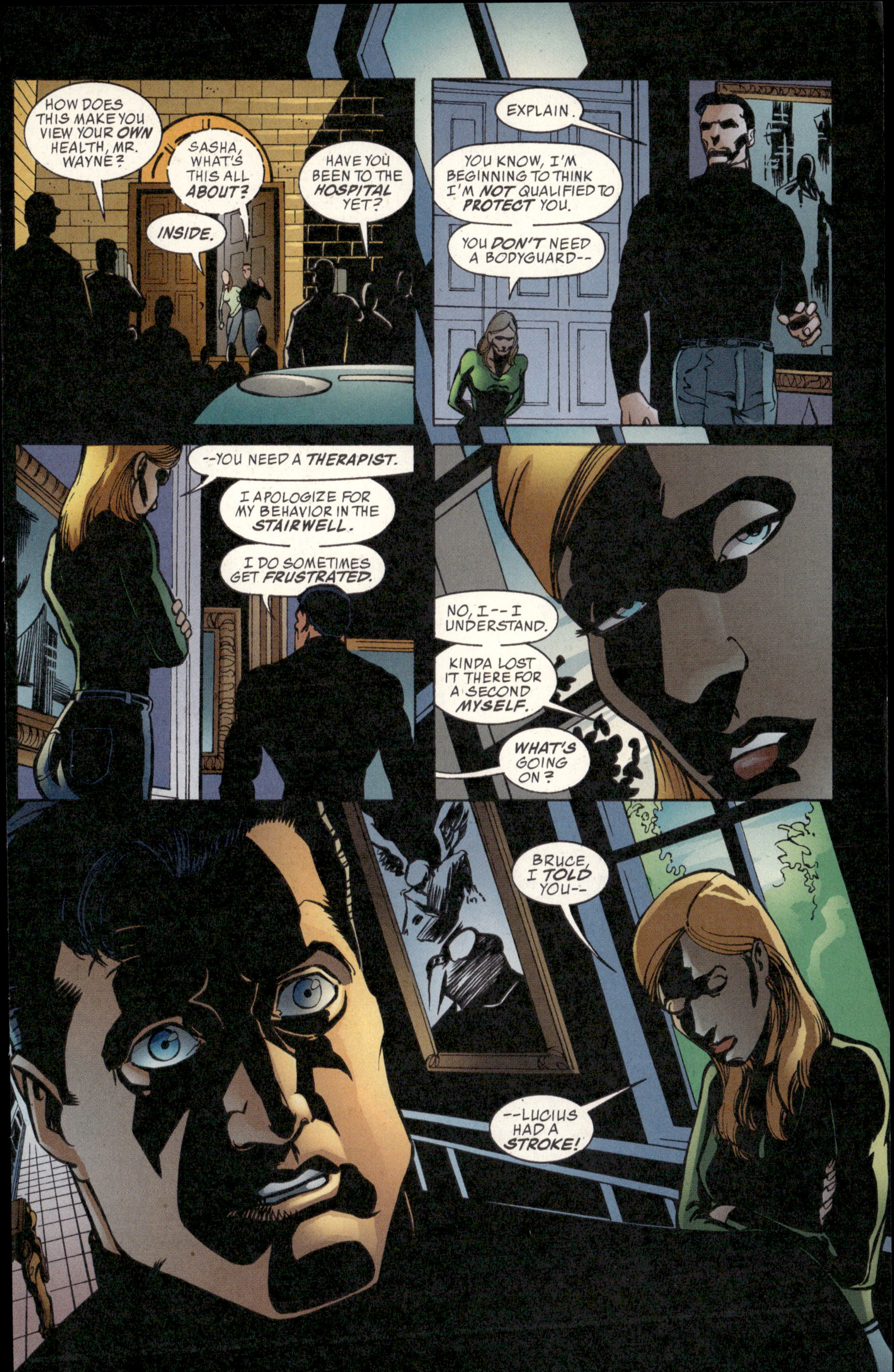
HOW DOES THIS MAKE YOU VIEW YOUR OWN HEALTH, MR. WAYNE?
SASHA, WHAT'S THIS ALL ABOUT?
INSIDE.
HAVE YOU BEEN TO THE HOSPITAL YET?
EXPLAIN.
YOU KNOW, I'M BEGINNING TO THINK I'M NOT QUALIFIED TO PROTECT YOU.
YOU DON'T NEED A BODYGUARD--
--YOU NEED A THERAPIST.
I APOLOGIZE FOR MY BEHAVIOR IN THE STAIRWELL.
I DO SOMETIMES GET FRUSTRATED.
NO, I-- I UNDERSTAND.
KINDA LOST IT THERE FOR A SECOND MYSELF.
WHAT'S GOING ON?
BRUCE, I TOLD YOU--
--LUCIUS HAD A STROKE!

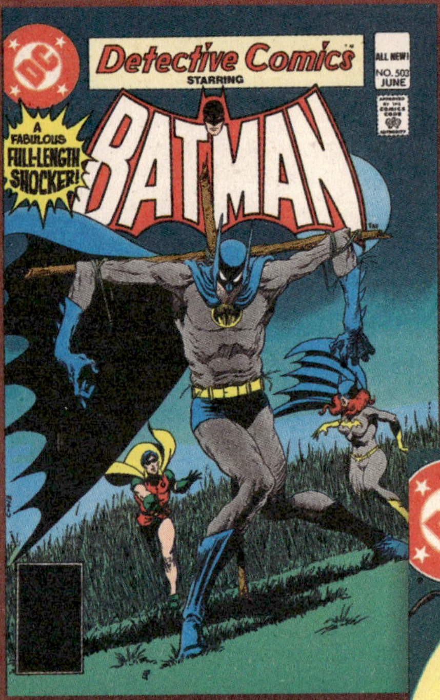
Detective Comics
STARRING
BATMAN
ALL NEW!
NO. 503
JUNE
A FABULOUS FULL-LENGTH SHOCKER!

HARVEST OF FEAR

The Scarecrow made only two appearances in the 1940s and really didn't make a serious bid for being one of Batman's deadliest opponents until the 1970s. Over the next few pages you will see how artists have expressed all the possibilities inherent in the master of fear. On this page: DETECTIVE COMICS #503 (June 1981) by Jim Starlin, BATMAN #373 (July 1984) by Ed Hannigan & Dick Giordano, BATMAN #296 (February 1978) by Sal Amendola & Al Milgrom.

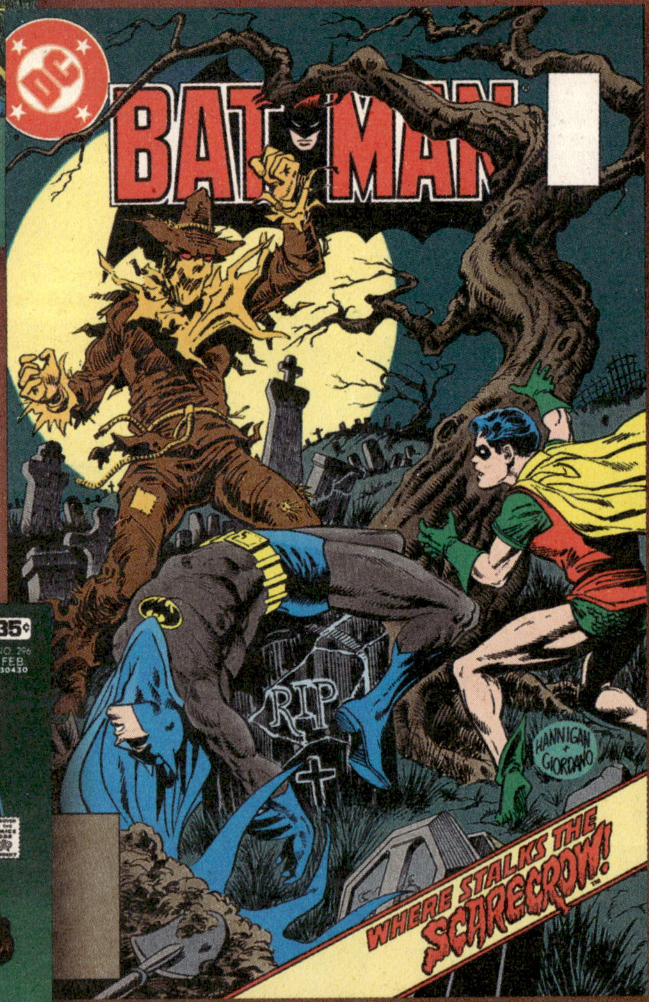
BATMAN
RIP
HANNIGAN + GIORDANO
WHERE STALKS THE SCARECROW!

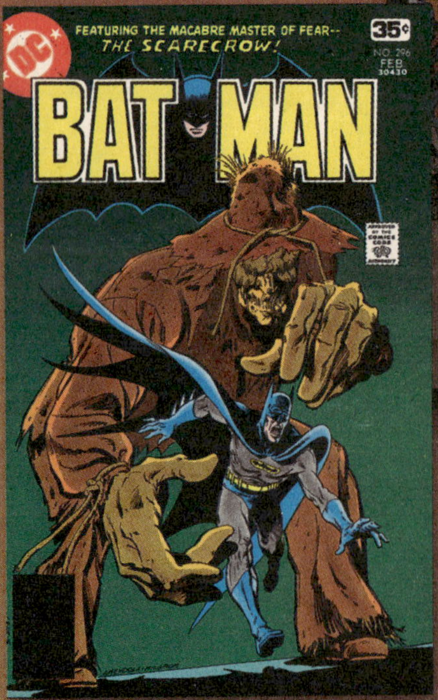
FEATURING THE MACABRE MASTER OF FEAR--
THE SCARECROW!
35¢
NO. 296
FEB
BATMAN

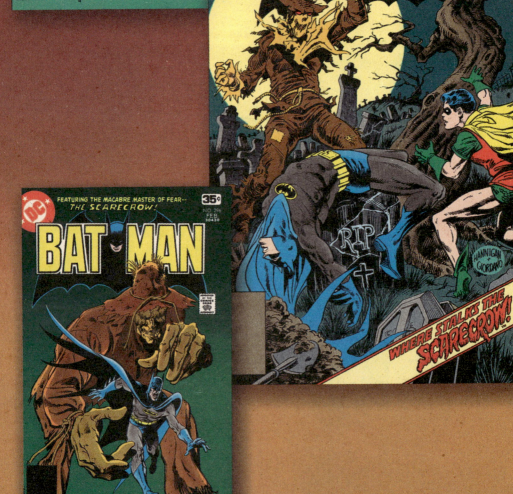

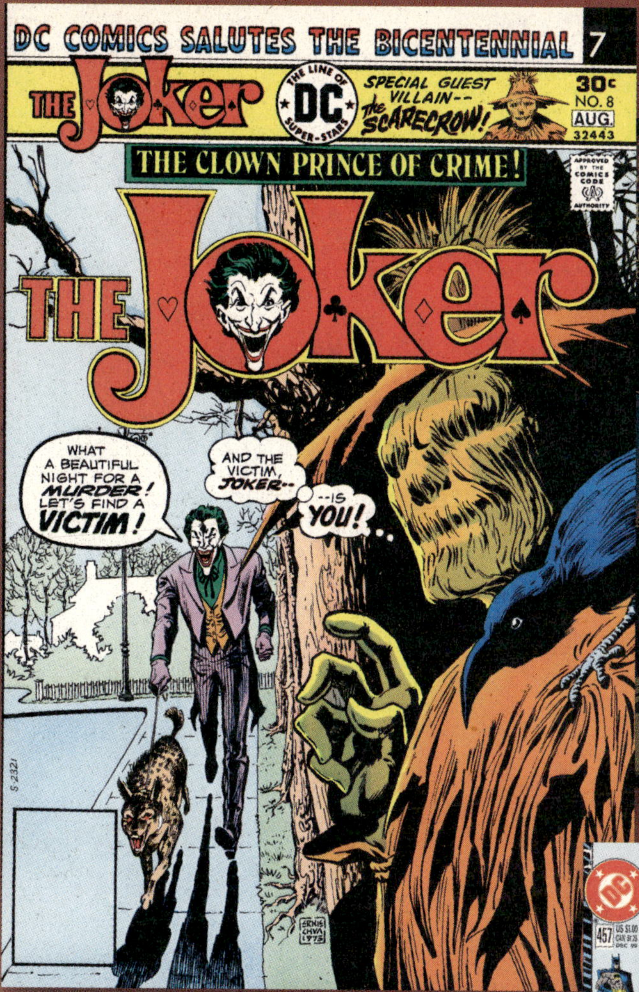
DC COMICS SALUTES THE BICENTENNIAL 7
THE JOKER
SPECIAL GUEST VILLAIN-- the SCARECROW!
30¢ NO. 8 AUG.
THE CLOWN PRINCE OF CRIME!
THE JOKER
WHAT A BEAUTIFUL NIGHT FOR A MURDER! LET'S FIND A VICTIM!
AND THE VICTIM, JOKER--
--IS YOU!...

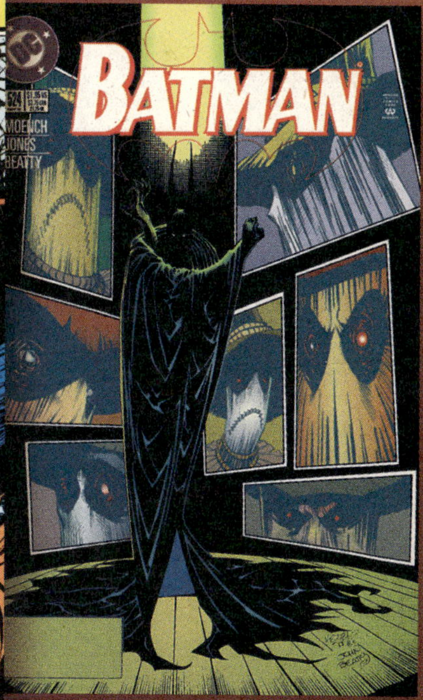
BATMAN
MOENCH
JONES
BEATTY

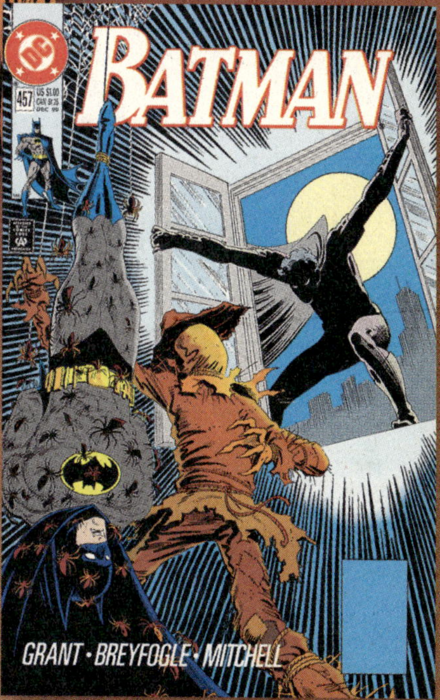
BATMAN
GRANT · BREYFOGLE · MITCHELL

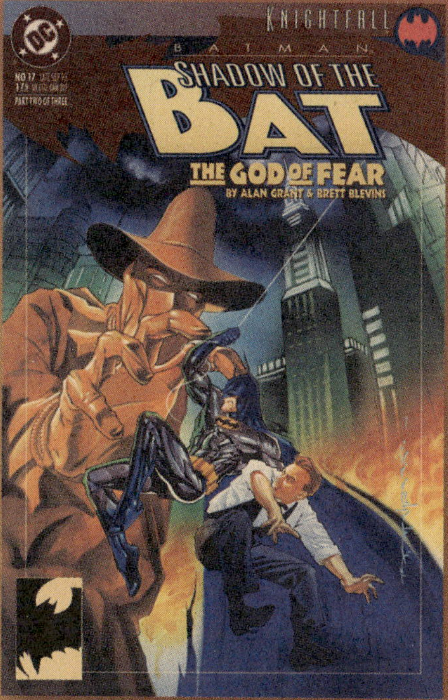
KNIGHTFALL
BATMAN
SHADOW OF THE BAT
THE GOD OF FEAR
BY ALAN GRANT & BRETT BLEVINS

While The Joker may have been the first villain to headline his own DC comic, he was far from the only Batman foe to appear in THE JOKER. THE JOKER #8 (July-August 1976) by Ernie Chan; BATMAN #524 (November 1995) by Kelley Jones & John Beatty, BATMAN #457 (December 1990) by Norm Breyfogle. SHADOW OF THE BAT #17 (September 1993) by Brian Stelfreeze.

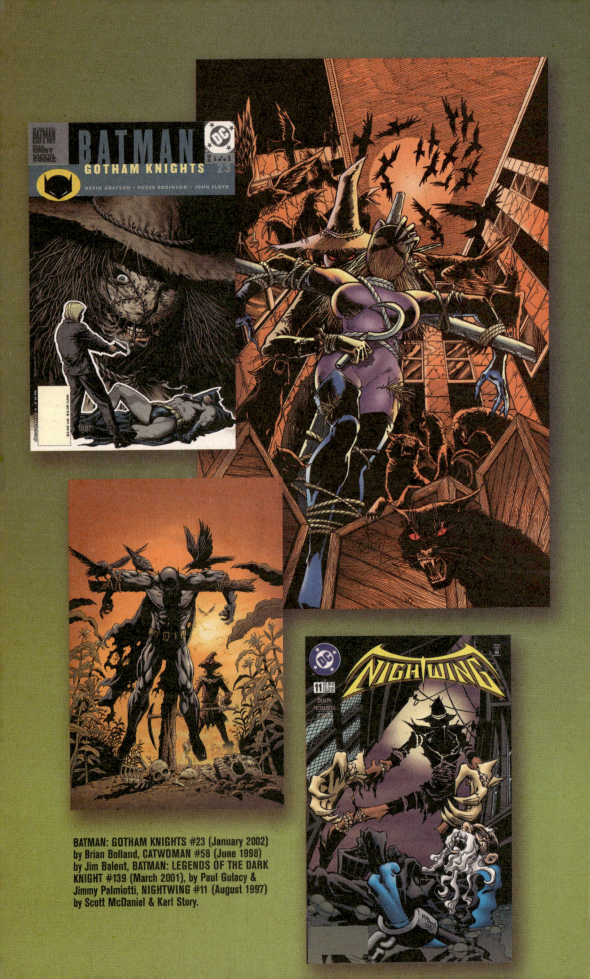

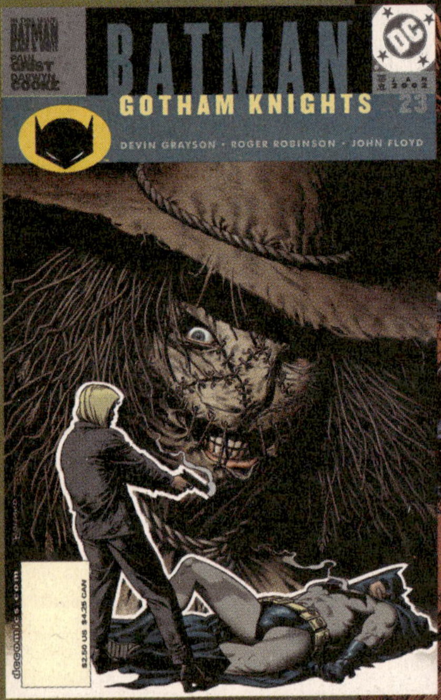
BATMAN
GOTHAM KNIGHTS
23
DEVIN GRAYSON · ROGER ROBINSON · JOHN FLOYD

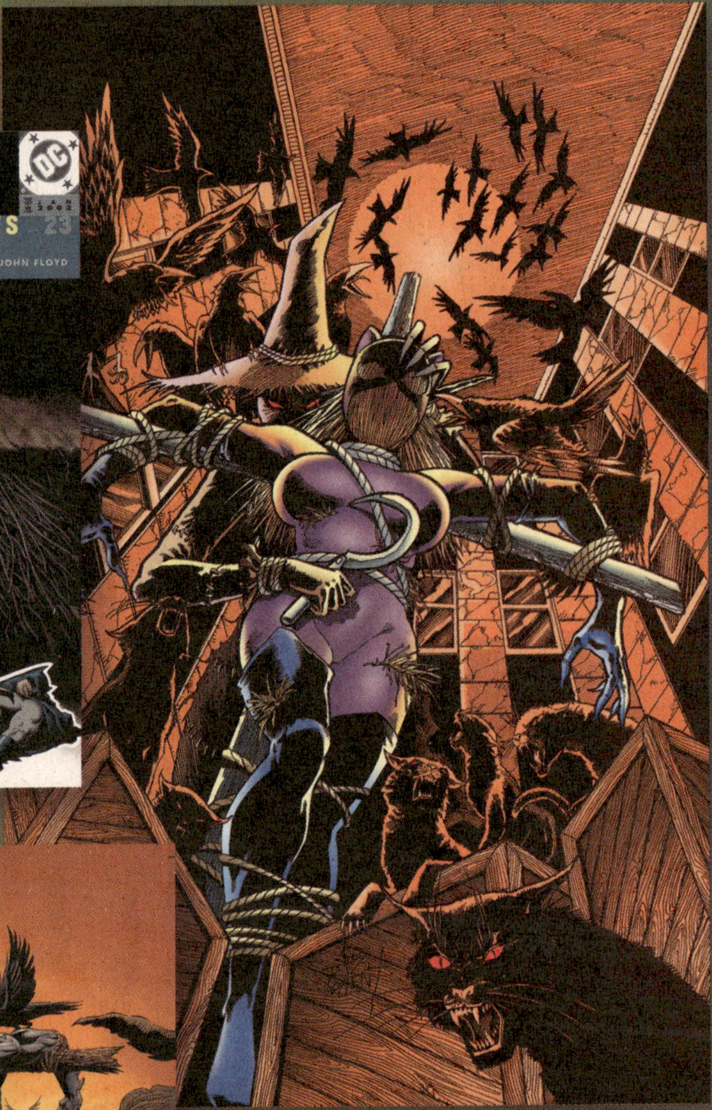

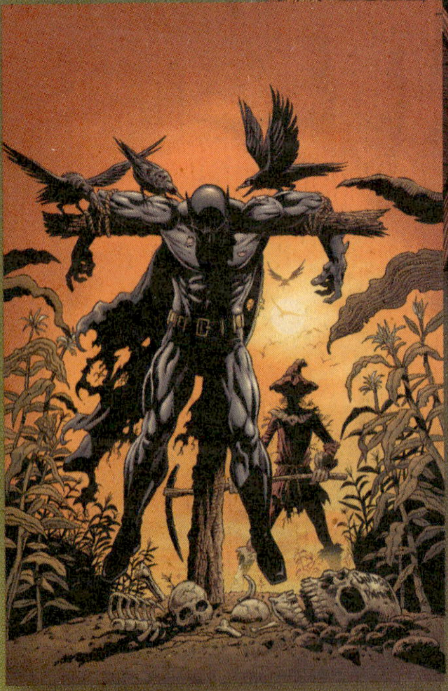

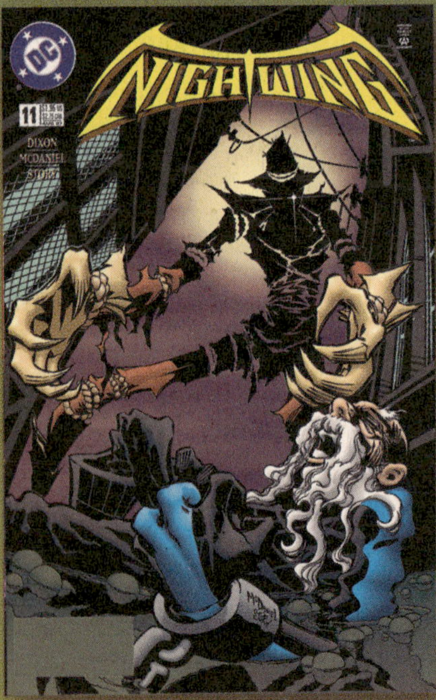
NIGHTWING
11
DIXON
McDANIEL
STORY

BATMAN: GOTHAM KNIGHTS #23 (January 2002) by Brian Bolland, CATWOMAN #58 (June 1998) by Jim Balent, BATMAN: LEGENDS OF THE DARK KNIGHT #139 (March 2001), by Paul Gulacy & Jimmy Palmiotti, NIGHTWING #11 (August 1997) by Scott McDaniel & Karl Story.

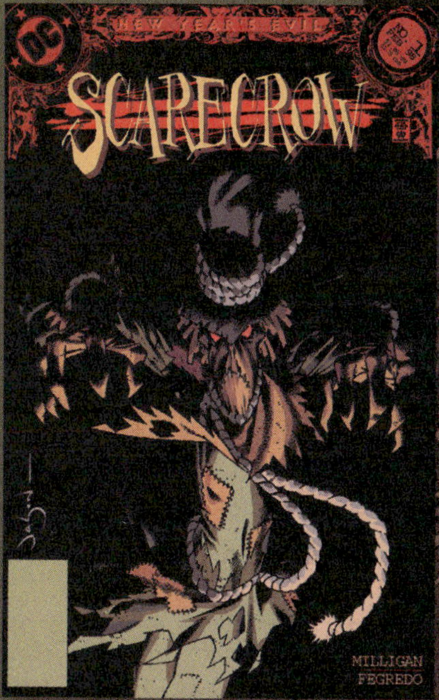
NEW YEAR'S EVIL
SCARECROW
MILLIGAN
FEGREDO

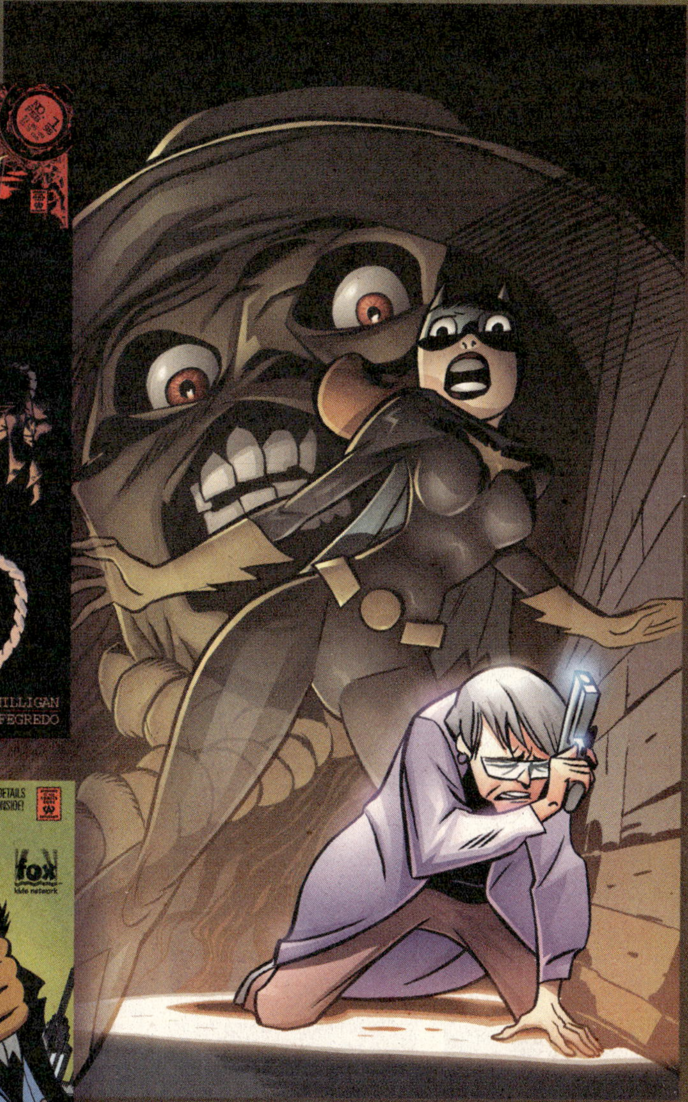

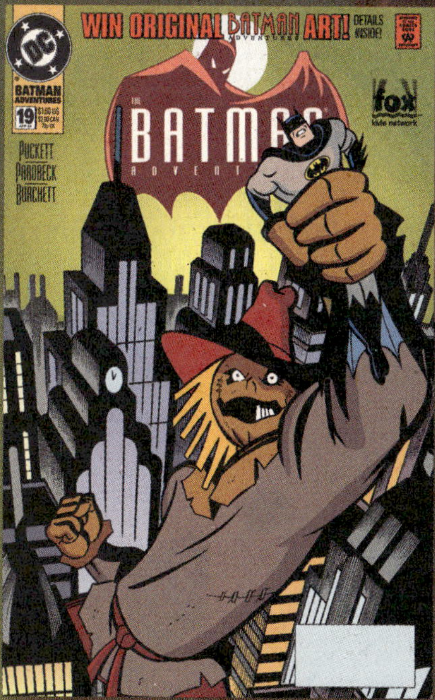
WIN ORIGINAL BATMAN ART! DETAILS INSIDE!
BATMAN ADVENTURES
19
PUCKETT
PAROBECK
BURCHETT
fox kids network

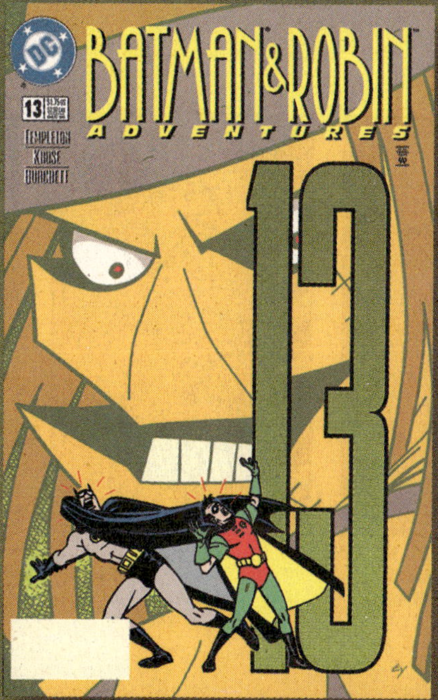
BATMAN & ROBIN
ADVENTURES
13
TEMPLETON
BURCHETT

For one week, DC unleashed several titles featuring an assortment of threats including the well-received SCARECROW (February 1998) by Jason Pearson, BATMAN BEYOND #13 (November 2000) by Ronnie DelCarmen, BATMAN ADVENTURES #19 (January 1994) by Mike Parobeck & Rich Burchett and finally BATMAN & ROBIN ADVENTURES #13 (December 1996) by Ty Templeton.

BATMAN COLLECTIONS

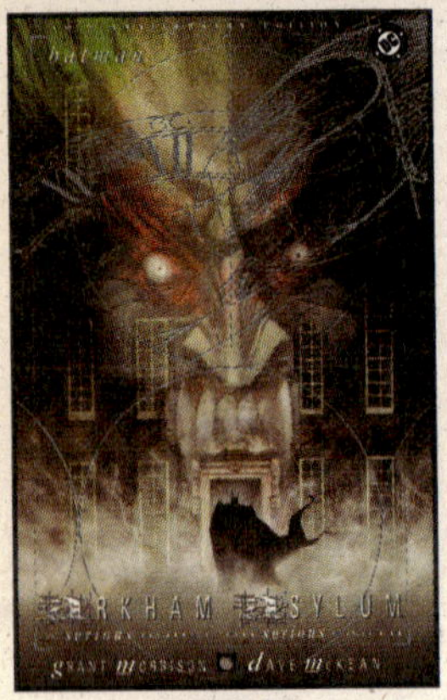

BATMAN: ARKHAM ASYLUM
Grant Morrison/Dave McKean
suggested for mature readers

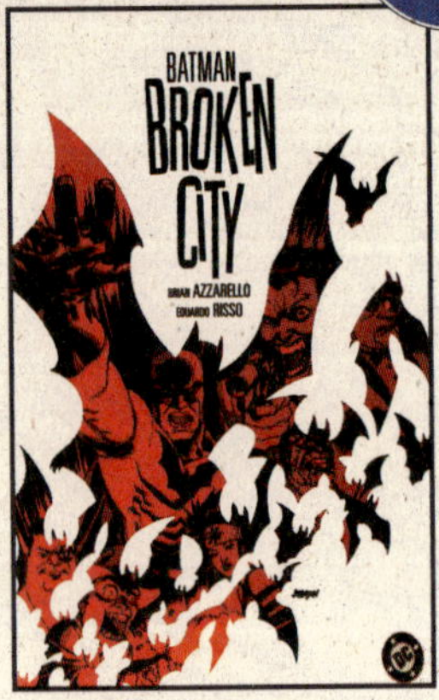
BATMAN
BROKEN CITY
BRIAN AZZARELLO
EDUARDO RISSO

BATMAN: BROKEN CITY
Brian Azzarello/Eduardo Risso

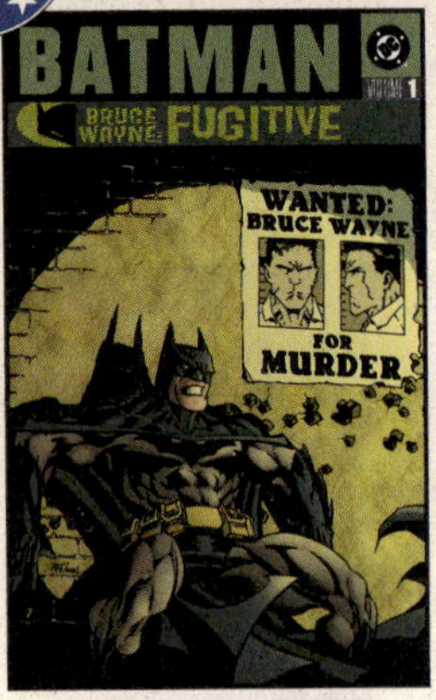
BATMAN
VOLUME 1
BRUCE WAYNE: FUGITIVE
WANTED: BRUCE WAYNE
FOR MURDER

BATMAN: BRUCE WAYNE — MURDERER?
BATMAN: BRUCE WAYNE — FUGITIVE VOLUMES 1-3
various

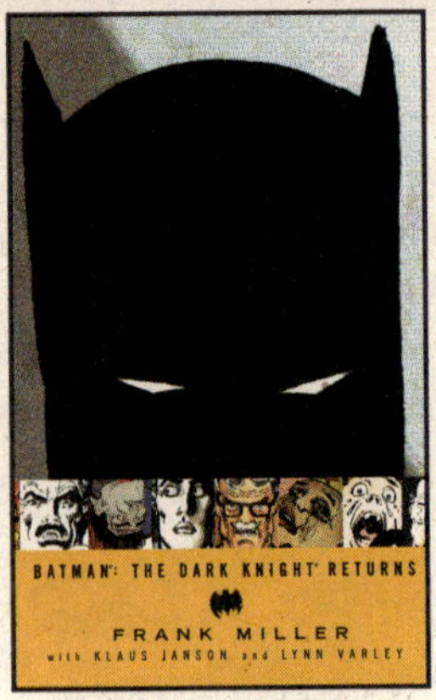
BATMAN: THE DARK KNIGHT RETURNS
FRANK MILLER
with KLAUS JANSON and LYNN VARLEY

BATMAN: THE DARK KNIGHT RETURNS
BATMAN: THE DARK KNIGHT STRIKES AGAIN!
Frank Miller

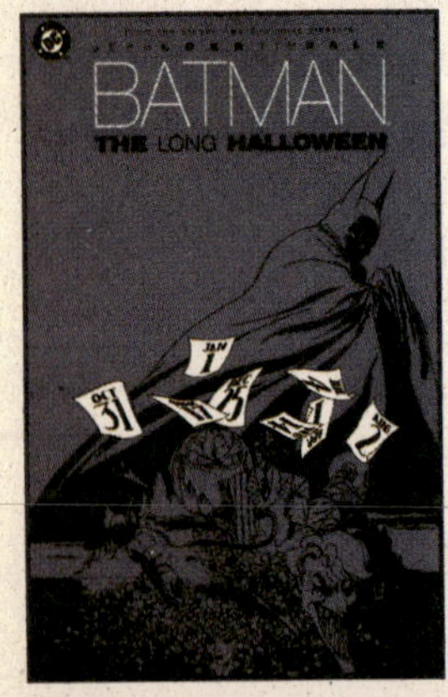
BATMAN
THE LONG HALLOWEEN

BATMAN: HAUNTED KNIGHT
BATMAN: THE LONG HALLOWEEN
BATMAN: DARK VICTORY
Jeph Loeb/Tim Sale

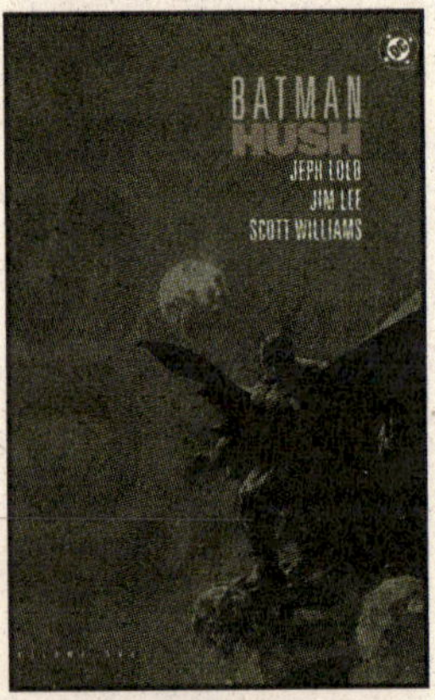
BATMAN
HUSH
JEPH LOEB
JIM LEE
SCOTT WILLIAMS

BATMAN: HUSH VOLUMES 1-2
Jeph Loeb/Jim Lee/ Scott Williams

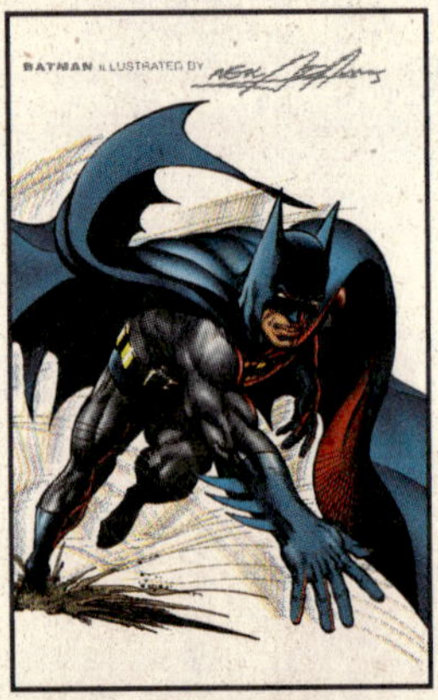

BATMAN ILLUSTRATED BY NEAL ADAMS VOLUMES 1-2
Dennis O'Neil/Neal Adams/various

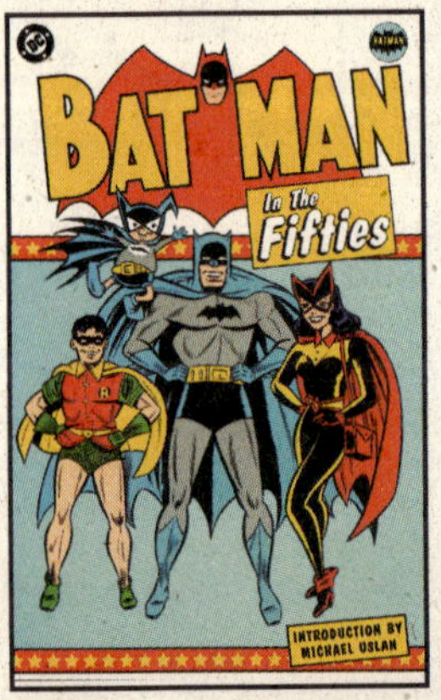
BATMAN
In The Fifties
INTRODUCTION BY MICHAEL USLAN

BATMAN IN THE FORTIES
BATMAN IN THE FIFTIES
BATMAN IN THE SIXTIES
BATMAN IN THE SEVENTIE
BATMAN IN THE EIGHTIES
various

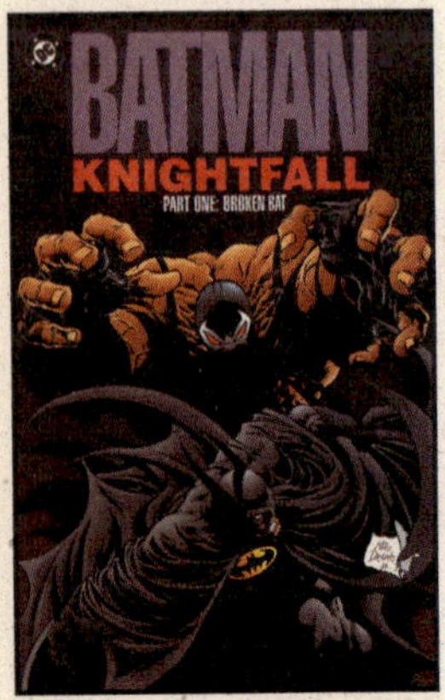
BATMAN
KNIGHTFALL
PART ONE: BROKEN BAT

BATMAN: KNIGHTFALL TPS
PART 1: BROKEN BAT
PART 2: WHO RULES THE NIGHT
PART 3: KNIGHT'S END
various

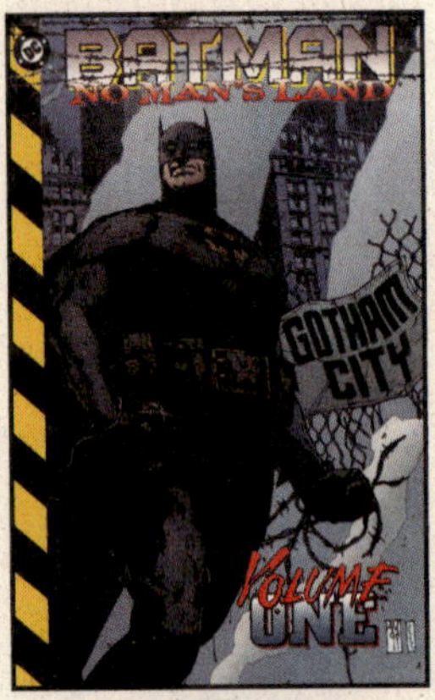
BATMAN
NO MAN'S LAND
GOTHAM CITY
VOLUME ONE

BATMAN: NO MAN'S LAND VOLUMES 1-5
various

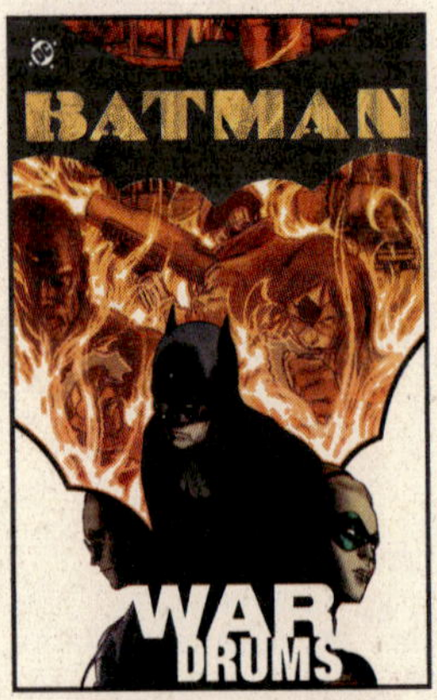
BATMAN
WAR DRUMS

BATMAN: WAR DRUMS
BATMAN: WAR GAMES VOL. 1
various

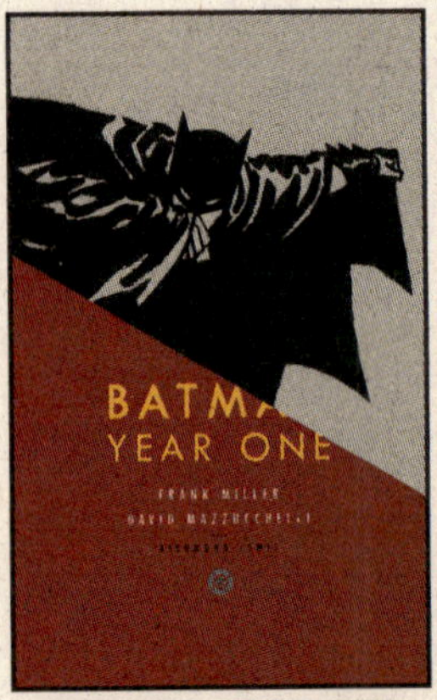
YEAR ONE

BATMAN: YEAR ONE
Frank Miller/David Mazzucchelli